CW01197161

1,000,000 Books
are available to read at

Forgotten Books

www.ForgottenBooks.com

Read online
Download PDF
Purchase in print

ISBN 978-1-330-70391-5
PIBN 10094593

This book is a reproduction of an important historical work. Forgotten Books uses state-of-the-art technology to digitally reconstruct the work, preserving the original format whilst repairing imperfections present in the aged copy. In rare cases, an imperfection in the original, such as a blemish or missing page, may be replicated in our edition. We do, however, repair the vast majority of imperfections successfully; any imperfections that remain are intentionally left to preserve the state of such historical works.

Forgotten Books is a registered trademark of FB &c Ltd.
Copyright © 2018 FB &c Ltd.
FB &c Ltd, Dalton House, 60 Windsor Avenue, London, SW19 2RR.
Company number 08720141. Registered in England and Wales.

For support please visit www.forgottenbooks.com

1 MONTH OF FREE READING

at

www.ForgottenBooks.com

By purchasing this book you are eligible for one month membership to ForgottenBooks.com, giving you unlimited access to our entire collection of over 1,000,000 titles via our web site and mobile apps.

To claim your free month visit:

www.forgottenbooks.com/free94593

* Offer is valid for 45 days from date of purchase. Terms and conditions apply.

English
Français
Deutsche
Italiano
Español
Português

www.forgottenbooks.com

Mythology Photography **Fiction** Fishing Christianity **Art** Cooking Essays Buddhism Freemasonry Medicine **Biology** Music **Ancient Egypt** Evolution Carpentry Physics Dance Geology **Mathematics** Fitness Shakespeare **Folklore** Yoga Marketing **Confidence** Immortality Biographies Poetry **Psychology** Witchcraft Electronics Chemistry History **Law** Accounting **Philosophy** Anthropology Alchemy Drama Quantum Mechanics Atheism Sexual Health **Ancient History** **Entrepreneurship** Languages Sport Paleontology Needlework Islam **Metaphysics** Investment Archaeology Parenting Statistics Criminology **Motivational**

EVENINGS WITH SHAKSPERE.

A Handbook to the Study of his Works

WITH

SUGGESTIONS FOR THE CONSIDERATION OF OTHER ELIZABETHAN LITERATURE

AND

CONTAINING SPECIAL HELP FOR SHAKSPERE SOCIETIES.

L. M. GRIFFITHS,

Honorary Secretary of the Clifton Shakspere Society.

"Turn him to any cause of policy,
The Gordian knot of it he will unloose."

LIBRARY
OF THE
UNIVERSITY

BRISTOL:
J. W. ARROWSMITH, 11 QUAY STREET.
LONDON:
SIMPKIN, MARSHALL, HAMILTON, KENT & COMPANY LIMITED.

1889.

ENGL. LIB. FD.

The rights of translation and reproduction are reserved.

I dedicate

THIS VOLUME

TO

THE LADY-MEMBERS

(PAST AND PRESENT)

OF THE

CLIFTON SHAKSPERE SOCIETY

WHOSE

READY CO-OPERATION

HAS GIVEN ME

GREAT ENCOURAGEMENT

IN MUCH ARDUOUS

SECRETARIAL WORK.

PREFACE.

IF this were a book about Shakspere of the kind with which we are too familiar, it would need some sort of prefatory apology. The world has had enough, perhaps too much, of instruction as to what it is to think about Shakspere. There will, therefore, in these pages be found no dogmatisms about Shakspere's "sweetest comedy" or his "weakest history" or his "gloomiest tragedy." Not even have I attempted to direct the reader to the "most wonderful passage" or to the poet's "greatest creation." I may have my opinions thereon, but it can be of no conceivable use that I should impertinently put them before other people to whom different parts of the author's work would appeal with as much force as other parts do to me. Persons possessed of ordinary intelligence should be left to form their own opinions on these and kindred points. I by no means assert that none of the analysis of Shakspere's work has any value. That would be equivalent to denying the existence of a critical insight keener than one's own; but it is nearly always the case that the Shaksperian commentator gives a mere exposition of his own views, and with a fog of words makes a clear view of the dramatist's meaning almost impossible. So much has been written to "explain" Shakspere that, with 'The Stranger in the Dress Circle,' we might well ask, "Does he then so greatly need interpretation?" (*The Universal Review*, May, 1889.)

I have tried to make the following pages a help to the enquirer who wishes to get an intelligent grasp of Shakspere and his surroundings, and who is unwilling to think by deputy. A traveller is grateful for a guide-book which will point out the situations of the most interesting objects and supply something of their history, without presuming to tell him what he is to think of them. In like manner I have endeavoured to act on behalf of the Shakspere-student, to whom it is of more importance to give close attention to the plays themselves than to other people's opinions about them. I have striven to indicate the lines upon which the work should be undertaken if it is desired to produce satisfactory and lasting results.

With this in view, nothing can be better than a study of the life which surrounded Shakspere, and which is strongly reflected in his own plays and in those of his contemporaries. Whilst his characters, differing from those of almost any other writer, are types for all ages, yet their actions are so often modified by the circumstances of the Elizabethan period, that in the absence of a familiarity with the customs, the use of words, and the tone of thought then prevalent, no true judgement can be formed. Having this knowledge and an acquaintance with the materials with which Shakspere worked, the student is in a far better position to appreciate the worth of the dramatist than if he should attempt to do so by assimilating ready-made opinions. But in any case, application and study of the work in detail will be necessary to see its true beauty. Without these, it is unreasonable to expect results in this field of labour more than in any other. An appreciation of Shakspere's worth is not to be gained by a listless skimming of his pages to pass an idle hour, or by the gratification of the æsthetic sense in a performance in which a stronger appeal is made to the eye than to the intellect.

It is too much the fashion to try to see in Shakspere one who set himself to teach his fellow-man. Shakspere wrote his plays for his theatre-audiences, and the enrichment of the coffers of the proprietors was certainly not a point of which he was regardless. Probably in not one of his plays is there any predetermined didactic purpose. His wise and genial sayings issued forth from his large soul and mighty mind because his heart was overflowing with all that was good and noble. From many a passage in his works, and from the general tendency of the whole, it is clear that, through a complete acquaintance with his Bible, he had gained an insight into the love of God differing only in degree from that vouchsafed to those of whom we commonly speak as inspired, and that by this, coupled with his marvellous knowledge of human nature, he was enabled to "justify the ways of God to men," and to lead the sinful and the sorrowing into ways of pardon and into paths of comfort.

The student is frequently led astray by dogmatic heresies

concerning the influences by which Shakspere was moved. It is irritating to be told that the poet founded various portions of a play upon definite works which, not altogether dissimilar in subject, are nevertheless but instances of other writers' variations in the treatment of not improbable incidents. Upon investigation, it will be found that often these emphatic utterances of commentators have no better authority than the deceptions of their own imaginations. In all these cases, I have cited the principal instances in which the subject-matter of the plays had been written about by others, although often the topics handed down for generations had become common literary property. The reader who seeks out these will be pleased to find that Shakspere, notwithstanding the ingenious attribution of his plots to other sources, was not wholly without the power of originality of treatment. The study will lead to many unfrequented byways of literature, and will dispel the fancy that Shakspere was such a poor being that he could not write *Twelfth Night* without first consulting *Apollonius and Silla*; or that, familiar as he must have been with the misanthropical doings of the traditional Timon, he could not be trusted to give his own, or put a patch on somebody else's, unscholarly version of them, but must have had Lucian immediately before him as a model.

It has been my aim to so set forth all the information on these and other points that it may be as useful to the solitary student as to those who prefer to work in combination; but to the latter, knowing from personal experience the pleasure, interest, and profit to be obtained by a conjoint systematic study of the Elizabethan

Drama, I have tried to give such hints about a Shakspere-society as may lead those who are desirous of forming such to set about it with as little difficulty as possible.

In the Reading-Tables and elsewhere there are so many figures that it is almost too much to hope that, either in computation or in printing, they are given without mistake; and I shall be grateful to those who will point out to me any errors they may discover. The names given in Chapter IX. of owners of the Quartos is of course singularly incomplete, and I am sorry that I could not make it otherwise. They are British with scarcely an exception. To the American Shaksperians, to whom we in the old country are under the greatest obligation for their enthusiastic and excellent work, I owe many apologies for the imperfect lists, which, if they could be made complete, might usefully be arranged in groups according to ownership.

In Chapter XII. I have tried to put into some sort of order the information at present known about the acting companies of Shakspere's time. The record of their movements is in an almost hopeless tangle. Something towards unravelling this has been done, more particularly by Collier, Halliwell-Phillipps, and Fleay, but much remains. The path along which one has to go in search of helps in the work is full of pitfalls, "and that craves wary walking." Dogmatic statements based only on probability are often made with as much assurance as if they were matters of fact, with the result that the enquirer is led widely astray. In work of this kind, where so much is yet incomplete, authorities should be quoted and references given for nearly every statement made. I should here like to modify one to which I referred with approval at p. 194. As a company described as the Queen's players was at Stratford-on-Avon in 1569 and in 1596, it will be more reasonable to consider that the actors playing there in 1587 were the Interluders (see p. 339) and not Elizabeth's special company of which James Burbage may have been a member, and which, established in 1583, had probably come to an end in 1594. It is of interest also to note that the youths licensed as performers in 1615 (see p. 232) were to travel "staying only fourteen days in a place, and not playing during church hours," and that when in 1618 they arrived at Exeter the Mayor would not allow them to play, as their manager had illegally added men to the Company. The Mayor however was not an enthusiast about dramatic performances; he considered that "those who spend their money on plays are ordinarily very poor people" (*Calendar of State Papers.* Domestic. 1611-1618, p. 549).

Metrical tests applied critically to Shakspere's plays have such an exasperating effect on many people, that I am almost afraid to say much about them. But the characteristics of the verse vary so much in different plays that their striking peculiarities cannot be ignored, although perhaps in some quarters too much has been made of them. I throw myself on the mercy of my readers for venturing to suggest another such test; and I beseech a tender consideration of Chapter XIII., in which I have explained it.

Distance from the British Museum has made it difficult to

prepare some of the details of this book; but I have been fortunate in having had free access to the excellent collections of books in the Bristol Museum and Library and in the library of the Clifton Shakspere Society.

The Reading-Tables, which formed the starting-point of the book, I owe to the industry of my wife, who, with a zeal commendable in its pertinacity, prepared them with the greatest accuracy. Miss Florence Herapath supplied me with the arrangement whereby the divided verse-lines of the non-Shaksperian plays can be gathered from their Reading-Tables, and in doing so brought to bear much metrical acumen on the problems, to the puzzling nature of which I have called attention at page 5. Miss Janet Smith, with most painstaking counting, which I fear must have often proved very wearisome, provided me with the table printed on page 353, without which the application of the test there given would have been impossible. The amount of labour involved in it can be appreciated only by those who have done similar work. To these ladies I am deeply indebted for the encouragement thereby given me, and to many other friends who have rendered me smaller but important services.

I should be ungrateful if I did not here express my most sincere thanks to my publisher and his staff for the great care they have bestowed on presenting my matter in a style of attractiveness which is, beyond all question, of the highest character.

Of the many shortcomings of the book I am perhaps more conscious than any who may set themselves to criticise it; but it must be remembered that the task I have set myself is a suggestive rather than a teaching one.

Feeling that one ought to offer to others that which from long experience has been found useful, and in the belief that

> "Never anything can be amiss
> When simpleness and duty tender it,"

I send forth the book with the hope that it will prove helpful to all students of the writer whom his own countrymen delight to honour as one who has led them to high places of delight and instruction, and whom all "corners of the world" acknowledge as the finest representative of an age which abounded with literary giants.

9 Gordon Road,
Clifton, Bristol,
November, 1889.

CONTENTS.

EVENINGS WITH SHAKSPERE.

LIBRARY OF THE UNIVERSITY OF CALIFORNIA

CHAPTER I.

The Method of the Work.

"Vouchsafe to read the purpose of my coming."
Love's Labour's Lost, II. i. 109.

THIS book is issued with a double purpose. At first, it was mainly intended to be a help in the reading-arrangements of the many Societies which exist for reading Shakspere's plays, by the distribution of the parts among the members.

The Reading-Tables, which form so large a part of the book, have been found indispensable in such a Society for many years, and it seemed likely that they would be useful in similar Societies. Prefixed to each play in Charles Knight's 'Cabinet' edition, and in Hunter's 'Annotated' *Shakespeare*, there is a list of the appearances of most of the persons represented, but no account is taken of many of the minor characters.

Recently a book entitled *Shakespeare Indexes* has been published, which gives a list of the scenes in which all the *dramatis personæ* speak.[1] As a help in the work of a Shakspere Reading Society this was a distinct gain, but it has the great and obvious disadvantage that the times of the speakers' appearances cannot be seen at a glance and the parts cannot be easily distributed so as to ensure that in any one scene a reader shall not have to take more than one part. This point is of prime importance in securing the success of the readings, and must be always kept in view.

But as there should be a Shakspere-Society, not only in every town, but in every set of people that can get together at least a dozen men and women with any literary desires, I have, out of an experience of many years as secretary, added some suggestions on the way of working such a society.

It is most desirable that persons busy with a daily occupation should have some outside intellectual diversion in which they can engage in a methodical manner. For this purpose nothing can be better than a Shakspere-Society with its endless ramifications of beauty, enjoyment, and interest. To people of leisure such a society offers boundless facilities for a zest and satisfaction in life which it would be difficult to obtain in any other way.

There will, of course, to the last days be scoffers who will throw ridicule on the idea of any good literary work being done by co-operation. But, without stopping to discuss this question, it will be sufficient to say that this is not quite the point involved in the existence of a Shakspere-Society. Beyond the pleasure of the meeting for the reading, experience has shown over and over again

[1] The book contains a second list, in which all the characters of the plays are given alphabetically, with a statement of the exact places in the plays where they can be found. This list, rather fuller than a similar one in Knight's *Pictorial Shakspere*, will be very useful.

how much is to be gained by the stimulus of others' exertions, and how association keeps up systematic study.

The literary criticism of which a society of ordinarily well-informed men and women is capable may not add anything to the knowledge of experts, but, at least, it will be a delight and an illumination to many to whom the wealth of the Elizabethan drama has not yet afforded much beyond the riches of Shakspere himself, or to whom, perhaps, his work is known only by a superficial acquaintance with the more frequently acted plays or, possibly, by a perfect familiarity with most of the well-quoted passages.

It is greatly to be feared that much of the nineteenth century admiration of Shakspere is akin to the prevailing sham of the present day. Many who talk of him as the greatest of poets, and who would be shocked if there were not a beautifully-bound edition of his works on the drawing-room table, would be puzzled to give the characteristics, or even the names, of the companions of the King in *Love's Labour's Lost*, or to write an intelligent outline of *The Two Gentlemen of Verona*, or they might be unable to say where Parolles is to be found, and, perhaps, as some one has said, would have to confess that they had never read *Cymbeline*. Books of "Extracts" or "Beauties" are, no doubt, greatly the cause of this deep ignorance, which is specially blameworthy as it is combined with so much pretence of knowledge. If there had been none of these books the world would have been the better, as it must then have gone to the text itself to find the gems. Ordinary intelligence and simple application are the only requirements for a fair grasp of the spirit and details of all Shakspere's plays. Technical criticism will, in addition, bring out a multitude of side questions of intense interest.

The Reading-Tables explain themselves.[1] At first they were prepared giving the mere appearances of the speakers, but afterwards it was decided to find out the number of lines in each part, in order that the grouping so often necessary might be arranged as equally as possible. It will be seen that this can sometimes be done exactly, and often when it cannot be so done the approximation is very close.

The tables of the Shakspere-plays are prepared from the 'Globe' edition. The various Lords, Messengers, and the like are not in every case differentiated. In many instances to do so would be to introduce confusion without any counterbalancing gain. Boys, Pages, Prologues, Epilogues, Choruses, Fairies are classed with the female characters. Most of the discrepancies between the totals of the scenes in the Tables and those in the 'Globe' are accounted for by the following:—

(*a*) Where a line of verse is divided between two or more speakers each speaker is in these Tables credited with a full line.

(*b*) Where two or more persons speak together the same words, each of these speakers is in these Tables credited with the words.

In the other instances the counting of the 'Globe' is wrong.[2] The tables of the other plays are compiled from the books mentioned in Chapter II., in which are given the reasons for their

[1] A few of them were printed in *Shakespeariana*, 1884-5.

[2] Counting the lines in a play is apparently a simple matter. Yet it seems difficult to be correct. Impressed with the inaccuracies in Mr. Fleay's tables (*Shakespeare Manual*, p. 135) Miss Rochfort Smith and Mr. Furnivall issued a re-numbering of the scene-lines (New Shakspere Society's *Transactions*, 1880—5, Part II.) Even in that there are many slight mistakes.

inclusion.[1] In all the editions that I have seen of the dramatists of Shakspere's time it is a matter of the greatest difficulty often to say what is prose and what is verse, and particularly so in instances where portions of speeches may go to make up one verse-line. No two persons would agree in the scansion of many of these, as it is frequently a question of individual judgement or caprice. But in many passages that admit of no doubt great injustice is done to playwrights by editors who print lines which as they stand are atrocious verse, but which would make excellent prose. It is most unscholarlike to print, for instance, *A New Way to Pay Old Debts* as verse throughout. Other cases will readily occur to the student, who was certainly justified in expecting that recent editors of Elizabethan plays would have attended to this and have made clear, in the way that has been done with Shakspere's plays, those instances where two or more speakers make up a line of verse between them.[2]

[1] In *British Dramatists* the length of a prose-line is sufficiently near that in the 'Globe' *Shakespeare* to enable a comparison of the length of the plays to be made.

[2] Many of the later Elizabethan dramatists are excessively fond of this metrical device. The reader may be pardoned for feeling irritated at meeting with passages printed thus, and such are of frequent occurrence.

"*Arb.* Is it? and, when I was return'd, thou know'st
Thou didst pursue it, till thou wound'st me in
To such a strange and unbelieved affection,
As good men cannot think on.
Gob. This I grant;
I think I was the cause.
Arb. Wert thou? Nay, more.
I think thou meant'st it.
Gob. Sir, I hate a lie.
As I love Heaven and honesty, I did;
It was my meaning.
Arb. Be thine own sad Judge."

A King and No King (ed. Darley, Vol. I., p. 76, col. 1.; *British Dramatists*, p. 288, col. 2; 'Mermaid Series,' Beaumont and Fletcher, Vol. II., p. 97).

The topics suggested for discussion cover only a very small portion of the ground, but they may be useful in indicating some lines upon which papers may be written. They are put in a dogmatic form on purpose to elicit discussion.[1] The statements are compiled in great measure, and often word for word, from books to which I have had access. Acknowledgement of the sources in each instance is not made, as it would prove wearisome and irritating. If there are any persons who seek further information on some of the points, I shall be glad to refer them to the books to which I have been indebted. It is almost needless to add that the statements contained in the "Suggestions" are not to be taken as representing my views.

The lists of extant Shakspere-editions have been obtained from the 'Cambridge' *Shakespeare.* I have kept the exact spelling of the names of printer and publisher. These supply further instances of the different ways in which in Shakspere's time the name of a person was often spelled. Much information in reference to the early editions can be obtained from books that should be familiar to the Shakspere-student, such as the *Variorum* of 1821, Mr. Halliwell-Phillipps's *Outlines of the Life of Shakespeare,*[2] Mr. Fleay's works containing many useful tables, the Rev. H. P. Stokes's book on the Chronological Order of the Plays, and Mr. Furnivall's Introduction to the 'Leopold' *Shakspere.* Particulars of the early editions of the plays by other writers have been gathered from various sources. It must be borne in mind that my lists do not give any editions later than the

[1] Unconscious testimony was rendered to the success of the intention I had when such questions were issued on a card to our members, for one of them innocently said to me, "There are several things here I shouldn't agree with."

[2] The edition from which my quotations are made is the Sixth. 1886.

date of the first Folio, except in those few instances where the earliest known edition is later than that year. Some writers have sought to fix the time of composition of many early plays by historical, meteorological, commercial, and such like allusions contained in them. As these are often—perhaps nearly always—misleading, I have not inserted them. They can be found in the pages of many imaginative commentators, who often also have fanciful theories about the sources of Shakspere's plots—theories which involve the assumption that he could easily read works in languages other than his own.[1] It is more reasonable to suppose that he learned the stories from his everyday companions, many of whom were scholars, and that the adaptation is one branch of his marvellous genius. These views are frequently not matters for dogmatic statements, but are open questions, and I have put some of them amongst the "Suggestions for Discussion."

In some instances, editions earlier than those known must either exist undiscovered or have been lost. Amongst the plays mentioned by Meres in 1598 are *The Two Gentlemen of Verona* and *The Comedy of Errors.* The earliest known editions of these are in the 1623 Folio. As frequent reference will be made to Meres, the full quotation of his mention of the writers whose plays are considered in this book is here given from the Allusion-Books issued by the New Shakspere Society:—

:: . . . . our Satyrifts, *Hall, the Author of Pigmalions*

[1] For instance, it is stated by more than one Shakspere-scholar that Shakspere founded *Timon of Athens* on Lucian's *Dialogues,* no English translation of which was in existence; and a recent medical writer, overlooking the fact that the incident of Juliet and the narcotic is taken direct from Arthur Brooke's poem, cites the names of learned writers to whom he considers Shakspere was probably indebted, but of whom it may be safely said Shakspere had never heard.

Image, and certain Satyres, Rankins, and ſuch others, are very profitable.

" . . . . the Engliſh tongue is mightily enriched, and gorgeouſlie inueſted in rare ornaments and reſplendent abiliments by ſir *Philip Sidney, Spencer, Daniel, Drayton, Warner, Shakeſpeare, Marlow* and *Chapman.*

" . . . . the ſweete wittie ſoule of *Ouid* liues in melli-fluous & hony-tongued *Shakeſpeare*, witnes his *Venus* and *Adonis*, his *Lucrece*, his ſugred Sonnets among his priuate friends, &c.

"As *Plautus* and *Seneca* are accounted the beſt for Comedy and Tragedy among the Latines: ſo *Shakeſpeare* among yᵉ Engliſh is the moſt excellent in both kinds for the ſtage; for Comedy, witnes his *Gẽtlemẽ of Verona*, his *Errors*, his *Loue labors loſt*, his *Loue labours wonne*, his *Midſummers night dreame*, & his *Merchant of Venice:* for Tragedy his *Richard the* 2. *Richard the* 3. *Henry the* 4. *King Iohn, Titus Andronicus* and his *Romeo* and *Iuliet.*

" . . . . the Muſes would ſpeak with *Shakeſpeares* fine filed phraſe, if they would ſpeake Engliſh.

"As *Muſæus*, who wrote the loue of *Hero* and *Leander*, had two excellent ſchollers, *Thamarus* & *Hercules:* ſo hath he in England two excellent Poets, imitators of him in the ſame argument and ſubiect, *Chriſtopher Marlow,* and *George Chapman.*"

[Quotations are then given from Ovid and Horace about the permanence of their works, and Meres speaks similarly of] "ſir *Philip Sidneys, Spencers, Daniels, Draytons, Shakeſpeares*, and *Warners workes.*

"As Italy had *Dante, Boccace, Petrarch, Taſſo, Celiano* and *Arioſto:* ſo England had *Mathew Roydon, Thomas Atchelow, Thomas Watſon, Thomas Kid, Robert Greene* & *George Peele.* . ."

[Among the chief lyric poets are named] "*Spencer*, (who excelleth in all kinds), *Daniel, Drayton, Shakeſpeare, Bretton.*

. . . . "these are our best for Tragedie, the Lord *Buckhurst*, Doctor *Leg* of Cambridge, Doctor *Edes* of Oxforde, maister *Edward Ferris*, the Authour of the *Mirrour for Magistrates*, *Marlow*, *Peele*, *Watson*, *Kid*, *Shakespeare*, *Drayton*, *Chapman*, *Decker*, and *Beniamin Iohnson*.

. . . . "the best for Comedy amongst vs bee, *Edward* Earle of Oxforde, Doctor *Gager* of Oxforde, Maister *Rowley* once a rare Scholler of learned Pembrooke Hall in Cambridge, Maister *Edwardes* one of her Maiesties Chappell, eloquent and wittie *Iohn Lilly*, *Lodge*, *Gascoyne*, *Greene*, *Shakespeare*, *Thomas Nash*, *Thomas Heywood*, *Anthony Mundye* our best plotter, *Chapman*, *Porter*, *Wilson*, *Hathway*, and *Henry Chettle*.

. . . . "these are the most passionate among vs to bewaile and bemoane the perplexities of Loue, *Henrie Howard* Earle of Surrey, sir *Thomas Wyat* the elder, sir *Francis Brian*, sir *Philip Sidney*, sir *Walter Rawley*, sir *Edward Dyer*, *Spencer*, *Daniel*, *Drayton*, *Shakespeare*, *Whetstone*, *Gascoyne*, *Samuell Page* sometimes fellowe of *Corpus Christi* Colledge in Oxford, *Churchyard*, *Bretton*."

[Reference is made to the ways in which Peele, Greene, and Marlowe met their deaths. Of the latter it is said] "our tragicall poet *Marlow* for his Epicurisme and Atheisme had a tragicall death; you may read of this *Marlow* more at large in the *Theatre of Gods iudgments*, in the 25. chapter entreating of Epicures and Atheists."

"*Palladis Tamia. Wits Treasvry, being the second part of Wits Commonwealth.* By Francis Meres Maister of Artes of both Vniuersities. 1598."

Meres gives the names of a large number of writers in addition to those mentioned above. From the length of the list, in which are many forgotten names, it must be concluded that he was a general, rather than a discriminating, admirer.

The chapter called "Notes on Editions of Shakspere's Works" contains summaries which I have not seen elsewhere, and which I trust may be found useful. Speaking for themselves they do not need any detailed explanation. I have added a table giving a list of many plays that have been issued separately, with notes or introduction. I have not ventured to appraise their literary worth. Some are nearly valueless, and others are almost indispensable. The list is given merely to save the enquirer much laborious searching.

The names of the companies acting the plays are those given on the title-pages of the editions. I shall be grateful for direct evidence of the performance of the plays about which I have made no statement. From the books already mentioned, and from Warton's *History of English Poetry*, I have in a separate chapter drawn up some information in reference to the companies who acted these plays and to the events which led to their formation.

I have left columns for the entry of the names of the present owners of the early editions of which so few copies exist. Many of those that I have given are from Bohn's edition of Lowndes' *Bibliographer's Manual*.[1] If a complete list could be given it would be of interest to the student. Many of the copies are in an imperfect state. I should have liked to have indicated this, but as the amount of imperfection varies considerably, no typographical device could convey a fair impression of its extent.

Immediately following I have endeavoured to reproduce the

[1] To this and the British Museum Catalogue of Early printed books, and to Hazlitt's *Handbook to Early English Literature*, I have been indebted for much information in reference to the early editions of nearly all the non-Shaksperian plays. Lowndes sometimes gives the date of an edition but no particulars about it. Of such I should be specially glad to get detailed information.

documentary evidence of the history—literary and otherwise—both of the play and its subject down to 1623, in such a way that the student may see at a glance all that is known of it.[1] In noting dates taken from records it must be remembered that before 1752, the official new year, synchronous with the renewal of Nature in the spring, began on the 25th of March.[2] In order to avoid confusion, I have, except where specially mentioned, given all dates according to the popular reckoning. Thus, Danter's entry of *Titus Andronicus*, dated February 6th, 1593 in the Stationers' Registers, is quoted by me as 1594.

The entries in Henslowe's *Diary*[3] are quoted direct from the Shakespeare Society's edition in 1845. The entries in the Stationers' Registers are taken from the *Transcript*, which the world owes to the painstaking labour of Mr. Arber.[4] I have endeavoured

[1] Many of the references to the early plays are, to put it mildly, under great suspicion. I have given them, adding a word of caution about their reception, because thereby the student may be introduced to that remarkable phase of Shakspere-investigation which is associated with the names of Collier, Cunningham, and others.

[2] This is a survival of the Hebrew sacred year. A trace of it, combined with a reminiscence of the Old Style, is still to be found in the arrangements of the Chancellor of the Exchequer's financial year, which begins on the 5th of April.

[3] Illiterate but useful Henslowe, at various times in many occupations, was also a theatrical manager. In this capacity he kept a record of his transactions from 1591 to 1609. The original MS. is in Dulwich College. A clerical friend of mine says that "after the Bible and the Prayer-book, Henslowe's *Diary* is the most interesting book in the English language."

[4] Judging from the facsimiles in Mr. Halliwell-Phillipps's *Outlines*, I cannot discover the reasons for the varieties of type in the *Transcript* entries. I have, however, literally adopted them.

Mr. Arber's *Transcript* would have been still more interesting and useful if the entries had been accompanied by notes after the manner of Collier in the volumes of the Registers (1557–1587), which he edited for the Shakespeare Society in 1848-9. Mr. Arber, in a praiseworthy desire to be clear, has been led into some mistakes, *e.g.*, in the entry of an interlude called *Edward Longe Shankes*, on August 14, 1600, (III. 169) he inserts [*III. surnamed*] after "*Edward*," and in the entry of March 2, 1618 (III. 621)

to give literally all the entries between 1584—the date of *Campaspe* —and 1623—the date of the first Shakspere-Folio—which refer to the plays comprehended in the scheme of study or to works apparently similar in subject.[1] It will be noted that there are instances where editions are in existence, but of which there are no entries in the Registers. On the other hand, plays were entered in the Registers and the books were either never published or have been lost. Entry in the Registers secured the copyright of the work. But as there were other authorities by which permission to print books could be granted, they are not a complete record of all literature. They also seem to have been imperfectly kept. This will be seen in many instances which occur in these pages, where the first entry is a transfer of rights from one publisher to another. Arber (*Transcript*, II. 24 and III. 18-19) calls attention to the fact "that the *Registers*—most precious as they are to posterity—are practically in their original intention the SUBSIDIARY CASH BOOKS of a London guild; that they were never intended as a record of the entire authorized literature; and that had they been so intended there were causes in operation—as the patents for whole classes of works as well as for single books; the books printed in other parts of Great Britain especially at the Universities and at Edinburgh, &c.

[1] An examination of the entries and of the history of the plays after this date is of great interest. I stopped at 1623, as it is such a noteworthy date in connection with Shakspere-work.

he reads "*Doctor. FAUSTUS 2 parte* [*s*]" where the [s] should not have been added, as the reference is to the sequel to *Faustus* originally entered to Burby on November 16, 1593.

Mr. Arber's volumes also stand in need of a copious index. Although indexes were not the only literary things which Collier seems to have manufactured, yet the care and detail with which he prepared these in the books which he edited have laid students under a perpetual obligation to him.

—which would have precluded the possibility of their ever becoming such a National Index of Printed Literature."

Feeling it would be convenient to have a Chronicle of Events connected with the writers and the plays that are to come within the consideration of a Shakspere-Society, I have put into that form those which seem to be of the greatest interest. In such a record it is difficult to know what to leave out. The dates of some of these events cannot be exactly ascertained. Those about which there may be a little doubt are printed in *Italic.*

CHAPTER II.

The Extent of the Work.

"When we mean to build,
We first survey the plot, then draw the model."
2 *Henry IV.*, I. iii. 41-2.

IF the attention is closely limited to the works of Shakspere alone, much of interest will be evoked but the view of the man and of his times will after all be but circumscribed.

To the members of a Shakspere-Society, a systematic consideration of Shakspere not only in his works but in his personal and literary environment will reveal matters of interest which are never presented to the ordinary reader.

Many of us are too prone to look upon Shakspere as a writer of single plays. Whilst it is an incontrovertible fact that the creator of Hamlet or the author of *Othello* would, if he had done nothing else, have had an enduring fame, yet it must be conceded that we shall get a truer view of him if we look at his work as a whole and take note of the influences which were around him. Devotees of Shakspere should be glad to survey him in conjunction with his contemporaries, as it will bring out his powers into greater prominence. It will, however, be a gain to most people to discover that, although there has been only one sun in the English system of the dramatic universe, there are—or perhaps one should say were—many stars, some of them being of the first magnitude. And Shakspere was so intimately connected with the play-writers of his time that a study of his work which leaves out that of his contemporaries must fall short of its best possible results. Joint authorship, appropriation of subjects, disagreements, quarrels, estrangements, were even then of such frequent occurrence amongst men of genius that a closer inspection showing that the greatest of them were very human will not be without its benefits, and certainly not without its interest.

These great writers seem to have been thrown together so much in their ordinary vocation as playwrights that to obtain a right appreciation of them, we must study them as a body as well as individually.

So to bring into view the set in which Shakspere mixed, plays by his contemporaries must be included in the scheme of work. It is, of course, only possible to make a selection of these. There would not be enough time in a society to deal with any considerable number of plays by each of the Elizabethan dramatists, and some, probably most, members of societies would be unwilling to incur the expense of buying separate editions of an author for the study of only one or two of his plays.

The difficulty can be got over by the use of two cheap books:

(1) *British Dramatists.* Edited by John S. Keltie.[1]

(2) The 'Tauchnitz' volume of *Doubtful Plays of Shakespeare.*[2]

[1] Published by Nimmo of Edinburgh, at 5/-.

[2] Published in paper covers at 1/6, in cloth at 2/-.

These books and the 'Globe' *Shakespeare* will be the text-books of each member of the Society.

British Dramatists contains twenty-one plays of the time between 1584 and 1639; but in the course of study for a Shakspere-Society the plays by Ford and Shirley are omitted.[1] The 'Tauchnitz' book has six plays which if at all connected with Shakspere, are so probably only to a very slight extent. *The Two Noble Kinsmen*, which is included in the scheme, can be obtained, edited with notes by Professor Skeat, in the Pitt Press Series, or the text only can be got in the last number of Cassell's serial issue of the 'Leopold' *Shakspere*, from which its Reading-Table here has been prepared. In many of these plays, as in several of Shakspere's, there is much in the phraseology to be lamented, from a nineteenth century point of view. But as vice is held up to reprobation and the general lesson of the play is a healthy one, these passages can always be eliminated without destroying the current of the story. It is a matter of common knowledge that in those times there was in all ranks of life an almost incredible freedom of expression. Fresh instances of this have just come to light in the details of the Hatfield House MSS. that have recently been made public. In reference to this it must be borne in mind that "morality is not outraged, or even in question: it is only a matter of fashion."[2] It is more than doubtful if the Elizabethan dramatists worded the title-pages of their plays, but it is not improbable that the publishers, knowing the views which the writers entertained of the topics they treated,

[1] An enthusiastic Society might be able to set apart extra evenings for these, or they could, with some plays not included in the book, be taken as a summer course. An inventive and laborious set of workers could find some way of indirectly introducing at the critical meetings something about the early plays to be found in *Dodsley* and about such writers as John Heywood, Kyd, Lodge, Nash, Chapman, Dekker, and Middleton.

[2] Mr. J. W. Mills in *The Academy*, May 5, 1888, p. 312.

endeavoured by lengthy titles to give the author's summary of the moral of the subject-matter of the play.

The session should consist of eight months in each year. One play should be taken in each of these months.[1] In England, October to May inclusive will be found the most convenient time.

It will be advisable to consider the plays in some definite order, and not leave their selection to hap-hazard chance. After trying more than one plan, we have settled down to the chronological order as being the most helpful. This, it is almost needless to say, can not be definitely ascertained, but a tolerably close approximation is possible. A society wishing for the sequence of its Shakspere-work to follow a great authority, can take Professor Dowden as a guide, and adopt the order which he gives in his *Shakspere Primer.*[2] The other plays taken also in chronological order, are to be worked in with the Shakspere ones. In each session five months are to be given to undoubted works of Shakspere, and three to others. This will be found a desirable proportion. The Poems and Sonnets must have two evenings devoted to their critical consideration, as they will not be read in parts. It will be most convenient to take them near the middle of the course.

Members can join at any time and the list can be repeated over and over again, as at the end of a course the *personnel* of the Society will so have changed that the oldest inhabitant will always be joined in a reconsideration of a play by companions of ever-varying modes of thought.

[1] This plan is put forth in defiance of a saying, I think, by Goethe, to the effect that "no one who did not wish to make shipwreck of his intellect should study more than one play of Shakspere in a twelvemonth."

[2] Published by Macmillan and Co. This is a book which everybody, whether belonging to a Shakspere-Society or not, should have.

The following list will make a comprehensive course, extending over eight years:—

1st Session.

Titus Andronicus
Campaspe
1 Henry VI.
2 Henry VI.
Faustus
3 Henry VI.
The Comedy of Errors
Friar Bacon

2nd Session.

The Two Gentlemen of Verona
Edward II.
Love's Labour's Lost
Richard II.
King David
A Midsummer-Night's Dream
Richard III.
Locrine

3rd Session.

Romeo and Juliet
Edward III.
John
The Taming of the Shrew
Every Man in his Humour
The Merchant of Venice
Much Ado about Nothing
Thomas, Lord Cromwell

4th Session.

1 Henry IV.
Antonio and Mellida
2 Henry IV.
The Merry Wives of Windsor
Antonio's Revenge
Henry V.
Poems and Sonnets
A Woman Killed with Kindness

5th Session.

As You Like It
The London Prodigal
Twelfth Night
Julius Cæsar
A Yorkshire Tragedy
Hamlet
The Silent Woman

6th Session.

All's Well that Ends Well
The Alchemist
Othello
Measure for Measure
Philaster
Lear
Timon of Athens
A King and No King

7th Session.	*8th Session.*
MACBETH	CYMBELINE
THE KNIGHT OF THE BURNING PESTLE	THE DUKE OF MILAN
PERICLES	THE WINTER'S TALE
ANTONY AND CLEOPATRA	THE TEMPEST
THE DUCHESS OF MALFI	THE BIRTH OF MERLIN
TROILUS AND CRESSIDA	HENRY VIII.
CORIOLANUS	THE TWO NOBLE KINSMEN
THE VIRGIN-MARTYR	A NEW WAY TO PAY OLD DEBTS

Love's Labour's Lost is usually placed earlier than in the foregoing list, but looking to the fact that the play, as we have it, is the 1598 edition, "presented before her Highnes this last Christmas. Newly corrected and augmented;" and considering that almost certainly that was the first appearance of the revised play, it ought rather—although containing much of Shakspere's early work—to be placed even later than I have given it. It is difficult to know where to put *The Taming of the Shrew*. The external evidence, such as it is, and which I have set forth opposite its reading-table, might justify a later position, but altogether it is best perhaps to take it before so many of the plays which are obviously more mature in workmanship. The position of *The Merry Wives of Windsor* is another difficulty. There is no entry or edition of it before 1602, and the edition published in that year is a mere sketch compared with the play in the 1623 Folio. I have later on called attention to it in reference to the other Falstaff-plays, and as it cannot be very much, if at all, out of its order I have, in the course, placed it between 2 *Henry IV.* and *Henry V.*, and thereby have avoided the shock of reviving Falstaff in his dissoluteness after the touching record of his death. The chronological position of many of the other plays is entirely matter of conjecture, and will form an interesting exercise for the individual student or for the members of a society. *Timon of Athens*, *Pericles*, and *Troilus and Cressida* are the most perplexing of them. Each is in itself so unequal that it is impossible to resist the conclusion that it is either the work of Shakspere and somebody else, or that it was written at vastly distant periods of Shakspere's life. In either case the order each play is to take in a list is, with the present evidence, an insoluble problem.

On account of the length of *Hamlet* it will be well to give two evenings to its reading. A similar time should be devoted to its critical consideration.

CHAPTER III.

Organisation.

"We have strict statutes and most biting laws."
Measure for Measure, I. iii. 19

AS the development of a Shakspere-Society will probably always be gradual, the best way of showing the mode of working one will be to trace the growth of the Society of which I have been Secretary from its beginning, and then to quote our rules and add some comments showing their desirability and their course of evolution.

In 1876 the idea was suggested that it would be a pleasant way of spending some evenings if a few people could meet regularly at one another's houses to read Shakspere's plays in parts. A small meeting of ladies and gentlemen to form a Society with this purpose was held at my house on March 11th of that year, and on March 25th *The Two Gentlemen of Verona* was read from a cast drawn up by the Secretary and one of the principal promoters. It was intended to have the readings twice a month, and this was done for four months. But it had very soon become apparent that much greater interest would be introduced if opportunities were afforded for talking over the excellencies and obscurities of many passages.

The Society had been formed as a Reading Party, and systematic Shaksperian criticism was a novelty to the members.[1] It was difficult to see how a satisfactory plan for such could be worked. As a tentative proceeding, it was decided to devote every fifth meeting to a consideration of the four plays that had just been read. This did not prove satisfactory.[2] Eventually it was agreed to have reading and critical meetings alternately. The admirable plan of taking a play each month has been followed since then, and it is difficult to see how a better arrangement could be made. Some members of a Shakspere-Society will care for the readings only and some for the criticism only, and so each will get a meeting once a month; whilst for those who care for both forms of occupation, the more frequent opportunities of joining with like-minded people in congenial work will be gladly seized.

In Shakspere's plays the *dramatis personæ* vary so much in number[3] that it will be well to have members enough for the frequent occasions when there are many characters in the same scene. Our number of seven ladies and eighteen gentlemen has been found very convenient, and in this book all the arrangements of preparing the cast when there are more characters than members have been made for this number.[4] And as the social character of

[1] To a member of a learned profession who belonged to a Shakspere Reading Party, I suggested not long ago that they should follow some such lines as ours. Amazed, he said to me, "What! criticise Shakspere!" Much misconception arises from the too frequent limitation of the word "criticism" to its adverse meaning. The process should be understood to be merely one of intelligent consideration. The word has got almost as much distorted as the Elizabethan "censure."

[2] See Chapter V.

[3] The men's characters range from 13 to 58, and the women's from 2 to 10.

[4] If it is desirable to modify the numbers, the grouping arrangements will be facilitated by taking the set of groups given in Chapter IX. as a point of departure.

the work is always to be kept in view, it will be well not to exceed the number, which well suits the capacity of most drawing-rooms.

We have been great sticklers for rule. The stability of a society will largely depend upon the strictness with which its laws are kept. Our rules have been modified and developed from time to time. Now they are as follows:—

1. The Society shall be called "The Clifton Shakspere Society."

The local form of title[1] will be better than any high-sounding name borrowed from histrionic association or derived from a fanciful nomenclature.

2. The object of the Society shall be the study of the works of Shakspere by reading and criticism. The plays shall be read by allotment of the parts to the members.

As additional light is thrown upon Shakspere's works by the study of the contemporary drama, the words of this rule may stand, unless a literalist wishes for an exact definition of the extent of the work. The mode of allotting is stated in Rule 10, and will be considered in detail in Chapter IV.

3. The Society shall consist of not more than twenty-five Members (seven ladies and eighteen gentlemen) and seven Associates (two ladies and five gentlemen), from whom shall be elected an Annual President, a Secretary, and an Assistant-Secretary. When the Society has its complement of Members

[1] Even this simple style may cause some misapprehension. At one of my visits to Stratford, I was with a lady who often makes somewhat long pauses in her speech. She was going to tell one of the librarians there something about our Society, but when she had got as far as "We have a Clifton Shakspere," an expression came over his face which seemed to denote a fear that a nineteenth-century rival to his hero had been found on the banks of another Avon, and that soon, perhaps, his occupation would be gone. He was, however, re-assured when she finished the sentence. It was only a momentary trouble, but it was a real one.

there may be elected seven Associates (two ladies and five gentlemen), who may attend the meetings, succeed to vacant Memberships without further election, and who may be requested to fill up vacancies in the cast. Any Member may after resignation be elected a Vice-President, provided the number of Vice-Presidents at any one time shall not exceed six.

For reasons stated above, I strongly recommend this number of members.

The introduction of Associates was one of the happiest thoughts ever conceived in the mind of a member of a Shakspere-Society. They form a class we have had for years. They should be always at their posts, and then they would prove the greatest comfort to a secretary perplexed by the inability of his members to come to the readings. The clause in the rule sufficiently defines their usefulness. They have no parts allotted in the original cast.

This rule could be improved by making provision for the admission of those who wish to join such a Society without having upon them the responsibility of taking part in the readings, which, according to Rule I., have to be undertaken by the members. The honour of Vice-President will be conferred upon those only who have rendered signal service to the Society.

It will introduce an element of freshness to have a new President every year; but it will be best to re-elect the Secretary if he is interested in the work and will give enough time to it. An Assistant-Secretary is a luxury that young societies will not need, and is one that we have only recently obtained. His share in the work will be mentioned under Rule 11.

4. Any person wishing to join the Society shall be proposed and

seconded at one meeting, and balloted for at the next. One adverse vote in ten to exclude.

Information of a vacancy should be given in the notice convening the meeting, so that all may have the same opportunity of proposing fresh names. In a small society the good sense of the members shown in bringing forward only fit persons will render the exercise of the adverse vote rarely necessary. Our provision for exclusion gives, perhaps, too much power to a single vote.

5. Each Member and Associate shall pay an entrance fee of 2/6, and an annual subscription of 3/6.

The annual subscription here named is ridiculously small for a literary society. A new society should fix its yearly contribution at not less than 5/-. Half-a-guinea should be the subscription for most societies. Our subscription remains at its original amount, which in our early days as a mere reading-party was ample. With enlarged aims more is wanted.

6. On the proposal of any Member or Associate, seconded by another, and unanimously adopted at a subsequent meeting, any lady or gentleman may be invited to become a corresponding member of the society and to send from time to time communications to be read at the critical meetings. Corresponding members shall pay no entrance-fee or subscription, and shall be entitled to all the privileges of ordinary members. The number of corresponding members at any one time shall not exceed ten, four of whom are to be resident outside the British Isles.

Corresponding members will only be thought of in a well-established society, with a thoroughly systematic course of criticism,

Referring to this rule the editor of *Shakespeariana*[1] said, "This is a valuable feature of Club-work, and indicates a way to bring in a breath of fresh air from the outer world, for which the ordinary, insulated Club would be the better." This is well put, as probably n every case a corresponding member will be one who is far in advance of most of the members in knowledge of special points, and who will be able to throw a flood of light on a technical question which would involve immense research on the part of one who had not made a particular study of it. Our corresponding members are a great strength to us. A meeting rarely passes without a communication from one or other of them. The number should be kept small, and should be limited to those who are known to have done good Shakspere-work.

7. The Society shall meet at 7.30 p.m. on the second and the fourth Saturday in each month, from October to May inclusive. An extra meeting shall be held on the first Saturday in October, at which the Secretary shall present a Report of the Society's work during the previous twelve months, the retiring President deliver an address, and the officers be elected.

It will rarely be possible to get a society together to begin work at half-past seven. We are summoned for that hour, but some little time is taken up by tea and by final arrangements about the readings. This, probably, will always be necessary.

The extra meeting is required for transaction of yearly business, which would encroach too much on the work of a reading or a critical evening.

It is convenient that the Secretary should every year bring together in a report the record of the Society's work.

[1] Vol. III. p. 572. 1886.

The Presidential address gives the opportunity of a wider survey than is often possible at an ordinary meeting.

Every session a card having the names of the plays and the dates on which they are to be taken should be sent to the members. We print upon it the list of the critical departments (see Chapter V.) and the names of Vice-Presidents, Past-Presidents, and Corresponding Members.

8. The first meeting of the month shall be devoted to the reading of the play, and the second meeting to criticism of it. At the critical meetings each Member and Associate is at liberty to introduce a visitor.

It has been sometimes thought that the order of the work might be reversed, and that the reading would be more attractive if the criticism had come first. But the advantages altogether are in favour of the order in the rule.

Visitors at the critical meetings should be encouraged to add to the discussions by pen or speech.

9. At the last meeting in each session the work for the next session shall be arranged.

It will be found convenient to have time in the recess for thinking over the way in which the plays shall be considered, and for preparing the list of subjects for discussion. (See Chapter V.)

10. The Secretary, twelve days before the evening for reading, shall send to each member a form for selecting the cast of the parts in the play to be read. The cast of the parts shall be made by the Secretary from the returns forwarded by the members.

Directions for preparing the cast will be found in Chapter IV.

11. The Assistant-Secretary shall, at least five days before the evening for reading, give to each person belonging to the Society notice of the meeting, with a copy of the final cast, and the same length of notice of the critical meetings.

In those societies that need, and have the good fortune to possess, an Assistant-Secretary the best arrangement will be for the Secretary to do the work of preparing the cast and to send a copy of the final cast to the Assistant-Secretary, who by means of one of the various copying processes will prepare the required number and send them out. The exact form of the notices for the reading and critical evenings will be sent to him by the Secretary, with whom it will be found less confusing to leave the arrangements, and who, keeping the minute-book, will know what matter it will be necessary to insert in the notices. It adds much to the interest of the work for each member to get a copy of the final cast, rather than a bare mention of the part to be read. It is not much extra trouble to print enough for the Vice-Presidents, Associates, and Corresponding Members.

12. Members with parts allotted are expected to make a special effort to attend the reading, on account of the inconvenience of re-arranging the cast; but in case there should be a positive inability to be present, it is requested that notice to that effect be sent to the Secretary not later than the Wednesday next before the reading.

Observations on this rule will be more conveniently placed in Chapter IV.

13. The Society shall subscribe annually to "The New Shakspere Society."

This will not be necessary in those unfortunate cases where critical work is not done.

14. The Library-Fund, formed and maintained by donations from Members and others, shall be managed by a Committee consisting of one lady and two gentlemen, with the President and the Secretary as members *ex officio*. From this fund no book shall be purchased for the Society without the approval of three members of the Committee.

15. The books and publications belonging to the Society shall be kept at the Secretary's house. Each Member and Associate shall be provided with a catalogue of the Library, and shall be able to obtain any book required, recording the loan in a register kept for the purpose.

A consideration of these rules will be found in Chapter VI.

16. Notice of a proposed alteration of, or addition to, the rules shall be given at one meeting and voted upon at the next. For such change a majority of two-thirds of those present shall be necessary.

It would be wise to add here a clause, requiring that the proposed alteration shall be stated in the circular convening the meeting. It is important that the whole Society should be informed of any contemplated change.

These rules will probably be found ample. Whatever code is adopted, it must be rigidly kept. It is better to have a few rules and permit no departure from them than to have a long array of paper-laws which are constantly being allowed to be trifled with or broken.

CHAPTER IV.

The Readings.

"It is not enough to speak, but to speak true."
A Midsummer-Night's Dream, V. i. 121.

THE mode of allotting the parts should be carried out so as not to throw an invidious task upon one person or any small number of persons. The plan which we have (Rule 10, p. 27) is perfect in theory, and only requires co-operation to make it a complete success in practice. A printed form containing a list of all the members is sent to each of them, with a request to return it[1] to the Secretary filled up in the way he or she would like the play to be read. If the *dramatis personæ* are so many as to require arrangement in groups, these are stated,[2] and any other information is added that is necessary for the purpose.[3]

[1] This can be done anonymously, if wished.

[2] Or, if the society is constituted with the numbers given in Rule 3 (p. 23), the members could be referred to this book for the groups.

[3] If this book is not used it will be necessary to give the designations of the characters not definitely mentioned in the list at the beginning of the play and to point out that some women's parts will be left out in the reading. For instance, in 2 *Henry IV.* we omit Doll Tearsheet, giving in II. iv. some of her sayings to the Hostess, and so preserving the continuity of the scene.

From the papers returned the Secretary compiles the final cast according to the votes given. The returns must be quite independent, as agreement between two or more members would violate the principle upon which the cast is made. A plan, not invidious in its mode and not involving trouble, has been suggested by which the parts would be distributed by lottery. This might bring out latent talent, but it would usually be so grotesque in its results that a society wishing to retain its reputation for sanity would do well not to adopt it. A society, not able to attain to the mode of allotment by intelligent vote, could read through a play by the speeches being taken in turn as the members happen to sit.

After the parts are allotted, the next thing is to get the people to the meeting to read. In every society there will most likely always be some members whom it will be impossible to make realise the responsibility to others which the mere act of membership involves. It should be a point of honour that the attendance at the readings should be as regular as possible. Only the most important matters should keep members from a reading. Not only does an absence throw upon the Secretary the work—often a troublesome one—of re-arranging the cast,[1] but it frequently gives to over-burdened readers other parts which they may have to take up at very short notice, or, sad to say, perhaps without any notice at all. A small money-fine never to be remitted for any excuse whatever would be the best way of bringing home to many persons the fact that their presence was important. I should recommend any society beginning work to have such a fine. When the society has been once established it will be difficult to introduce it. In some societies a certain number of consecutive failures to attend is considered equivalent to

[1] The point mentioned on p. 2 must always be kept in view.

a resignation. Also, as it is more pleasing to the society generally to hear the parts well distributed, the attendance of all members is desirable in order to avoid the concentration of a vast number of parts upon one reader. Holofernes, who said, "I will play three myself," would find in a modern Shakspere-Society that his powers would be subject to a severer strain than that. He would have to admit that such a limitation would be a "simple coming-in for one man" who on a single evening "plays many parts."

Although the 'Globe' edition is the society's standard of reference for the Shakspere-plays, it will not be desirable to insist that it shall be the only book used for the reading. Not many people who are over forty can read such type easily, especially at night, and most persons will prefer to choose their own text. But in order to prevent confusion, members should always compare their own editions with it, as editors do not all follow the same early authorities, and sometimes there is much discrepancy between modern copies.[1]

All 'Bowdlerised' editions must be avoided. They leave passages in which should be out and omit parts which ought to stay in. Even the Clarendon Press series, which at present does not include half the number of plays, is faulty in this respect, and must occasionally prove very embarrassing to teachers, for whom they are especially intended. Any necessary expurgation must be done by members themselves. When it comes in the middle of a speech, it should be left to the individual reader. When it affects the cues, it should be an arrangement between the persons concerned; but sometimes it will be better for the Secretary to arrange it for them. At times it occurs that a reader's part, not itself requiring mutilation,

[1] Similar comparison should be made with the editions of the other plays read by the society.

is, through an omission of this kind, brought on much sooner than it otherwise would be. Notice of this should always be given to the reader, or an awkward pause may take place and some confusion ensue.[1]

Nothing should be left out of any play for the purpose of shortening it. If it is too long for the evening's reading, it will be best to carry on part for reading at the beginning of the critical evening; but this must be done as rarely as possible. In our earlier days we cut out much of the long plays, but such practice is one to be carefully avoided. Long ago one of our members tersely put it, "Parts to be left out must be on account of breadth and not of length." It may be convenient to have a five-minutes' interval about half-way through the reading.

Opinions will vary much as to the mode of society-reading, that is, whether the elocution should be dramatic or commonplace. Most persons, probably, will prefer the former in moderation. Passages should be "well spoken, with good accent," "not too tame," "with discretion as the tutor." It comes somewhat as a shock to see in the text a speaker chidden for violence of manner whose words have been rendered by the reader in the mildest manner possible. In fact, Hamlet's advice to the player, leaving out the directions as to action, may be taken as applicable to members of dramatic reading-societies. In some societies it is the custom for all the readers in a scene to stand whilst it is being read.

[1] I have all the plays marked so that they can be read aloud by a society of ladies and gentlemen. I shall be happy to give them to any publisher who would print them, and thereby confer a boon not only on Shakspere-Societies, but upon individuals wishing to read the plays aloud. A most admirable and useful volume might be compiled, consisting of all the plays comprehended in this scheme of study, arranged in the order given, and treated in the manner I have named.

The songs may be sung, but on no account must the realism be interfered with by allowing songs which are obviously solos to be rendered as part-songs. From the frequency with which this has been done it is clear that although many of the composers who have set the songs to music may have been great musicians, they were certainly not students of Shakspere. In singing in society there should be no break in the text by having to go to a piano and finding out music. If the singing involve this, it should be done without accompaniment or the song should be read. If the song comes in the part of one who cannot or will not sing, there should be no difficulty in transferring it.

It is not fair to the society generally that members should from their own choice, or through the default of others, read parts at sight. There may be some omission to be made which requires a little looking at beforehand. Again, although nearly all Shakspere's verse-lines have rhythm as well as sense, it is necessary to be familiar with their metrical form, and this it is not always easy to see at a glance. Every part should be carefully gone over before the reading. A misplaced accent will destroy the music of a line, and a disregard of the proper pronunciation of some parts of speech may at times be truly horrifying. It may make some persons shiver to hear an Oberon say

"The imperial votaress pass'd on,"

or a Gratiano declare that he gave the ring to

"a little scrubb'd boy,"

or a Juliet with a reiterated lamentation that her

"Romeo is banish'd."

Members by being well on the alert to take up their parts at the proper moment can add much to the pleasure of a reading. It is a tantalising disillusion to find that there is in the party a Bottom, who every now and then, from some cause or other, practically says, "When my cue comes, *call* me."

The Reading-evenings, if carefully managed in reference to many of the foregoing particulars, will prove pleasant and popular. But in order that they should be so, it will be necessary that the Secretary should be loyally supported by the members, who must render him every assistance by regular attendance and a promptness in taking up parts required.

CHAPTER V.

The Criticism.

"I am nothing, if not critical."
Othello II. i. 120.

ALL Shakspere Reading-Societies should make provision for something more than elocutionary consideration of the plays they read. To get a satisfactory plan for this was with us, at first, a great difficulty.

Some of the members who were with us in our early days, when we began our critical work by setting apart every fifth meeting for a retrospect of four plays, often recall with astonishment our mode of procedure then. Novices in the art, we essayed little beyond comment on the unusual words, and, as a result, the whole evening was spent upon the earlier portion of the first of the four plays and the other three were not touched. Much the same sort of thing was repeated with the next series of four. When, in May, 1877, it was proposed to make every fourth meeting a critical one, a lady-member, who has been one of our greatest reformers, boldly proposed an entire departure from the original plan of a mere reading-party, and succeeded in getting the time of the society equally divided between reading and criticism. The plan we followed for some time was that described in the sixth by-law (p. 43), and it was not till April, 1878, that our first paper on a play was read. Since that time we have almost always had one or more papers at each critical meeting. An arrangement which for a time was very popular was the division of the critical work into sections, which were allotted to members who brought forward reports in connection therewith. The following is a list of them :—

Æsthetic Criticism.
Anachronisms.
Animals.
Arts and Sciences.
Biblical and Religious Allusions.
Classical and Mythical Allusions.
Coins, Weights, and Measures.
Demonology and Witchcraft.
Dress and Social Customs.
Early Dramatic Representations.
Fine Art.
Geography.
Grammar.
Historical References.
Law and Heraldry.
Meats and Drinks.
Medicine and Surgery.
Metre and Authorship.
Music and Ballads.
Oaths and Exclamations.
Personal Histories.
Plants.

Play-craft.
Puns and Jests.
Rare Words and Phrases.
Satire and Irony.
Similes and Metaphors.
Sources and History.
Sports and Pastimes.
Trade and Commerce.
Tradition and Folk-lore.
Various Readings.

But since we have had a good supply of papers of a more general character this plan has, I think unfortunately, fallen much into disuse. To the most busy, the most nervous, or the most recent critics, it offers a convenient opportunity for taking some share in that which to many is the most interesting part of the society's work. Rarely should a critical meeting pass without half-a-dozen short departmental reports. They need not attempt to be exhaustive. It would often be most useful to get a two or three minutes' paper on one point within the survey of a critical department.

It will be a distinct gain if a society can get systematic consideration of Shakspere's marvellous characterisation. This may be done by getting one or more members with inclination and ability for this particular work to promise to bring at each meeting a critical analysis of one or more of the characters; or, better still, by getting several people to write very short papers on the same character or characters. This latter plan has the advantage of getting the characters looked at simultaneously from several points of view. Many persons are too much inclined to take recorded opinions as final, rather than enquire closely for themselves whether such opinions are justified. Some most utter nonsense has been written about Shakspere's characters. There is still plenty of room for analysis of these, if people will give up writing about them as mere abstractions of various virtues and vices and will look upon them as flesh-and-blood beings whose analogues may be met with in every-day life. They are to be paralleled amongst our own friends and acquaintances, who, if the external conditions were alike, would act in much the same style as the people in the plays. If this is not so, we should have to say that Shakspere's creations are not true to life.

The "Suggestions for Discussion," to be found later on, will serve to prompt many with ideas that may not have occurred to them. It is not meant thereby to lay down any limit to the subjects to be brought forward. Many members will, of course, prefer to work out a line of thought that may be quite independent of them. The aim should be to get at each meeting one general paper dealing with the play as a whole and some smaller papers or departmental reports upon minor questions or on side-issues. Discussion on papers is more likely to be general if their titles can be announced beforehand.

Beyond the multitudinous points of intense interest to be found by a close study of the text itself, there are many others which should engage the attention of members of a society. A consideration of so-called sources of the plot of a play will always be interesting. Although in many cases it will be merely a view of the treatment of the same subject by other writers, the comparison will be of value. In some instances, such as the Chronicles, Plutarch's *Lives*, and older plays, from which Shakspere derived not only facts but expressions, the connection is undoubted. Many of the historical plays should also be compared with the verse-histories of Drayton and Daniel.

A comparison of the textual values of the Quartos and the 1623 Folio, with an examination of the emendations of various editors, will show to what an extent the generally-received modern text deviates from the early copies.

Many a play that is commonly accepted as the production of a single playwright was either the conjoint work of two or more writers, or the completion by a second writer of another's unfinished drama, or the copy altered to suit the requirements of a theatrical manager, dependent upon the changing taste of a fickle public. Familiarity with the individual styles of the writers of the period, including a knowledge of their metrical peculiarities, will enable a critic to assign, perhaps with an approach to accuracy, the different parts of such plays. In cases where the question of Shakspere's authorship is involved, the attempt to do this must not be made with a preconceived determination to allot him all the best parts of a play in which there is reason to believe work of a second writer exists in conjunction with his. The nineteenth century has had painful experience in finding that poets who occupy the front rank can at times write much that is unpleasing and inharmonious; and in investigating the alleged composite authorship of any play in which it is supposed that Shakspere was only partly concerned, it may remove some difficulties if we admit that he may sometimes have nodded or that occasionally he may have put pen to paper when he was dyspeptic.

Theatrical companies did not generally receive plays indiscriminately from writers, but kept to their own set. Much, therefore, may be learned from an investigation of the records which show by which companies certain plays were first acted. The later stage-history of the play should be followed, and at each critical meeting there should be a paper on this subject, showing the mangling the plays have undergone at the hands of many from whom better things might have been expected, and also lamenting the outrages which have been inflicted upon the text in its preparation for the stage.

The ordinary reader of Shakspere, delighted with the language or with the story, or with both, does not see in the plays any veiled allusions to contemporary persons or events. But there can be very little doubt that such references exist. When we take into consideration the fondness of his age for far-fetched conceits or obscure allusion, it is impossible to believe that Shakspere would not find some opportunity of introducing into the plays his views of the great social and political movements of the period. Through the lapse of time it becomes increasingly difficult to fix many of these references. An allusion quite patent to an Elizabethan audience may be completely lost upon us, without in the least interfering with the charm which is upon the surface of the play. Some investigation into these matters has been made, but its result for the most part lies unheeded in the pages of discarded magazines or neglected books.[1] A search into the State Papers might often bring out the connection of a passage in the plays with some contemporary episode.

The reading of Mr. P. A. Daniel's *Time-Analysis* will always afford interest. It would be an admirable thing if somebody would on the same lines do the time-analysis of other plays as they come before the society.

[1] Much of interest in reference to such points will be found in Richard Simpson's books and articles.

The introduction of non-Shaksperian plays into the work of the society will afford various opportunities of dealing with the relation of Shakspere to his fellow-dramatists, and of those to one another. The theory that the playwrights often pilloried one another in their plays is one worth working out in connection with plays by many of the writers whose work is here comprehended.

At the critical evenings on these writers, there should always be a paper dealing with the writers generally and giving an outline of their work, besides that coming immediately before the meeting. Some consideration in detail should also be given to the dedications with which their plays are so frequently introduced. It is easy to adduce from the plays various illustrations of life and manners in that age of energy, and these will be of perennial interest.

There should be some by-laws for the conduct of the critical meetings. On paper ours look needlessly harsh. They are intended more to be kept in reserve than for common use, and are as follows:

1. Papers, and discussions thereon, shall take precedence of other discussion, and unless the President, or the Chairman for the time being, shall decide otherwise, the meetings shall close at 10.15 p.m.
2. All speakers shall address the Chair.
3. The President, or the Chairman for the time being, shall decide at what period any person to whom questions may have been put shall reply.
4. As far as practicable, the discussion on one point shall be closed before raising another.
5. When two or more papers are read on the same evening, each paper shall, so far as time will allow, be discussed before another is read, unless the Chairman decide otherwise.

6. When time permits after the disposal of the papers and discussions thereon, or in the absence of any paper, the criticism of the play shall be conducted in the following manner:—Taking scene by scene, the reader of each part, if present, shall be asked to bring before the society any difficulty or interesting point met with in the reading of that particular part. At the close of the discussion which may arise from this, any other person may call attention to points in that particular part not introduced by its reader. If the reader of the part should be absent, or should not start any point for discussion, the part may be then dealt with by the society generally.

Most of these are formal. The second, which to some persons will seem peculiarly terrifying, is intended to prevent the conversation on the papers getting broken up among a few groups.

It may be wise occasionally to have a written criticism of the elocutionary powers of the members. It may do good to some indifferent but self-contented readers to have their faults pointed out with an unsparing hand. It will be better that a communication of this kind should be anonymous. It should come not oftener than once a session.

CHAPTER VI.

The Library.

"In such indexes, although small pricks
To their subsequent volumes, there is seen
The baby figure of the giant mass
Of things to come at large."

Troilus and Cressida, I. iii. 343-6.

IF the society is to do any critical work, it must have some books of reference. Whether its library is to be large or small will depend upon many circumstances.

In a society altogether wealthy, there would be no difficulty in the provision of funds; but if, as will almost certainly be the case, the purses of the members vary greatly in their contents, a poll-tax for a library-fund would be very unequal in its incidence, and therefore very unpopular, and it might excite rebellion. The problem is then presented of having to raise sufficient money to enable the society to get the books necessary for its work, and whilst getting contributions from the society generally, to exercise no uncomfortable pressure upon any individuals; and yet, at the same time, in getting the nucleus of a library, to have the sum provided quickly, for if the appeal is spread over a long period the interest taken in the matter will probably become most languid.

At first our library had a painfully slow development, depending on an occasional present, or the purchase of some small book by means of a tiny subscription. When much troubled how to get a more satisfactory library, I was cheered by a suggestion from one of our practical members, who, towards the establishment of a library-fund, offered to give three guineas if four other members would each give a similar sum, and if the rest of the society would contribute something fairly substantial. These conditions were so easily fulfilled that the society quickly found itself the possessor of about £40 wherewith to buy books. Since then, by occasional helps, the fund for library-purposes has exceeded £50. With this amount, aided by gifts of books from members and others, the society has at its command a library which is of fair working usefulness, but of course falls far short of that which a Shakspere-society ought to have.

It is a matter of great difficulty to say what books a society must possess. All the following will be found useful, and some of them indispensable. A society that had them all would be well off. I have arranged them in classes, as our own catalogue is arranged. There are many in this list that we have not yet been able to get.

Biography.

Skottowe's *Life of Shakspeare.*

Neil's *Shakespere: a Critical Biography.*

Halliwell-Phillipps's *Outlines of the Life of Shakespeare.*

Fleay's *Life and Work of Shakespeare.*

Books on Stratford by Wheler, Bellew, Walter, and Wise; and on New Place by Halliwell [Phillipps] will be found of interest.

Books on the Sonnets by Armitage Brown, Henry Brown, and Massey may be mentioned here as bearing largely upon Shakspere's life.

Texts.

The 1821 *Variorum.*

The 'Cambridge' *Shakespeare.*

Reprint of 1623 Folio.[1]

Facsimile Quartos.[2]

Furness's Editions.

The 'Bankside' *Shakespeare.*[3]

The 'Leopold' *Shakspere.*

The 'Henry Irving' *Shakespeare.*

Dodsley's *Old English Plays* (Hazlitt).

Complete editions of all the authors included in the society's work.

The series of Pseudo-Shakespearean Plays, edited by Drs. Proescholdt and Warnke.

Works of General Shaksperian Interest.

Douce's *Illustrations of Shakspeare.*

Drake's *Shakespeare and his Times.*

Hunter's *New Illustrations.*

Mrs. Cowden-Clarke's *Concordance.*

Cohn's *Shakespeare in Germany.*

Watkiss Lloyd's *Critical Essays.*

Gervinus's *Commentaries*; either in its original form or in Miss Bunnètt's translation.

Fleay's *Shakespeare Manual* and *Introduction to Shakespearian Study.*

Hazlitt's *Literature of the Age of Elizabeth.*

[1] Either that published by Booth, or that by Chatto and Windus, or both.

[2] These can now be got at a moderate price. Forty-three are in the set in course of publication by Quaritch.

[3] Published by the Shakespeare Society of New York, and consisting of the earliest known version parallel with that of 1623.

Simpson's *School of Shakspere.*

Dowden's *Shakspere: a Critical Study.*

Hudson's *Shakespeare: his Life, Art, and Characters.*

Mrs. Furness's *Concordance to the Poems.*

Schmidt's *Shakespeare-Lexicon.*

Nares's *Glossary.*

Dyce's *Glossary.*

Works on Separate Plays.

There is no need to mention these; every such book should be got.

There are many works that are more especially useful in the Critical Departments, under which I have placed them. Many books previously mentioned deal largely with some of the following subjects; their names are not repeated. The publications of Shakspere-societies would, in many cases, be almost exclusively of use in connection with some of these departments:

Sources and History.

Hazlitt's *Shakespeare's Library.*

Skeat's *Shakespeare's Plutarch.*

Metre and Authorship.

Walker's *Shakespeare's Versification.*

Bathurst's *Differences in Shakespeare's Versification.*

Grammar.

Craik's edition of *Julius Cæsar.*

Ellis's *Early English Pronunciation.*

Abbott's *Shakespearian Grammar.*

Shakspere's Play-craft.

Daniel's *Time-Analysis.*

Stokes's *Chronological Order.*

Aesthetic Criticism.

The number of works of this description is legion.

Historical References.

Courtenay's *Commentaries.*

Classical and Mythical Allusions.

Miss Carey's translation of Stapfer's *Shakespeare and Classical Antiquity.*

Similes and Metaphors.

The literature of these is scattered about in various books. Shakspere's use of them should be presented in a methodical form.

Dress and Social Customs.

Rye's *England as Seen by Foreigners.*

Hall's *Society in the Elizabethan Age.*

Goadby's *The England of Shakespeare.*

Plants and Animals.

Ellacombe's *Plant-Lore.*

Grindon's *Shakspere Flora.*

Harting's *Ornithology of Shakespeare.*

Miss Phipson's *Animal Lore.*

Geography.

References to Shakspere's knowledge of geography must be sought for in many books of general comment.

Law and Heraldry.

Campbell's *Shakespeare's Legal Acquirements,* and some of Rushton's works.

Medicine and Surgery.

Bucknill's *Medical Knowledge* and *Mad Folk.*

Music and Ballads.

Chappell's *Popular Music of the Olden Time.*

Demonology and Witchcraft.

Fairy Tales, edited by Hazlitt.

Early Dramatic Representations.

Hone's *Ancient Mysteries.*

Dictionary of Plays by Halliwell [Phillipps].

Collier's *History of English Dramatic Poetry.*

Schlegel's *Dramatic Art.*

Kelly's *Notices of Leicester.*

The English Drama and Stage (1543—1664).

Ward's *English Dramatic Literature.*

Coins, Weights, and Measures.

Information concerning these will be found in most of the copiously annotated editions and in that invaluable book Nares's *Glossary.*

Sports and Pastimes.

Strutt's *Sports and Pastimes.*

Puns and Jests.

There is room for a book on these. There is a section on Shakspere's Puns in Ellis's *Early English Pronunciation.*

Arts and Sciences.

There is no definite work on Shakspere's allusions to these. One would be interesting.

Anachronisms.

These have been a delight to many a small critic. The

members of a society not caring to work out the subject for themselves, will readily meet with observations thereon in the pages of many an exhausting commentator.

Rare Words and Phrases.

Dictionary of Archaic Words by Halliwell [Phillipps].
Minsheu's *Guide into the Tongues.*
Cotgrave's *Dictionary.*

Various Readings.

The 'Cambridge' *Shakespeare* and Ingleby's *Still Lion* will supply all that is wanted in respect of these.

Biblical and Religious Allusions.

Bishop Wordsworth's *Shakspeare's Knowledge and Use of the Bible.*

Fine Art.
Meats and Drinks.
Trade and Commerce.

The notes of the 1821 *Variorum* must be the authority for much of the information in reference to the foregoing.

Tradition and Folk-lore.

Thiselton Dyer's *Folk Lore of Shakespeare.*

Satire and Irony.

Shakspere's use of the above, compared with that of other writers, would form an admirable subject for a book.

Oaths and Exclamations.

In addition to the notes in the larger editions, the Glossaries which the society must have will supply all needed information in reference to this very interesting subject.

Personal Histories.

French's *Shakspeareana Genealogica.*

Contemporary Literature.

Most of Arber's and Bullen's Reprints will be helpful; and many of the works issued by Shakspere and other literary societies and presses should be obtained.

Transactions of Shakspere-Societies.

All that have been ever issued should find a place in the society's library. As previously mentioned, they would be appropriately classified under many of the headings already given.

Bibliography.

There are some lists dealing with Shakspere literature, both ancient and current, that will be useful. Those by Thimm and Cohn should be had. The catalogue of the Birmingham Shakespeare Library will be found of great interest.

Miscellaneous.

Shakespeariana should, of course, be taken in. Interesting volumes can be formed by binding together Shakspere magazine articles, of which there is an unlimited supply of good, bad, and indifferent. Members should be reminded from time to time of the desirability of collecting such for the society. We have at present five volumes thus formed, and are constantly on the look-out for more.

A society possessing the books here mentioned will be well supplied. The aim should be to obtain, not only books that are useful in work, but each society should endeavour to get together such a collection of Shakspere literature that will be representative, if not comprehensive, of the multitudinous phases that this branch of literary investigation has produced. Such a library would have much that would be curious rather than valuable, and would include many of the criticisms of the eighteenth century, and the books which illustrate the history of those peculiar results known as Shakspere crazes and forgeries.

Of course each member will, in addition to the three text-books of the society, have a Dowden's *Shakspere Primer,* and the Clarendon Press Edition of the plays.

The rules for the management of the library should be simple. The books must be kept where the critical meetings are held. All persons belonging to the society must have the opportunity of taking out books, and some provision must be adopted in reference to the purchase of books.[1]

[1] Our Rule 14 (see p. 29) answers well. Members should always be encouraged to add books to the library.

CHAPTER VII.

Some Minor Matters.

"Have a care of your entertainments."
The Merry Wives of Windsor, IV. v. 77

IN some societies entertainments of a nature lighter than that of the ordinary meetings are sometimes held. Even a society so serious as the New Shakspere Society had, as long as it could afford it, an annual musical entertainment. These diversions, probably, in all cases contain an element of danger. Introduced often, they would doubtless tend to the demoralisation of the more regular work. Presumably, their object is to increase the attractiveness of a society; but if the perennial interest and diversified character of an organised study of the Elizabethan drama do not draw, the singing of songs and asking of conundrums will not be likely to create a literary taste. Extraneous devices will fail to goad persons into a love for that which meets with no responsive chord in their natures. It has been said[1] that it is common to find in English people an absolute insensibility to Art, literary and otherwise, and that this is irremediable; and Dr. Clifford Allbutt, in words addressed primarily to medical students, but really of far wider applicability, speaking in reference to advice often given about keeping up literary attainments, said: "To give such advice is like urging

[1] "Elementary Principles in Art." A Lecture. *Macmillan's Magazine*, May, 1867. The whole is wonderfully bright and fresh, and should be read.

all men to have a taste for music. Some, perhaps most persons, lack an ear for literature. Take up your Bible, or the collects in the Prayer-book, and read them with a nice attention to the words as well as to the matter. If to the power and melody of those words you find an answering delight in yourself, you have an ear for literature—a sense of style. It is a precious possession, and you may well cherish it. If you have it not, you cannot make it, and you had better take your pleasure in the breeding of fox-terriers."[1] If there is a slight taste for the special work of a Shakspere-Society, it will be better to foster it by application in its own particular line than by the administration of stimulating condiments. Appetite will grow by what it feeds on.

But a Shakspere-Society will fail if its meetings are cold, formal, and dry. The social element is a prime factor of success. Therefore an occasional off-meeting, not arranged for in the programme of the society, will be useful for affording opportunities for the members getting to know one another better. This could be attained by an outing of some kind in the period between the sessions. If Stratford is accessible, nothing better than a day there could be desired. Pleasant gatherings would be afforded by a spontaneous invitation to the society from members who have facilities for giving a half-day's entertainment. An annual dinner might be permitted. Possibly a reading in winter, to which the public would be admitted, or one or two private open-air readings in the summer, might be desirable introductions. But trivialities, such as regular musical evenings, members citing their favourite passages or setting and working out Shakspere-puzzles, and the like, should be all sternly discountenanced.

[1] *British Medical Journal*, 1883. Vol. II. p. 664.

CHAPTER VIII.

The Publications.

"Heaven doth with us as we with torches do,
Not light them for themselves; for if our virtues
Did not go forth of us, 'twere all alike
As if we had them not."

Measure for Measure, I. i. 33–6.

A SHAKSPERE-SOCIETY will not have fulfilled its mission if it does not, by publishing its transactions, show to the world something of what it has done. This applies not only to those societies which exist principally for the purpose of publication, but to every private society that does regular and honest work. To the larger societies I have no suggestion to offer further than to say that I think it would be wise to issue more parallel-texts, and perhaps, as one of our members says, an Etymological Dictionary of Shakspere-words.

A society will probably have to be at work for some time before it thinks of printing any of its papers. When such a determination has been arrived at, the difficulty will arise as to the best way of doing it. This will, as in the case of the library, be very much a question of money.

Probably the best form would be a selection of the papers in a yearly volume, published at not more than five shillings. The society might either publish on the chance of finding a buying public, or it may prefer to be cautious and not print till it has a sufficient number of subscribers to assure it from loss.

In the first case a guarantee-fund must be formed. Members willing to become guarantors would probably be found in most societies that had existed long enough to think of printing, and had worked hard enough to produce good papers. If subscribers are to be obtained before publication, an earnest appeal must be made by members in their own circles and generally to literary people outside.

Every society should keep before it as a distinct aim the publication of some of its papers. It is a duty which it owes to all Shakspere-students. The riches of Shakspere are not yet exhausted, and will last on well into the coming centuries. An editor would have to be appointed for the publication. He should have absolute power in the selection of the papers to be printed.

CHAPTER IX.

Reading-Tables.

"Will you with counters sum
The past proportion of his infinite?"
Troilus and Cressida, II. ii. 28–9.

Suggestions for Discussion.

"All kind of arguments and question deep."
A Lover's Complaint, 121.

Lists of Early Editions.

"In print I found it."
The Two Gentlemen of Verona, II. i. 175.

History of the Plays.

"Let us from point to point this story know."
All's Well that Ends Well, V. iii. 325.

TITUS ANDRONICUS.

Total Number of Lines.	CHARACTERS.	I.	II.				III.		IV.				V.		
		1	1	2	3	4	1	2	1	2	3	4	1	2	3
209	SATURNINUS	105	...	5	35	...	...	...	...	...	...	55	...	...	9
63	BASSIANUS	48	...	1	14	...	...	...	...	...	...	...	...	...	...
303	MARCUS	74	...	3	...	47	41	10	47	...	19	...	...	1	61
6	CAPTAIN	6	...	...	...	...	...	...	...	...	...	...	...	...	...
718	TITUS	136	...	15	9	...	190	73	58	...	76	...	...	132	29
196	LUCIUS	30	...	...	...	...	46	..	...	..	...	...	41	...	79
52	CHIRON	1	20	...	10	4	...	...	...	13	...	...	...	4	..
94	DEMETRIUS	10	33	2	13	6	...	...	...	28	...	...	...	2	...
3	TRIBUNE	3	...	...	...	...	...	...	...	...	...	...	..	...	...
4	MUTIUS	4	...	..	...	...	...	...	...	...	...	...	...	...	...
28	QUINTUS	4	...	...	24	...	...	...	...	...	...	...	...	...	...
31	MARTIUS	2	...	...	29	...	...	...	...	...	...	...	...	...	...
4	"ALL"	2	...	...	...	...	...	...	...	...	...	...	...	...	2
355	AARON	...	89	...	41	...	19	...	...	110	...	...	86	...	10
7	MESSENGER	...	...	...	...	...	7	...	...	...	...	...	...	...	...
15	PUBLIUS	...	...	...	...	...	...	...	...	...	9	...	...	6	...
24	CLOWN	...	...	...	...	...	...	...	...	...	17	7	...	...	...
21	ÆMILIUS	...	...	...	...	...	...	...	...	...	...	8	6	..	7
12	1ST GOTH	...	...	...	...	...	...	...	...	...	...	...	11	...	1
21	2ND GOTH	...	...	...	...	...	...	...	...	...	...	...	21	...	...
3	3RD GOTH	...	...	...	...	...	...	...	...	...	...	...	3	...	...
257	TAMORA	66	...	...	85	...	...	...	...	...	...	43	...	61	2
58	LAVINIA	10	...	2	46	...	...	...	...	...	...	...	...	...	...
44	YOUNG LUCIUS	...	...	...	...	...	...	2	25	13	...	...	...	...	4
19	NURSE	...	...	...	...	...	...	...	...	19	...	...	...	...	...
2547		501	142	28	306	57	303	85	130	183	121	113	168	206	204
2523	Actual Number of Lines	495	135	26	306	57	301	85	129	180	121	113	165	206	204

SCHEME FOR ARRANGING THE PARTS WITH EIGHTEEN MEN

SIXTEEN CHARACTERS SINGLY AND TWO GROUPS.

MUTIUS 4 } 7 TRIBUNE 3 } 10
3RD GOTH 3 } MESSENGER 7 }

SUGGESTIONS FOR DISCUSSION.

1. *Titus Andronicus* and some of the so-called doubtful plays were written by Shakspere between 1584 and 1590.
2. The savage atrocities of the story are distinct proof that Shakspere did not write *Titus Andronicus*.
3. *Titus Andronicus* was an ironical censure on Marlowe's style.

LIST OF EARLIEST KNOWN EDITIONS.

Date.	*Printer.*	*Publisher.*	*Acted by*	*Present Owners.*
1600	I. R.	Edward White	Earl of Pembroke's servants; Earl of Derby's ,,; Earl of Sussex's ,,; Lord Chamberlain's ,,	University of Edinburgh. Lady Ellesmere.
1611	——	Eedward White	The King's servants	British Museum. Bodleian Library. Trinity College, Cambridge. Duke of Devonshire.

Upon several occasions, the first of which is April 11, 1592, the acting of "tittus and Vespacia" by "my lord Stranges mene" is recorded by Henslowe (*Diary*, pp. 24—30). In the "Tragædia von Tito Andronico," a German play, acted about 1600 by English players in Germany, and reprinted with a translation in Cohn's *Shakespeare in Germany*, one of the characters is called Vespasian. It has, therefore, been thought that Shakspere's play bears some relation to that mentioned by Henslowe. But dealing with events in connection with the destruction of Jerusalem there were some early works in which Titus and Vespasian were principal characters. There are MSS. of such in the British Museum, and one "in Englishe meter," entered in the Stationers' Registers on January 5, 1598, may be the play referred to by Meres, who said that "Doctor *Leg* hath penned two famous tragedies, ye one of *Richard the 3.* the other of the destruction of *Ierusalem*," although there is reason to believe that Legge's play, not known at present, was written in Latin (see p. 87).

Dated January 23, 1594, Henslowe has an entry of "titus and ondronicus" as a new play, acted by "the earle of Susex his men" (*Diary*, p. 33). Henslowe's prefix further negatives the theory of the connection between this play and that acted in 1592.

In the Stationers' Registers is the following record:—

1594. February 6.

John Danter. Entred for his Copye vnder thandes of bothe the wardens a booke intituled *a Noble Roman Historye of Tytus Andronicus* vjd

John Danter. Entred alsoe vnto him by warraunt from Master **Woodcock** the ballad thereof. vjd

There is no other evidence that the reference is to Shakspere's play. In Percy's *Reliques of Ancient English Poetry* is a ballad called "Titus Andronicus's Complaint." The date of this is unknown. In subject it is very similar to the play.

Henslowe (*Diary*, pp. 35, 36) has entries of the performance of "andronicous" by "my Lord Admeralle and my Lorde chamberlen men" at Newington, in June, 1594.

In 1598 Meres mentions "Titus Andronicus" as one of Shakspere's tragedies.

In 1600 appeared anonymously the first of the editions mentioned in the table, and described as "The most lamentable Romaine Tragedie of Titus Andronicus."

The following entry is to be found in the Stationers' Registers:—

1602. April 19.

Thomas pavier Entred for his copies by assignement from **Thomas millington** these bookes folowinge, *Saluo Jure cuiuscunque*

viz

. . . .

The first and *Second parte of Henry the VJt* ij bookes xijd
A booke called *Titus and Andronicus* vjd
Entred by warrant vnder master **Setons** hand.

There is no record of an entry to Millington. It will be seen that a statement was inserted to guard any pre-existent right.

In 1611, without author's name, was published the second of the known editions as "The most lamentable Tragedie of Titus Andronicus."

Ben Jonson's reference to "Andronicus" in 1614 (Induction to *Bartholomew Fair*) is too vague for the purpose of fixing date.

The title of the play in the 1623 Folio is "The Lamentable Tragedy of Titus Andronicus."

CAMPASPE.

Total Number of Lines.	CHARACTERS.	Prologues.		I.			II.		III.					IV.					V.				Epilogues.	
		Black-friars.	Court.	1	2	3	1	2	1	2	3	4	5	1	2	3	4	5	1	2	3	4	Black-friars.	Court.
57	CLYTUS	...	...	32	...	...	...	...	...	...	...	14	...	...	...	11	...	...	...	...	...	...	...	...
71	PARMENIO	...	...	23	...	...	...	...	...	...	...	14	...	...	...	34	...	...	...	...	...	...	...	...
355	ALEXANDER	...	...	28	...	45	...	89	...	...	...	70	...	...	...	...	...	...	...	...	...	123	...	...
157	HEPHÆSTION	...	...	5	...	11	...	95	...	...	...	14	...	...	...	...	...	...	...	...	...	32	...	...
132	MANES	...	...	...	50	...	17	...	...	45	...	...	2	16	...	...	...	...	2	...	...	...	...	...
129	PSYLLUS	...	...	...	51	...	24	...	...	37	...	...	6	11	...	...	...	...	...	...	...	...	...	...
60	GRANICHUS	...	...	...	33	...	20	...	...	...	...	...	...	7	...	...	...	...	...	...	...	...	...	...
34	MELIPPUS	...	...	...	...	34	...	...	...	...	...	...	...	...	...	...	...	...	...	...	...	...	...	...
21	PLATO	...	...	...	...	21	...	...	...	...	...	...	...	...	...	...	...	...	...	...	...	...	...	...
27	ARISTOTLE	...	...	...	...	27	...	...	...	...	...	...	...	...	...	...	...	...	...	...	...	...	...	...
10	CLEANTHES	...	...	...	...	10	...	...	...	...	...	...	...	...	...	...	...	...	...	...	...	...	...	...
8	ANAXARCHUS	...	...	...	...	8	...	...	...	...	...	...	...	...	...	...	...	...	...	...	...	...	...	...
4	CRATES	...	...	...	...	4	...	...	...	...	...	...	...	...	...	...	...	...	...	...	...	...	...	...
5	CRISIPPUS	...	...	...	...	5	...	...	...	...	...	...	...	...	...	...	...	...	...	...	...	...	...	...
175	DIOGENES	...	...	...	...	11	27	16	...	...	...	7	...	56	...	...	...	...	30	...	8	20	...	...
256	APELLES	...	...	...	...	...	...	3	15	...	36	35	89	...	18	...	14	8	...	22	...	16	...	...
9	CRYSUS	...	...	...	...	...	...	...	...	...	...	9	...	...	...	...	...	...	...	...	...	...	...	...
8	SOLINUS	...	...	...	...	...	...	...	...	...	...	...	...	8	...	...	...	...	...	...	...	...	...	...
7	"POPULUS"	...	...	...	...	...	...	...	...	...	...	...	...	7	...	...	...	...	...	...	...	...	...	...
28	SYLVIUS	...	...	...	...	...	...	...	...	...	...	...	...	...	...	...	...	...	28	...	...	...	...	...
2	MILO	...	...	...	...	...	...	...	...	...	...	...	...	...	...	...	...	...	2	...	...	...	...	...
5	PERIM	...	...	...	...	...	...	...	...	...	...	...	...	...	...	...	...	...	5	...	...	...	...	...
13	TRICO	...	...	...	...	...	...	...	...	...	...	...	...	...	...	...	...	...	13	...	...	...	...	...
11	MILECTUS	...	...	...	...	...	...	...	...	...	...	...	...	...	...	...	...	...	...	...	11	...	...	...
11	PHRYGIUS	...	...	...	...	...	...	...	...	...	...	...	...	...	...	...	...	...	...	...	11	...	...	...
47	"BLACKFRIARS PROLOGUE"	47	...	...	...	...	...	...	...	...	...	...	...	...	...	...	...	...	...	...	...	...	...	...
25	"COURT PROLOGUE"	...	25	...	...	...	...	...	...	...	...	...	...	...	...	...	...	...	...	...	...	...	...	...
24	TIMOCLEA	...	...	24	...	...	...	...	...	...	...	...	...	...	...	...	...	...	...	...	...	...	...	...
134	CAMPASPE	...	...	10	...	...	...	...	11	...	29	3	...	...	40	...	33	...	...	...	...	8	...	...
9	PAGE	...	...	...	...	...	...	1	...	...	...	...	...	...	...	...	...	5	...	...	...	3	...	...
24	LAIS	...	...	...	...	...	...	...	...	...	...	...	...	...	...	...	...	...	...	...	24	...	...	...
20	"BLACKFRIARS EPILOGUE"	...	...	...	...	...	...	...	...	...	...	...	...	...	...	...	...	...	...	...	...	...	20	...
26	"COURT EPILOGUE"	...	...	...	...	...	...	...	...	...	...	...	...	...	...	...	...	...	...	...	...	...	...	26
1912		47	25	122	134	170	88	204	26	82	65	166	97	105	58	45	47	13	80	22	54	202	20	26
1904	... Actual Number of Lines ...	47	25	122	126	170	88	204	26	82	65	166	97	105	58	45	47	13	80	22	54	202	20	26

SCHEME FOR ARRANGING THE PARTS WITH EIGHTEEN MEN AND SEVEN LADIES.

Men's Parts.

THIRTEEN CHARACTERS SINGLY AND FIVE GROUPS.

MILECTUS 11, PERIM 5 } 16	PHRYGIUS 11, CRISIPPUS 5, MILO 2 } 18	CRATES 4, TRICO 13 } 17
CLEANTHES 10, SOLINUS 8 } 18		ANAXARCHUS 8, CRYSUS 9 } 17

Ladies' Parts.

Omit LAIS.

SUGGESTIONS FOR DISCUSSION.

1. Lyly's work is marred by the way in which he used his superficial learning to curry favour with Queen and Court.
2. Dramatic literature is indebted to Lyly for the introduction of vivacious prose-dialogue.
3. In *Midas* Lyly replied to the attack made upon him in the early draft of *Love's Labour's Lost.*

LIST OF EARLIEST KNOWN EDITIONS.

Date.	*Printer.*	*Publisher.*	*Acted by*	*Present Owners.*
1584	— — —	Thomas Cadman	Her Majesty's Children; The Children of Paul's	British Museum.; Bodleian Library.
1584	— — —	Thomas Cadman	Her Majesty's Children; The Children of Paul's	
1591	Thomas Orwin	William Broome	Her Majesty's Children; The Children of Paul's	British Museum.

In the first mentioned of these editions the play is called "Campaspe," and it is said to have been "Played beefore the Queenes Maiestie on newyeares day at night." In the other edition of the same year it is called "A moste excellent Comedie of Alexander, Campaspe, and Diogenes," and the title-page mentions its performance before the Queen "on twelfe day at night." Fairholt (*The Dramatic Works of John Lilly.* 1858. Vol. I. pp. xxvi. xxvii. 284) thinks that the edition with the longer title was the earlier of these editions. It is not a matter of much importance. As the year 1584 began in March, the "twelfe day," if his view is correct, must have been January 6, 1583-4, and the "newyeares day" January 1, 1584-5. It seems, however, more reasonable to consider the "newyeares day" to have been the 25th of March, 1584, and the "twelfe day" to have been January 6, 1584-5. Against this view it may be stated that in the official accounts of the Treasurer of the Chamber, quoted by Mr. Halliwell-Phillipps (*Outlines*, II. 166) New year's day is undoubtedly the 1st of January. Anyway, it is unlikely that two editions would be published referring to performances on days so near to one another as the 1st and 6th of the same month. The 1591 title is merely "Campaspe," and refers also to a twelfth-day performance. Fairholt seems to think that the two short titles would be consecutive, but he states that the head-line in all these editions is "Alexander and Campaspe." Neither edition gave the author's name.

In the Stationers' Registers are the following entries:—

1565. July 22—1566. July 22. **purfoote**	Recevyd of **Thomas purfoote** for his lycense for prynting of a ballett intituled *an history of* ALEXANDER CAMPASPES *and* APELLES *and of the ffaythfull fryndeshippe betwene them*	iiij[d]
1597. April 12. **Jone brome** widowe.	Entred for her copies in full courte holden this Day. iiij bookes: called . . . . CAMPASPE, To enioy Duringe her widowe or that she shalbe a free Stationers wife of this companye The which copies were **Thomas Cadmans**	ij[s]
1601. August 23. **George potter.**	Entred for his copies in full Court holden this Day these copies folowinge whiche belonged to mystres **Brome** Lately Deceased *viz* . . . . CAMPASPE	vj[s]

There is no entry either to Cadman or to Master Broome.

I HENRY VI.

Total Number of Lines.	CHARACTERS.	I.						II.					III.				IV.							V.				
		1	2	3	4	5	6	1	2	3	4	5	1	2	3	4	1	2	3	4	5	6	7	1	2	3	4	5
76	Bedford	46						6	10					14														
183	Gloucester	24		42									51			1	36							18				11
59	Exeter	22											15				14							6				2
96	Winchester	15		19									32				1							11			18	
43	1st Messenger	18			4				9	6									6									
7	2nd Messenger	7																										
45	3rd Messenger	45																										
133	Charles		48				22	12						5	12								11		7		16	
49	Alençon		18				2	8						1	7										2		11	
59	Reignier		21				4	4						6												20	4	
29	Bastard		13					4						5	3								4					
3	1st Warder			3																								
10	1st Serving-man			4									5										1					
1	2nd Warder			1																								
5	Woodvile			5																								
21	Mayor			11									10															
6	Officer			6																								
18	Master Gunner				18																							
15	Salisbury				15																							
406	Talbot				67	32		20	28	33				56		12	33	29			24	41	31					
2	Gargrave				2																							
1	Glansdale				1																							
4	Sergeant							4																				
4	1st Sentinel							4																				
44	Burgundy							6	12					9	12								3		2			
8	Soldier							5						3														
6	Captain								1					3						2								
1	Porter									1																		
184	Plantagenet										45	37	9				9		27							10	47	
174	Suffolk										11															103		60
64	Somerset										37		5				5			17								
72	Warwick										27		26				4										15	
29	Vernon										11					8	10											
4	Lawyer										4																	
88	Mortimer											88																
4	1st Gaoler											4																
2	2nd Serving-man												2															
10	3rd Serving-man												10															
1	"All"												1															
2	Watch													2														
8	Fastolfe													4			4											
25	Basset															10	15											
27	General																	27										
77	Lucy																		20	27			30					
47	John Talbot																				31	16						
1	Legate																							1				
5	Scout																								5			
24	Shepherd																										24	
254	Joan		50			7	3	12						30	57								16		5	34	40	
4	Boy				4																							
45	Countess									45																		
179	King												41			14	63							26				35
33	Margaret																									33		
2697		177	150	91	111	39	31	85	60	85	135	129	207	138	91	45	194	56	53	46	55	57	96	62	21	200	175	108
2678	Actual No. of Lines	177	150	91	111	39	31	82	60	82	134	129	201	137	91	45	194	56	53	46	55	57	96	62	21	195	175	108

SCHEME FOR ARRANGING THE PARTS WITH EIGHTEEN MEN.

SEVEN CHARACTERS SINGLY AND ELEVEN GROUPS.

Character	Lines	Total
Bedford	76	82
Gargrave	2	
Legate	1	
1st Warder	3	
Somerset	64	84
Master Gunner	18	
Watch	2	
Warwick	72	83
Captain	6	
Scout	5	
Exeter	59	84
Salisbury	15	
Sergeant	4	
Officer	6	
John Talbot	47	85
Bastard	29	
2nd Messenger	7	
2nd Servant	2	
Fastolfe	8	85
Shepherd	24	
1st Messenger	43	
1st Servant	10	
Lucy	77	83
Glansdale	1	
Porter	1	
1st Sentinel	4	
Woodvile	5	82
Vernon	29	
Burgundy	44	
1st Gaoler	4	
Mayor	21	84
Reignier	59	
Lawyer	4	
Basset	25	84
Alençon	49	
3rd Servant	10	
General	27	81
Soldier	8	
2nd Warder	1	
3rd Messenger	45	

SUGGESTIONS FOR DISCUSSION.

1. The extraordinary popularity of 1 *Henry VI.* upon its first production is a true measure of Shakspere's early genius.
2. The display of book-learning in 1 *Henry VI.* is not uncharacteristic of a beginner, and is to be found in some of Shakspere's undoubted plays.
3. The travesty of the noble character of Joan of Arc is proof that Shakspere did not write 1 *Henry VI.*

THE EARLIEST KNOWN EDITION IS THE 1623 FOLIO.

Under date of March 3, 1592, Henslowe has an entry of "henery the vj" acted by "my lord Stranges mene" (*Diary*, p. 22).

In 1599 1 *Henry VI.* is referred to in the epilogue of *Henry V.*

In the Stationers' Registers there is the record of an assignment on April 19, 1602, from Thomas Millington to Thomas Pavier of "*The first* and *Second parte of* HENRY *the* VJ^{t} ij bookes" (see p. 59); these are the plays now known as the second and third parts. Millington was the publisher of *The Contention* and *The True Tragedy* (see pp. 65, 69).

In the entry of the 1623 Folio in the Registers this play is described as "The thirde parte of HENRY ye SIXT." In the Folio itself it is called "The first Part of Henry the Sixt."

The subject of many of the historical plays was treated in verse by Daniel, who in his "Poems on the Civil Wars," reprinted in Chalmers's *English Poets*, briefly reviews the history of England from the Conquest to the death of Edward III., and then dwells with great detail upon the time from the accession of Richard II. down to the return of Warwick from his mission to the Lady Bona. In the Registers on October 11, 1594, this entry was made:—

Symon waterson Entred for his copie vnder the wardens handes, a booke intituled, *The discention betwixt the houses of* YORKE *and* LANCASTER *in verse* penned by SAMUELL DANYELL, vppon Condicon that before yt be printed he shall procure sufficient aucthority for the printinge of yt vj^{d}

2 HENRY VI.

Total Number of Lines.	CHARACTERS.	I.				II.				III.			IV.										V.		
		1	2	3	4	1	2	3	4	1	2	3	1	2	3	4	5	6	7	8	9	10	1	2	3
298	Suffolk	20	...	46	...	13	...	2	...	62	97	...	58	...	...	...	...	...	...	...	...	...	...	...	...
314	King	26	...	10	...	36	...	27	...	43	76	15	...	...	...	17	...	...	...	...	31	...	32	1	...
16	"All"	1	...	1	...	...	...	...	...	...	2	...	...	5	...	...	...	...	2	4	1	...	...	...	...
306	Gloucester	61	25	22	...	75	...	14	40	69	...	...	...	...	...	...	...	...	...	...	...	...	...	...	...
104	Cardinal	31	...	3	...	24	...	...	...	30	2	14	...	...	...	...	...	...	...	...	...	...	...	...	...
96	Salisbury	29	...	2	...	...	9	5	...	...	28	1	...	...	...	...	...	...	...	...	...	...	14	...	8
132	Warwick	15	...	7	...	...	17	...	...	...	64	3	...	...	...	...	...	...	...	...	...	...	8	12	6
380	York	55	...	15	31	...	58	12	...	94	...	...	...	...	...	...	...	...	...	...	...	...	90	13	12
74	Buckingham	7	...	8	8	12	...	...	...	4	...	...	...	...	...	6	...	...	...	10	3	...	16	...	...
25	Somerset	6	...	5	...	...	...	...	...	7	1	...	...	...	...	...	...	...	...	...	3	...	3	...	...
26	1st Messenger	...	3	...	...	...	...	...	...	...	...	...	...	...	...	11	...	...	4	...	8	...	...	...	...
32	Hume	...	28	...	4	...	...	...	...	...	...	...	...	...	...	...	...	...	...	...	...	...	...	...	...
10	1st Petitioner	...	...	10	...	...	...	...	...	...	...	...	...	...	...	...	...	...	...	...	...	...	...	...	...
6	2nd Petitioner	...	...	6	...	...	...	...	...	...	...	...	...	...	...	...	...	...	...	...	...	...	...	...	...
29	Peter	...	...	16	...	...	...	13	...	...	...	...	...	...	...	...	...	...	...	...	...	...	...	...	...
22	Horner	...	...	11	...	...	...	11	...	...	...	...	...	...	...	...	...	...	...	...	...	...	...	...	...
24	Bolingbroke	...	...	...	24	...	...	...	...	...	...	...	...	...	...	...	...	...	...	...	...	...	...	...	...
4	Townsman	...	...	...	...	4	...	...	...	...	...	...	...	...	...	...	...	...	...	...	...	...	...	...	...
24	Simpcox	...	...	...	...	24	...	...	...	...	...	...	...	...	...	...	...	...	...	...	...	...	...	...	...
3	Mayor	...	...	...	...	3	...	...	...	...	...	...	...	...	...	...	...	...	...	...	...	...	...	...	...
2	Beadle	...	...	...	...	2	...	...	...	...	...	...	...	...	...	...	...	...	...	...	...	...	...	...	...
3	1st Neighbour	...	...	...	...	...	...	3	...	...	...	...	...	...	...	...	...	...	...	...	...	...	...	...	...
2	2nd Neighbour	...	...	...	...	...	...	2	...	...	...	...	...	...	...	...	...	...	...	...	...	...	...	...	...
2	3rd Neighbour	...	...	...	...	...	...	2	...	...	...	...	...	...	...	...	...	...	...	...	...	...	...	...	...
2	1st Prentice	...	...	...	...	...	...	2	...	...	...	...	...	...	...	...	...	...	...	...	...	...	...	...	...
2	2nd Prentice	...	...	...	...	...	...	2	...	...	...	...	...	...	...	...	...	...	...	...	...	...	...	...	...
2	Servingman	...	...	...	...	...	...	...	2	...	...	...	...	...	...	...	...	...	...	...	...	...	...	...	...
2	Herald	...	...	...	...	...	...	...	2	...	...	...	...	...	...	...	...	...	...	...	...	...	...	...	...
4	Sheriff	...	...	...	...	...	...	...	4	...	...	...	...	...	...	...	...	...	...	...	...	...	...	...	...
7	Stanley	...	...	...	...	...	...	...	7	...	...	...	...	...	...	...	...	...	...	...	...	...	...	...	...
6	Post	...	...	...	...	...	...	...	...	6	...	...	...	...	...	...	...	...	...	...	...	...	...	...	...
5	1st Murderer	...	...	...	...	...	...	...	...	...	5	...	...	...	...	...	...	...	...	...	...	...	...	...	...
2	2nd Murderer	...	...	...	...	...	...	...	...	...	2	...	...	...	...	...	...	...	...	...	...	...	...	...	...
11	Vaux	...	...	...	...	...	...	...	...	...	11	...	...	...	...	...	...	...	...	...	...	...	...	...	...
64	Captain	...	...	...	...	...	...	...	...	...	...	...	64	...	...	...	...	...	...	...	...	...	...	...	...
7	1st Gentleman	...	...	...	...	...	...	...	...	...	...	...	7	...	...	...	...	...	...	...	...	...	...	...	...
1	Master	...	...	...	...	...	...	...	...	...	...	...	1	...	...	...	...	...	...	...	...	...	...	...	...
1	Mate	...	...	...	...	...	...	...	...	...	...	...	1	...	...	...	...	...	...	...	...	...	...	...	...
1	2nd Gentleman	...	...	...	...	...	...	...	...	...	...	...	1	...	...	...	...	...	...	...	...	...	...	...	...
18	Whitmore	...	...	...	...	...	...	...	...	...	...	...	18	...	...	...	...	...	...	...	...	...	...	...	...
18	Bevis	...	...	...	...	...	...	...	...	...	...	...	...	16	...	...	...	...	2	...	...	...	...	...	...
21	Holland	...	...	...	...	...	...	...	...	...	...	...	...	16	...	...	...	...	5	...	...	...	...	...	...
276	Cade	...	...	...	...	...	...	...	...	...	...	...	...	90	16	...	...	12	79	31	...	48	...	...	...
42	Dick	...	...	...	...	...	...	...	...	...	...	...	...	27	4	...	...	2	9	...	...	...	...	...	...
21	Smith	...	...	...	...	...	...	...	...	...	...	...	...	15	...	...	...	3	3	...	...	...	...	...	...
3	Clerk	...	...	...	...	...	...	...	...	...	...	...	...	3	...	...	...	...	...	...	...	...	...	...	...
5	Michael	...	...	...	...	...	...	...	...	...	...	...	...	5	...	...	...	...	...	...	...	...	...	...	...
16	Stafford	...	...	...	...	...	...	...	...	...	...	...	...	16	...	...	...	...	...	...	...	...	...	...	...
7	William Stafford	...	...	...	...	...	...	...	...	...	...	...	...	7	...	...	...	...	...	...	...	...	...	...	...
48	Say	...	...	...	...	...	...	...	...	...	...	...	...	...	...	7	...	...	41	...	...	...	...	...	...
5	2nd Messenger	...	...	...	...	...	...	...	...	...	...	...	...	...	...	5	...	...	...	...	...	...	...	...	...
8	Scales	...	...	...	...	...	...	...	...	...	...	...	...	...	...	...	8	...	...	...	...	...	...	...	...
5	1st Citizen	...	...	...	...	...	...	...	...	...	...	...	...	...	...	...	5	...	...	...	...	...	...	...	...
1	Soldier	...	...	...	...	...	...	...	...	...	...	...	...	...	...	...	...	1	...	...	...	...	...	...	...
56	Clifford	...	...	...	...	...	...	...	...	...	...	...	...	...	...	...	...	...	...	27	3	...	21	5	...
51	Iden	...	...	...	...	...	...	...	...	...	...	...	...	...	...	...	...	...	...	...	...	42	9	...	...
1	Edward	...	...	...	...	...	...	...	...	...	...	...	...	...	...	...	...	...	...	...	...	...	1	...	...
24	Richard	...	...	...	...	...	...	...	...	...	...	...	...	...	...	...	...	...	...	...	...	...	10	6	8
45	Young Clifford	...	...	...	...	...	...	...	...	...	...	...	...	...	...	...	...	...	...	...	...	...	3	42	...
317	Queen	9	...	57	...	10	...	12	...	68	127	...	...	...	...	14	...	...	...	...	...	...	9	11	...
119	Duchess	...	51	7	4	...	...	1	56	...	...	...	...	...	...	...	...	...	...	...	...	...	...	...	...
9	Spirit	...	...	...	9	...	...	...	...	...	...	...	...	...	...	...	...	...	...	...	...	...	...	...	...
4	Jourdain	...	...	...	4	...	...	...	...	...	...	...	...	...	...	...	...	...	...	...	...	...	...	...	...
8	Wife to Simpcox	...	...	...	...	8	...	...	...	...	...	...	...	...	...	...	...	...	...	...	...	...	...	...	...
3179		260	107	226	84	211	84	108	111	383	415	33	150	200	20	60	13	18	145	72	49	90	216	90	34
3161	... Actual Number of Lines ...	259	107	226	84	204	82	108	110	383	412	33	147	200	20	60	13	18	145	72	49	90	216	90	33

SCHEME FOR ARRANGING THE PARTS WITH EIGHTEEN MEN.

EIGHT CHARACTERS SINGLY AND TEN GROUPS.

Character	Lines	Group total
Edward	1	80
Captain	64	
Clerk	3	
1st Petitioner	10	
2nd Neighbour	2	
Richard	24	84
Whitmore	18	
Horner	22	
Bevis	18	
Servingman	2	
Somerset	25	81
Mate	1	
Hume	32	
Smith	21	
Beadle	2	
Buckingham	74	80
Master	1	
Herald	2	
Soldier	1	
3rd Neighbour	2	
Clifford	56	80
Scales	8	
Wm. Stafford	7	
1st Murderer	5	
Townsman	4	
Young Clifford	45	80
Holland	21	
2nd Messenger	5	
1st Neighbour	3	
Post	6	
Say	48	80
Simpcox	24	
2nd Murderer	2	
Sheriff	4	
2nd Prentice	2	
Stafford	16	75
2nd Gentleman	1	
Peter	29	
Mayor	3	
1st Messenger	26	
Stanley	7	80
Vaux	11	
Iden	51	
Michael	5	
2nd Petitioner	6	
Bolingbroke	24	80
1st Gentleman	7	
Dick	42	
1st Citizen	5	
1st Prentice	2	

SUGGESTIONS FOR DISCUSSION.

1. *The Contention* was a garbled and spurious version of Shakspere's 2 *Henry VI.*
2. The striking excellence of many passages in 2 *Henry VI.* and its obvious connection with the other historical plays prove Shakspere to be the only possible author.
3. The misrepresentation of the motive of Cade's insurrection is not at all in Shakspere's manner.

LIST OF EARLIEST KNOWN EDITIONS.

Date.	*Printer.*	*Publisher.*	*Acted by*	*Present Owners.*
1594	Thomas Creed	Thomas Millington		Bodleian Library.
1600	Valentine Simmes	Thomas Millington		Bodleian Library. Trinity College, Cambridge. Duke of Devonshire.

In the Bodleian there is (with a manuscript title) an edition said to have been printed by W. W. for Thomas Millington in 1600.

These editions are of the play known as *The Contention*, which was thus entered in the Stationers' Registers :—

1594. March 12.

Thomas mylling-ton Entred for his copie vnder the handes of bothe the wardens a booke intituled, *the firste parte of the Contention of the twoo famous houses of* YORK *and* LANCASTER *with the deathe of the good Duke* HUMFREY *and the banishement and Deathe of the Duke of* SUFFOLK *and the tragicall ende of the prowd Cardinall of* WINCHESTER *with the notable rebellion of* JACK CADE *and the Duke of* YORKES *ffirste clayme vnto the Crowne* vj[d]

The 1594 edition was published anonymously, with the title worded in the same way as the entry.
The 1600 edition, also without author's name, had the same title.
On April 19, 1602, Millington transferred the copyrights of "The first and Second parte of Henry the VJ[t]" to Pavier (For copy of the entry see p. 59). The play now known as 2 *Henry VI.* was then described as the first part. In the Folio it is called "The second Part of Henry the Sixt, with the death of the Good Duke Hvmfrey."

The connections of *The Contention* and *The True Tragedy* (see p. 69) with 2 and 3 *Henry VI.* are amongst the most vexed questions of Shaksperian criticism. The two plays described as "The Whole Contention betweene the two Famous Houses, Lancaster and Yorke. With the Tragicall ends of the good Duke Humfrey, Richard Duke of Yorke, and King Henrie the sixt. Diuided into two Parts: And newly corrected and enlarged" and said to be "written by William Shake-speare, Gent." were, with *Pericles*, published in one volume in 1619 by T. P. Copies of this edition are in the British Museum, Trinity College at Cambridge, and the Duke of Devonshire's library. The 1623 Folio is the earliest known copy of the plays as we now have them (see pp. 63, 69). They are not named in the list of plays in the entry of that book in the Stationers' Registers. As the publishers of the Folio entered those plays only which "are not formerly entered to other men," it looks as if they considered Shakspere to have been the author of both the early forms. These are easily accessible to the student as they are reprinted in Hazlitt's *Shakespeare's Library*.

FAUSTUS.

Total Number of Lines.	CHARACTERS.	Chorus.	I.				II.		Chorus.	III.	Chorus.	IV.				V.				Chorus.
			1	2	3	4	1	2		1		1	2	3	4	1	2	3	4	
677	Faustus	...	109	...	74	...	109	72	...	48	...	...	42	37	21	56	...	109	...	...
59	Wagner	...	1	20	...	28	...	...	...	...	...	...	...	2	...	8	...	...	...	...
11	Evil Angel ...	...	4	...	...	...	3	4	...	...	...	...	...	...	...	...	...	...	...	...
22	Valdes	...	22	...	...	...	...	...	...	...	...	...	...	...	...	...	...	...	...	...
16	Cornelius	...	16	...	...	...	...	...	...	...	...	...	...	...	...	...	...	...	...	...
43	1st Scholar ...	...	...	13	...	...	...	...	...	...	...	...	...	...	...	13	...	12	5	...
32	2nd Scholar ...	...	...	11	...	...	...	...	...	...	...	...	...	...	...	2	...	10	9	...
169	Mephistophilis ..	...	...	...	30	...	69	18	...	27	...	...	...	15	...	10	...	...	...	...
36	Clown	...	...	...	...	36	...	...	...	...	...	...	...	...	...	...	...	...	...	...
25	Lucifer	...	...	...	...	...	...	25	...	...	...	...	...	...	...	...	...	...	...	...
7	"Wrath"	...	...	...	...	...	...	7	...	...	...	...	...	...	...	...	...	...	...	...
15	"Gluttony" ...	...	...	...	...	...	...	15	...	...	...	...	...	...	...	...	...	...	...	...
2	"Lechery" ...	...	...	...	...	...	...	2	...	...	...	...	...	...	...	...	...	...	...	...
15	Pope	...	...	...	...	...	...	...	...	15	...	...	...	...	...	...	...	...	...	...
15	Friar	...	...	...	...	...	...	...	...	15	...	...	...	...	...	...	...	...	...	...
3	Cardinal	...	...	...	...	...	...	...	...	3	...	...	...	...	...	...	...	...	...	...
23	Robin	...	...	...	...	...	...	...	...	...	...	23	...	...	...	...	...	...	...	...
11	Ralph	...	...	...	...	...	...	...	...	...	...	11	...	...	...	...	...	...	...	...
53	Emperor	...	...	...	...	...	...	...	...	...	...	...	53	...	...	...	...	...	...	...
16	Knight	...	...	...	...	...	...	...	...	...	...	...	16	...	...	...	...	...	...	...
45	Horse-courser ...	...	...	...	...	...	...	...	...	...	...	...	...	45	...	...	...	...	...	...
11	Duke	...	...	...	...	...	...	...	...	...	...	...	...	...	11	...	...	...	...	...
16	3rd Scholar ...	...	...	...	...	...	...	...	...	...	...	...	...	...	...	3	...	8	5	...
28	Old Man	...	...	...	...	...	...	...	...	...	...	...	...	...	...	19	9	...	...	...
65	"Chorus"	28	...	...	...	...	...	...	11	...	17	...	...	...	...	...	...	...	...	9
10	Good Angel ...	...	4	...	...	...	3	3	...	...	...	...	...	...	...	...	...	...	...	...
8	"Pride"	...	...	...	...	...	...	8	...	...	...	...	...	...	...	...	...	...	...	...
6	"Covetousness"	...	...	...	...	...	...	6	...	...	...	...	...	...	...	...	...	...	...	...
8	"Envy"	...	...	...	...	...	...	8	...	...	...	...	...	...	...	...	...	...	...	...
6	"Sloth"	...	...	...	...	...	...	6	...	...	...	...	...	...	...	...	...	...	...	...
12	Duchess	...	...	...	...	...	...	...	...	...	...	...	...	...	12	...	...	...	...	...
1465		28	156	44	104	64	184	174	11	108	17	34	111	99	44	111	9	139	19	9
1457	Actual No. of Lines	28	156	44	104	64	182	174	11	108	17	34	111	99	44	111	9	133	19	9

For the division of Acts and Scenes, see Dr. Wagner's edition.

SCHEME FOR ARRANGING THE PARTS WITH EIGHTEEN MEN.

TWELVE CHARACTERS SINGLY AND SIX GROUPS.

POPE	15	26	CARDINAL	3	19	RALPH	11	26	KNIGHT	16	18	FRIAR	15	26	3RD SCHOLAR	16	23
DUKE	11		CORNELIUS	16		"GLUTTONY"	15		"LECHERY"	2		EVIL ANGEL	11		"WRATH"	7	

Four of "The Seven Deadly Sins" are to be given to the ladies with many apologies.

SUGGESTIONS FOR DISCUSSION.

1. Marlowe took the plot of *Faustus* from Spies' *Historia*, brought from Germany by one of the English actors.
2. Of the additions to *Faustus* by Dekker, Bird, and Rowley, those by Dekker are indistinguishable from Marlowe's own writing.
3. *Faustus* is a dramatic failure.

LIST OF EARLIEST KNOWN EDITIONS.

Date.	*Printer.*	*Publisher.*	*Acted by*	*Present Owners.*
1604	V. S.	Thomas Bushell	Earl of Nottingham's servants	Bodleian Library.
1609	G. E.	John Wright		Hamburg Town Library.
1611	G. B.	John Wright		
1616		Iohn Wright		British Museum.
1620		Iohn Wright		British Museum.

In the Stationers' Registers is the following entry:—

1589. February 28.

Ric Jones Allowed vnto him for his Copie, *A ballad of the life and deathe of Doctor* FFAVSTVS *the great Cunngerer*. Allowed vnder the hand of the Bishop of LONDON, and master warden **Denhams** hand beinge to the Copie vj^{d}

The relation of this ballad to Marlowe's play is uncertain. Prof. Ward thinks it was founded on the play (Introduction to *Doctor Faustus* in Clarendon Press Series). Dr. Wagner thinks it was not (Introduction to *Doctor Faustus*. Longmans). Both these editions should be studied. The reasoning is largely based on the supposition that the ballad which Prof. Ward prints in full and which Dr. Wagner largely quotes is the one entered in 1589. It is taken from the Roxburghe collection in the British Museum. It should be noted that Richard Jones, to whom the ballad was entered, printed Marlowe's *Tamburlaine* in 1590.

In 1592 (see British Museum Catalogue) was printed the book of which there is an entry in the Stationers' Registers in 1596 (see below).

Marlowe died in May, 1593.

In the Registers is also this record:—

1593. November 16.

Cutbert. Burbye. Entred for his copie vnder thandes of bothe the wardens. *The seconde Reporte of Doctour John* FFAVSTVS. *with the ende of* WAGNERS *life* · vj^{d}

Prof. Ward says that this is an English version "of the Wagnerbuch—an imitation or continuation professing to give an account of the doings of Doctor Faustus's famulus Wagner." Marlowe's play, as we have it, has nothing about the death of Wagner.

Henslowe has many entries of the acting of *Faustus*, the earliest of which, by "my Lord Admeralle and my Lord chamberlen men" at Newington, is September 30, 1594 (*Diary*, p. 42).

The following entry is in the Stationers' Registers:—

1596. April 5.

Edward white. Entred for his copie (he havinge thinterest of **abell Jeffes** thereto) *The history of the Damnable Life and Deserued Death of Doctor John* FAVSTVS vj^{d}

Copies of this and the book entered in 1593 are in the Bodleian. They are reprinted in Thoms's *Early Prose Romances*.

Henslowe records (1) that he "Pd unto Thomas Dickers, the 20 of Desembr 1597, for adycyons to Fostus twentie shellinges" (*Diary*, p. 71); (2) that in "The Enventary tacken of all the properties for my Lord Admeralles men, the 10 of Marche 1598" was "j dragon in fostes" (*Diary*, p. 273).

In 1600 S. Rowland in *The Knave of Clubs* alludes to "Allen playing Faustus."

The first of the known editions was thus entered in the Stationers' Registers:—

1601. January 7.

Thomas Busshell Entred for his copye vnder the handes of master Doctor BARLOWE, and the Wardens a booke called *the plaie of Doctor* FAUSTUS vj^{d}

Henslowe notes that he "Lent unto the companye, the 22 of novmbr 1602, to paye unto Wm Birde and Samwell Rowley, for ther adicyones in Docter Fostes, the some of iiijli" (*Diary*, p. 228).

In 1604 was published the first of the known editions as "The Tragicall History of Dr. Faustus" and "written by Ch. Marl." The authorship of the 1609 edition was described in the same way. Its title was worded as in the 1610 entry.

On October 16, 1609, the copyright of the English Wagner-book was assigned by Mistress Burby to Master Welby.

In the Stationers' Registers the transfer of Bushell's edition is thus noted:—

1610. September 13.

John Wrighte. Assigned ouer to him from **Thomas Busshell** and with Consent of master **Adames** warden vnder his hand, these 2 Copyes followinge xij^{d}

viz

. . . .

The tragicall history of the horrible life and Death of Doctor FFAUSTUS, written by C. M:

Lowndes and Cunningham mention the 1611 edition, but say nothing about its ownership.

On March 2, 1618, Master Welby transferred to Master Snodham the rights he had acquired from Mistress Burby. (For the entries of both transfers see p. 93).

John Wright, in 1620, obtained an interest also in the book entered to White in 1596. The following is the entry:—

1620. December 13.

Master **Pauier** and **John Wright.** Assigned ouer vnto them by **Edward White** and by consent of both the wardens all the state the said **Edward white** hath in theis twelue copies followinge vj^{s}

viz

. . . .

The history of Doctor FFAUSTUS

The 1616 and 1620 editions have much the same title as the 1609 copy. The 1620 title-page contains the words "with new additions."

3 HENRY VI.

Total Number of Lines.	CHARACTERS.	I.				II.						III.			IV.								V.						
		1	2	3	4	1	2	3	4	5	6	1	2	3	1	2	3	4	5	6	7	8	1	2	3	4	5	6	7
436	Warwick	45	...	...	...	80	5	17	...	...	31	...	...	91	...	28	28	...	...	22	...	22	34	33	...	...	...	...	...
173	York	37	37	...	99	...	...	...	...	...	...	...	...	...	...	...	...	...	...	...	...	...	...	...	...	...	...	...	...
429	Edward	5	9	...	...	40	38	15	...	...	23	...	57	...	63	...	11	...	8	...	43	10	28	4	16	6	23	...	30
15	Montague	5	3	...	...	...	...	...	...	...	...	...	...	...	5	...	...	...	...	...	...	1	1	...	...	...	...	...	...
390	Richard	6	21	...	...	65	20	13	6	...	23	...	93	...	22	...	...	...	18	...	12	3	19	...	4	...	12	44	9
3	Norfolk	3	...	...	...	...	...	...	...	...	...	...	...	...	...	...	...	...	...	...	...	...	...	...	...	...	...	...	...
362	King Henry ...	75	...	...	...	...	23	...	...	78	...	69	...	...	...	...	...	...	...	46	...	22	...	...	...	...	...	49	...
30	Northumberland	13	...	...	15	...	2	...	...	...	...	...	...	...	...	...	...	...	...	...	...	...	...	...	...	...	...	...	...
140	Clifford	18	...	26	13	...	46	...	7	...	30	...	...	...	...	...	...	...	...	...	...	...	...	...	...	...	...	...	...
11	Westmoreland ...	11	...	...	...	...	...	...	...	...	...	...	...	...	...	...	...	...	...	...	...	...	...	...	...	...	...	...	...
17	Exeter	12	...	...	...	...	...	...	...	3	...	...	...	...	...	...	...	...	...	...	...	2	...	...	...	...	...	...	...
37	1st Messenger ...	...	4	...	...	24	6	...	...	...	...	...	...	...	...	...	...	...	...	...	...	...	1	...	...	2	...	...	...
1	Sir John Mortimer	...	1	...	...	...	...	...	...	...	...	...	...	...	...	...	...	...	...	...	...	...	...	...	...	...	...	...	...
3	Tutor	...	...	3	...	...	...	...	...	...	...	...	...	...	...	...	...	...	...	...	...	...	...	...	...	...	...	...	...
105	George	...	...	...	...	...	7	11	...	...	3	...	8	...	24	1	...	...	...	9	...	3	22	...	4	...	7	...	6
22	A Son	...	...	...	...	...	...	...	...	22	...	...	...	...	...	...	...	...	...	...	...	...	...	...	...	...	...	...	...
27	A Father	...	...	...	...	...	...	...	...	27	...	...	...	...	...	...	...	...	...	...	...	...	...	...	...	...	...	...	...
18	1st Keeper	...	...	...	...	...	...	...	...	...	...	18	...	...	...	...	...	...	...	...	...	...	...	...	...	...	...	...	...
14	2nd Keeper	...	...	...	...	...	...	...	...	...	...	14	...	...	...	...	...	...	...	...	...	...	...	...	...	...	...	...	...
2	Nobleman	...	...	...	...	...	...	...	...	...	...	...	2	...	...	...	...	...	...	...	...	...	...	...	...	...	...	...	...
66	King Lewis	...	...	...	...	...	...	...	...	...	...	...	...	66	...	...	...	...	...	...	...	...	...	...	...	...	...	...	...
35	Oxford	...	...	...	...	...	...	...	...	...	...	...	...	19	...	...	2	...	...	2	...	1	1	1	...	8	1	...	...
29	Post	...	...	...	...	...	...	...	...	...	...	...	...	4	18	...	...	...	...	7	...	...	...	...	...	...	...	...	...
33	Somerset	...	...	...	...	...	...	...	...	...	...	...	...	...	1	...	1	...	...	13	...	...	1	12	...	4	1	...	...
20	Hastings	...	...	...	...	...	...	...	...	...	...	...	...	...	8	...	...	...	2	...	10	...	...	...	...	...	...	...	...
3	"All"	...	...	...	...	...	...	...	...	...	...	...	...	...	...	1	...	...	...	...	1	1	...	...	...	...	...	...	...
8	1st Watchman ...	...	...	...	...	...	...	...	...	...	...	...	...	...	...	...	8	...	...	...	...	...	...	...	...	...	...	...	...
7	2nd Watchman ...	...	...	...	...	...	...	...	...	...	...	...	...	...	...	...	7	...	...	...	...	...	...	...	...	...	...	...	...
9	3rd Watchman ...	...	...	...	...	...	...	...	...	...	...	...	...	...	...	...	9	...	...	...	...	...	...	...	...	...	...	...	...
7	Rivers	...	...	...	...	...	...	...	...	...	...	...	...	...	...	...	...	7	...	...	...	...	...	...	...	...	...	...	...
2	Huntsman	...	...	...	...	...	...	...	...	...	...	...	...	...	...	...	...	...	2	...	...	...	...	...	...	...	...	...	...
3	Lieutenant	...	...	...	...	...	...	...	...	...	...	...	...	...	...	...	...	...	...	3	...	...	...	...	...	...	...	...	...
5	Mayor	...	...	...	...	...	...	...	...	...	...	...	...	...	...	...	...	...	...	...	5	...	...	...	...	...	...	...	...
14	Montgomery ...	...	...	...	...	...	...	...	...	...	...	...	...	...	...	...	...	...	...	...	14	...	...	...	...	...	...	...	...
3	Soldier	...	...	...	...	...	...	...	...	...	...	...	...	...	...	...	...	...	...	...	3	...	...	...	...	...	...	...	...
1	2nd Messenger ...	...	...	...	...	...	...	...	...	...	...	...	...	...	...	...	...	...	...	...	...	...	1	...	...	...	...	...	...
5	Somerville	...	...	...	...	...	...	...	...	...	...	...	...	...	...	...	...	...	...	...	...	...	5	...	...	...	...	...	...
279	Queen Margaret	42	...	...	53	...	22	...	...	6	...	...	...	73	...	...	...	...	...	...	...	...	...	...	...	50	33	...	...
46	Prince	4	...	...	...	...	8	...	...	3	...	...	...	6	...	...	...	...	...	...	...	...	...	...	...	12	13	...	...
24	Rutland	...	...	24	...	...	...	...	...	...	...	...	...	...	...	...	...	...	...	...	...	...	...	...	...	...	...	...	...
73	Lady Grey	...	...	...	...	...	...	...	...	...	...	...	36	...	8	...	...	28	...	...	...	...	...	...	...	...	...	...	1
9	Bona	...	...	...	...	...	...	...	...	...	...	...	...	9	...	...	...	...	...	...	...	...	...	...	...	...	...	...	...
2916		276	75	53	180	209	177	56	13	139	110	101	196	268	149	30	66	35	30	102	88	65	113	50	24	82	90	93	46
2905	Actual No. of Lines	273	75	52	180	209	177	56	13	139	110	101	195	265	149	30	64	35	29	102	88	65	113	50	24	82	90	93	46

EIGHT CHARACTERS SINGLY AND TEN GROUPS.

Somerset 33, Norfolk 3, Huntsman 2 } 38	Exeter 17, Hastings 20, Mortimer 1 } 38	Northumberland 30, 2nd Messenger 1, 2nd Watchman 7 } 38	Westmoreland 11, Somerville 5, Son 22 } 38
	Oxford 35, Tutor 3 } 38	Nobleman 2, 1st Messenger 37 } 39	
Montague 15, Mayor 5, 1st Keeper 18 } 38	Rivers 7, Soldier 3, Post 29 } 39	Montgomery 14, 2nd Keeper 14, 3rd Watchman 9 } 37	Lieutenant 3, Father 27, 1st Watchman 8 } 38

SUGGESTIONS FOR DISCUSSION.

1. *The True Tragedy* was a surreptitious and tinkered version of Shakspere's 3 *Henry VI.*
2. Shakspere's wonderful power of differentiating his characters comes out very strongly in 3 *Henry VI.*
3. The treatment of the character of Margaret of Anjou in 2 and 3 *Henry VI.* is conclusive evidence against the Shaksperian authorship.

LIST OF EARLIEST KNOWN EDITIONS.

Date.	*Printer.*	*Publisher.*	*Acted by*	*Present Owners.*
1595	P. S.	Thomas Millington	Earl of Pembroke's servants	Bodleian Library.
1600	W. W.	Thomas Millington	Earl of Pembroke's servants	British Museum. Bodleian Library. Duke of Devonshire. Mr. Halliwell-Phillipps.

These editions are of the play known as *The True Tragedy*. They were both published anonymously, and had the title worded alike: "The true Tragedie of Richard Duke of Yorke, and the death of good King Henrie the Sixt, with the whole contention betweene the two Houses Lancaster and Yorke as it was sundrie times acted by the Right Honourable the Earle of Pembrooke his seruants." It was printed in 1619 with two other plays in one volume. The full title of this and other matters connected with this play are given at p. 65.

In the Stationers' Registers the only entry of *The True Tragedy* is the transfer of the copyright in 1602, where the play is called the "Second parte of Henry the VJ^t" (see p. 59). In the entry of the 1623 Folio, which is the earliest authority of the play as we now have it, the play named "the Thirde Parte of Henry the Sixt" is that now known as the first part (see p. 63). The known existence of Millington's editions, and of the copy of 1619 which had Shakspere's name on the title-page, was to the Folio publishers evidence of the Shaksperian authorship and therefore for the reason there given this play was not then mentioned. In the Folio itself the title of the play is "The third part of Henry the Sixt, with the death of the Duke of Yorke."

The student should carefully examine the Introduction to *The Contention* and *The True Tragedy*, edited by Mr. Halliwell [Phillipps] for the Shakespeare Society in 1843, and Mr. Fleay's article, "Who Wrote Henry VI.?" in *Macmillan's Magazine*, November, 1875, and also Miss Jane Lee's comparison of these plays with 2 and 3 *Henry VI.* (New Shakspere Society's *Transactions*, 1875-6, Part II.)

THE COMEDY OF ERRORS.

Total Number of Lines.	CHARACTERS.	I.		II.		III.		IV.				V.
		1	2	1	2	1	2	1	2	3	4	1
143	ÆGEON	110	...	...	...	...	...	...	...	...	...	33
91	DUKE	48	...	...	...	...	...	...	...	...	...	43
1	GAOLER	1	...	...	...	...	...	...	...	...	...	...
15	1ST MERCHANT	...	15	...	...	...	...	...	...	...	...	...
279	ANTIPHOLUS OF S. ...	...	55	...	84	...	86	...	...	27	5	22
248	DROMIO OF S.	...	2	...	67	14	62	16	25	44	7	11
161	DROMIO OF E.	...	33	32	...	30	...	1	...	...	44	21
212	ANTIPHOLUS OF E. ...	...	...	...	...	47	...	48	...	...	44	73
26	BALTHAZAR	...	...	...	...	26	...	...	...	...	...	...
77	ANGELO	...	...	...	...	2	10	34	...	...	...	31
34	2ND MERCHANT	...	...	...	...	...	...	11	...	...	...	23
13	OFFICER	...	...	...	...	...	...	3	...	...	10	...
12	PINCH	...	...	...	...	...	...	...	...	...	12	...
15	SERVANT	...	...	...	...	...	...	...	...	...	...	15
260	ADRIANA	...	...	55	63	2	...	...	34	...	31	75
96	LUCIANA	...	...	30	8	...	36	...	10	...	5	7
8	LUCE...	...	...	...	...	8	...	...	...	...	...	...
35	COURTEZAN	...	...	...	...	...	...	...	...	26	6	3
73	ABBESS	...	...	...	...	...	...	...	...	...	...	73
1799		159	105	117	222	129	194	113	69	97	164	430
1778	Actual Number of Lines	159	105	116	221	123	190	113	66	97	162	426

In Scheme for arranging the parts with seven ladies omit COURTEZAN.

SUGGESTIONS FOR DISCUSSION.

1. The brevity of *The Comedy of Errors* is accounted for by the fact that the play as we have it is only an abridged acting edition.

2. The description of *The Comedy of Errors* as a mere farce is, considering the tragic background of the play, singularly inappropriate.

3. The portraiture of Adriana represents a phase in Shakspere's home-life.

THE EARLIEST KNOWN EDITION IS THE 1623 FOLIO.

In the Stationers' Registers is this entry :—

1594. June 10.
Thomas Creede Entred for his Copie vnder thande of Master **Cawood** a booke entituled *Menachmi beinge A pleasant and fine Conceyted Comedye taken out of the moste excellent wittie Poett.* PLAUTUS *chosen purposely from out the reste as leaste harmefull and yet moste delightfull* **vjdC**

In the reprint of a contemporary record it is stated that at Gray's Inn on December 28, 1594, ". . . a Comedy of Errors like to Plautus his Menechmus was played by the players . . ."

In 1595 the book entered in the previous year was issued. The printer states that the author, W.W., "having diverse of this Poettes Comedies Englished, for the use and delight of his private friends" had reluctantly allowed this one to be published. It is reprinted in Hazlitt's *Shakespeare's Library.*

In 1598 Meres, referring to Shakspere as a writer of comedy, commends him for "his Errors."

Manningham on February 2, 1602, in a note on the performance of *Twelfth Night*, likens it to "the Commedy of Errores," as if this were a well-known play. The passage from his Diary is given in full in connection with *Twelfth Night.*

There is a record that in 1604, "on Inosents Night The Plaie of Errors," by "Shaxberd," was performed at Whitehall "by his Matis Plaiers." The genuineness of this has been questioned. A Judicial summing-up in favour of the accuracy of the fact is given by Mr. Halliwell-Phillipps (*Outlines*, Vol. II., pp. 161–7). The entry of this and several other plays is printed in *Extracts from the Accounts of the Revels at Court*, which Peter Cunningham edited for the Shakespeare Society in 1842, and is in manuscript among the Malone Papers in the Bodleian. Reprinted from the *Stratford-upon-Avon Herald* may be found in *Shakespeariana*, May, 1888, some notes by E. H. Hathaway, dealing with the alleged forgeries of Cunningham, but making no mention of the corroborative Malone MS.

There is no reason for connecting with this play either *The Historie of Error*, acted in 1577 by the Children of Paul's, or a play called, perhaps by a misprint, *The Historic of Ferrar*, that was performed at Windsor in 1583.

FRIAR BACON.

Total Number of Lines.	CHARACTERS.	I.			II.				III.		IV.					V.	
		1	2	3	1	2	3	4	1	2	1	2	3	4	5	1	2
159	Lacy	23	...	18	...	...	50	...	30	...	...	...	6	...	32	...	...
49	Warren	11	...	...	...	10	...	22	...	...	...	...	...	..	6	..	...
33	Ermsby	6	...	...	...	12	...	7	...	...	...	...	...	...	8	...	...
136	Ralph	58	...	...	...	26	...	32	...	...	...	...	20	...	...	...	...
248	Prince Edward	85	...	...	...	24	28	...	81	16	...	...	9	...	...	...	5
344	Bacon	...	75	...	...	36	25	..	...	57	...	72	...	54	...	...	25
242	Miles	...	42	...	...	23	...	30	...	23	...	72	...	...	...	52	...
43	Burden	...	31	...	...	...	...	12	...	...	...	...	...	...	...	...	...
31	Clement	...	12	...	...	...	...	19	...	...	...	...	...	...	...	...	...
31	Mason	...	9	..	...	...	...	22	...	...	...	...	...	...	..	..	...
10	Thomas	...	...	10	...	...	...	...	...	...	...	...	...	...	...	...	...
5	Richard	...	...	5	...	...	...	...	...	...	...	...	...	...	..	...	...
104	King Henry	...	...	...	34	...	...	...	...	22	...	...	20	...	...	...	28
26	King of Castile	...	...	...	8	...	...	..	...	7	...	...	11	...	...	...	...
52	Emperor	...	...	...	15	...	...	...	...	25	...	...	9	...	...	...	3
73	Bungay	...	...	...	...	...	30	...	...	31	...	...	...	12	...	...	...
6	Constable	...	...	...	...	...	...	6	...	...	...	...	...	...	...	...	...
84	Vandermast	...	...	...	...	...	...	...	...	84	...	...	...	...	...	...	...
7	"Hercules"	...	...	...	...	...	...	...	...	7	...	...	...	...	...	...	...
48	Lambert	...	...	...	...	...	...	...	...	...	33	...	...	15	...	...	...
37	Serlsby	...	...	...	...	...	...	...	...	...	29	...	...	8	...	...	...
25	Keeper	...	...	...	...	...	...	...	...	...	11	...	...	...	14	...	...
15	Post	...	..	...	...	...	...	...	...	..	15	...	...	...	...	...	...
3	"The Brazen Head"...	...	...	...	...	...	...	...	...	...	...	3	...	...	...	...	...
11	1st Scholar	...	...	...	...	...	...	...	...	...	...	...	...	11	...	...	...
9	2nd Scholar	...	...	...	...	...	...	...	...	...	...	...	...	9	...	...	...
2	Friend	...	...	...	...	...	...	...	...	...	...	...	...	...	2	...	...
21	Devil	...	...	..	..	...	...	...	...	...	...	...	...	...	...	21	...
18	Hostess	...	18	...	...	...	...	...	...	...	...	...	...	...	...	...	...
295	Margaret	...	...	48	...	...	51	...	53	...	83	...	...	...	52	.	8
9	Joan	...	...	9	...	...	...	...	...	...	...	...	...	...	...	...	...
34	Elinor	...	...	..	10	...	...	...	...	6	...	...	10	...	...	...	8
2210		183	187	90	67	131	184	150	164	278	171	147	85	109	114	73	77
2209	Actual Number of Lines	183	187	90	67	131	184	150	164	278	171	146	85	109	114	73	77

The Clarendon Press edition might have divided the play into Acts as well as Scenes. In *British Dramatists* there is no division of either.

ELEVEN CHARACTERS SINGLY AND SEVEN GROUPS.

King of Castile 26, 1st Scholar 11, Constable 6	43	Ermsby 33, 2nd Scholar 9, "The Brazen Head" 3	45	Mason 31, Richard 5, "Hercules" 7	43

Burden 43, Friend 2	45	Clement 31, Post 15	46	Keeper 25, Devil 21	46	Serlsby 37, Thomas 10	47

SUGGESTIONS FOR DISCUSSION.

1. Of the Elizabethan dramatists, Greene alone had the literary characteristics of Shakspere.
2. Margaret in *Friar Bacon* is the finest delineation of woman-character in the pre-Shaksperian drama.
3. Greene's references to Shakspere show no more than a protest against the admission of an uneducated man amongst University playwrights.

LIST OF EARLIEST KNOWN EDITIONS.

Date.	*Printer.*	*Publisher.*	*Acted by*	*Present Owners.*
1594.	— —	Edward White	Her Majesty's servants	British Museum. Bodleian Library. Lady Ellesmere.
1599.				Bodleian Library.

Henslowe has several entries of the acting of *Friar Bacon*. The earliest is by "my lord Stranges mene" on February 19, 1592 (*Diary*, p. 20).

Greene died on the 3rd of September, 1592.

The entry of the 1594 edition in the Stationers' Registers reads thus:

1594. May 14.

Edward White. Entred for his Copie vnder thandes of bothe the wardens a booke entituled *the Historye of ffryer Bacon and ffryer Boungaye* vj^{d}C.

The name of Adam Islip was first inserted and then struck out.

The edition was published as "The Honorable Historie of frier Bacon, and frier Bongay."

Henslowe "Lent unto Thomas Downton, the 14 of desembr 1602, to paye unto Mr Mydelton for a prologe and epeloge for the playe of Bacon for the corte, the some of v^{s}" (*Diary*, p. 228). Nothing is now known of this prologue and epilogue.

In connection with this play should be studied "The Famous Historie of frier Bacon: containing the wonderful things that he did in his life: also the Manner of his death, with the Lives and Deaths of the two Conjurers, Bungye and Vandermast," which Prof. Ward (Clarendon Press edition) says was "a popular story-book probably written towards the end of the sixteenth century, and founded upon the accretions of the legendary history of Friar Bacon." It is reprinted in Thoms's *Early Prose Romances*.

THE TWO GENTLEMEN OF VERONA.

Total Number of Lines.	CHARACTERS.	I.			II.							III.		IV.				V.			
		1	2	3	1	2	3	4	5	6	7	1	2	1	2	3	4	1	2	3	4
393	VALENTINE	43	...	...	65	...	...	112	...	...	...	77	...	23	...	...	...	...	...	...	73
465	PROTEUS	68	...	29	...	17	...	49	...	43	...	75	42	...	57	...	30	...	15	...	40
226	SPEED	51	...	...	100	...	...	3	28	...	...	40	...	4	...	...	...	...	...	...	...
35	ANTONIO	...	...	35	...	...	...	...	...	...	...	...	...	...	...	...	...	...	...	...	...
46	PANTHINO	...	...	28	...	1	17	...	...	...	...	...	...	...	...	...	...	...	...	...	...
242	LAUNCE	...	..	...	...	...	48	...	35	..	...	104	...	...	...	...	55	...	...	...	...
56	THURIO	...	...	...	...	...	...	14	...	...	...	...	14	...	7	...	...	...	16	...	5
200	DUKE	...	...	...	...	...	...	18	...	...	...	102	42	...	...	...	...	...	18	...	20
22	1ST OUTLAW	...	...	...	...	...	...	...	...	...	...	...	...	15	...	...	...	...	...	6	1
16	2ND OUTLAW	...	...	...	...	...	...	...	...	...	...	...	...	14	...	...	...	...	...	1	1
26	3RD OUTLAW	...	...	...	...	...	...	...	...	...	...	...	...	20	...	..	...	...	...	5	1
26	HOST	...	...	...	...	...	...	...	...	...	...	...	...	...	26	...	...	...	...	...	...
29	EGLAMOUR	...	...	...	...	...	...	...	...	...	...	...	...	...	...	19	...	10	...	...	...
323	JULIA	...	91	...	...	4	...	...	...	...	72	...	...	..	27	...	99	...	10	...	20
72	LUCETTA	...	54	...	...	...	...	...	...	...	18	...	...	...	...	...	...	...	...	...	...
159	SILVIA	...	...	...	18	...	...	24	...	...	...	...	...	...	29	32	29	3	...	3	21
2336		162	145	92	183	22	65	220	63	43	90	398	98	76	146	51	213	13	59	15	182
2294	Actual No. of Lines	161	140	91	182	21	65	214	63	43	90	397	98	76	140	47	210	12	56	15	173

In II. 2, Proteus's lines should be 16, and in V. 1, Eglamour's should be 9.

SUGGESTIONS FOR DISCUSSION.

1. *The Two Gentlemen of Verona* was founded upon an early play of which *Julio und Hyppolita* was a translation.
2. The repetition in the later plays of the incidents of *The Two Gentlemen of Verona* shows that Shakspere was dissatisfied with the crude way in which he had at first sketched them, and proves that he would not have included the play in an edition of his works.
3. The versification of *The Two Gentlemen of Verona* is more harmonious than most of the poetry of Shakspere.

THE EARLIEST KNOWN EDITION IS THE 1623 FOLIO.

Meres in 1598 names the "Gẽtlemẽ of Verona" as one of Shakspere's comedies.

Till it was entered with the other plays of the First Folio on November 8, 1623, there is no mention of it in the Stationers' Registers.

"Julio und Hyppolita," with an English translation, is reprinted in Cohn's *Shakespeare in Germany*, where, and in a similarly named and earlier published section of Thoms's *Three Notelets on Shakespeare*, much of interest will be found in reference to the English actors who went to Germany about 1600 and performed plays in various towns. Thomas Heywood, in his *Apology for Actors*, 1612 (ed. Shakespeare Society, 1841, pp. 40, 58) has something to say about English comedians who were acting on the continent about that time. "Julio und Hyppolita" and the "Tragædia von Tito Andronico" (see p. 59) are reprinted by Cohn from *Englische Comedien und Tragedien*, first published in 1620. The *Titus Andronicus*, with many other plays, had been reprinted by Tieck in 1817 in his *Deutsches Theater*, a work intended to comprise the most noteworthy of the less known early German plays, but which came to an end before it had fulfilled its purpose.

EDWARD II.

Total Number of Lines.	CHARACTERS.	I.				II.						III.		IV.						V.					
		1	2	3	4	1	2	3	4	5	6	1	2	1	2	3	4	5	6	1	2	3	4	5	6
159	GAVESTON	86	...	5	18	...	21	...	2	21	6	...	...	...	...	...	...	...	...	...	...	...	...	...	...
4	1ST POOR MAN	4	...	...	...	...	...	...	...	...	...	...	...	...	...	...	...	...	...	...	...	...	...	...	...
4	2ND POOR MAN	4	...	...	...	...	...	...	...	...	...	...	...	...	...	...	...	...	...	...	...	...	...	...	...
6	3RD POOR MAN	6	...	...	...	...	...	...	...	...	...	...	...	...	...	...	...	...	...	...	...	...	...	...	...
717	KING EDWARD	58	...	...	138	...	86	...	9	...	...	87	39	...	...	36	...	4	49	124	...	35	...	52	...
149	LANCASTER	14	17	...	32	...	53	9	8	9	...	...	7	...	...	...	...	...	...	...	...	...	...	...	...
40	ELDER MORTIMER	2	5	...	33	...	...	...	...	...	...	...	...	...	...	...	...	...	...	...	...	...	...	...	...
449	YOUNGER MORTIMER	13	22	...	91	...	58	9	9	21	...	...	12	5	21	...	13	25	...	...	58	...	64	...	28
120	KENT	16	...	...	1	...	18	7	...	...	...	...	2	14	7	...	1	23	...	...	13	9	9	...	...
86	WARWICK	3	9	...	19	...	7	3	1	28	9	...	7	...	...	...	...	...	...	...	...	...	...	...	...
8	BISHOP OF COVENTRY	8	...	...	...	...	...	...	...	...	...	...	...	...	...	...	...	...	...	...	...	...	...	...	...
31	ARCHBISHOP OF CANTERBURY	...	16	...	13	...	...	...	...	...	...	...	...	...	...	...	...	...	...	...	...	...	2	...	...
36	PEMBROKE	...	...	...	8	...	3	1	...	23	...	...	1	...	...	...	...	...	...	...	...	...	...	...	...
1	BEAUMONT	...	...	...	1	...	...	...	...	...	...	...	...	...	...	...	...	...	...	...	...	...	...	...	...
50	BALDOCK	...	...	...	...	23	3	...	...	...	...	4	3	...	...	...	...	2	15	...	...	...	...	...	...
117	YOUNGER SPENSER	...	...	...	...	36	2	...	1	...	...	29	15	...	...	16	...	3	15	...	...	...	...	...	...
5	MESSENGER	...	...	...	...	...	1	...	...	...	...	...	...	...	...	2	...	...	...	...	2	...	...	...	...
3	GUARD	...	...	...	...	...	3	...	...	...	...	...	...	...	...	...	...	...	...	...	...	...	...	...	...
41	ARUNDEL	...	...	...	...	...	...	...	...	16	...	24	...	...	...	1	...	...	...	...	...	...	...	...	...
5	JAMES	...	...	...	...	...	...	...	...	...	5	...	...	...	...	...	...	...	...	...	...	...	...	...	...
18	ELDER SPENSER	...	...	...	...	...	...	...	...	...	...	9	7	...	...	...	...	2	...	...	...	...	...	...	...
17	HERALD	...	...	...	...	...	...	...	...	...	...	17	...	...	...	...	...	...	...	...	...	...	...	...	...
6	LEVUNE	...	...	...	...	...	...	...	...	...	...	...	6	...	...	...	...	...	...	...	...	...	...	...	...
21	SIR JOHN	...	...	...	...	...	...	...	...	...	...	...	...	...	17	...	2	2	...	...	...	...	...	...	...
22	RICE AP HOWEL	...	...	...	...	...	...	...	...	...	...	...	...	...	...	...	...	10	12	...	...	...	...	...	...
9	ABBOT	...	...	...	...	...	...	...	...	...	...	...	...	...	...	...	...	...	9	...	...	...	...	...	...
2	1ST MONK	...	...	...	...	...	...	...	...	...	...	...	...	...	...	...	...	...	2	...	...	...	...	...	...
2	MOWER	...	...	...	...	...	...	...	...	...	...	...	...	...	...	...	...	...	2	...	...	...	...	...	...
29	LEICESTER	...	...	...	...	...	...	...	...	...	...	...	...	...	...	...	...	...	15	14	...	...	...	...	...
13	BISHOP OF WINCHESTER	...	...	...	...	...	...	...	...	...	...	...	...	...	...	...	...	...	...	6	7	...	...	...	...
3	TRUSSEL	...	...	...	...	...	...	...	...	...	...	...	...	...	...	...	...	...	...	3	...	...	...	...	...
8	BERKELEY	...	...	...	...	...	...	...	...	...	...	...	...	...	...	...	...	...	...	8	...	...	...	...	...
45	MATREVIS	...	...	...	...	...	...	...	...	...	...	...	...	...	...	...	...	...	...	...	3	14	...	24	4
23	GURNEY	...	...	...	...	...	...	...	...	...	...	...	...	...	...	...	...	...	...	...	2	8	...	13	...
4	1ST SOLDIER	...	...	...	...	...	...	...	...	...	...	...	...	...	...	...	...	...	...	...	...	1	3	...	...
49	LIGHTBORN	...	...	...	...	...	...	...	...	...	...	...	...	...	...	...	...	...	...	...	...	...	15	34	...
4	CHAMPION	...	...	...	...	...	...	...	...	...	...	...	...	...	...	...	...	...	...	...	...	...	4	...	...
3	1ST LORD	...	...	...	...	...	...	...	...	...	...	...	...	...	...	...	...	...	...	...	...	...	...	...	3
3	2ND LORD	...	...	...	...	...	...	...	...	...	...	...	...	...	...	...	...	...	...	...	...	...	...	...	3
261	QUEEN ISABELLA	...	14	...	72	...	8	...	39	...	...	12	...	...	27	...	14	16	...	...	31	...	6	...	22
27	NIECE	...	...	...	...	23	3	...	1	...	...	...	...	...	...	...	...	...	...	...	...	...	...	...	...
1	HORSE-BOY	...	...	...	...	...	...	...	...	1	...	...	...	...	...	...	...	...	...	...	...	...	...	...	...
81	PRINCE EDWARD	...	...	...	...	...	...	...	...	...	...	5	...	...	13	...	...	2	...	...	7	...	12	...	42
2682		214	83	5	426	82	266	29	70	119	20	187	99	19	85	55	30	89	119	155	123	67	115	123	102
2623	Actual Number of Lines ...	208	82	5	423	82	261	28	68	107	19	184	96	17	82	55	30	87	118	155	117	67	113	119	100

In *British Dramatists* this play is not divided into Acts or Scenes. The arrangement in the Table is the same as that of Fleay's edition (Collins' Series) and Tancock's edition (Clarendon Press Series).

SCHEME FOR ARRANGING THE PARTS WITH EIGHTEEN MEN.

NINE CHARACTERS SINGLY AND NINE GROUPS.

Canterbury 31, Berkeley 8, 2nd Lord 3, 2nd Poor Man 4 — 46	Coventry 8, Leicester 29, Champion 4, Messenger 5 — 46	Winchester 13, Sir John 21, Abbot 9, Guard 3 — 46	Pembroke 36, 1st Monk 2, 1st Lord 3, James 5 — 46
Elder Spenser 18, Beaumont 1, Gurney 23, 1st Poor Man 4 — 46	Arundel 41, 3rd Poor Man 6 — 47; Matrevis 45, Mower 2 — 47	Elder Mortimer 40, Levune 6 — 46	Trussel 3, Rice ap Howel 22, Herald 17, 1st Soldier 4 — 46

SUGGESTIONS FOR DISCUSSION.

1. *Edward II.*, at the time of its production, was the master-piece of history-plays.
2. The attacks made by Nash and Greene upon Marlowe show that his influence upon dramatic verse is commonly over-estimated.
3. The death-scene of Edward II. moves pity and terror beyond any scene ancient or modern.

LIST OF EARLIEST KNOWN EDITIONS.

Date.	*Printer.*	*Publisher.*	*Acted by*	*Present Owners.*
1594		William Jones	Earl of Pembroke's servants	Library at Cassel.
1598	Richard Bradocke	William Jones	Earl of Pembroke's servants	British Museum. Bodleian Library.
1612		Roger Barnes	Earl of Pembroke's servants	British Museum.
1622		Henry Bell	The late Queen's servants	British Museum. Bodleian Library.

Marlowe died in May, 1593.

The first of the known editions was thus entered in the Stationers' Registers:—

1593. July 6.

William Jones Entred for his copie vnder thandes of Master Richard Judson and the Wardens. A booke. Intituled *The troublesom Reign and Lamentable Death of Edward the Second, king of England, with the tragicall fall of proud Mortymer* vj^d w.

The edition itself was issued with its title in the words of the entry.

In the Registers there are these entries:—

1593. December 3.

Nicholas Linge **John Busbie** Entred for theire Copie vnder the handes of the Wardens and master Hartwell A booke entituled *Pierse Gaviston Erle of Cornewall his life deathe and fortune* vj^d

1596. April 15.

Matthew Lownes. Entred for his copie vnder the handes of the wardens a booke called *mortimeriados the lamentable Civill warres betwene Edward the Second and the Barons* vj^d.

This poem by Drayton was published in the same year, and on October 8, 1601, its copyright was transferred to Master Linge, who in the following year brought out an edition in which the title was somewhat modified and the structure of the verse altered. It is reprinted in Chalmers's *English Poets.*

The following entries are in the Registers:—

1611. December 16.

Roger Barnes. Entred for his Copy by assignement from **William Jones** and vnder master warden **Lownes** his hand, A booke called *the troublesome raygne and lamentable deathe of Edward the 2d* by Chr Marlowe gent vj^d.

1617. April 17.

Henry Bell Assigned ouer vnto him by **Roger Barnes** and Consent of master warden **Lownes** a booke Called *The tragedie of Edward the seconde* written by Christofer Marloe vj^d.

The titles of the last three of the editions are in the words of the 1593 entry, with the addition of "And also the life and death of Peirs Gaueston, the great Earle of Cornewall, and mighty fauorite of King Edward the second."

In the New Shakspere Society's *Transactions*, 1875-6, Part II., is given Dr. Rudolf Genée's list of the chief textual differences between the 1594 edition and modern editions.

LOVE'S LABOUR'S LOST.

Total Number of Lines.	CHARACTERS.	I.		II.	III.	IV.			V.	
		1	2	1	1	1	2	3	1	2
322	KING	117	...	47	...	...	...	76	...	82
70	LONGAVILLE	14	...	6	...	...	...	33	...	17
91	DUMAIN	8	...	2	...	...	...	44	...	37
627	BIRON	128	...	18	51	...	...	237	...	193
32	DULL	9	7	...	...	...	13	...	3	...
202	COSTARD	44	13	...	40	26	3	4	14	58
255	ARMADO	...	96	...	58	...	...	...	48	53
234	BOYET	...	...	67	...	64	...	...	...	103
2	1ST LORD	...	...	2	...	...	...	...	...	...
5	FORESTER	...	...	...	...	5	...	...	...	...
80	NATHANIEL	...	...	...	...	...	45	...	13	22
200	HOLOFERNES	...	...	...	...	...	104	...	60	36
4	MERCADE	...	...	...	...	...	...	...	...	4
168	MOTH	...	70	...	60	...	...	...	24	14
18	JAQUENETTA	...	6	...	...	...	8	4	...	...
289	PRINCESS	...	...	67	...	50	...	...	...	172
42	MARIA	...	...	22	...	4	...	...	...	16
46	KATHARINE	...	...	8	...	...	...	...	...	38
178	ROSALINE	...	...	30	...	11	...	...	...	137
2865		320	192	269	209	160	173	398	162	982
2789	Actual Number of Lines	318	192	258	207	151	173	386	162	942

SUGGESTIONS FOR DISCUSSION.

1. The evidences that Shakspere in the 1598 Quarto had "corrected and augmented" his *Love's Labour's Lost* are to be found in the play itself.
2. *Love's Labour's Lost*, being the only play for the plot of which Shakspere was solely responsible, shows that the bent of his mind was decidedly comic.
3. In *Love's Labour's Lost* some of the anti-Martinist writers are satirised, and all the chief characters are drawn from living originals.

EARLIEST KNOWN EDITION.

Date.	*Printer.*	*Publisher.*	*Acted by*	*Present Owners.*
1598.	W. W.	Cutbert Burby		British Museum. Bodleian Library. Trinity College, Cambridge. University of Edinburgh. Duke of Devonshire. Lady Ellesmere. Mr. Halliwell-Phillipps.

Meres, in 1598, mentions "Loue labors lost" as one of Shakspere's comedies.

The title of the 1598 edition is "A Pleasant Conceited Comedie called, Loues labors lost." As it is described on its title-page as "newly corrected and augmented. By W. Shakespere," there must have been an earlier form, which seems to be referred to in R.T.'s *The Months Minde of a Melancholy Lover*, 1598, where the play is thus mentioned:

"LOVES LABOR LOST, I once did see a Play,
Ycleped so . . . . , ... "

and also in a letter from Sir Walter Cope in 1604 to the "Lorde Vycount Cranborne," in which, lamenting that there is "no new playe that the quene hath not seene," he speaks of the players having "Revyved an olde one, Cawled *Loves Labore lost.*"

In the suspected entry of the Court Revels of 1605 (see p. 71) is this record: "By his Matis plaiers, Betwin Newers Day and Twelfe day A play of Loues Labours Lost."

The first entry in the Stationers' Registers in reference to this play is as follows:

1607. January 22.

Master **Linge** Entred for his copies by direccon of A Court and with consent of Master **Burby** vnder his handwrytinge These. iij copies

viz.

ROMEO and JULIETT.
Loues Labour Loste.
The taminge of A Shrewe **xviij**d*R*

There is also this entry:

1607. November 19.

John Smythick. Entred for his copies vnder thandes of the wardens. these bookes followinge Whiche dyd belonge to **Nicholas Lynge**

viz.

. . . .

6 A booke called *HAMLETT* **vj**d

. . . .

9 *The taminge of a Shrewe* **vj**d
10 *ROMEO and JULETT* **vj**d
11 *Loues Labour Lost* **vj**d

. . . .

John Smythick (appearing as I. Smithweeke) was one of those at whose charges the 1623 Folio was printed, in which the play is entitled "Loues Labour's lost."

In the consideration of this play, Mr. S. L. Lee's "A New Study of *Love's Labour Lost*" (*Gentleman's Magazine*, October, 1880), and Dr. F. Landmann's "Shakspere and Euphuism" (New Shakspere Society's *Transactions*, 1880–5, Part II.), should be consulted.

RICHARD II.

Total Number of Lines.	CHARACTERS.	I.				II.				III.				IV.	V.					
		1	2	3	4	1	2	3	4	1	2	3	4	1	1	2	3	4	5	6
755	RICHARD	57	...	74	40	41	...	...	...	...	146	104	...	134	63	...	...	...	96	...
192	GAUNT	8	16	62	...	106	...	...	...	...	...	...	...	...	...	...	...	...	...	...
414	BOLINGBROKE	59	...	78	...	...	...	56	...	38	...	55	...	39	...	...	56	...	...	33
135	MOWBRAY	83	...	52	...	...	...	...	...	...	...	...	...	...	...	...	...	...	...	...
25	MARSHAL	...	...	25	...	...	...	...	...	...	...	...	...	...	...	...	...	...	...	...
85	AUMERLE	...	...	5	15	...	...	...	...	...	12	3	...	26	...	11	13	...	...	...
6	1ST HERALD	...	...	6	...	...	...	...	...	...	...	...	...	...	...	...	...	...	...	...
7	2ND HERALD	...	...	7	...	...	...	...	...	...	...	...	...	...	...	...	...	...	...	...
32	GREEN	...	...	...	5	...	25	...	...	2	...	...	...	...	...	...	...	...	...	...
39	BUSHY	...	...	...	4	...	33	...	...	2	...	...	...	...	...	...	...	...	...	...
1	"ALL"	...	...	...	1	...	...	...	...	...	...	...	...	...	...	...	...	...	...	...
288	YORK	...	...	...	...	74	41	49	...	2	...	13	...	11	...	70	28	...	...	...
142	NORTHUMBERLAND	...	...	...	...	50	...	35	...	...	...	30	...	15	7	...	...	...	...	5
22	ROSS	...	...	...	...	20	...	2	...	...	...	...	...	...	...	...	...	...	...	...
12	WILLOUGHBY	...	...	...	...	10	...	2	...	...	...	...	...	...	...	...	...	...	...	...
17	SERVANT	...	...	...	...	...	5	...	...	...	...	...	10	...	...	...	...	2	...	...
22	BAGOT	...	...	...	...	...	9	...	...	...	...	...	...	13	...	...	...	...	...	...
45	PERCY	...	...	...	...	...	...	21	...	...	...	8	...	5	...	...	6	...	...	5
8	BERKELEY	...	...	...	...	...	...	8	...	...	...	...	...	...	...	...	...	...	...	...
15	CAPTAIN	...	...	...	...	...	...	...	15	...	...	...	...	...	...	...	...	...	...	...
20	SALISBURY	...	...	...	...	...	...	...	9	...	11	...	...	...	...	...	...	...	...	...
63	CARLISLE	...	...	...	...	...	...	...	...	...	14	...	...	49	...	...	...	...	...	...
37	SCROOP	...	...	...	...	...	...	...	...	...	37	...	...	...	...	...	...	...	...	...
52	GARDENER	...	...	...	...	...	...	...	...	...	...	...	52	...	...	...	...	...	...	...
27	FITZWATER	...	...	...	...	...	...	...	...	...	...	...	...	23	...	...	...	...	...	4
5	LORD	...	...	...	...	...	...	...	...	...	...	...	...	5	...	...	...	...	...	...
10	SURREY	...	...	...	...	...	...	...	...	...	...	...	...	10	...	...	...	...	...	...
10	ABBOT	...	...	...	...	...	...	...	...	...	...	...	...	10	...	...	...	...	...	...
21	EXTON	...	...	...	...	...	...	...	...	...	...	...	...	...	...	...	...	10	6	5
12	GROOM	...	...	...	...	...	...	...	...	...	...	...	...	...	...	...	...	...	12	...
6	KEEPER	...	...	...	...	...	...	...	...	...	...	...	...	...	...	...	...	...	6	...
58	DUCHESS OF GLOUCESTER	...	58	...	...	...	...	...	...	...	...	...	...	...	...	...	...	...	...	...
115	QUEEN	...	...	...	...	1	39	...	...	...	...	...	43	...	32	...	...	...	...	...
6	LADY	...	...	...	...	...	...	...	...	...	...	...	6	...	...	...	...	...	...	...
93	DUCHESS OF YORK	...	...	...	...	...	...	...	...	...	...	...	...	...	...	45	48	...	...	...
2797		207	74	309	65	302	152	173	24	44	220	213	111	340	102	126	151	12	120	52
2756	Actual Number of Lines	205	74	309	65	299	149	171	24	44	218	209	107	334	102	117	146	12	119	52

In II. 3 Bolingbroke's lines should be 55. The total lines should be 2755, as the total of V. 4 should be 11.

TEN CHARACTERS SINGLY AND EIGHT GROUPS.

Surrey	10	42	Fitzwater	27	42	Scroop	37	44	Bushy	39	45
Green	32		Captain	15		2nd Herald	7		1st Herald	6	
Berkeley	8	43	Ross	22	45	Salisbury	20	46	Bagot	22	46
Abbot	10		Keeper	6		Exton	21		Willoughby	12	
Marshal	25		Servant	17		Lord	5		Groom	12	

SUGGESTIONS FOR DISCUSSION.

1. *Richard II.* was written by Shakspere in two parts, the first of which was the play seen by Dr. Simon Forman.
2. Shakspere wrote *Richard II.* as a warning against the Court-party favoured by Elizabeth.
3. On account of its unity of design *Richard II.* deserves to be called the most admirable of all historical plays.

LIST OF EARLIEST KNOWN EDITIONS.

Date.	*Printer.*	*Publisher.*	*Acted by*	*Present Owners.*
1597	Valentine Simmes	Androw Wise	Lord Chamberlain's servants	Trinity College, Cambridge. Duke of Devonshire. Mr. A. H. Huth.
1598	Valentine Simmes	Andrew Wise	Lord Chamberlain's servants	British Museum. Bodleian Library. Trinity College, Cambridge.
1608	W. W.	Mathew Law	Lord Chamberlain's servants	British Museum. Trinity College, Cambridge,
1608	W. W.	Mathew Law	The King's servants	Bodleian Library. Duke of Devonshire.
1615	———	Mathew Law	The King's servants	British Museum. Bodleian Library. Trinity College, Cambridge,

In the Stationers' Registers is this entry:—

1597. August 29.

Andrew Wise. Entred for his Copie by appoyntment from master Warden **man** *The Tragedye of* *Richard the Second* **vj^d^**

Thus described the edition was issued in the same year without author's name. The 1598 edition "by William Shakespeare" had the same title. In 1598 Meres mentions "Richard the 2" as one of Shakspere's tragedies.

Sir John Hayward had been imprisoned for writing a work introducing the death of Richard II. In the Stationers' Registers on January 9, 1599, it is called "the ffirste parte of the Life and Reign of Kinge Henry the ffourthe extending to the ende of the ffirst yere of his Reign." The British Museum has a copy.

On February 7, 1601, the day before the outbreak of Essex's rebellion, his friends, in order to foment popular hatred against Elizabeth, paid the Lord Chamberlain's company, to which Shakspere then belonged, for a special performance of "the playe of the deposyng and kyllyng of Kyng Rychard the Second." Augustine Phillipps, one of the company, says that they at first demurred to acting this as it was "so old, and so long out of yous." Sir Gelly Meyrick, Essex's steward, in his official examination, said, in reference to the same performance, that "the playe was of Kyng Harry the iiij.th and of the kyllyng of Kyng Richard the Second" (From documents in the Public Record Office). Competent critics are not agreed about the identity of this play with Shakspere's, in which it is believed that the portion first printed in 1608 (IV. i. 154—318) formed part of the original play, but had for political purposes been withheld.

The following entry occurs in the Registers:—

1603. June 25.

Mathew Lawe Entred for his copies in full courte Holden this Day. These ffyve copies folowinge **ij^s^vj^d^**

viz

iij enterludes or playes

The ffirst is of *Richard the* . 3.

The second of *Richard the* . 2.

The Third of *Henry the* . 4 *the firste part.* all kinges.

. . . .

all whiche by the consent of the Company are sett ouer to him from **Andrew Wyse**

The 1608 editions are alike except in the title-pages. The play has there the same description and authorship as in the 1598 edition. It was in 1608 that the copies first contained the "new additions of the Parliament Sceane, and the deposing of King Richard."

Simon Forman left a MS. account of a performance of *Richard II.* which he saw at the Globe on April 30, 1611 (see under *Macbeth*).

The edition of 1615 had the full title-page that appeared in 1608.

In the 1623 Folio the play is called "The life and death of King Richard the Second."

In connection with *Richard II.* should be read Holinshed's *Chronicle* and Daniel's *Poems on the Civil Wars.* As bearing upon the subject Prof. Henry Morley, in his edition of the play in Cassell's National Library, prints Langland's *Richard the Redeless* and a passage from Gower's *Confessio Amantis.*

KING DAVID.

Total Number of Lines.	CHARACTERS.	I.			II.	III.				IV.					V.		
		Prologue.	1	2	1	Chorus.	1	2	3	1	2	3	4	5	Chorus.	1	2
571	DAVID	...	72	...	79	...	63	...	82	86	...	61	...	...	...	...	128
113	CUSAY	...	19	8	7	...	7	...	...	7	54	...	...	...	...	1	10
213	JOAB	...	...	48	...	...	...	...	38	...	...	7	...	41	...	34	45
16	ABISAI	...	...	8	...	...	...	...	4	...	...	2	...	...	...	...	2
74	URIAS	...	...	9	65	...	...	...	...	...	...	...	...	...	...	...	...
18	HANON	...	...	8	...	...	...	...	10	...	...	...	...	...	...	...	...
7	MACHAAS	...	...	7	...	...	...	...	...	...	...	...	...	...	...	...	...
223	ABSALON	...	...	...	51	...	...	20	19	...	63	...	...	70	...	...	...
65	NATHAN	...	...	...	...	...	49	...	...	...	...	...	...	...	...	...	16
5	1ST SERVANT	...	...	...	...	...	5	...	...	...	...	...	...	...	...	...	...
13	AMNON	...	...	...	...	...	...	13	...	...	...	...	...	...	...	...	...
14	JONADAB	...	...	...	...	...	...	2	12	...	...	...	...	...	...	...	...
15	ADONIA	...	...	...	...	...	...	6	9	...	...	...	...	...	...	...	...
14	SADOC	...	...	...	...	...	...	...	...	10	4	...	...	...	..	...	...
26	AHIMAAS	...	...	...	...	...	...	...	...	4	2	11	...	...	...	5	4
8	JONATHAN...	...	...	...	...	...	...	...	...	5	...	3	...	...	...	...	...
27	ITHAY	...	...	...	...	...	...	...	...	22	...	5	...	...	...	...	...
41	ACHITOPHEL	...	...	...	...	...	...	...	...	...	17	...	24	...	..	...	...
17	AMASA	...	...	...	...	...	...	...	...	...	5	...	...	...	...	12	...
1	"ALL"	...	...	...	..	...	...	...	...	...	1	...	...	...	...	...	...
1	ABIATHAR...	...	...	...	...	...	...	...	...	...	1	...	...	...	...	...	...
55	SEMEI	...	...	...	...	...	...	...	...	...	...	55	...	..	...	...	...
23	SOLDIER	...	...	...	...	...	...	..	...	...	...	...	...	23	...	...	...
39	SALOMON	...	...	...	...	...	...	...	...	...	...	...	...	...	...	...	39
4	MESSENGER	..	...	...	...	...	...	...	...	...	...	...	...	...	...	...	4
23	"PROLOGUE"	23	...	...	...	...	...	...	...	...	...	...	...	...	...	...	..
101	BETHSABE	...	42	...	...	...	27	...	...	...	...	...	...	...	...	...	32
23	THAMAR	...	...	...	23	...	...	...	...	...	...	...	...	...	...	...	...
35	"CHORUS"	...	...	...	...	23	...	...	...	...	...	...	...	...	12	...	...
31	WOMAN OF THECOA ..	...	...	...	...	...	...	...	31	...	...	...	...	...	...	...	...
9	1ST CONCUBINE	...	...	...	...	...	...	...	...	...	9	...	...	...	...	...	...
9	2ND CONCUBINE	...	...	...	...	...	...	...	...	..	9	...	...	...	...	...	...
1834		23	133	88	225	23	151	41	205	134	165	144	24	134	12	52	280
1833	Actual Number of Lines	23	133	88	225	23	150	41	205	134	165	144	24	134	12	52	280

The play in *British Dramatists* should have been divided into Acts and Scenes as in the Table.

SCHEME FOR ARRANGING THE PARTS WITH EIGHTEEN MEN.

TWELVE CHARACTERS SINGLY AND SIX GROUPS.

ABIATHAN	1	19	ABISAI	16	21	AMASA	17	21
HANON	18		1ST SERVANT	5		MESSENGER	4	
ADONIA	15	22	JONADAB	14	22	AMNON	13	27
MACHAAS	7		JONATHAN	8		SADOC	14	

SUGGESTIONS FOR DISCUSSION.

1. Peele's early work was over-praised by Nash, who thereby hoped to depreciate Marlowe.

2. *King David*, with nothing to recommend it but harmonious versification, strikingly displays Peele's lack of power of invention.

3. Peele's writings largely influenced Milton.

EARLIEST KNOWN EDITION.

Date.	*Printer.*	*Publisher.*	*Acted by*	*Present Owners.*
1599	Adam Islip	———		British Museum. Bodleian Library.

The following entries are to be found in the Stationers' Registers:

1561. July 22—1562. July 24.

Recevyd of **Thomas hackett** for his lycense for pryntinge *an new interlude of the ij synnes of kynge DAVID* iiij[d]

1594. May 14.

Edward White. Entred for his Copie vnder thandes of bothe the wardens a booke called *the booke of DAVID and BETHSABA* vj[d]C.

The name of Adam Islip was first entered and then struck out.

In 1598 Meres speaks of Peele's death.

The edition of 1599 was issued as "The Love of King David & fair Bethsabe. With the Tragedie of Absalon. As it hath ben diuers times plaied on the stage. Written by George Peele."

A MIDSUMMER-NIGHT'S DREAM.

Total Number of Lines.	CHARACTERS.	I.		II.		III.		IV.		V.
		1	2	1	2	1	2	1	2	1
242	THESEUS	65	...	...	...	...	...	41	...	136
41	EGEUS	30	...	...	...	...	...	11	...	...
142	DEMETRIUS	2	...	23	2	...	62	25	...	28
178	LYSANDER	53	...	...	44	...	59	10	...	12
134	QUINCE	...	51	...	...	39	...	...	9	35
279	BOTTOM	...	54	...	...	94	...	51	19	61
58	FLUTE	...	5	...	...	7	...	...	12	34
14	STARVELING	...	2	...	...	3	...	..	2	7
24	SNOUT	...	2	...	...	10	...	...	...	12
16	SNUG	...	3	...	...	...	...	...	4	9
206	PUCK	...	...	37	18	11	101	3	...	36
224	OBERON	...	...	79	8	...	63	46	...	28
24	PHILOSTRATE	...	...	...	...	...	...	...	...	24
36	HIPPOLYTA	5	...	...	...	...	...	7	...	24
165	HERMIA	56	...	...	26	...	80	3	...	...
229	HELENA	43	...	34	32	...	116	4	...	...
52	FAIRY	...	...	28	24	...	...	...	...	...
143	TITANIA	...	...	72	8	34	...	25	...	4
5	PEASEBLOSSOM	...	...	...	...	4	...	1	...	...
5	COBWEB	...	...	...	...	4	...	1	...	...
3	MOTH	...	...	...	...	3	...	...	...	...
6	MUSTARDSEED	...	...	...	...	4	...	2	...	...
2226		254	117	273	162	213	481	230	46	450
2180	Actual Number of Lines	251	114	268	162	206	463	225	46	445

Contrary to the usual practice of classing Fairies with the female characters, Oberon and Puck are here put amongst the men, as the parts for the ladies are sufficiently numerous without them.

SCHEME FOR ARRANGING THE PARTS WITH SEVEN LADIES.

FIVE CHARACTERS SINGLY AND TWO GROUPS.

COBWEB	5	57	HIPPOLYTA	36	39
FAIRY	52		MOTH	3	

SUGGESTIONS FOR DISCUSSION.

1. *A Midsummer-Night's Dream* was written to order for Lord Southampton's marriage.
2. The introduction of supernatural influences renders *A Midsummer-Night's Dream* unfit for stage-representation.
3. The varying interpretations of II. i. 148—168 show that the passage is not allegorical.

LIST OF EARLIEST KNOWN EDITIONS.

Date.	*Printer.*	*Publisher.*	*Acted by*	*Present Owners.*
1600	———	Thomas Fisher	Lord Chamberlain's servants	British Museum. Bodleian Library. Trinity College, Cambridge. Duke of Devonshire. Mr. A. H. Huth.
1600	Iames Roberts	———	Lord Chamberlain's servants	British Museum. Bodleian Library. Trinity College, Cambridge. Duke of Devonshire. Mr. Halliwell-Phillipps.

In 1598 Meres, referring to Shakspere's comedies, mentions "his Midsummers night dreame."

The first of the editions named above stands in the Stationers' Registers thus:—

1600. October 8.

Thomas ffyssher Entred for his copie vnder the handes of master RODES and the Wardens. A booke called *A mydsommer nightes Dreame* vj[d]

There is no entry of the Roberts Quarto.

Both the editions "written by William Shakespeare" were published with the same short title.

The following entry occurs in the Registers:—

1608. August 13.

Master **Pavyer.** Entred for his copie vnder thandes of Master WILSON and the Wardens. A booke beinge *A history of TYTANA and THESEUS* vj[d]

In the British Museum is a copy dated 1636 of "The Historie of Titana and Theseus," by W. Bettie and published by R. Bird.

The title of the play in the 1623 Folio is "A Midsommer Nights Dreame."

Prof. Henry Morley, in his edition of the play in Cassell's National Library, prints several poems on the subject of Pyramus and Thisbe, all earlier than the play. Much in reference to Robin Goodfellow can be seen in Hazlitt's *Fairy Mythology*. Plutarch's *Life of Theseus*, Halpin's *Oberon's Vision* and *Fairy Mythology* by Halliwell [Phillipps] (eds. Shakespeare Society 1843 and 1845), should also be consulted.

RICHARD III.

Total Number of Lines.	CHARACTERS	I.				II.				III.							IV.					V.				
		1	2	3	4	1	2	3	4	1	2	3	4	5	6	7	1	2	3	4	5	1	2	3	4	5
1161	Gloucester	125	154	125	...	41	19	...	...	56	...	...	32	69	...	73	...	83	26	198	...	...	...	154	6	...
174	Clarence	22	...	...	142	...	...	...	...	...	...	...	...	...	...	...	...	...	...	...	...	...	...	10	...	...
39	Brackenbury	8	...	...	25	...	...	...	...	...	...	...	...	...	...	...	6	...	...	...	...	...	...	...	...	...
149	Hastings	10	...	5	...	3	1	...	...	6	70	...	49	...	...	...	...	...	...	...	...	...	...	5	...	...
2	Gentleman	...	2	...	...	...	...	...	...	...	...	...	...	...	...	...	...	...	...	...	...	...	...	...	...	...
55	Rivers	...	...	18	...	4	12	...	...	...	...	17	...	...	...	...	...	...	...	...	...	...	...	4	...	...
13	Grey	...	...	6	...	...	...	...	...	...	...	4	...	...	...	...	...	...	...	...	...	...	...	3	...	...
374	Buckingham	...	...	12	...	12	24	...	...	58	7	...	12	27	...	156	...	29	...	...	...	27	...	10	...	...
107	Derby	...	...	8	...	5	...	...	...	...	13	...	8	...	...	...	11	3	...	17	12	...	...	21	...	9
15	Dorset	...	...	3	...	4	7	...	...	...	...	...	...	...	...	...	1	...	...	...	...	...	...	...	...	...
62	Catesby	...	...	2	...	...	...	...	...	5	16	...	...	...	...	14	...	2	4	8	...	...	...	4	7	...
66	1st Murderer	...	...	7	59	...	...	...	...	...	...	...	...	...	...	...	...	...	...	...	...	...	...	...	...	...
69	2nd Murderer	...	...	...	69	...	...	...	...	...	...	...	...	...	...	...	...	...	...	...	...	...	...	...	...	...
64	King Edward	...	...	...	...	64	...	...	...	...	...	...	...	...	...	...	...	...	...	...	...	...	...	...	...	...
8	1st Citizen	...	...	...	...	...	...	8	...	...	...	...	...	...	...	...	...	...	...	...	...	...	...	...	...	...
13	2nd Citizen	...	...	...	...	...	...	13	...	...	...	...	...	...	...	...	...	...	...	...	...	...	...	...	...	...
28	3rd Citizen	...	...	...	...	...	...	28	...	...	...	...	...	...	...	...	...	...	...	...	...	...	...	...	...	...
12	Archbishop	...	...	...	...	...	...	...	12	...	...	...	...	...	...	...	...	...	...	...	...	...	...	...	...	...
30	1st Messenger	...	...	...	...	...	...	...	9	...	15	...	...	...	...	...	...	...	...	5	...	...	...	1	...	...
17	Mayor	...	...	...	...	...	...	...	...	1	...	...	...	11	...	5	...	...	...	...	...	...	...	...	...	...
9	Cardinal	...	...	...	...	...	...	...	...	9	...	...	...	...	...	...	...	...	...	...	...	...	...	...	...	...
3	Pursuivant	...	...	...	...	...	...	...	...	...	3	...	...	...	...	...	...	...	...	...	...	...	...	...	...	...
1	Priest	...	...	...	...	...	...	...	...	...	1	...	...	...	...	...	...	...	...	...	...	...	...	...	...	...
30	Ratcliff	...	...	...	...	...	...	...	...	...	...	3	2	...	...	...	...	...	...	10	...	...	...	15	...	...
5	Vaughan	...	...	...	...	...	...	...	...	...	...	1	...	...	...	...	...	...	...	...	...	...	...	4	...	...
7	Ely	...	...	...	...	...	...	...	...	...	...	...	7	...	...	...	...	...	...	...	...	...	...	...	...	...
3	Lovel	...	...	...	...	...	...	...	...	...	...	...	1	2	...	...	...	...	...	...	...	...	...	...	...	...
14	Scrivener	...	...	...	...	...	...	...	...	...	...	...	...	...	14	...	...	...	...	...	...	...	...	...	...	...
1	"Another"	...	...	...	...	...	...	...	...	...	...	...	...	...	...	1	...	...	...	...	...	...	...	...	...	...
37	Tyrrel	...	...	...	...	...	...	...	...	...	...	...	...	...	...	...	...	8	29	...	...	...	...	...	...	...
3	2nd Messenger	...	...	...	...	...	...	...	...	...	...	...	...	...	...	...	...	...	...	3	...	...	...	...	...	...
7	3rd Messenger	...	...	...	...	...	...	...	...	...	...	...	...	...	...	...	...	...	...	7	...	...	...	...	...	...
10	4th Messenger	...	...	...	...	...	...	...	...	...	...	...	...	...	...	...	...	...	...	10	...	...	...	...	...	...
8	Urswick	...	...	...	...	...	...	...	...	...	...	...	...	...	...	...	...	...	...	...	8	...	...	...	...	...
2	Sheriff	...	...	...	...	...	...	...	...	...	...	...	...	...	...	...	...	...	...	...	...	2	...	...	...	...
136	Richmond	...	...	...	...	...	...	...	...	...	...	...	...	...	...	...	...	...	...	...	...	...	19	85	...	32
2	Oxford	...	...	...	...	...	...	...	...	...	...	...	...	...	...	...	...	...	...	...	...	...	2	...	...	...
1	Herbert	...	...	...	...	...	...	...	...	...	...	...	...	...	...	...	...	...	...	...	...	...	1	...	...	...
8	Blunt	...	...	...	...	...	...	...	...	...	...	...	...	...	...	...	...	...	...	...	...	...	2	6	...	...
1	Surrey	...	...	...	...	...	...	...	...	...	...	...	...	...	...	...	...	...	...	...	...	...	...	1	...	...
10	Norfolk	...	...	...	...	...	...	...	...	...	...	...	...	...	...	...	...	...	...	...	...	...	...	10	...	...
9	Ghost of Henry VI.	...	...	...	...	...	...	...	...	...	...	...	...	...	...	...	...	...	...	...	...	...	...	9	...	...
3	"Lords"	...	...	...	...	...	...	...	...	...	...	...	...	...	...	...	...	...	...	...	...	...	...	3	...	...
165	Anne	...	118	...	...	...	...	...	...	...	...	...	...	...	...	...	39	...	...	...	...	...	...	8	...	...
274	Queen Elizabeth	...	...	50	...	7	21	...	15	...	...	...	...	...	...	...	32	...	...	149	...	...	...	...	...	...
218	Queen Margaret	...	...	124	...	...	...	...	...	...	...	...	...	...	...	...	...	...	...	94	...	...	...	...	...	...
140	Duchess of York	...	...	...	...	...	44	...	26	...	...	...	...	...	...	...	16	...	...	54	...	...	...	...	...	...
21	Boy	...	...	...	...	...	21	...	...	...	...	...	...	...	...	...	...	...	...	...	...	...	...	...	...	...
9	Girl	...	...	...	...	...	9	...	...	...	...	...	...	...	...	...	...	...	...	...	...	...	...	...	...	...
47	Duke of York	...	...	...	...	...	...	...	16	23	...	...	...	...	...	...	...	...	...	...	...	...	...	8	...	...
51	Prince	...	...	...	...	...	...	...	...	43	...	...	...	...	...	...	...	...	...	...	...	...	...	8	...	...
6	Page	...	...	...	...	...	...	...	...	...	...	...	...	...	...	...	...	6	...	...	...	...	...	...	...	...
8	Ghost of Prince Edward	...	...	...	...	...	...	...	...	...	...	...	...	...	...	...	...	...	...	...	...	...	...	8	...	...
3707		165	274	360	295	140	158	49	78	201	125	25	111	109	14	249	105	131	59	555	20	29	24	377	13	41
3620	Actual Number of Lines	162	263	356	290	140	154	49	73	200	124	25	109	109	14	247	104	126	57	540	20	29	24	351	13	41

Much confusion will occur in the reading of this play if a very careful comparison of the text is not made beforehand, as the Quarto and Folio editions vary so much.

In V. 3 the lines of Clarence, Ghost of Henry VI., Ghost of Prince Edward should be respectively 8, 7, 6, and the total lines should be 3618, as the total of II. 3 should be 47.

RATCLIFF 30, SHERIFF 2, PURSUIVANT 3 — 47		URSWICK 8, SCRIVENER 14, 2ND CITIZEN 13 — 48	GENTLEMAN 2, 1ST CITIZEN 8, 1ST MESSENGER 30 — 40	NORFOLK 10, DORSET 15, MAYOR 17 — 42
OXFORD 2, GHOST OF HENRY VI. 9, 3RD CITIZEN 28, 4TH MESSENGER 10 — 49	SURREY 1, 2ND MURDERER 69 — 70	TYRREL 37, BLUNT 8, PRIEST 1, 2ND MESSENGER 3 — 49	VAUGHAN 5, 1ST MURDERER 66 — 71	LOVEL 3, HERBERT 1, BRACKENBURY 39, 3RD MESSENGER 7 — 50

Ladies' Parts.

FOUR CHARACTERS SINGLY AND THREE GROUPS.

BOY 21, GHOST OF PRINCE EDWARD 8 — 29	DUKE OF YORK 47, GIRL 9 — 56	PRINCE 51, PAGE 6 — 57

SUGGESTIONS FOR DISCUSSION.

1. The Quartos of *Richard III.* are pirated copies of Shakspere's text which appears in the 1623 Folio.
2. There is no justification for the disregard of historic truth in *Richard III.*
3. The continuity of the character of Richard in 3 *Henry VI.* and *Richard III.* proves that the two plays are by the same author.

LIST OF EARLIEST KNOWN EDITIONS.

Date.	*Printer.*	*Publisher.*	*Acted by*	*Present Owners.*
1597	Valentine Sims	Andrew Wise	Lord Chamberlain's servants	British Museum. Bodleian Library. Duke of Devonshire. Mr. A. H. Huth.
1598	Thomas Creede	Andrew Wise	Lord Chamberlain's servants	British Museum. Bodleian Library. Trinity College, Cambridge.
1602	Thomas Creede	Andrew Wise	Lord Chamberlain's servants	British Museum. Trinity College, Cambridge.
1605	Thomas Creede	Mathew Lawe	Lord Chamberlain's servants	British Museum. Bodleian Library.
1612	Thomas Creede	Mathew Lawe	The King's servants	British Museum. Trinity College, Cambridge.
1622	Thomas Purfoot	Mathew Law	The King's servants	British Museum. Bodleian Library. Trinity College, Cambridge.

In 1579 Dr. Thomas Legge, Vice-Chancellor of Cambridge, wrote a play in Latin called "Richardus Tertius;" and, with a like title, Henry Lacey of the same University in 1586 wrote a play, copies of which are among the Harleian MSS. in the British Museum. On June 19, 1594, was entered in the Stationers' Registers, and in the same year was published, an enterlude entitled "The True Tragedie of Richard the Third: Wherein is showne the death of Edward the fourth, with the smothering of the two yoong Princes in the Tower: With a lamentable ende of Shores wife, an example for all wicked women. And lastly the coniunction and ioyning of the two noble Houses, Lancaster and Yorke. As it was playd by the Queenes Maiesties Players." It was entered to, and printed by, Thomas Creede, and published by William Barley. Legge's play and that of 1594 have been printed by the Shakespeare Society and by Hazlitt in *Shakespeare's Library.* Shakspere was indebted to neither play.

The earliest known edition of Shakspere's *Richard III.* was thus entered in the Stationers' Registers:—

1597. October 20.

Andrewe wise Entred for his copie vnder thandes of master BARLOWE, and master warden **man.** *The tragedie of kinge* RICHARD *the* THIRD *with the death of the Duke of* CLARENCE vjd

The edition itself, which is anonymous, is called "The Tragedy of King Richard the third. Containing, His treacherous Plots against his brother Clarence: the pittiefull murther of his innocent nephewes: his tyrannicall vsurpation: with the whole course of his detested life, and most deserued death." The 1598 edition has the same title, adding "By William Shakespeare." In 1598 Meres mentions "Richard the 3" as one of Shakspere's tragedies.

In 1602 the title-page describes the play as "newly augmented"; but there is no additional matter.

On June 25, 1603, the copyright was transferred from Wise to Mathew Lawe. (For the full entry see p. 81.)

The title of the 1605 and following editions is the same as that of 1602. In the Folio the title is "The Tragedy of Richard the Third: with the Landing of Earle Richmond, and the Battell at Bosworth Field."

Before and after Shakspere's play, in addition to the works mentioned above, much was written on the life and times of Richard III. "A tragicall Report of Kinge Richard the 3" was, amongst several "ballades," entered in the Stationers' Registers to Henry Carre on August 15, 1586. In 1600 was printed Thomas Heywood's *Edward IV.*, in which Richard appears much concerned about the "prophecy of G." Included with payment "for new adicyons for Jeronymo," Henslowe "lent unto bengemy Johnsone, at the apoyntment of E. Alleyn and Wm Birde, the 24 of June 1602, in earneste of a boocke called Richard crockbacke the some of xli" (*Diary*, p. 223). Probably this play was never finished. Henslowe has also (pp. 214, 251) entries about "the Booke of Shoare" and about "a playe wherein Shores wiffe is writen," in connection with which the names of "Thomas hewod," "John Ducke," "harey Chettell," and "John Daye" are mentioned.

From 1559, the date of the first edition of *A Myrroure for Magistrates*, down to 1610, several poems by Baldwin, Higgens, Churchyard, and Niccols appeared, referring to the incidents of the same historical period. Many are mentioned by Mr. F. A. Marshall in the 'Henry Irving' *Shakespeare.* On May 14, 1614, was entered to Laurence Lisle, and in the same year C.B. issued, *The Ghost of Richard III.*, which has been reprinted by the Shakespeare Society from the unique copy in the Bodleian Library.

Mr. James Spedding and Mr. E. H. Pickersgill have made elaborate comparisons of the Quarto and Folio versions of *Richard III.* Their papers are in the New Shakspere Society's *Transactions*, 1875-6, Part I.

LOCRINE.

Total Number of Lines.	CHARACTERS.	I.				II.							III.							IV.					V.					
		Chorus.	1	2	3	Chorus.	1	2	3	4	5	6	Chorus.	1	2	3	4	5	6	Chorus.	1	2	3	4	Chorus.	1	2	3	4	5
143	BRUTUS	...	143	...	...	...	...	...	...	...	...	...	...	...	...	...	...	...	...	...	...	...	...	...	...	...	...	...	...	...
38	ASSARACUS	...	12	...	...	...	...	...	...	...	...	...	...	...	...	...	...	...	...	...	4	...	...	...	...	20	...	2	...	...
165	CORINEUS	...	70	...	...	...	...	...	...	...	...	...	...	13	...	...	12	10	...	...	30	...	...	...	...	...	...	...	30	...
136	THRASIMACHUS ...	...	11	...	4	...	...	7	17	...	7	...	...	23	...	...	9	...	...	...	...	...	...	...	...	25	17	...	5	11
4	DEBON	...	2	...	...	...	...	...	2	...	...	...	...	...	...	...	...	...	...	...	...	...	...	...	...	...	...	...	...	...
330	LOCRINE	...	19	...	10	...	...	...	...	...	...	...	...	33	...	...	30	...	...	...	88	...	36	...	...	46	...	11	13	44
31	CAMBER	...	1	...	...	...	...	...	...	...	...	...	...	13	...	...	6	...	...	...	4	...	...	...	...	7	...	...	...	...
218	STRUMBO	...	...	74	...	...	...	36	37	3	7	...	...	...	...	30	...	...	...	...	...	31	...	...	...	...	...	...	...	...
38	TROMPART	...	...	3	...	...	...	14	2	...	19	...	...	...	...	...	...	...	...	...	...	...	...	...	...	...	...	...	...	...
274	HUMBER	...	...	...	...	...	56	...	...	15	19	21	...	...	28	...	...	...	52	...	...	49	...	34	...	...	...	...	...	...
54	HUBBA...	...	...	...	...	...	31	...	...	...	...	4	...	...	15	...	...	4	...	...	...	...	...	...	...	...	...	...	...	...
14	SEGAR	...	...	...	...	...	4	...	...	...	...	...	...	...	10	...	...	...	...	...	...	...	...	...	...	...	...	...	...	...
16	CAPTAIN	...	...	...	...	...	...	16	...	...	...	...	...	...	...	...	...	...	...	...	...	...	...	...	...	...	...	...	...	...
146	ALBANACT	...	...	...	...	...	...	...	39	9	62	...	...	...	18	...	...	...	2	...	...	5	...	11	...	...	...	...	...	...
11	OLIVER	...	...	...	...	...	...	...	...	...	...	...	...	...	...	11	...	...	...	...	...	...	...	...	...	...	...	...	...	...
5	WILLIAM	...	...	...	...	...	...	...	...	...	...	...	...	...	...	5	...	...	...	...	...	...	...	...	...	...	...	...	...	...
7	1ST SOLDIER	...	...	...	...	...	...	...	...	...	...	...	...	...	...	...	...	...	...	...	7	...	...	...	...	...	...	...	...	...
5	2ND SOLDIER	...	...	...	...	...	...	...	...	...	...	...	...	...	...	...	...	...	...	...	5	...	...	...	...	...	...	...	...	...
101	"ATE"	21	...	...	...	17	...	...	...	...	...	...	17	...	...	...	...	...	...	16	...	...	...	...	18	...	...	...	...	12
120	GUENDOLEN	...	7	...	...	...	...	...	...	...	...	...	...	6	...	...	...	...	...	...	...	...	...	...	...	...	35	...	15	57
26	DOROTHY	...	...	8	...	...	...	18	...	...	...	...	...	...	...	...	...	...	...	...	...	...	...	...	...	...	...	...	...	...
105	ESTRILD	...	...	...	...	...	18	...	...	...	...	4	...	...	...	...	...	...	...	...	49	...	...	...	...	9	...	3	3	19
9	MARGERY	...	...	...	...	...	...	...	...	...	...	...	...	...	...	9	...	...	...	...	...	...	...	...	...	...	...	...	...	...
3	PAGE	...	...	...	...	...	...	...	...	...	...	...	...	...	...	...	...	...	...	...	...	...	...	...	...	3	...	...	...	...
4	MADAN...	...	...	...	...	...	...	...	...	...	...	...	...	...	...	...	...	...	...	...	...	...	...	...	...	...	4	...	...	...
62	SABREN	...	...	...	...	...	...	...	...	...	...	...	...	...	...	...	...	...	...	...	...	...	...	...	...	...	...	...	...	62
2065		21	265	85	14	17	109	91	97	27	114	29	17	88	71	55	57	14	54	16	187	85	36	45	18	110	56	16	66	205
2049	Actual No. of Lines	21	263	85	14	17	109	79	95	27	114	29	17	88	71	55	57	14	54	16	187	85	36	45	18	110	56	16	66	205

SCHEME FOR ARRANGING THE PARTS WITH SEVEN LADIES.

SIX CHARACTERS SINGLY AND ONE GROUP.

MADAN 4 } 7
PAGE 3 }

SUGGESTIONS FOR DISCUSSION.

1. The 'dumb show' of *Locrine* fixes the date of its production.
2. *Locrine* was written by Peele as a mock-heroic travesty in ridicule of Greene's work.
3. The comic scenes in *Locrine* are undeniably Shakspere's.

EARLIEST KNOWN EDITION.

Date.	*Printer.*	*Publisher.*	*Acted by*	*Present Owners.*
1595	Thomas Creede	————		British Museum. Trinity College, Cambridge. Duke of Devonshire.

In the Stationers' Registers is this entry:—

1594. July 20.
Thomas Creede. Entred for his Copie vnder thandes of the Wardens. *The lamentable Tragedie of* LOCRINE, *the eldest sonne of Kinge* BRUTUS. *discoursinge the warres of the Brittans &c.* **vj**d

The edition was published with the "&c." of the entry expanded in the title into "& Hunnes, with their discomfiture: The Britaines victorie with their Accidents & the death of Albanact. No lesse pleasant then profitable. Newly set foorth, ouerseene and corrected, By W.S."

In connection with this play reference should be made to the Chronicles containing the legendary story, and to the poems which had dealt with the episodes such as Spenser's *Faerie Queene* and Drayton's *Poly-Olbion*. In later times Milton introduced part of the story in *Comus*.

ROMEO AND JULIET.

Total Number of Lines.	CHARACTERS.	Prologue.	I.					Prologue.	II.						III.					IV.					V.		
			1	2	3	4	5		1	2	3	4	5	6	1	2	3	4	5	1	2	3	4	5	1	2	3
41	Sampson	...	41	...	...	...	...	...	...	...	...	...	...	...	...	...	...	...	...	...	...	...	...	...	...	...	...
24	Gregory	...	24	...	...	...	...	...	...	...	...	...	...	...	...	...	...	...	...	...	...	...	...	...	...	...	...
5	Abraham	...	5	...	...	...	...	...	...	...	...	...	...	...	...	...	...	...	...	...	...	...	...	...	...	...	...
161	Benvolio	...	51	20	...	13	1	...	9	...	...	14	...	...	53	...	...	...	...	...	...	...	...	...	...	...	...
36	Tybalt	...	5	...	...	...	17	...	...	...	...	...	...	...	14	...	...	...	...	...	...	...	...	...	...	...	...
6	1st Citizen	...	2	...	...	...	...	...	...	...	...	...	...		4	...	...	...	...	...	...	...	...	...	...	...	...
269	Capulet	...	3	33	...	...	56	...	...	...	...	...	...	...	...	...	...	31	63	...	26	...	19	28	...	...	10
41	Montague	...	28	...	...	...	...	...	...	...	...	...	...	...	3	...	...	...	...	...	...	...	...	...	...	...	10
75	Prince	...	23	...	...	...	...	...	...	...	...	...	...	...	16	...	...	...	...	...	...	...	...	...	...	...	36
618	Romeo	...	65	29	...	34	27	...	2	86	25	54	...	12	36	...	71	...	24	...	...	...	...	...	71	...	82
69	Paris	...	...	4	...	...	...	...	...	...	...	...	...	...	...	...	...	4	...	23	...	...	...	6	...	...	32
38	1st Servant	...	...	21	5	...	11	...	...	...	...	...	...	...	...	...	...	...	...	...	...	...	1	...	...	...	...
273	Mercutio	...	...	...	...	73	...	...	34	...	...	95	...	...	71	...	...	...	...	...	...	...	...	...	...	...	...
14	2nd Servant	...	...	...	...	...	7	...	...	...	...	...	...	...	...	...	...	...	...	...	5	...	2	...	...	...	...
3	2nd Capulet	...	...	...	...	...	3	...	...	...	...	...	...	...	...	...	...	...	...	...	...	...	...	...	...	...	...
350	Friar Laurence	...	...	...	...	...	...	...	...	...	72	...	...	18	...	...	87	...	...	56	...	...	...	25	...	17	75
37	Peter	...	...	...	...	...	...	...	...	...	...	7	...	...	...	...	...	...	...	...	...	...	...	30	...	...	...
16	1st Musician	...	...	...	...	...	...	...	...	...	...	...	...	...	...	...	...	...	...	...	...	...	...	16	...	...	...
6	2nd Musician	...	...	...	...	...	...	...	...	...	...	...	...	...	...	...	...	...	...	...	...	...	...	6	...	...	...
1	3rd Musician	...	...	...	...	...	...	...	...	...	...	...	...	...	...	...	...	...	...	...	...	...	...	1	...	...	...
32	Balthasar	...	...	...	...	...	...	...	...	...	...	...	...	...	...	...	...	...	...	...	...	...	...	...	11	...	21
7	Apothecary	...	...	...	...	...	...	...	...	...	...	...	...	...	...	...	...	...	...	...	...	...	...	...	7	...	...
13	Friar John	...	...	...	...	...	...	...	...	...	...	...	...	...	...	...	...	...	...	...	...	...	...	...	...	13	...
19	1st Watchman	...	...	...	...	...	...	...	...	...	...	...	...	...	...	...	...	...	...	...	...	...	...	...	...	...	19
1	2nd Watchman	...	...	...	...	...	...	...	...	...	...	...	...	...	...	...	...	...	...	...	...	...	...	...	...	...	1
3	3rd Watchman	...	...	...	...	...	...	...	...	...	...	...	...	...	...	...	...	...	...	...	...	...	...	...	...	...	3
14	"Prologue"	14	...	...	...	...	...	...	...	...	...	...	...	...	...	...	...	...	...	...	...	...	...	...	...	...	...
115	Lady Capulet	...	1	...	36	...	1	...	...	...	...	...	...	...	11	...	...	2	37	...	3	3	3	13	...	...	5
3	Lady Montague	...	3	...	...	...	...	...	...	...	...	...	...	...	...	...	...	...	...	...	...	...	...	...	...	...	...
290	Nurse	...	...	...	61	...	15	...	...	2	...	63	38	...	...	31	21	...	25	...	2	...	4	28	...	...	...
541	Juliet	...	...	...	8	...	19	...	...	114	...	...	43	7	...	116	...	...	105	48	12	56	...	...	...	...	13
14	"Chorus"	...	...	...	...	...	...	14	...	...	...	...	...	...	...	...	...	...	...	...	...	...	...	...	...	...	...
9	Page	...	...	...	...	...	...	...	...	...	...	...	...	...	...	...	...	...	...	...	...	...	...	...	...	...	9
3144		14	251	107	110	120	157	14	45	202	97	233	81	37	208	147	179	37	254	127	48	59	29	153	89	30	316
3052	Actual No. of Lines	14	244	106	106	114	147	14	42	190	94	233	80	37	202	143	175	36	241	126	47	58	27	150	86	30	310

The total lines should be 3053, as the total of IV. 4 should be 28.

SCHEME FOR ARRANGING THE PARTS WITH EIGHTEEN MEN.

FOURTEEN CHARACTERS SINGLY AND FOUR GROUPS.

2ND CAPULET	3	23	1ST CITIZEN	6	23	FRIAR JOHN	13	24	APOTHECARY	7	24
1ST WATCHMAN	19		2ND SERVANT	14		ABRAHAM	5		1ST MUSICIAN	16	
3RD MUSICIAN	1		3RD WATCHMAN	3		2ND MUSICIAN	6		2ND WATCHMAN	1	

SUGGESTIONS FOR DISCUSSION.

1. Internal evidence proves that the original draft of *Romeo and Juliet* was written as early as 1591.
2. It is a weighty testimony to the massive healthiness of Shakspere's character, that, among the heroes of his plays, Romeo alone falls a victim to love.
3. The nurse in *Romeo and Juliet* has her original in Marlowe's *Dido*.

LIST OF EARLIEST KNOWN EDITIONS.

Date.	*Printer.*	*Publisher.*	*Acted by*	*Present Owners.*
1597	Iohn Danter	———	Lord Hunsdon's servants	British Museum. Bodleian Library. Trinity College, Cambridge. Duke of Devonshire.
1599	Thomas Creede	Cuthbert Burby	Lord Chamberlain's servants	British Museum. Bodleian Library. Trinity College, Cambridge. University of Edinburgh. Mr. A. H. Huth.
——	———	Iohn Smethwicke	The King's servants	British Museum. Bodleian Library. Trinity College, Cambridge. Mr. A. H. Huth.
1609	———	Iohn Smethwick	The King's servants	British Museum. Bodleian Library. Trinity College, Cambridge. Duke of Devonshire.

In the Stationers' Registers is this entry:—

1562. July 22—1563. July 22.

master **Tottle** Recevyd of master **Tottle** for his lycense for pryntinge of *the Tragicall history of the Romeus and Juliett with sonettes* iiij^d

This is Arthur Brooke's poem which, on November 19, 1562, without the Sonnets, was printed with the title "The Tragicall Historye of Romeus and Iuliet, written first in Italian by Bandell, and nowe in Englishe by Ar. Br." It has been reprinted, amongst other places, in the 1821 *Variorum*, Vol. VI., and in Hazlitt's *Shakespeare's Library*. In the address "To the Reader" Brooke refers to a version of the story he had seen on the stage. In 1567 was published the second volume of Painter's *Palace of Pleasure*, which contained as "The XXV. Nouell," translated from a French version, "The goodly Hystory of the true, and constant Loue betweene Rhomeo and Iulietta, the one of whom died of Poyson, and the other of sorrow, and heuinesse: wherein be comprysed many aduentures of Loue, and other deuises touchinge the same." This is also printed by Hazlitt. In 1583, on February 18, "master Tottell" was licensed to print "Romeo and Juletta," and several other books. There is no edition known of this date. In 1587 Brooke's poem was republished as "The Tragicall historie of Romeus and Iuliet, contayning in it a rare example of true constancie: with the Subtill Counsels and practises of an old Fryer, and their ill euent." The student who wishes to pursue the story to more remote sources will find references to them in many annotated editions of the play, and especially in the reprint of the work of Brooke and Painter which has been edited by Mr. P. A. Daniel for the New Shakspere Society.

The following entry occurs in the Registers:—

1596. August 5.

Edward White. Entred for his Copie vnder the wardens handes. these twoo ballades followinge

viz

The one intituled. *A newe ballad of Romeo and Juliett* vj^d

. . . .

The 1597 edition is called "An Excellent conceited Tragedie of Romeo and Iuliet, As it hath been often (with great applause) plaid publiquely." The title of the 1599 edition is "The most excellent and lamentable Tragedie, of Romeo and Iuliet. Newly corrected, augmented, and amended." Both these were anonymous. "Romeo and Iuliet" is given by Meres in 1598 in his list of Shakspere's tragedies.

In 1607 the play is mentioned twice in the Registers. On January 22, it was entered with *Love's Labour's Lost* and *The Taming of a Shrew* to Ling from Burby, and on November 19 Ling transferred the three plays and "A booke called *Hamlett*" to Smythick (for the full entries see p. 79). It has been thought that the undated edition (some copies of which are anonymous and some have the name of "W. Shake-speare") may have been published soon after the entry. The British Museum copy has no name of author. The known copies of the 1609 edition are anonymous, and have the same title as the 1599 edition. The Folio version is called "The Tragedie of Romeo and Ivliet."

The "Tragædia von Romio und Julietta" in Cohn's *Shakespeare in Germany* should be studied, and, on the question of conjoint authorship, Mr. Fleay's article in *Macmillan's Magazine*, July, 1877, and Mr. Spalding's paper in the New Shakspere Society's *Transactions*, 1877-9, Part I.

EDWARD III.

Total Number of Lines.	CHARACTERS.	I.		II.		III.					IV.							V.
		1	2	1	2	1	2	3	4	5	1	2	3	4	5	6	7	1
739	EDWARD	78	32	225	123	...	...	87	...	55	...	40	...	...	...	...	...	99
59	ARTOIS	38	...	...	...	...	...	9	...	6	...	...	...	...	...	6	...	...
104	AUDLEY	2	...	..	12	...	...	8	...	13	...	...	...	45	...	9	15	...
39	LORRAIN	19	2	...	...	9	...	...	9	...	...	...	...	...	...	...	...	...
282	PRINCE	19	...	...	4	...	...	47	...	37	...	...	...	89	...	11	48	27
121	WARWICK	4	8	109	...	..	...	...	...	...	...	...	...	...	...	...	...	...
13	MOUNTAGUE	9	4	...	...	...	...	...	...	...	...	...	...	...	...	...	...	...
33	DAVID	...	33	...	...	...	...	...	...	...	...	...	...	...	...	...	...	...
4	DOUGLAS	...	4	...	...	...	...	...	...	...	...	...	...	...	...	...	...	...
8	1ST MESSENGER ...	...	8	...	...	...	...	...	...	...	...	...	...	...	...	...	...	...
1	2ND MESSENGER ...	...	1	...	...	...	...	...	...	...	...	...	...	...	...	...	...	...
46	LODOWICK	...	...	40	6	...	...	...	...	...	...	...	...	...	...	...	...	...
44	DERBY	...	...	...	19	...	...	12	...	5	...	7	...	...	...	...	...	1
271	JOHN	...	...	...	...	92	...	57	4	...	...	...	17	...	78	18	1	4
85	CHARLES	...	...	...	...	6	...	2	...	...	...	...	40	...	26	11	...	..
3	BOHEMIA	...	..	...	...	3	...	...	...	...	...	...	...	...	...	...	...	...
66	MARINER	..	...	...	...	66	...	...	...	...	...	...	...	...	...	...	...	...
32	PHILIP	...	...	...	...	9	...	3	...	...	...	...	...	...	13	7	...	...
4	POLISH CAPTAIN ...	...	...	...	...	4	...	...	...	...	...	...	...	...	...	...	...	...
22	1ST FRENCHMAN ...	...	...	...	...	...	13	...	...	...	...	9	...	...	...	...	...	...
19	2ND FRENCHMAN ...	...	...	...	...	...	19	...	..	...	...	...	...	...	...	...	...	...
5	3RD FRENCHMAN ...	...	...	...	...	...	5	...	...	...	...	...	...	...	...	...	...	...
31	4TH FRENCHMAN ...	...	...	...	...	...	31	...	..	...	...	...	...	...	...	...	...	...
2	GOBIN	...	...	...	...	...	...	2	...	...	...	...	...	...	...	...	...	...
1	"ALL"	...	...	...	...	...	...	1	...	...	...	...	...	...	...	...	...	...
9	MONTFORT	...	...	...	...	...	...	...	...	...	9	...	...	...	...	...	...	...
92	SALISBURY	...	...	...	...	...	...	...	...	...	31	...	...	...	6	...	...	55
31	VILLIERS	...	...	...	...	...	...	...	...	...	3	...	28	...	...	...	...	...
18	PERCY	...	...	...	...	...	...	...	...	...	...	18	...	...	..	...	...	...
16	FRENCH CAPTAIN ...	...	...	...	...	...	...	...	...	...	...	11	...	...	5	...	...	...
20	1ST HERALD	..	..	...	...	...	...	...	...	...	...	...	...	11	...	...	...	9
6	2ND HERALD	...	..	...	...	...	...	...	...	...	...	...	...	6	...	...	...	...
10	3RD HERALD	...	...	...	...	...	...	...	...	...	...	...	...	10	...	...	...	...
1	1ST ESQUIRE	...	...	...	...	...	...	...	...	...	...	...	...	...	...	1	...	...
1	2ND ESQUIRE	...	...	...	...	...	...	...	...	...	...	...	...	...	...	1	...	...
9	1ST CITIZEN	...	...	...	...	...	...	..	...	...	..	...	...	..	...	...	...	9
7	2ND CITIZEN	...	...	...	...	...	...	...	...	...	...	...	...	...	...	...	...	7
17	COPLAND	..	...	...	...	...	...	...	...	...	...	...	...	...	...	...	...	17
214	COUNTESS	...	74	89	51	...	...	...	...	...	...	...	...	...	...	...	...	...
8	WOMAN	...	...	...	...	...	8	...	...	..	...	...	...	...	...	...	...	...
17	QUEEN	...	...	...	...	...	...	...	...	...	...	...	...	...	...	...	...	17
2510		169	166	463	215	189	76	228	13	116	43	85	85	161	128	64	64	245
2493	Actual No. of Lines	169	166	459	212	189	76	227	13	114	43	85	85	161	126	62	64	242

SCHEME FOR ARRANGING THE PARTS WITH EIGHTEEN MEN.

Derby	44 ⎫	Percy	18 ⎫	Gobin	2 ⎫	Bohemia	3 ⎫
2nd Messenger	1 ⎬ 50	Villiers	31 ⎬ 50	Lorrain	39 ⎬ 50	French Captain	16 ⎬ 50
3rd Frenchman	5 ⎭	1st Esquire	1 ⎭	1st Citizen	9 ⎭	4th Frenchman	31 ⎭
Copland	17 ⎫	1st Herald	20 ⎫	Montague	13 ⎫	Montfort	9 ⎫
Douglas	4 ⎬ 50	1st Frenchman	22 ⎬ 50	Philip	32 ⎬ 51	David	33 ⎬ 50
2nd Frenchman	19 ⎬	1st Messenger	8 ⎭	2nd Herald	6 ⎭	2nd Citizen	7 ⎬
3rd Herald	10 ⎭					2nd Esquire	1 ⎭
		Lodowick	46 ⎫ 50				
		Polish Captain	4 ⎭				

SUGGESTIONS FOR DISCUSSION.

1. The varying proportion of rhyme-lines to verse-lines in *Edward III.* shows that I. 2—II. 2 is the only part written by Shakspere.
2. In *Edward III.*, the chief part of which must have been written by Peele, the mode of treating history is un-Shaksperian.
3. Shakspere's gallery of female characters is incomplete without the Countess of Salisbury.

LIST OF EARLIEST KNOWN EDITIONS.

Date.	Printer.	Publisher.	Acted by	Present Owners.
1596	——	Cuthbert Burby		{ British Museum. { Trinity College, Cambridge.
1599	Simon Stafford	Cuthbert Burby		⎰ British Museum. ⎹ Bodleian Library. ⎱ Trinity College, Cambridge. ⎱ Mr. Halliwell-Phillipps.

The first-mentioned of the editions was thus entered in the Stationers' Registers:—
1595. December 1.
Cutbert Burby   Entred for his copie vnder the handes of the wardens A book Intitled *Edward the Third and the Blacke Prince their warres with kinge John of Fraunce*   vj^d

In the following year the edition was published anonymously as "The Raigne of King Edward the third. As it hath bin sundrie times plaied about the Citie of London." The 1599 edition has the same title.

In the Registers are these entries:—
1609. October 16.
Master Welby   Assigned ouer vnto hym by mistres **Burby** in full Court holden this daye and with the consent of the master wardens and Assistentes here present in Court All her right in these copies folowinge vnder this condycon that yf there shalbe found any indirecte Dealinge herein by any of the parties to the same Then these copies to be at the disposicon of the .Company and this entrance to be void   xix[s]
viz in

     27. *Edward the third* . . . .

     30. *Doctor ffaustus the 2 parte* . . . . . .

     37. her parte with master **Burre**, in *every man in his humour*

1618. March 2.
Master Snodham   Assigned ouer vnto him by master **Welbey** with Consente of the master and wardens all his Right in theis Copies followinge   xxj[s]
vizt

     Henry the 4th by D Haywarde . . . .

     Edward the 3^d the play. . . . . .

     Doctor . Faustus 2 parte . . . . . .

     Every man in his humor. his parte

Drs. Warnke and Proescholdt in their edition in "Pseudo-Shakespearian Plays" (Halle: Max Niemeyer, 1886), in which they argue against the Shaksperian authorship of *Edward III.*, say "The greater part . . . . . is based on Holinshed's Chronicle of England, ... on Holinshed's Chronicle of Scotland and on Painter's Palace of Pleasure," but that to the latter "the poet was indebted . . . . . merely for the leading idea" of the Countess-episode. Mr. J. W. Mills asks "If it be not Shakspere, who was the great unknown that could write lines so different from the diction of any known contemporary?" and Miss Emma Phipson points out many similarities between this play and Shakspere's later work (*Academy*, June 25, 1887, p. 455).

JOHN.

Total Number of Lines.	CHARACTERS.	I.	II.	III.				IV.			V.						
		1	1	1	2	3	4	1	2	3	1	2	3	4	5	6	7
435	KING JOHN	48	104	34	3	64	...	...	119	...	27	...	8	...	...	...	28
41	CHATILLON	16	25	...	...	...	...	...	...	...	...	...	...	...	...	...	...
3	ESSEX	3	...	...	...	...	...	...	...	...	...	...	...	...	...	...	...
522	BASTARD	143	123	9	8	5	...	...	22	57	43	53	...	...	...	20	39
22	ROBERT FAULCONBRIDGE	22	...	...	...	...	...	...	...	...	...	...	...	...	...	...	...
1	GURNEY	1	...	...	...	...	...	...	...	...	...	...	...	...	...	...	...
154	LEWIS	...	28	8	...	...	18	...	...	...	...	83	...	...	17	...	...
35	AUSTRIA	...	27	8	...	...	...	...	...	...	...	...	...	...	...	...	...
193	KING PHILIP	...	119	48	...	...	26	...	...	...	...	...	...	...	...	...	...
64	1ST CITIZEN	...	64	...	...	...	...	...	...	...	...	...	...	...	...	...	...
12	FRENCH HERALD	...	12	...	...	...	...	...	...	...	...	...	...	...	...	...	...
13	ENGLISH HERALD	...	13	...	...	...	...	...	...	...	...	...	...	...	...	...	...
158	SALISBURY	...	...	6	...	...	...	...	28	53	...	32	...	19	...	...	20
165	PANDULPH	...	...	72	...	...	67	...	...	...	11	15	...	...	...	...	...
140	HUBERT	...	...	...	...	8	...	43	35	25	...	...	1	...	...	28	...
2	1ST EXECUTIONER	...	...	...	...	...	...	2	...	...	...	...	...	...	...	...	...
79	PEMBROKE	...	...	...	...	...	...	...	56	13	...	...	...	4	...	...	6
28	MESSENGER	...	...	...	...	...	...	...	14	...	...	...	8	...	6	...	...
1	PETER	...	...	...	...	...	...	...	1	...	...	...	...	...	...	...	...
9	BIGOT	...	...	...	...	...	...	...	...	9	...	...	...	...	...	...	...
39	MELUN	...	...	...	...	...	...	...	...	...	...	...	...	39	...	...	...
55	ELINOR	29	21	2	...	3	...	...	...	...	...	...	...	...	...	...	...
15	LADY FAULCONBRIDGE ...	15	...	...	...	...	...	...	...	...	...	...	...	...	...	...	...
120	ARTHUR	...	9	1	...	1	...	99	...	10	...	...	...	...	...	...	...
263	CONSTANCE	...	48	141	...	...	74	...	...	...	...	...	...	...	...	...	...
42	BLANCH	...	15	27	...	...	...	...	...	...	...	...	...	...	...	...	...
29	PRINCE HENRY	...	...	...	...	...	...	...	...	...	...	...	...	...	...	...	29
2640		277	608	356	11	81	185	144	275	167	81	183	17	62	23	48	122
2570	Actual Number of Lines	276	598	347	10	73	183	134	269	159	79	180	17	61	22	44	118

SCHEME FOR ARRANGING THE PARTS WITH EIGHTEEN MEN.

FIFTEEN CHARACTERS SINGLY AND THREE GROUPS.

GURNEY	1	13	BIGOT	9	10	ESSEX	3	5
FRENCH HERALD	12		PETER	1		1ST EXECUTIONER	2	

SUGGESTIONS FOR DISCUSSION.

1. For the outline of *John*, Shakspere was solely indebted to *The Troublesome Raigne*, to the author of which belongs the great merit of presenting an intelligent dramatic record of that period.

2. In *John*, Shakspere altered history to make the play a protest against foreign intervention in the political troubles of England in his own day.

3. The Character of James Gurney is a striking instance of Shakspere's power in very small matters.

THE EARLIEST KNOWN EDITION IS THE 1623 FOLIO.

In 1598 Meres, recounting Shakspere's excellence in tragedy, mentions "his . . . . King Iohn."

"The Troublesome Raigne of Iohn King of England, with the discouerie of King Richard Cordelions Base sonne (vulgarly named, The Bastard Fawconbridge): also the death of King Iohn at Swinstead Abbey," is connected with Shakspere's play. The following editions are in existence:—

Date.	*Printer.*	*Publisher.*	*Acted by*	*Present Owners.*
1591	———	Sampson Clarke	The Queen's players	Trinity College, Cambridge.
1611	Valentine Simmes	Iohn Helme	The Queen's players	British Museum. Bodleian Library. Trinity College, Cambridge. Duke of Devonshire.
1622	Aug: Mathewes	Thomas Dewe		British Museum. Trinity College, Cambridge. Duke of Devonshire.

The 1591 edition was published anonymously. It is reprinted in Hazlitt's *Shakespeare's Library*. The 1611 edition was said to be by "W. Sh." and the 1622 edition by "W. Shakespeare."

In the Stationers' Registers is this entry:—

1614. November 29.

John Beale. Entred for his Coppie by Direction from the wardens a booke called *the history of George lord ffauconbridg basterd sonne to Richard Cordelion* which said Coppie was master **Barleyes** vj^{d}.

William Barley was the publisher of "The True Tragedie of Richard the Third" in 1594 (see p. 87).

As the publishers of the 1623 Folio did not include *John* in the list of plays "not formerly entred to other men," it must be inferred that they looked upon the earlier form as the work of Shakspere, although there is no entry of *The Troublesome Raigne* in the Stationers' Registers. In the Folio the play is called "The life and death of King Iohn."

THE TAMING OF THE SHREW.

Total Number of Lines.	CHARACTERS.	Induction.		I.		II.	III.		IV.					V.	
		1	2	1	2	1	1	2	1	2	3	4	5	1	2
68	SLY	10	54	4	...	...	...	...	...	...	...	...	...	...	...
137	LORD	106	31	...	...	...	...	...	...	...	...	...	...	...	...
9	1ST HUNTSMAN	9	...	...	...	...	...	...	...	...	...	...	...	...	...
3	2ND HUNTSMAN	3	...	...	...	...	...	...	...	...	...	...	...	...	...
21	1ST SERVANT	2	14	1	...	...	3	...	1	...	...	...	...	...	...
5	PLAYER	5	...	...	...	...	...	...	...	...	...	...	...	...	...
12	2ND SERVANT	...	12	...	...	...	...	...	...	...	...	...	...	...	...
12	3RD SERVANT	...	12	...	...	...	...	...	...	...	...	...	...	...	...
2	"ALL"	...	1	...	...	...	...	...	1	...	...	...	...	...	...
8	MESSENGER	...	8	...	...	...	...	...	...	...	...	...	...	...	...
190	LUCENTIO	...	...	92	7	...	28	6	...	5	...	11	...	16	25
295	TRANIO	...	...	63	34	46	...	42	...	66	...	27	...	13	4
175	BAPTISTA	...	...	23	...	70	...	36	...	...	...	20	...	14	12
172	GREMIO	...	...	27	39	56	...	34	...	...	...	...	...	13	3
213	HORTENSIO	...	...	30	78	15	29	...	...	25	11	...	8	...	17
118	BIONDELLO	...	...	6	2	...	...	47	...	8	...	30	...	20	5
585	PETRUCHIO	...	...	...	78	162	...	62	72	...	88	...	42	18	63
187	GRUMIO	...	...	...	49	...	...	2	98	...	38	...	...	...	...
32	CURTIS	...	...	...	...	...	...	...	32	...	...	...	...	...	...
5	NATHANIEL	...	...	...	...	...	...	...	5	...	...	...	...	...	...
1	PHILIP	...	...	...	...	...	...	...	1	...	...	...	...	...	...
1	JOSEPH	...	...	...	...	...	...	...	1	...	...	...	...	...	...
1	NICHOLAS	...	...	...	...	...	...	...	1	...	...	...	...	...	...
2	PETER	...	...	...	...	...	...	...	2	...	...	...	...	...	...
54	PEDANT	...	...	...	...	...	...	...	...	15	...	21	...	18	...
1	HABERDASHER	...	...	...	...	...	...	...	...	...	1	...	...	...	...
18	TAILOR	...	...	...	...	...	...	...	...	...	18	...	...	...	...
51	VINCENTIO	...	...	...	...	...	...	...	...	...	...	...	9	40	2
5	HOSTESS	5	...	...	...	...	...	...	...	...	...	...	...	...	...
16	PAGE	...	15	1	...	...	...	...	...	...	...	...	...	...	...
220	KATHARINA	...	...	13	...	52	...	30	3	...	45	...	22	4	51
70	BIANCA	...	...	4	...	16	33	1	...	6	...	...	...	2	8
11	WIDOW	...	...	...	...	...	...	...	...	...	...	...	...	...	11
2700		140	147	264	287	417	93	260	217	125	201	109	81	158	201
2648	Actual Number of Lines	138	147	259	282	412	92	254	214	120	198	109	79	155	189

In Induction I. the Lord's lines should be 105, and in II. 1 Tranio's 47.

SCHEME FOR ARRANGING THE PARTS WITH EIGHTEEN MEN.

TWELVE CHARACTERS SINGLY AND SIX GROUPS.

Joseph 1, Tailor 18	19	1st Servant 21, Haberdasher 1	22	Vincentio 51, Nicholas 1	52
Philip 1, Messenger 8, 1st Huntsman 9	18	Peter 2, Player 5, 3rd Servant 12	19	Nathaniel 5, 2nd Huntsman 3, 2nd Servant 12	20

SUGGESTIONS FOR DISCUSSION.

1. Greene's references to the original of *The Taming of the Shrew* and to *Faire Em* prove that the latter play was written by Shakspere.
2. It can be proved from *The Taming of the Shrew* that Shakspere had been to Italy.
3. If *The Taming of the Shrew* is to be taken seriously, it shows Shakspeare's ignorance of human nature.

THE EARLIEST CERTAIN EDITION IS THE 1623 FOLIO.

There is a copy without a title-page, which, not improbably, may be of a date between 1607 and 1610.

The following is a list of the earliest known editions of *The Taming of a Shrew*, which must be studied with the play in its present form :—

Date.	*Printer.*	*Publisher.*	*Acted by*	*Present Owners.*
1594	Peter Short	Cutbert Burbie	Earl of Pembroke's servants	Duke of Devonshire.
1596	P. S.	Cuthbert Burbie	Earl of Pembroke's servants	British Museum. Lady Ellesmere.
1607	V. S.	Nicholas Ling	Earl of Pembroke's servants	Bodleian Library. Duke of Devonshire.

The first of these editions was thus entered in the Stationers' Registers :—

1594. May 2.
Peter Shorte Entred vnto him for his copie vnder master warden **Cawoodes** hande a booke intituled *A plesant Conceyted historie called 'the Tayminge of a Shrowe'* **vj**[d]

The edition itself, without author's name, has the same title. It has been reprinted by the Shakespeare Society and in Hazlitt's *Shakespeare's Library*.

On June 11, 1594, Henslowe records (*Diary*, p. 36) that "the tamynge of a shrowe" was played at Newington by "my Lord Admeralle and my Lorde chamberlen men."

The following entry, probably referring to the subject of the play, occurs in the Registers :—

1594. October 16.
Thomas Gosson **Joseph Hunte** Entred for their copie vnder thandes of master warden **Binge**, a ballad intituled, *the coolinge of curst* KATE **vj**[d]

The 1596 edition is an anonymous one, with the same title as that of 1594.

On August 27, 1596, there is in the Registers, in connection with Thomas Millington's name, a mention of "the ballad entituled The Taming of a Shrew" (see p. 155). The ballad in Percy's *Reliques of Ancient English Poetry* called "The Frolicksome Duke" deals only with the incident of the Induction, which in some such form was a frequent one in literature.

The transfers of the copyright of *A Shrew* were made from Burby to Ling on January 22, 1607, and from Ling to Smythick on November 19, 1607, (see p. 79). Ling's edition in 1607 was published anonymously, and had the same title as the previous issue. Smythick was one of those who brought out the 1623 Folio, in the entry of which in the Registers *The Taming of the Shrew* is not named, as the publishers did not include those copies which had been "formerly entred to other men." They evidently considered that it was practically a play by Shakspere which in 1607 had been assigned to Smythick, who, in 1631, brought out another quarto, the text of which follows that of the Folio.

The facts mentioned above point to a date for the present play later than that usually ascribed to it (see a paper by Mr. A. R. Frey in *Shakespeariana*, June, 1887. He unaccountably states that Shakspere's name is on the title-page of the 1607 edition of *A Shrew*).

Lord Pembroke's company acted *Titus Andronicus* (see p. 59). Beyond this there is no record that they performed any other play with which Shakspere was connected except *The True Tragedy* (see p. 69).

As a supplement to this play the student should read Fletcher's *The Woman's Prize*, in which the tables are turned on the husband.

In reference to the authorship of *The Taming of the Shrew* consideration should be given to Mr. Fleay's paper and the discussion thereon (New Shakspere Society's *Transactions*, 1874, Part I.).

EVERY MAN IN HIS HUMOUR.

Total Number of Lines.	CHARACTERS.	Prologue.	I.				II.			III.			IV.									V.
			1	2	3	4	1	2	3	1	2	3	1	2	3	4	5	6	7	8	9	1
313	KNOWELL...	..	165	...	...	...	...	...	86	..	...	2	...	...	...	19	...	...	...	23	...	18
380	BRAINWORM	...	8	27	...	...	...	62	57	28	8	...	2	...	5	58	...	15	26	...	40	44
248	STEPHEN ...	...	52	52	...	...	...	39	...	38	23	...	8	...	...	...	6	...	...	...	19	11
27	SERVANT ...	...	18	...	...	...	...	...	...	...	...	..	...	...	...	...	...	..	...	...	...	9
298	ED. KNOWELL...	...	...	78	...	...	...	21	...	72	45	...	20	...	13	...	42	...	...	...	...	7
202	MATHEW ...	...	...	...	24	64	1	...	...	23	2	...	23	...	...	...	12	...	42	...	9	2
251	COB ...	...	...	...	83	...	1	...	...	...	74	53	...	27	...	...	...	...	..	10	...	3
404	BOBADILL...	...	...	...	...	123	8	...	...	64	39	...	8	...	...	...	116	...	27	...	6	13
432	KITELY	...	...	...	...	...	165	...	...	...	116	34	22	...	...	...	...	51	...	28	...	16
86	CASH	...	...	...	...	...	2	...	...	...	73	...	8	...	...	...	...	1	...	2	...	...
149	DOWNRIGHT	...	...	...	...	...	53	...	...	...	...	..	56	...	...	...	11	...	...	...	21	8
258	WELLBRED	...	...	...	...	...	...	...	...	69	35	...	46	...	23	...	...	76	..	...	..	9
1	"ALL" ...	...	...	...	...	...	...	...	...	...	1	...	...	..	...	...	...	...	...	...	...	...
236	CLEMENT...	...	...	...	...	...	...	...	...	...	...	41	...	...	...	...	...	...	...	...	...	195
31	FORMAL ...	...	...	...	...	...	...	...	...	...	...	6	...	...	...	16	...	...	...	...	...	9
30	"PROLOGUE" ...	30	...	...	...	...	...	...	...	...	...	...	...	...	...	...	...	...	...	...	...	...
33	TIB ...	...	...	...	...	6	...	...	...	...	...	...	..	9	...	...	...	...	...	15	...	3
72	DAME KITELY	...	...	...	...	...	16	..	...	..	...	...	17	...	...	...	...	14	...	18	...	7
30	BRIDGET ...	...	..	...	...	...	...	...	...	...	...	...	18	...	...	...	...	12	...	...	...	...
3481		30	243	157	107	193	246	122	143	294	416	136	228	36	41	93	187	169	95	96	95	354
3458	Actual No. of Lines	30	242	157	107	193	243	122	143	294	402	136	228	36	41	93	187	169	95	91	95	354

SUGGESTIONS FOR DISCUSSION.

1. The success of *Every Man in his Humour* led to the attack upon Jonson by Marston and Dekker.
2. Ben Jonson's frequent references to *The Spanish Tragedy* are evidence of his high opinion of Kyd, whom he had helped in his work.
3. Critics have been misled in thinking that, in the Prologue to *Every Man in his Humour*, Ben Jonson refers to Shakspere.

LIST OF EARLIEST KNOWN EDITIONS.

Date.	*Printer.*	*Publisher.*	*Acted by*	*Present Owners*
1601	———	Walter Burre	Lord Chamberlain's servants	British Museum.
1616	W. Stansby	Richard Meighen	Lord Chamberlain's servants	British Museum and others. [This is the Folio.]

This play was "Acted in the yeere 1598. By the then Lord Chamberlaine his seruants" (see the first volume of the Folio edition of Ben Jonson's works).

On August 4, 1600 (it must be then, although the year is not named), occurs this entry in the Stationers' Registers:—

As you like yt a booke
HENRY the FFIFT a booke
Euery man in his humour a booke
The commedie of 'muche A doo about nothing' a booke
} to be staied

The restriction was soon removed, for this entry is met with:—

1600. August 14.

Master Burby Entred for yeir copie vnder the handes of master PASVILL and ye Wardens. a
Walter Burre. booke called *Euery man in his humour* vjd

On the title-page of the 1601 edition it is stated that the play "hath been sundry times publickly acted." It is designated by the short form of the 1600 entry.

At the Court Revels in 1605 it is said that "On Candelmas night A playe Euery one in his Umor" was acted "By his Matis plaiers." (On the genuineness of this entry see p. 71).

On October 16, 1609, Burby's widow transferred her share in the copyright of this and thirty-seven other works to Welby (see p. 93).

In 1616 was published the first volume of Ben Jonson's collected works. It was printed by W. Stansby for R. Meighen. This does not seem to have disturbed the copyright originally entered to Burby and Burre, for on March 2, 1618, Welby, who had become possessed of Mistress Burby's share, transferred it to Snodham (see p. 93).

The Lord Chamberlain's servants mentioned in the 1616 Folio had become the King's servants in 1603.

THE MERCHANT OF VENICE.

Total Number of Lines.	CHARACTERS.	I.			II.									III.					IV.		V.
		1	2	3	1	2	3	4	5	6	7	8	9	1	2	3	4	5	1	2	1
188	ANTONIO	46	...	39	...	...	...	...	...	6	...	...	..	...	...	19	...	...	66	...	12
109	SALARINO	41	...	...	...	...	...	3	...	5	...	34	...	22	...	4	...	...	...	...	...
59	SALANIO	11	...	...	...	...	...	3	...	...	...	21	...	24	...	...	...	..	...	...	...
341	BASSANIO	51	...	16	...	38	...	...	...	...	...	...	...	...	144	...	...	...	50	...	42
181	LORENZO	6	...	...	...	...	..	27	...	21	...	...	...	...	5	...	12	34	...	...	76
178	GRATIANO	34	...	...	...	18	...	3	...	20	...	...	...	...	31	...	...	...	33	5	34
18	SERVANT	...	5	...	...	..	...	...	...	...	...	...	11	2	...	...	...	...	...	...	...
364	SHYLOCK	...	...	134	...	...	...	...	39	...	...	...	...	72	...	16	...	...	103	...	...
103	MOROCCO	...	...	...	32	...	..	...	...	...	71	...	...	...	...	...	...	...	...	...	...
188	LAUNCELOT ...	...	...	...	...	120	5	6	15	...	...	...	...	...	...	...	...	35	...	...	7
41	OLD GOBBO ...	...	...	...	...	41	...	...	...	...	...	...	...	...	...	...	...	...	...	...	...
2	LEONARDO	...	...	...	...	2	...	...	...	...	...	...	...	...	...	...	...	...	...	...	...
66	ARRAGON	...	...	...	...	...	...	...	...	...	...	...	66	...	...	...	...	...	...	...	...
16	TUBAL	...	...	...	...	...	...	...	...	...	...	...	...	16	...	...	...	...	...	...	...
9	MUSICIAN	...	...	...	..	...	...	...	...	...	...	...	...	...	9	...	...	...	...	...	...
1	"ALL"	...	...	...	...	...	...	...	...	...	...	...	...	...	1	...	...	...	...	...	...
24	SALERIO	...	...	...	..	...	...	...	...	...	...	...	...	...	20	...	...	...	4	...	...
1	BALTHASAR ..	..	...	...	...	...	...	...	...	...	...	...	...	...	...	...	1	...	...	...	...
57	DUKE	...	...	...	...	...	...	...	...	...	...	...	...	...	...	...	...	...	57	...	...
8	STEPHANO	...	...	...	..	..	...	...	...	...	...	...	...	...	...	...	...	...	...	...	8
589	PORTIA	...	96	...	17	...	...	...	...	...	9	...	20	...	118	...	71	...	138	12	108
110	NERISSA	...	46	...	...	...	...	...	...	...	...	...	6	...	5	...	2	...	22	4	25
89	JESSICA	...	...	...	...	...	16	...	4	18	...	...	...	...	7	...	1	29	...	...	14
2742		189	147	189	49	219	21	42	58	70	80	55	103	136	340	39	87	98	473	21	326
2662	Actual No. of Lines	186	147	183	46	215	21	40	57	68	79	53	101	136	330	36	84	96	458	19	307

SCHEME FOR ARRANGING THE PARTS WITH EIGHTEEN MEN.

SEVENTEEN CHARACTERS SINGLY AND ONE GROUP.

LEONARDO 2 } 3
BALTHASAR 1 }

SUGGESTIONS FOR DISCUSSION.

1. The influence of Marlowe's *Jew of Malta* is clearly seen in *The Merchant of Venice.*
2. Shakspere was induced to take up the story of *The Merchant of Venice* by his own money-lending habits.
3. The sympathy which is aroused on behalf of Shylock is entirely adventitious.

LIST OF EARLIEST KNOWN EDITIONS.

Date.	*Printer.*	*Publisher.*	*Acted by*	*Present Owners.*
1600	J. Roberts	———		British Museum. Bodleian Library. Trinity College, Cambridge. Duke of Devonshire. Mr. A. H. Huth.
1600	I. R.	Thomas Heyes	Lord Chamberlain's servants	British Museum. Bodleian Library. Trinity College, Cambridge. Duke of Devonshire.

When "my Lord Admeralle and my Lorde chamberlen men" were playing at Newington they often acted "the Venesyon comodey," which on August 25, 1594, was a new play (Henslowe's *Diary*, p. 40). Beyond the indication afforded by the title, there is no evidence that this was Shakspere's play.

In the Stationers' Registers are these entries:—

1598. July 22.
James Robertes. Entred for his copie vnder the handes of both the wardens, a booke of *the Marchaunt of Venyce or otherwise called the Jewe of Venyce*
PROUIDED that yt bee not prynted by the said **James Robertes** or anye other whatsoeuer without lycence first had from the Right honorable the lord Chamberlen **vjd**

1600. October 28.
Thomas haies Entred for his copie vnder the handes of the Wardens and by Consent of master **Robertes.** A booke called *the booke of the merchant of Venyce* **vjd**

Many words have been expended about the relative order and value of the two 1600 editions, each of which had the name of "Shakespeare" on its title-page. The general opinion gives the Roberts Quarto the doubtful honour of first appearance, as it is commonly credited with being a surreptitious copy. The Heyes Quarto is usually considered to be the better of the two texts, which were issued with much the same title. That of the second mentioned is "The most excellent Historie of the Merchant of Venice. With the extreame crueltie of Shylocke the Iewe towards the sayd Merchant, in cutting a iust pound of his flesh: and the obtayning of Portia by the choyse of three chests." In each of the editions, with a little variety of spelling, the head-line throughout is "The Comicall History of the Merchant of Venice."

In Cunningham's record of the 1605 performances at Whitehall (see p. 71) is this entry: "By his Matis plaiers. On Shrousunday A play of the Marchant of Venis. Shaxberd." The same authority says that by the King's command the play was acted again on the Tuesday following.

The following entry occurs in the Registers:—

1619. July 8.
Laurence Hayes Entred for his Copies by Consent of a full Court theis two Copies following which were the Copies of **Thomas Haies** his fathers

vizt.

A play Called *The Marchant of Venice,*

. . . . **xijd**

The title of the play in the Folio is simply "The Merchant of Venice."

On the sources, fanciful and probable, of the two stories a great deal has been written, and a summary of it will be found in most of the Editors' introductions to the play. In addition to the pieces printed by Hazlitt (*Shakespeare's Library*) the student will find much of interest in "The Original of Shylock," by Mr. Sidney L. Lee (*Gentleman's Magazine*, February, 1880).

MUCH ADO ABOUT NOTHING.

Total Number of Lines.	CHARACTERS.	I.			II.			III.					IV.		V.			
		1	2	3	1	2	3	1	2	3	4	5	1	2	1	2	3	4
357	LEONATO	35	14	...	39	...	46	...	4	...	...	17	69	...	108	...	...	25
34	MESSENGER	30	...	...	...	...	...	...	...	...	...	2	...	...	...	...	...	2
356	DON PEDRO	66	...	...	71	...	71	...	51	...	...	...	12	...	71	...	7	7
474	BENEDICK...	99	...	...	85	...	88	...	9	...	...	...	52	...	25	66	...	50
125	DON JOHN	2	...	46	12	19	...	...	38	...	...	...	8	...	...	...	...	...
293	CLAUDIO	40	...	...	28	...	37	...	35	...	...	...	59	...	58	...	15	21
57	ANTONIO	...	15	...	7	...	...	...	...	...	...	...	...	...	32	...	...	3
41	CONRADE	...	...	15	...	...	...	...	...	20	...	...	...	6	...	...	...	...
140	BORACHIO...	...	...	16	4	39	...	...	...	53	...	...	...	4	24	...	...	...
32	BALTHASAR	...	...	...	6	...	26	...	...	...	...	...	...	...	...	...	...	...
198	DOGBERRY	...	...	...	...	...	...	...	...	72	...	41	...	50	35	...	...	...
30	VERGES	...	...	...	...	...	...	...	...	14	...	9	...	5	2	...	...	...
32	1ST WATCH	...	...	...	...	...	...	...	...	26	...	...	...	6	...	...	...	...
11	2ND WATCH	...	...	...	...	...	...	...	...	8	..	...	...	3	...	...	...	...
84	FRIAR	...	...	..	...	...	...	...	...	...	...	...	75	...	...	...	...	9
17	SEXTON	...	...	...	...	...	...	...	...	...	...	...	...	17	...	...	...	...
11	LORD	...	...	...	...	...	...	...	...	...	...	...	...	...	...	...	11	...
309	BEATRICE...	57	...	...	124	...	8	10	...	...	18	...	57	...	...	24	...	11
135	HERO	2	...	...	11	...	..	78	...	...	18	...	18	...	...	...	...	8
75	MARGARET	...	...	...	6	...	...	1	...	...	58	...	...	...	...	10	...	...
51	URSULA	...	...	...	11	...	...	29	...	...	5	...	...	...	...	6	...	...
2	BOY	...	...	...	...	...	2	...	...	...	...	...	...	...	...	...	...	...
2864		331	29	77	404	58	278	118	137	193	99	69	350	91	355	106	33	136
2826	Actual No. of Lines	330	29	77	404	58	273	116	137	193	99	69	340	90	341	106	33	131

The actual number of lines should be 2829, as the total of II. 3 should be 276. In the 'Globe' three lines of the second verse of the song are not printed in full.

SUGGESTIONS FOR DISCUSSION.

1. *Much Ado about Nothing* is the play mentioned by Meres as *Loue labours wonne.*
2. In Benedick and Beatrice, Shakspere meant his audience to see Lord Herbert and a niece of the Earl of Nottingham.
3. The conduct of Hero's love-matters is contemptible and unJustifiable.

EARLIEST KNOWN EDITION.

Date.	*Printer.*	*Publishers.*	*Acted by*	*Present Owners.*
1600	V.S.	Andrew Wise, and William Aspley	Lord Chamberlain's servants	British Museum. Bodleian Library. Trinity College, Cambridge. Mr. A. H. Huth.

This play was one of those entered in the Stationers' Registers on August 4, 1600, and marked "to be staied" (see p. 99). It was, however, soon allowed to be printed, as appears by this entry :—

1600. August 23.

Andrewe Wyse **William Aspley** Entred for their copies vnder the handes of the wardens Two bookes. the one called *Muche a Doo about nothinge.* Thother *the second parte of the history of kinge HENRY the IIIJth with the humours of Sir JOHN FFALLSTAFF:* Wrytten by master SHAKESPERE **xijd**

The title-page of the edition has the statement that "it hath been sundrie times publikely acted," and that it was "Written by William Shakespeare." "Much adoe about Nothing" is the title given to the play both in Quarto and Folio.

During the festivities which took place at Court in 1613, at the time of the marriage of the Princess Elizabeth with Frederick V., this play, under different names, was acted twice. A MS. in the Bodleian contains "The Accompte of the right honourable the Lord Stanhope of Harrington, Treaſurer of his Majeſties Chamber, for all ſuch Somes of money as hath beine receaved and paied by him within his Office from the feaſte of St. Michaell Tharchangell, Anno Regni Regis Jacobi Decimo (1612), untill the feaſte of St. Michaell, Anno Regni Regis Jacobi undecimo (1613), conteyning one whole yeare.

"Item paid to John Heminges uppon lyke warrant, dated att Whitehall ix° die Julij 1613 for himſelf and the rest of his fellowes, his Majeſties ſervauntes and Players for preſentinge a playe before the Duke of Savoyes Embaſſadour on the viijth daye of June, 1613, called Cardenna, the ſome of vj li. xiij s. iiij d.

"Item paid to John Heminges uppon the Cowncells warrant dated att Whitehall xx° die MaiJ 1613, for preſentinge before the Princes Highnes the Lady Elizabeth and the Prince Pallatyne Elector fowerteene ſeverall playes, viz: one playe called Filaſter, One other called the Knott of ffooles, One other Much adoe abowte nothinge, The Mayeds Tragedy, The merye dyvell of Edmonton, The Tempeſt, A kinge and no kinge, The Twins Tragedie The Winters Tale, Sir John ffalſtaffe, The Moor of Venice, The Nobleman, Cæſars Tragedye, And one other called Love lyes a bleedinge, All which Playes weare played with-in the tyme of this Accompte, viz: paid the ſome of iiijxxxiij li. vj s. viij d.

"Item paid to the ſaid John Heminges uppon the lyke warrant, dated att Whitehall xx° die MaiJ 1613, for preſentinge ſixe ſeverall playes, viz: one playe called a bad begininninge makes a good endinge, One other called the Capteyne, One other the Alcumiſt. One other Cardenno One other The Hotſpur And one other called Benedicte and Betteris, All played within the tyme of this Accompte viz: paid Fortie powndes, And by waye of his Majeſties rewarde twentie powndes, In all lx li." (*Shakespeare's Centurie of Prayse*, pp. 103–4).

Ayrer's "Comedia von der schönen Phaenicia," given in German and English form in Cohn's *Shakespeare in Germany* should be compared with *Much Ado about Nothing.* The exact date of Ayrer's play is unknown. The two plays were almost contemporaneous.

THOMAS, LORD CROMWELL.

Total Number of Lines.	CHARACTERS.	I.			II.				III.			IV.						V.				
		1	2	3	Chorus.	1	2	3	1	2	3	Chorus.	1	2	3	4	5	1	2	3	4	5
143	Hodge	11	6	...	...	...	43	...	43	38	...	...	...	2	...	...	...	...	...	...	...	...
6	Will	6	...	...	...	...	...	...	...	...	...	...	...	...	...	...	...	...	...	...	...	...
6	Tom	3	3	...	...	...	...	...	...	...	...	...	...	...	...	...	...	...	...	...	...	...
464	Cromwell	...	51	...	...	37	51	...	35	42	18	...	14	28	...	36	...	10	9	28	...	105
42	Old Cromwell	...	37	...	...	...	...	...	...	...	...	...	...	5	...	...	...	...	...	...	...	...
50	Bowser	...	13	...	...	...	...	37	...	...	...	...	...	...	...	...	...	...	...	...	...	...
104	Bagot	...	...	43	...	...	44	17	...	...	...	...	...	...	...	...	...	...	...	...	...	...
106	Frescobald	...	...	41	...	...	...	...	28	...	...	...	...	29	...	8	...	...	...	...	...	...
40	Banister	...	...	10	...	...	...	7	...	...	...	...	...	23	...	...	...	...	...	...	...	...
3	Post	...	...	...	...	3	...	...	...	...	...	...	...	...	...	...	...	...	...	...	...	...
40	Governor (Antwerp)	...	...	...	...	...	...	40	...	...	...	...	...	...	...	...	...	...	...	...	...	...
94	Bedford	...	...	...	...	...	...	...	...	43	...	...	13	...	...	...	6	18	...	3	...	11
7	Host	...	...	...	...	...	...	...	...	7	...	...	...	...	...	...	...	...	...	...	...	...
9	Servant	...	...	...	...	...	...	...	...	7	1	...	...	...	...	...	1	...	...	...	...	...
22	Governor (Bologna)	...	...	...	...	...	...	...	...	22	...	...	...	...	...	...	...	...	...	...	...	...
12	1st Citizen	...	...	...	...	...	...	...	...	1	...	...	...	...	...	...	...	...	...	...	11	...
19	Messenger	...	...	...	...	...	...	...	...	12	...	...	...	...	...	...	...	4	3	...	...	...
60	Hales	...	...	...	...	...	...	...	...	...	52	...	8	...	...	...	...	...	...	...	...	...
28	Wolsey	...	...	...	...	...	...	...	...	...	28	...	...	...	...	...	...	...	...	...	...	...
15	More	...	...	...	...	...	...	...	...	...	11	...	4	...	...	...	...	...	...	...	...	...
43	Norfolk	...	...	...	...	...	...	...	...	...	...	...	12	6	...	...	14	...	...	7	...	4
143	Gardiner	...	...	...	...	...	...	...	...	...	...	...	19	15	...	...	82	...	...	14	...	13
20	Suffolk	...	...	...	...	...	...	...	...	...	...	...	7	...	...	...	9	...	...	3	...	1
21	Seely	...	...	...	...	...	...	...	...	...	...	...	...	21	...	...	...	...	...	...	...	...
18	Newton	...	...	...	...	...	...	...	...	...	...	...	...	...	18	...	...	...	...	...	...	...
10	Crosby	...	...	...	...	...	...	...	...	...	...	...	...	...	10	...	...	...	...	...	...	...
1	Usher	...	...	...	...	...	...	...	...	...	...	...	...	...	...	1	...	...	...	...	...	...
6	1st Witness	...	...	...	...	...	...	...	...	...	...	...	...	...	...	...	6	...	...	...	...	...
8	2nd Witness	...	...	...	...	...	...	...	...	...	...	...	...	...	...	...	8	...	...	...	...	...
4	Herald	...	...	...	...	...	...	...	...	...	...	...	...	...	...	...	...	...	...	4	...	...
2	Sergeant	...	...	...	...	...	...	...	...	...	...	...	...	...	...	...	...	...	...	2	...	...
23	2nd Citizen	...	...	...	...	...	...	...	...	...	...	...	...	...	...	...	...	...	...	...	23	...
5	Lieutenant	...	...	...	...	...	...	...	...	...	...	...	...	...	...	...	...	...	...	...	...	5
6	Sadler	...	...	...	...	...	...	...	...	...	...	...	...	...	...	...	...	...	...	...	...	6
1	Executioner	...	...	...	...	...	...	...	...	...	...	...	...	...	...	...	...	...	...	...	...	1
1	Officer	...	...	...	...	...	...	...	...	...	...	...	...	...	...	...	...	...	...	...	...	1
55	Mistress Banister	...	...	20	...	18	...	9	...	...	...	...	...	8	...	...	...	...	...	...	...	...
38	"Chorus"	...	...	...	10	...	...	...	...	15	...	13	...	...	...	...	...	...	...	...	...	...
10	Joan	...	...	...	...	...	...	...	...	...	...	...	...	10	...	...	...	...	...	...	...	...
2	Young Cromwell	...	...	...	...	...	...	...	...	...	...	...	...	...	...	...	...	...	...	...	...	2
1687		20	110	114	10	58	138	110	106	187	110	13	77	147	28	45	126	32	12	61	34	149
1675	Actual Number of Lines	20	110	114	10	58	138	110	106	187	108	13	75	146	28	44	122	32	12	59	34	149

SCHEME FOR ARRANGING THE PARTS WITH EIGHTEEN MEN.

TEN CHARACTERS SINGLY AND EIGHT GROUPS.

SUFFOLK 20 NEWTON 18 POST 3 } 41	WOLSEY 28 HOST 7 WILL 6 } 41	SEELY 21 1ST CITIZEN 12 2ND WITNESS 8 } 41	MORE 15 GOVERNOR (BOLOGNA) 22 LIEUTENANT 5 } 42
CROSBY 10 TOM 6 1ST WITNESS 6 MESSENGER 19 } 41	BANISTER 40 EXECUTIONER 1 USHER 1 } 42	GOVERNOR(ANTWERP) 40 SERGEANT 2 OFFICER 1 } 43	SADLER 6 2ND CITIZEN 23 HERALD 4 SERVANT 9 } 42

SUGGESTIONS FOR DISCUSSION.

1. *Thomas, Lord Cromwell* was a continuation of the series of plays written by Chettle and others on the incidents of the reign of Henry VIII.

2. In *Thomas, Lord Cromwell* the character and fate of the minister of Henry VIII. are adapted so as to fit the history of Essex, the favourite of Henry's daughter.

3. By his observations on *Thomas, Lord Cromwell*, Schlegel shows himself to be an incompetent Shaksperian critic.

LIST OF EARLIEST KNOWN EDITIONS.

Date.	*Printer.*	*Publisher.*	*Acted by*	*Present Owners.*
1602	———	William Iones	Lord Chamberlain's servants	Bodleian Library.
1613	Thomas Snodham	———	The King's servants	British Museum. Bodleian Library. Trinity College, Cambridge. Duke of Devonshire.

Here is an instance of a play entered in the Stationers' Registers to one whose name does not appear on the title-page of the work. The following is the entry:—

1602. August 11.

William Cotton Entred for his Copie vnder thandes of master JACKSON and master **waterson** warden A booke called '*the lyfe and Deathe of the Lord* CROMWELL' *as yt was lately Acted by the Lord Chamberleyn his servantes* **vjd**

The title of the 1602 book "written by W. S." is "The True Chronicle Historie of the whole life and death of Thomas Lord Cromwell." It is said to have "beene sundrie times publikely Acted."

In the Registers is this entry:—

1611. December 16.

John Browne. Entred for his Copyes by assignement from **william Jones** and vnder master warden **Lownes** his hand, ... and one other booke called, *the lyfe and death of the Lord* CROMWELL, by W: S. **xijd.**

The 1613 edition has its title worded in the same way as the 1602.

A transfer of copyright is thus recorded:—

1617. February 16.

Master **Barrett** Assigned ouer vnto him by master **Leake** and by order of a full Courte all theis Copies followinge **xiiijs.**

vizt.

. . . .

VENUS and ADONIS

. . . .

Idem Allowed vnto him also by the same Court all the Copies that belonged to master **Cotton** *vizt*

. . . .

Life and death of lord CROMWELL

This play was first added to Shakspere's plays in the third Folio in 1664.

I HENRY IV.

Total Number of Lines.	CHARACTERS.	I.			II.				III.			IV.				V.				
		1	2	3	1	2	3	4	1	2	3	1	2	3	4	1	2	3	4	5
341	KING	75	...	45	...	...	...	...	...	130	...	...	...	...	...	47	...	...	19	25
41	WESTMORELAND ...	33	...	...	...	...	...	...	...	...	...	...	7	...	...	...	...	...	1	...
688	FALSTAFF	...	90	...	...	63	...	248	...	...	127	...	67	...	...	22	...	27	44	...
616	PRINCE HENRY ..	...	98	...	...	31	...	256	...	44	47	...	9	...	...	29	...	9	78	15
87	POINS	...	52	...	...	11	...	24	...	...	...	...	...	...	...	...	...	...	...	...
189	WORCESTER	...	...	63	...	...	...	...	16	...	...	22	...	4	...	47	34	...	...	3
26	NORTHUMBERLAND	...	...	26	...	...	...	...	...	...	...	...	...	...	...	...	...	...	...	...
566	HOTSPUR	...	...	171	...	...	72	...	109	...	...	77	...	73	...	...	39	9	16	...
41	BLUNT	...	...	7	...	...	...	...	...	7	...	...	...	20	...	...	...	7	...	...
25	1ST CARRIER ...	...	...	...	24	...	...	1	...	...	...	...	...	...	...	...	...	...	...	...
1	OSTLER	...	...	...	1	...	...	...	...	...	...	...	...	...	...	...	...	...	...	...
20	2ND CARRIER ...	...	...	...	20	...	...	...	...	...	...	...	...	...	...	...	...	...	...	...
47	GADSHILL	...	...	...	40	3	...	4	...	...	...	...	...	...	...	...	...	...	...	...
21	CHAMBERLAIN ...	...	...	...	21	...	...	...	...	...	...	...	...	...	...	...	...	...	...	...
31	BARDOLPH	...	...	...	...	3	...	12	...	...	13	...	3	...	...	...	...	...	...	...
14	PETO	...	...	...	...	1	...	13	...	...	...	...	...	...	...	...	...	...	...	...
6	1ST TRAVELLER ...	...	...	...	...	6	...	...	...	...	...	...	...	...	...	...	...	...	...	...
3	SERVANT	...	...	...	...	...	3	...	...	...	...	...	...	...	...	...	...	...	...	...
18	FRANCIS	...	...	...	...	...	...	18	...	...	...	...	...	...	...	...	...	...	...	...
5	VINTNER	...	...	...	...	...	...	5	...	...	...	...	...	...	...	...	...	...	...	...
8	SHERIFF	...	...	...	...	...	...	8	...	...	...	...	...	...	...	...	...	...	...	...
60	MORTIMER	...	...	...	...	...	...	...	60	...	...	...	...	...	...	...	...	...	...	...
80	GLENDOWER	...	...	...	...	...	...	...	80	...	...	...	...	...	...	...	...	...	...	...
46	DOUGLAS	...	...	...	...	...	...	...	...	...	...	13	...	4	...	...	6	15	8	...
7	1ST MESSENGER ...	...	...	...	...	...	...	...	...	...	...	6	...	...	...	...	1	...	...	...
66	VERNON	...	...	...	...	...	...	...	...	...	...	25	...	20	...	...	21	...	...	...
34	ARCHBISHOP	...	...	...	...	...	...	...	...	...	...	...	...	...	34	...	...	...	...	...
8	SIR MICHAEL ...	...	...	...	...	...	...	...	...	...	...	...	...	...	8	...	...	...	...	...
1	2ND MESSENGER ...	...	...	...	...	...	...	...	...	...	...	...	...	...	...	...	1	...	...	...
8	LANCASTER	...	...	...	...	...	...	...	...	...	...	...	...	...	...	...	...	...	6	2
58	LADY PERCY ...	...	...	...	...	...	47	...	11	...	...	...	...	...	...	...	...	...	...	...
57	HOSTESS	...	...	...	...	...	...	14	...	...	43	...	...	...	...	...	...	...	...	...
3219		108	240	312	106	118	122	603	276	181	230	143	86	121	42	145	102	67	172	45
3180	Actual No. of Lines	108	240	302	106	118	120	603	271	180	230	136	86	113	41	144	101	65	172	44

The total lines should be 3177, as the total of V. should be 169.

Character	Lines	Total
Lancaster	8	40
1st Carrier	25	
1st Messenger	7	
Sir Michael	8	42
Bardolph	31	
Servant	3	
Francis	18	44
1st Traveller	6	
2nd Carrier	20	
Blunt	41	47
Vintner	5	
Ostler	1	
Archbishop	34	48
Peto	14	
Westmoreland	41	49
Sheriff	8	
Northumberland	26	48
Chamberlain	21	
2nd Messenger	1	

SUGGESTIONS FOR DISCUSSION.

1. In 1 *Henry IV.* Shakspere introduces the wild pastime only to show out more clearly the virtue of serious business.
2. 1 *Henry IV.* is Shakspere's finest play, so far as characterisation is concerned.
3. In the representation of Prince Henry in 1 *Henry IV.* Shakspere meant to describe himself.

LIST OF EARLIEST KNOWN EDITIONS.

Date.	*Printer.*	*Publisher.*	*Acted by*	*Present Owners.*
1598	P. S.	Andrew Wise		British Museum. Trinity College, Cambridge. Duke of Devonshire.
1599	S. S.	Andrew Wise		British Museum. Bodleian Library. Trinity College, Cambridge. Duke of Devonshire. Mr. A. H. Huth.
1604	Valentine Simmes	Mathew Law		Bodleian Library. Trinity College, Cambridge.
1608	———	Mathew Law		British Museum. Bodleian Library. Duke of Devonshire.
1613	W. W.	Mathew Law		British Museum. Bodleian Library. Trinity College, Cambridge.
1622	T. P.	Mathew Law		British Museum. Bodleian Library. Trinity College, Cambridge.

The first notice of this play in the Stationers' Registers is the following:—

1598. February 25.

Andrew Wyse. Entred for his Copie vnder thandes of Master Dix: and master Warden **man a** booke intituled *The historye of Henry the IIIJth with his battaile of Shrewsburye against Henry Hottspurre of the Northe with the conceipted mirthe of Sir John Ffalstoff* vjd.

The edition itself, which was anonymous, had its title worded much in the same way. In 1598 Meres mentions "Henry the 4" among Shakspere's tragedies.

On January 9, 1599, Sir John Hayward's book on the events of the first year of the reign of Henry IV. was entered in the Registers to "Master Woolff." This is the book for writing which Hayward was imprisoned (see p. 81). The 1599 edition of 1 *Henry IV.* is said on its title to be "Newly corrected by W. Shake-speare." This appears also in the three following editions, whose titles were all worded much alike.

The copyright of Hayward's book was assigned by Woolff's widow to Burby on April 14, 1603.

The date of the transfer of 1 *Henry IV.* to "Mathew Lawe" was on June 25, 1603 (see p. 81).

Of the 1613 edition the British Museum has two copies, which are not quite alike.

Among the plays acted before a Court-Party in 1613, that which is described as "The Hotspur" (see p. 103) was most likely this play.

On March 2, 1618, Welby transferred the right he had acquired in Hayward's book to Snodham (see p. 93).

The title of the play in the 1623 Folio is "The First Part of Henry the Fourth, with the Life and Death of Henry Sirnamed Hot-Spvrre."

"The Famous Victories of Henry the fifth," printed in 1598 (see p. 117), should be studied in connection with 1 and 2 *Henry IV.* and *Henry V.* It is reprinted in Hazlitt's *Shakespeare's Library* and in the edition of 1 *Henry IV.* in Cassell's National Library. It will be of interest to give some attention to the Introduction by Mr. Halliwell [Phillipps] in the Shakespeare Society Reprint (1845) of the Deryng *Henry IV.* MS.

ANTONIO AND MELLIDA.

Total Number of Lines.	CHARACTERS.	Induction.	Prologue.	I.	II.	III.			IV.	V.		Epilogue.
				1	1	1	2	3	1	1	2	
40	GALEATZO	6	...	...	8	...	...	...	3	...	23	...
195	PIERO	8	...	37	17	...	18	31	20	...	64	...
97	ALBERTO	59	...	4	17	...	...	...	...	17	...	...
194	BALURDO	4	...	1	39	...	26	5	26	55	38	...
34	FOROBOSCO	10	...	2	22	...	...	...	...	...	...	...
245	FELICE	38	...	21	44	...	91	22	1	21	7	...
359	ANTONIO	41	...	116	52	...	...	27	111	...	12	...
19	MATZAGENTE	5	...	...	8	...	...	...	...	...	6	...
44	DILDO	...	...	...	29	...	9	...	5	1	...	...
36	CATZO	...	...	...	27	...	9	...	...	...	...	...
51	CASTILIO	...	...	...	12	...	31	7	...	...	1	...
232	ANDRUGIO	...	...	...	...	87	...	...	97	...	48	...
60	LUCIO	...	...	...	..	31	...	...	25	...	4	...
10	PAINTER	...	...	...	...	...	...	...	...	10	...	...
23	"PROLOGUE"	...	23	...	...	...	...	...	...	...	...	...
100	MELLIDA	...	...	23	23	...	...	3	34	...	17	...
39	FLAVIA	...	...	2	17	...	11	4	...	...	5	...
162	ROSSALINE	...	...	54	29	...	7	...	...	...	72	...
1	PAGE...	...	...	...	...	...	...	...	1	...	...	...
12	"EPILOGUE"	...	...	...	...	...	..	...	...	...	...	12
1953		171	23	260	344	118	202	99	323	104	297	12
1937	Actual Number of Lines	170	23	257	339	116	202	96	321	104	297	12

The play can be divided into more scenes than are given in *British Dramatists*. In Act III. "Enter Felice" should be the beginning of the second scene. In this scene some of the speeches are given to wrong characters. On p. 356, col. 2, the lines beginning "But 'tis not crossed" should be Catzo's, and in the next column "All beyond all," &c., should be Dildo's. Antonio's first speech on p. 357 should begin a third scene, and the stage-directions should be altered. In col. 2, p. 360, the speech beginning "A sudden horror" should be Antonio's. In the table the necessary corrections have been made.

SUGGESTIONS FOR DISCUSSION.

1. *Antonio and Mellida* affords a good illustration of the way in which Elizabethan dramatists satirised one another.
2. Marston's engagement by the Lord Admiral's servants is celebrated allegorically in *Wily Beguiled*.
3. It is a matter for regret that Marston's greatest beauties of detail are to be found in his coarsest works.

EARLIEST KNOWN EDITION.

Date.	*Printer.*	*Publishers.*	*Acted by*	*Present Owner.*
1602	———	Mathewe Lownes, & Thomas Fisher	The Children of Paul's	British Museum.

This play and its second part, known as *Antonio's Revenge*, were thus entered in the Stationers' Registers:—

1601. October 24.

mathew Lownes Entred for their Copye vnder the handes of the wardens a booke called The ffyrst
Thomas ffyssher and second partes of the play called *ANTHONIO and MELIDA* vj^d^
PROVIDED that he gett laufull licence for yt.

The edition was soon after issued as "The History of Antonio and Mellida. The first part." The title-page said it had "beene sundry times acted," and that it was "Written by I. M."

2 HENRY IV.

Total Number of Lines.	CHARACTERS.	Induction.	I.			II.				III.		IV.					V.					Epilogue.
			1	2	3	1	2	3	4	1	2	1	2	3	4	5	1	2	3	4	5	
86	Lord Bardolph	...	40	...	46	...	...	...	...	...	...	...	...	...	...	...	...	...	...	...	...	...
4	Porter	...	4	...	...	...	...	...	...	...	...	...	...	...	...	...	...	...	...	...	...	...
106	Northumberland	...	87	...	...	...	...	19	...	...	...	...	...	...	...	...	...	...	...	...	...	...
16	Travers	...	16	...	...	...	...	...	...	...	...	...	...	...	...	...	...	...	...	...	...	...
78	Morton	...	78	...	...	...	...	...	...	...	...	...	...	...	...	...	...	...	...	...	...	...
719	Falstaff	...	...	185	...	57	...	...	122	...	140	...	...	108	...	...	33	...	36	...	38	...
162	Lord Chief Justice	...	...	63	...	42	...	...	...	...	...	...	...	...	...	...	...	50	...	...	7	...
13	Servant	...	...	13	...	...	...	...	...	...	...	...	...	...	...	...	...	...	...	...	...	...
149	Archbishop	...	...	...	33	...	...	...	...	...	...	91	25	...	...	...	...	...	...	...	...	...
56	Mowbray	...	...	...	6	...	...	...	...	...	...	43	7	...	...	...	...	...	...	...	...	...
57	Hastings	...	...	...	28	...	...	...	...	...	...	16	13	...	...	...	...	...	...	...	...	...
10	Fang	...	...	...	...	10	...	...	...	...	...	...	...	...	...	...	...	...	...	...	...	...
3	Snare	...	...	...	...	3	...	...	...	...	...	...	...	...	...	...	...	...	...	...	...	...
8	Gower	...	...	...	...	8	...	...	...	...	...	...	...	...	...	...	...	...	...	...	...	...
308	Prince Henry	...	...	...	...	...	93	...	37	...	...	...	...	...	...	81	...	70	...	...	27	...
82	Poins	...	...	...	...	...	70	...	12	...	...	...	...	...	...	...	...	...	...	...	...	...
57	Bardolph	...	...	...	...	...	17	...	11	...	22	...	...	1	...	...	1	...	5	...	...	...
12	1st Drawer	...	...	...	...	...	...	...	12	...	...	...	...	...	...	...	...	...	...	...	...	...
13	2nd Drawer	...	...	...	...	...	...	...	13	...	...	...	...	...	...	...	...	...	...	...	...	...
81	Pistol	...	...	...	...	...	...	...	38	...	...	...	...	...	...	...	...	...	28	...	15	...
6	Peto	...	...	...	...	...	...	...	6	...	...	...	...	...	...	...	...	...	...	...	...	...
294	King Henry IV.	...	...	...	...	...	...	...	...	80	...	...	...	...	76	138	...	...	...	...	...	...
77	Warwick	...	...	...	...	...	...	...	...	31	...	...	...	...	18	15	...	13	...	...	...	...
223	Shallow	...	...	...	...	...	...	...	...	...	136	...	...	...	...	...	36	...	38	...	13	...
47	Silence	...	...	...	...	...	...	...	...	...	16	...	...	...	...	...	...	...	31	...	...	...
13	Mouldy	...	...	...	...	...	...	...	...	...	13	...	...	...	...	...	...	...	...	...	...	...
2	Shadow	...	...	...	...	...	...	...	...	...	2	...	...	...	...	...	...	...	...	...	...	...
2	Wart	...	...	...	...	...	...	...	...	...	2	...	...	...	...	...	...	...	...	...	...	...
13	Feeble	...	...	...	...	...	...	...	...	...	13	...	...	...	...	...	...	...	...	...	...	...
14	Bullcalf	...	...	...	...	...	...	...	...	...	14	...	...	...	...	...	...	...	...	...	...	...
4	Messenger	...	...	...	...	...	...	...	...	...	...	4	...	...	...	...	...	...	...	...	...	...
110	Westmoreland	...	...	...	...	...	...	...	...	...	...	81	17	1	11	...	...	...	...	...	...	...
109	Lancaster	...	...	...	...	...	...	...	...	...	...	...	67	23	...	1	...	7	...	...	11	...
9	Colevile	...	...	...	...	...	...	...	...	...	...	...	...	9	...	...	...	...	...	...	...	...
17	Gloucester	...	...	...	...	...	...	...	...	...	...	...	...	...	9	3	...	5	...	...	...	...
23	Clarence	...	...	...	...	...	...	...	...	...	...	...	...	...	13	6	...	4	...	...	...	...
8	Harcourt	...	...	...	...	...	...	...	...	...	...	...	...	...	8	...	...	...	...	...	...	...
39	Davy	...	...	...	...	...	...	...	...	...	...	...	...	...	...	...	28	...	11	...	...	...
11	1st Beadle	...	...	...	...	...	...	...	...	...	...	...	...	...	...	...	...	...	...	11	...	...
3	1st Groom	...	...	...	...	...	...	...	...	...	...	...	...	...	...	...	...	...	...	...	3	...
1	2nd Groom	...	...	...	...	...	...	...	...	...	...	...	...	...	...	...	...	...	...	...	1	...
40	"Rumour"	40	...	...	...	...	...	...	...	...	...	...	...	...	...	...	...	...	...	...	...	...
35	Page	...	...	17	...	...	16	...	2	...	...	...	...	...	...	...	...	...	...	...	...	...
189	Hostess	...	...	...	...	89	...	...	90	...	...	...	...	...	...	...	...	...	...	10	...	...
5	Lady Northumberland	...	...	...	...	...	...	5	...	...	...	...	...	...	...	...	...	...	...	...	...	...
46	Lady Percy	...	...	...	...	...	...	46	...	...	...	...	...	...	...	...	...	...	...	...	...	...
93	Doll Tearsheet	...	...	...	...	...	...	...	79	...	...	...	...	...	...	...	...	...	...	14	...	...
37	Dancer	...	...	...	...	...	...	...	...	...	...	...	...	...	...	...	...	...	...	...	...	37
3490		40	225	278	113	209	196	70	422	111	358	235	129	142	135	244	98	149	149	35	115	37
3446	Actual Number of Lines	40	215	278	110	209	196	68	421	108	358	228	123	142	132	241	98	145	147	35	115	37

SCHEME FOR ARRANGING THE PARTS WITH EIGHTEEN MEN.

NINE CHARACTERS SINGLY AND NINE GROUPS.

HARCOURT	8	96	MOWBRAY	56	96	MORTON	78	97	PISTOL	81	97
LORD BARDOLPH	86		DAVY	39		PETO	6		MOULDY	13	
SHADOW	2		2ND GROOM	1		FEEBLE	13		SNARE	3	

CLARENCE	23	95	GLOUCESTER	17	95	WARWICK	77	96	SERVANT	13	96	GOWER	8	97
COLEVILE	9		BARDOLPH	57		WART	2		HASTINGS	57		POINS	82	
TRAVERS	16		FANG	10		PORTER	4		BULLCALF	14		1ST GROOM	3	
SILENCE	47		1ST BEADLE	11		2ND DRAWER	13		1ST DRAWER	12		MESSENGER	4	

In Ladies' Parts omit DOLL TEARSHEET (see p. 30).

SUGGESTIONS FOR DISCUSSION.

1. Shakspere wrote 2 *Henry IV.* to show that State-hypocrisy and plebeian cheating, being one and the same thing in principle, are equally disastrous in their results.
2. Animosity against the Commons is the inspiring thought of 2 *Henry IV.*
3. The changes made in connection with the names of Oldcastle and Falstaff prove that Shakspere's sympathies were with the Protestant party.

EARLIEST KNOWN EDITION.

Date.	*Printer.*	*Publishers.*	*Acted by*	*Present Owners.*
1600	V. S.	Andrew Wise, and William Aspley	Lord Chamberlain's servants	British Museum. Bodleian Library. Trinity College, Cambridge. Duke of Devonshire. Mr. A. H. Huth.

There was some confusion in the printing of this edition, some copies of which have not the first scene of the third act.

This play was first entered in the Stationers' Registers on August 23, 1600 (see p. 103).

The book was published with the title "The Second part of Henrie the fourth, continuing to his death, and coronation of Henrie the fift. With the humours of sir Iohn Falstaffe, and swaggering Pistoll." It was stated to have "been sundrie times publikely acted," and to have been "Written by William Shakespeare."

In the 1613 Stanhope record (see p. 103) the play of "Sir John ffalstaffe" may be either this or *The Merry Wives of Windsor* (see pp. 107, 113).

In the Folio the title of the play is "The Second Part of Henry the Fourth, Containing his Death: and the Coronation of King Henry the Fift."

Henry Morley, in his edition of the play in Cassell's National Library, prints "The Death of Henry IV." from Daniel (see p. 63).

THE MERRY WIVES OF WINDSOR.

Total Number of Lines.	CHARACTERS.	I.				II.			III.					IV.						V.				
		1	2	3	4	1	2	3	1	2	3	4	5	1	2	3	4	5	6	1	2	3	4	5
137	SHALLOW	55	...	...	...	20	...	20	14	7	...	13	...	...	4	...	...	...	...	...	4	...	...	...
163	SLENDER	107	...	...	...	...	...	3	3	4	...	23	...	...	...	...	...	...	...	...	5	...	...	18
265	EVANS	85	12	...	...	...	...	...	57	..	15	...	...	39	11	..	12	9	...	...	...	...	4	21
174	PAGE	26	...	...	...	29	...	8	16	12	13	8	...	...	8	...	22	...	...	...	7	...	...	25
488	FALSTAFF...	19	...	52	...	...	120	...	...	...	40	...	105	...	15	...	...	44	...	28	...	...	...	65
29	BARDOLPH	6	...	2	...	...	5	...	...	...	...	...	5	...	...	5	...	6	...	...	...	...	...	...
61	PISTOL	6	...	28	...	13	7	...	...	...	...	...	...	...	...	...	...	...	...	...	...	...	...	7
37	NYM	6	...	21	...	10	...	...	...	...	...	...	...	...	...	...	...	...	...	...	...	...	...	...
51	SIMPLE	3	1	...	15	...	...	...	8	...	...	...	...	...	...	...	...	24	...	...	...	...	...	...
131	HOST	...	...	11	...	12	...	35	18	7	...	...	...	...	..	9	...	32	7	...	...	...	...	...
11	RUGBY	...	...	...	4	...	...	7	...	...	...	...	...	...	...	...	...	...	..	...	...	...	...	...
114	CAIUS	...	...	...	44	...	...	33	13	3	8	...	...	...	...	...	...	6	...	...	...	1	...	6
100	FENTON	...	...	...	14	...	...	...	...	...	...	27	...	...	...	...	...	...	48	...	..	...	...	11
339	FORD...	...	...	...	...	34	115	...	..	39	30	...	29	..	50	...	12	...	...	2	...	...	...	28
1	"ALL"	...	...	...	...	...	...	...	...	1	...	..	...	...	...	...	...	...	...	...	...	...	...	...
4	1ST SERVANT	...	...	...	...	...	...	...	...	...	1	...	...	...	3	...	...	...	...	...	...	...	...	...
2	2ND SERVANT	...	...	...	...	...	...	...	...	...	...	...	...	...	2	...	...	...	...	...	...	...	...	...
76	ANNE PAGE	13	...	..	...	..	...	...	...	...	...	18	...	...	...	...	...	...	...	...	...	...	...	45
254	MISTRESS QUICKLY	...	...	...	103	2	81	...	...	...	...	21	16	18	...	...	...	11	...	2	...	..	...	...
361	MISTRESS PAGE ...	...	...	...	...	83	...	...	...	18	67	8	...	17	80	...	43	...	...	...	...	19	...	26
209	MISTRESS FORD ...	...	...	...	...	45	...	...	...	...	75	...	...	...	67	...	7	...	...	...	...	5	...	10
15	ROBIN	...	...	...	...	...	1	...	...	3	11	...	...	...	...	...	...	...	...	...	...	...	...	...
13	WILLIAM PAGE ...	...	...	...	...	...	...	...	...	...	...	...	...	13	...	...	...	...	...	...	...	...	...	...
3035		326	13	114	180	248	329	106	129	94	260	118	155	87	240	14	96	132	55	32	16	25	4	262
3019	Actual No. of Lines	326	13	114	180	248	329	102	129	93	260	115	155	87	240	14	91	132	55	32	16	25	4	259

The 'Globe' gives the part of the Queen of the Fairies in V. 5 to Mistress Quickly. It should be taken by Anne Page (see IV. vi. 20).

SUGGESTIONS FOR DISCUSSION.

1. The confusion of time in *The Merry Wives of Windsor* confirms the tradition that the play was written in haste.
2. The low tone of *The Merry Wives of Windsor* was intended by Shakspere for the taste of the barbarian aristocrats, for whom it was especially ordered.
3. Shakspere introduced Falstaff as the hero of *The Merry Wives of Windsor* on purpose to degrade him.

LIST OF EARLIEST KNOWN EDITIONS.

Date.	*Printer.*	*Publisher.*	*Acted by*	*Present Owners.*
1602	T. C.	Arthur Iohnson	Lord Chamberlain's servants	Bodleian Library. Trinity College, Cambridge. Duke of Devonshire. Mr. A. H. Huth.
1619	— —	Arthur Johnson		British Museum. Bodleian Library. Trinity College, Cambridge.

Under date of January 18, 1602, are the following entries in the Stationers' Registers:—

John Busby Entred for his copie vnder the hand of master **Seton** A booke called *An excellent and pleasant conceited commedie of Sir Jon*N *FFAULSTOF and the merry wyves of Windesor* } vj^d *Conceited Commedie*

Arthure Johnson Entred for his Copye by assignement from **John Busbye**, A booke Called *an excellent and pleasant conceyted Comedie of Sir Jon*N *FFAULSTAFE and the merye wyves of Windsor* vj^1

To these entries Mr. Arber appends this note: "The word *conceited* not being very clearly written in the text, it is repeated at the side as here printed. It is quite clear that the *Merry Wives of Windsor* was printed by **J. Busby** before this date, but not entered in the Registers until he came to assign it to **A. Johnson.** See the similar case of *King Lear*." Mr. Furnivall, commenting upon this note (*Some 300 Fresh Allusions to Shakspere*, xxix.), says: "there is no reason whatever for supposing" this. The 1602 edition, reprinted by the Shakespeare Society and in Hazlitt's *Shakespeare's Library*, is a mere sketch compared with the Folio version. Its title is "A Most pleasaunt and excellent conceited Comedie, of Syr Iohn Falstaffe, and the merrie Wiues of Windsor. Entermixed with sundrie variable and pleasing humors, of Syr Hugh the Welch Knight, Iustice Shallow, and his wise Cousin M. Slender. With the swaggering vaine of Auncient Pistoll and Corporal Nym." It is said to be "By William Shakespeare," and to have been acted "Both before her Maiestie, and else-where."

The record that this play was acted at Whitehall early in November, 1604, is open to suspicion (see p. 71). In Cunningham's *Extracts* the entry follows a notice of a play acted on November 1, 1604 (see p. 143), and reads thus: "By his Ma^tis plaiers. .The Sunday ffollowinge A Play of the Merry Wiues of Winsor."

It is most likely that the play acted at Court in 1613, under the name of "Sir John ffalstaffe," was this play (compare the title in the 1602 entry and in the Quarto editions, and see pp. 103, 111).

The 1619 edition, having its title shorn of the mention of the middle group of characters, is practically a reprint of the 1602 copy.

In the 1623 Folio the title is simply "The Merry Wiues of Windsor."

Critics try to show that for the incidents of this comedy Shakspere had to consult many out-of-the-way sources. Some of these are printed in the 1821 *Variorum*, in Hazlitt's *Shakespeare's Library*, and by Henry Morley in his edition of the play in Cassell's National Library. According to many commentators it would seem that the invention of some of the situations of the play might have come within the powers of a Straparola, but that it was quite beyond a Shakspere. It is, however, not too much to believe that Shakspere was equal to devising its plot, and that if there is any likeness to the stories quoted, it is only through indirect influence and not direct inspiration. The alleged sources of this play can be ignored, unless the student wishes to learn how remotely-similar incidents were treated by writers of whom it is probable Shakspere had never heard.

The determination of the relative order of this and the other Falstaff-plays will be an exercise full of interest to the student, who must closely examine the introduction to the Shakespeare Society Edition of the 1602 Sketch, edited by Mr. Halliwell [Phillipps].

ANTONIO'S REVENGE.

Total Number of Lines.	CHARACTERS.	Prologue.	I.				II.		III.		IV.			V.		
			1	2	3	4	1	2	1	2	1	2	3	1	2	3
447	PIERO	...	91	...	...	36	88	59	7	...	...	122	...	...	...	44
63	STROTZO	...	19	..	...	8	...	8	...	...	...	28	...	...	...	...
25	LUCIO	...	...	19	...	...	...	3	...	...	3	...	...	...	...	...
549	ANTONIO	...	...	...	74	34	...	113	146	10	53	19	39	...	16	45
7	MATZAGENTE	...	...	...	7	...	...	..	...	...	...	...	...	...	..	...
68	ALBERTO	...	...	...	5	9	...	5	...	...	8	14	5	...	16	6
160	BALURDO	...	...	...	34	3	28	...	...	37	...	23	...	...	31	4
17	GALEATZO	...	...	...	7	...	...	...	...	...	...	...	...	...	...	10
254	PANDULPHO	...	...	...	5	44	65	2	1	...	...	...	77	...	34	26
5	FOROBOSCO	...	...	...	...	1	...	...	2	...	...	2	...	...	...	..
94	ANDRUGIO	...	...	...	...	...	...	...	22	25	...	...	...	25	...	22
1	FELICE	...	...	...	...	...	...	...	1	...	...	...	...	...	...	...
13	1ST SENATOR	...	...	...	...	...	...	...	...	...	...	1	...	...	...	12
8	2ND SENATOR	...	...	...	...	...	...	...	...	...	...	2	...	...	...	6
33	"PROLOGUE"	33	...	...	...	...	...	...	...	...	...	...	...	...	...	...
158	MARIA	..	...	39	13	4	...	11	23	17	5	30	...	...	...	16
31	NUTRICE	...	...	12	...	...	...	...	1	18	...	...	...	...	...	...
54	MELLIDA	...	...	..	...	...	...	34	...	...	...	20	...	...	...	...
1	1ST PAGE...	...	...	...	...	...	...	...	1	...	...	...	...	...	...	...
1	2ND PAGE	...	...	...	...	...	...	...	1	...	...	...	...	...	...	...
12	JULIO	...	...	...	...	...	...	...	12	...	...	...	...	...	...	...
2001		33	110	70	145	139	181	235	217	107	69	261	121	25	97	191
1976	Actual Number of Lines	33	110	69	143	138	181	228	214	107	69	253	120	25	97	189

For convenience of distribution of parts, the division of scenes is left as in *British Dramatists*. But Scenes 2 and 3 of Act I. should be one scene.

SUGGESTIONS FOR DISCUSSION.

1. Although Marston freely imitated Shakspere, there is also evidence that he furnished Shakspere with hints.
2. Marston's chief merits as a playwright are to be found in his comedies.
3. Taken altogether, Marston brings discredit on the Elizabethan drama.

EARLIEST KNOWN EDITION.

Date.	*Printer.*	*Publisher.*	*Acted by*	*Present Owner.*
1602	— —	Thomas Fisher	The Children of Paul's	British Museum.

This play, which is the second part of *Antonio and Mellida*, was entered in the Stationers' Registers on October 24, 1601 (see p. 109).

The title of the edition is "Antonio's Reuenge. The second part." The acting and authorship are referred to in the same words as in the first part.

Collier says that to one of these plays there may be a reference in Henslowe's note that he "Lent unto Wm Borne, the 28 of septembr 1599, to lend unto Mr maxton, the new poete (Mr Mastone), in earneste of a Boocke called ———, the some of xxxxs." (*Diary*, p. 156).

HENRY V.

Total Number of Lines.	CHARACTERS.		I.			II.					III.								IV.									V.		
		Prologue.	1	2	Prologue.	1	2	3	4	Prologue.	1	2	3	4	5	6	7	Prologue.	1	2	3	4	5	6	7	8	Prologue.	1	2	Epilogue.
223	Canterbury... ...	...	82	141	...	...	...	...	...	...	...	...	...	...	...	...	...	...	...	...	...	...	...	...	...	...	...	...	...	...
27	Ely	...	20	7	...	...	...	...	...	...	...	...	...	...	...	...	...	...	...	...	...	...	...	...	...	...	...	...	...	...
1063	King Henry... ...	...	...	120	...	...	137	...	...	...	34	...	51	...	...	45	...	...	213	...	95	...	...	12	65	58	...	...	233	...
130	Exeter	...	...	16	...	...	11	...	57	...	...	...	...	...	...	...	...	...	...	...	4	...	...	27	2	5	...	...	8	...
27	Westmoreland ...	...	...	14	...	...	3	...	...	...	...	...	...	...	...	...	...	...	...	...	7	...	...	...	...	...	...	...	3	...
17	1st Ambassador ...	...	...	17	...	...	...	...	...	...	...	...	...	...	...	...	...	...	...	...	...	...	...	...	...	...	...	...	...	...
34	Bardolph	...	...	...	...	26	...	6	...	...	...	2	...	...	...	...	...	...	...	...	...	...	...	...	...	...	...	...	...	...
53	Nym	...	...	...	...	42	...	5	...	...	...	6	...	...	...	...	...	...	...	...	...	...	...	...	...	...	...	...	...	...
163	Pistol	...	...	...	...	43	...	16	...	...	...	13	...	...	...	21	...	...	17	...	...	30	...	...	...	...	...	23	...	...
7	Bedford	...	...	...	...	...	3	...	...	...	...	...	...	...	...	...	...	...	...	...	4	...	...	...	...	...	...	...	...	...
13	Scroop	...	...	...	...	...	13	...	...	...	...	...	...	...	...	...	...	...	...	...	...	...	...	...	...	...	...	...	...	...
15	Cambridge	...	...	...	...	...	15	...	...	...	...	...	...	...	...	...	...	...	...	...	...	...	...	...	...	...	...	...	...	...
13	Grey	...	...	...	...	...	13	...	...	...	...	...	...	...	...	...	...	...	...	...	...	...	...	...	...	...	...	...	...	...
96	French King ...	...	...	...	...	...	...	...	42	...	...	...	...	...	28	...	...	...	...	...	...	...	...	...	...	...	...	...	26	...
121	Dauphin...	...	...	...	...	...	...	...	38	...	...	...	...	...	11	...	56	...	...	10	...	...	6	...	...	...	...	...	...	...
126	Constable	...	...	...	...	...	...	...	12	...	...	...	...	...	21	...	60	...	...	29	...	...	4	...	...	...	...	...	...	...
6	Messenger	...	...	...	...	...	...	...	2	...	...	...	...	...	...	...	3	...	...	1	...	...	...	...	...	...	...	...	...	...
310	Fluellen	...	...	...	...	...	...	...	...	...	...	48	...	...	...	66	...	...	17	...	...	...	...	...	83	43	...	53	...	...
75	Gower	...	...	...	...	...	...	...	...	...	...	14	...	...	...	23	...	...	4	...	...	...	...	...	15	1	...	18	...	...
12	Jamy	...	...	...	...	...	...	...	...	...	...	12	...	...	...	...	...	...	...	...	...	...	...	...	...	...	...	...	...	...
24	Macmorris	...	...	...	...	...	...	...	...	...	...	24	...	...	...	...	...	...	...	...	...	...	...	...	...	...	...	...	...	...
7	Governor	...	...	...	...	...	...	...	...	...	...	...	7	...	...	...	...	...	...	...	...	...	...	...	...	...	...	...	...	...
18	Bourbon	...	...	...	...	...	...	...	...	...	...	...	...	...	9	...	...	...	...	...	...	...	9	...	...	...	...	...	...	...
54	Montjoy	...	...	...	...	...	...	...	...	...	...	...	...	...	...	25	...	...	...	...	13	...	...	...	16	...	...	...	...	...
5	Gloucester ...	...	...	...	...	...	...	...	...	...	...	...	...	...	...	1	...	...	2	...	1	...	...	...	1	...	...	...	...	...
49	Orleans	...	...	...	...	...	...	...	...	...	...	...	...	...	...	...	41	...	...	3	...	...	5	...	...	...	...	...	...	...
11	Rambures	...	...	...	...	...	...	...	...	...	...	...	...	...	...	...	9	...	...	2	...	...	...	...	...	...	...	...	...	...
7	Erpingham	...	...	...	...	...	...	...	...	...	...	...	...	...	...	...	...	...	7	...	...	...	...	...	...	...	...	...	...	...
2	Court	...	...	...	...	...	...	...	...	...	...	...	...	...	...	...	...	...	2	...	...	...	...	...	...	...	...	...	...	...
21	Bates	...	...	...	...	...	...	...	...	...	...	...	...	...	...	...	...	...	21	...	...	...	...	...	...	...	...	...	...	...
81	Williams	...	...	...	...	...	...	...	...	...	...	...	...	...	...	...	...	...	46	...	...	...	...	...	12	23	...	...	...	...
18	Grandpré	...	...	...	...	...	...	...	...	...	...	...	...	...	...	...	...	...	...	18	...	...	...	...	...	...	...	...	...	...
9	Salisbury	...	...	...	...	...	...	...	...	...	...	...	...	...	...	...	...	...	...	...	9	...	...	...	...	...	...	...	...	...
2	York	...	...	...	...	...	...	...	...	...	...	...	...	...	...	...	...	...	...	...	2	...	...	...	...	...	...	...	...	...
20	French Soldier	...	...	...	...	...	...	...	...	...	...	...	...	...	...	...	...	...	...	...	...	20	...	...	...	...	...	...	...	...
1	Warwick	...	...	...	...	...	...	...	...	...	...	...	...	...	...	...	...	...	...	...	...	...	...	...	...	1	...	...	...	...
1	English Herald	...	...	...	...	...	...	...	...	...	...	...	...	...	...	...	...	...	...	...	...	...	...	...	...	1	...	...	...	...
68	Burgundy	...	...	...	...	...	...	...	...	...	...	...	...	...	...	...	...	...	...	...	...	...	...	...	...	...	...	...	68	...
2	"All"	...	...	...	...	...	...	...	...	...	...	...	...	...	...	...	...	...	...	...	...	...	...	...	...	...	...	...	2	...
223	"Chorus"	34	...	...	42	...	...	...	...	35	...	...	...	...	...	...	...	53	...	...	...	...	...	...	...	...	45	...	...	14
47	Hostess	...	...	...	...	17	...	30	...	...	...	...	...	...	...	...	...	...	...	...	...	...	...	...	...	...	...	...	...	...
80	Boy	...	...	...	...	5	...	9	...	...	...	34	...	...	...	...	...	...	...	...	...	32	...	...	...	...	...	...	...	...
73	Katharine	...	...	...	...	...	...	...	...	...	...	...	...	42	...	...	...	...	...	...	...	...	...	...	...	...	...	...	31	...
33	Alice	...	...	...	...	...	...	...	...	...	...	...	...	24	...	...	...	...	...	...	...	...	...	...	...	...	...	...	9	...
24	Isabel	...	...	...	...	...	...	...	...	...	...	...	...	...	...	...	...	...	...	...	...	...	...	...	...	...	...	...	24	...
3411		34	102	315	42	133	195	66	151	35	34	153	58	66	69	181	169	53	329	63	135	82	24	39	194	132	45	94	404	14
3380	Actual No. of Lines	34	98	310	42	133	193	66	146	35	34	153	58	66	68	181	169	53	326	63	132	82	23	38	191	131	45	94	402	14

SCHEME FOR ARRANGING THE PARTS WITH EIGHTEEN MEN.

ELEVEN CHARACTERS SINGLY AND SEVEN GROUPS.

SALISBURY	9	66	SCROOP	13	68	WESTMORELAND	27	67
WARWICK	1		MONTJOY	54		JAMY	12	
ERPINGHAM	7		E. HERALD	1		BATES	21	
ORLEANS	49					GOVERNOR	7	

CAMBRIDGE	15	67	GLOUCESTER	5	68	BEDFORD	7	68	YORK	2	69
MACMORRIS	24		ELY	27		COURT	2		GREY	13	
RAMBURES	11		BOURBON	18		NYM	53		BARDOLPH	34	
1ST AMBASSADOR	17		GRANDPRÉ	18		MESSENGER	6		F. SOLDIER	20	

SUGGESTIONS FOR DISCUSSION.

1. The Quartos of *Henry V.* were pirated copies of Shakspere's work, which, for stage-purposes, he had shortened from the original play as it appears in the Folio.
2. *Henry V.* contains a manifesto of the political scheme of the friends of Essex.
3. Henry V. is Shakspere's ideal of highest manhood.

LIST OF EARLIEST KNOWN EDITIONS.

Date.	*Printer.*	*Publisher.*	*Acted by*	*Present Owners.*
1600	Thomas Creede	Tho. Millington and Iohn Busby	Lord Chamberlain's servants	British Museum. Bodleian Library. Trinity College, Cambridge. Duke of Devonshire. Mr. A. H. Huth.
1602	Thomas Creede	Thomas Pauier	Lord Chamberlain's servants	Trinity College, Cambridge. Duke of Devonshire.
1608	———	T. P.	Lord Chamberlain's servants	British Museum. Bodleian Library. Trinity College, Cambridge. Duke of Devonshire. Mr. A. H. Huth.

In the Stationers' Registers is this entry :—

1594. May 14.
Thomas Creede. Entred for his copie vnder thand of master **Cawood** warden a booke intituled. *The famous victories of HENRYE the FFYFT conteyninge the honorable battell of Agincourt* vj[d] C

This play was acted by the Queen's servants. The earliest known edition is one of 1598 (see p. 107).

Henslowe notes several performances of "harey the v," the first of which is on November 28, 1595, when the play was marked as a new one (*Diary*, p. 61).

In 1600 the first of the editions mentioned in the table was brought out, entitled "The Cronicle History of Henry the fift, With his battell fought at Agin Court in France. Togither with Auntient Pistoll." It had no author's name, but was said to have "bene sundry times playd."

On August 4, 1600, "Henry the ffift" was entered in the Registers (see p. 99) with a memorandum of restriction as to printing. In the same month is this entry :—

1600. August 14.
Thomas Pavyer Entred for his Copyes by Direction of master **white** warden vnder his hand wrytinge. These Copyes followinge beinge thinges formerlye printed and sett over to the sayd **Thomas Pavyer.**

viz

. . . .

The historye of HENRY the Vth with the battell of Agencourt vj[d]

. . . .

The 1602 edition has the same title as its predecessor, and is also anonymous.

Cunningham records (see p. 71) a performance of this play at Whitehall in 1605. "By his Matis plaiers. On the 7 of January was played the play of Henry the fift."

The title of the 1608 edition differs only in spelling from that of the others. There is no author's name.

In the Folio the play is called "The Life of Henry the Fift."

In 1603 *Henry V.* was referred to as "the p'aie of Ancient Pistoll" (Halliwell-Phillipps, *Outlines*, II. 330). This is another instance of plays being sometimes known by subordinate portions of their titles (see pp. 107, 111, 113).

On the question of the relation of the Quartos to the Folio, the student should consult Mr. P. A. Daniel's Introduction to the Parallel Text edition of the play issued by the New Shakspere Society, and Dr. Brinsley Nicholson's paper in the Society's *Transactions*, 1880—2, Part I.

POEMS AND SONNETS.

SUGGESTIONS FOR DISCUSSION.

1. *Venus and Adonis* is not so fine a poem as *Hero and Leander*.
2. *Venus and Adonis* and *Lucrece* were written before Shakspere left Stratford.
3. *The Passionate Pilgrim*, regarded in the light of the facts connected with its first publication, should be excluded from all future editions of Shakspere's works.
4. The 'W. H.' of the Sonnets is Shakspere's brother-in-law.
5. The 'Dark Woman' of the Sonnets (identified as Mary Fitton) can be traced through all the early plays.
6. It is astounding that for fame Shakspere relied only upon the Sonnets, looking to the fact that, except as connected with his life, they are wearisome and uninteresting.

VENUS AND ADONIS.

LIST OF EARLIEST KNOWN EDITIONS.

Date.	*Printer.*	*Publisher.*	*Present Owners.*
1593	Richard Field	———	Bodleian Library.
1594	Richard Field	———	British Museum. Bodleian Library. Mr. A. H. Huth.
1596	R. F.	Iohn Harison	British Museum. Bodleian Library.
1599	———	William Leake	Sir Charles Isham.
1602	———	William Leake	British Museum.
1602	———	William Leake	Bodleian Library.
1617	———	W. B.	Bodleian Library.
1620	———	I. P.	Bodleian Library. Trinity College, Cambridge.

The entries of this poem in the Stationers' Registers before 1623 are as follows:—

1593. April 18.

Richard ffeild Entred for his copie vnder thandes of the Archbisshop of CANTERBURY and master warden **Stirrop**, a booke intituled *VENUS and ADONIS*. **vj^d S.**

Assigned ouer to master **Harrison** *senior* 25 *Junij* 1594

1594. June 25.

Master **Harrison** *Senior*. Assigned ouer vnto him from **Richard ffeild** in open Court holden this Day a book called *VENUS and ADONIS* **vj^d**

The which was before entred to **Richard ffeild**. 18. *aprilis* 1593

1596. June 25.

William leeke Assigned ouer vnto him for his copie from master **harrison** thelder, in full Court holden this day. by the said master **harrisons** consent. A booke called. *VENUS and ADONIS* **vj^d**

In 1607 Robert Raworth, a master-printer, who, with John Monger, had bought Adam Islip's business, was "suppresst for printing anothers Copy" of *Venus and Adonis*.

In 1617 Leake transferred the copyright to Barrett (see p. 105), who afterwards assigned it to Parker:—

1620. March 8.

John Parker. Assigned ouer vnto him with the consent of Master **Barrett**, and order of a full Court holden this Day all his right in theis Copies following **viij^s vj^d**

vizt

. . . .

VENUS and ADONIS

. . . .

Neither of the editions has the author's name on the title-page, but each has a dedication signed "William Shakespeare." The editors of the 'Cambridge' *Shakespeare* name an edition of 1600, said to have been published by Harrison; but this copy, which is in the Bodleian, has its title-page in manuscript. Looking at the history of the copyright given above, it is impossible that Harrison could have issued an edition in that year. The 'Cambridge' editors say of the 1602 editions that "a comparison of the two proves to demonstration that they were different editions."

It is not necessary to imagine that for the incidents of this poem Shakspere had to turn to any written authorities.

LUCRECE.

LIST OF EARLIEST KNOWN EDITIONS.

Date.	*Printer.*	*Publisher.*	*Present Owners.*
1594	Richard Field	Iohn Harrison	British Museum. Bodleian Library. Sion College. Duke of Devonshire. Mr. A. H. Huth.
1598	P. S.	Iohn Harrison	Trinity College, Cambridge.
1600	I. H.	Iohn Harrison	Bodleian Library.
1607	N. O.	Iohn Harrison	Trinity College, Cambridge. Lady Ellesmere.
1616	T. S.	Roger Iackson	Bodleian Library.
1616	J. G.	J. Stafford	British Museum.

The following is the first entry of this poem in the Stationers' Registers :—

1594. May 9.

Master **harrison** *Senior* Entred for his copie vnder thand of master **Cawood** Warden, a booke intituled *the Ravyshement of Lucrece* **vjd C**

In the Bodleian there are two copies, which are not alike.

There is in the Registers this entry :—

1608. June 3.

John Busby **Nathanael Butter.** Entred for their copie vnder thandes of Sir George Buck. knight and the Wardens. A Booke called . *A Romane tragedie called 'The Rape of Lucrece'* **vjd**

This is Thomas Heywood's play, which afterwards went through several editions.

The transfer of the copyright of the poem is thus recorded :—

1614. March 1.

Roger Jackson Entred for his Coppies by consent of Master **John Harrison** the eldest and by order of a Court, these 4 bookes followinge **ijs**

vizt

. . . .

Lucrece.

The editions from 1594 to 1607 give no name of author on title-page, but, as in *Venus and Adonis*, each is accompanied by a dedication bearing the signature "William Shakespeare," whose name in 1616 appeared on the title-page of the editions published in that year, the date when the poem was said to be "newly reuised." Each edition has an "argument," giving the story in a short prose-outline, the authorship of which is uncertain.

The incidents recorded in this poem had early found their way into ballad-literature. "The grevious complaynt of Lucrece," entered in the Registers in 1568-9; "The Death of Lucryssia," 1569-70, are instances of the popular treatment of a subject which had engaged the attention of various writers from Chaucer onwards.

It would be interesting to have a paper on the notices which Shakspere's poems received from his contemporaries, who seem to have been more favourably impressed by the poems than they were by the plays.

THE PASSIONATE PILGRIM.

LIST OF EARLIEST KNOWN EDITIONS.

Date.	*Printer.*	*Publisher.*	*Present Owners.*
1599	For W. Iaggard	W. Leake	Trinity College, Cambridge.
1612	W. Iaggard		Bodleian Library.

This collection of poems, by various authors, was not entered in the Stationers' Registers.

The title of the 1599 edition is merely "The Passionate Pilgrime. By W. Shakespeare."

On the title-page the 1612 edition is called the third edition. It is entitled "The Passionate Pilgrime. or Certaine Amorous Sonnets, betweene Venus and Adonis, newly corrected and augmented. By W. Shakespere. The third Edition. Whereunto is newly added two Loue-Epistles, the first from Paris to Hellen, and Hellens answere backe againe to Paris." These love-epistles were from a work by Thomas Heywood, who took exception to their Shaksperian association in the title. He speaks (*Apology for Actors*, ed. Shakespeare Society, p. 62) of the inJury done to his "Britaines Troy" by printing these poems "in a lesse volume under the name of another"—a strange and slightingly vague way of alluding to Shakspere in the year 1612. The Bodleian copy has two title-pages, in one of which Shakspere's name is omitted.

A full analysis of the contents of the 1599 edition is given in the 1821 *Variorum*. A very useful account may be found in Halliwell-Phillipps's *Outlines* (Vol. I. pp. 375-8), and a briefer one in Furnivall's Introduction to the 'Leopold' *Shakspere* (pp. xxxv.-vi.).

In almost the same words three of the sections of *The Passionate Pilgrim* were in the 1598 *Love's Labour's Lost*. That one which comes in "Sonnets To sundry notes of Musicke"—a separate part of the 1599 collection--was also printed in 1600 in *England's Helicon* as "The Passionate Shepherd's Song," with "W. Shakespeare" attached. *England's Helicon* contained some other parts of *The Passionate Pilgrim*.

THE PHŒNIX AND THE TURTLE.

This poem, over the name of "William Shake-speare," is first met with in a book published in 1601 under the following title: "Loves Martyr: or, Rosalins Complaint. Allegorically shadowing the truth of Loue, in the constant Fate of the Phœnix and Turtle. A Poeme enterlaced with much varietie and raritie; now first translated out of the venerable Italian Torquato Cæliano, by Robert Chester. With the true legend of famous King Arthur, the last of the nine Worthies, being the first Essay of a new Brytish Poet: collected out of diuerse Authenticall Records. To these are added some new compositions, of seuerall moderne Writers whose names are subscribed to their seuerall workes, vpon the first subiect: viz. the Phœnix and Turtle." The Rev. Alexander B. Grosart, in his edition of *Love's Martyr*, issued as one of the New Shakspere Society's volumes, says "by the 'Phœnix' Shakespeare intended Elizabeth, and by the 'Dove' Essex, and the 'Phœnix and Turtle,' hitherto regarded as a mere enigmatical epicedial lay . . . . will be recognized as of rarest interest" (pp. lx.-i.). The whole of Dr. Grosart's Introduction should be studied. Mr. Furnivall controverts Dr. Grosart's views (New Shakspere Society's *Transactions*, 1877-9, Part III.).

THE SONNETS.

EARLIEST KNOWN EDITION.

Date.	*Printer.*	*Publisher.*	*Present Owners*
1609	G. Eld for T. T.	Iohn Wright	British Museum. Bodleian Library. Trinity College, Cambridge. Bentinck's Library, Varel.

Of this edition some copies, of which the British Museum has one, have "William Aspley' on the title-page in place of Wright's name.

In 1598 Meres, referring to Shakspere, mentions "his sugred sonnets among his priuate friends." It is not known what these were.

In substantially the same form, two of the Sonnets are first seen in print in the 1599 *Passionate Pilgrim*.

In the Stationers' Registers is this entry:—

1609. May 20.
Thomas Thorpe Entred for his copie vnder thandes of master WILSON and master **Lownes** Warden a Booke called SHAKESPEARES *sonnettes* vj^d

The edition has the title "Shake-speares Sonnets. Neuer before Imprinted."

The critical student of the Sonnets can always find occupation in demolishing the theories that have been offered in their explanation.

The edition edited by William Sharp and published by Walter Scott (1887) is a useful companion.

A LOVER'S COMPLAINT.

"A Louers complaint. By William Shake-speare," was printed at the end of the edition of the Sonnets.

A WOMAN KILLED WITH KINDNESS.

Total Number of Lines.	CHARACTERS.	Prologue.	I.		II.		III.				IV.					V.				Epilogue.
			1	2	1	2	1	2	3	4	1	2	3	4	5	1	2	3	4	
183	SIR FRANCIS ACTON ...	...	49	...	16	...	...	...	35	...	23	...	...	...	...	27	...	...	33	...
370	SIR CHARLES MOUNTFORD	...	45	...	67	...	27	...	48	...	...	87	...	...	...	87	...	...	9	...
248	WENDOLL	...	6	...	8	15	...	114	...	23	...	...	28	...	...	...	...	54	...	...
427	FRANKFORD	...	12	...	...	55	...	...	...	127	...	...	52	...	125	..	23	...	33	...
39	CRANWELL	...	4	...	2	...	6	...	...	5	...	...	11	...	1	...	5	...	5	...
31	MALBY	...	1	...	...	...	5	...	6	...	6	...	...	...	...	2	..	...	11	...
133	JENKIN	...	...	22	...	13	...	19	...	21	...	...	3	23	4	...	...	16	12	...
149	NICHOLAS...	...	...	17	...	18	...	19	...	47	...	...	9	...	18	...	4	15	2	...
16	JACK SLIME	...	...	16	...	...	...	...	...	...	...	...	...	...	...	...	...	...	...	...
3	ROGER BRICKBAT	...	...	3	...	...	...	...	...	...	...	...	...	...	...	...	...	...	...	..
5	"ALL"	...	...	2	...	...	...	...	...	...	...	...	...	...	2	...	...	...	1	...
1	FALCONER...	...	...	...	1	...	...	...	...	...	...	...	...	...	...	...	...	...	...	...
9	SHERIFF	..	...	...	9	...	...	...	...	...	...	...	...	...	...	...	...	...	...	...
17	KEEPER	...	...	...	...	...	2	...	...	...	...	15	...	...	...	...	...	...	...	...
38	SHAFTON	...	...	...	...	...	19	...	19	...	...	...	...	...	...	...	...	...	...	...
6	BUTLER	...	...	...	...	...	...	...	...	6	...	...	...	...	...	...	...	...	...	...
7	OLD MOUNTFORD	...	..	...	...	...	...	...	...	...	7	...	..	...	...	...	...	...	...	...
5	SANDY	...	...	...	...	...	...	...	...	...	5	...	...	...	...	...	...	...	...	...
4	RODER	...	...	...	...	...	...	...	...	...	4	...	...	...	...	...	...	...	...	...
4	TIDY	...	...	...	...	...	...	...	...	...	4	...	...	...	...	...	...	...	...	.
7	SERVING-MAN	...	...	...	...	...	...	...	...	...	...	...	...	7	...	...	...	...	...	...
2	CARTER	...	...	...	..	...	...	...	...	...	...	...	...	...	...	...	...	2	...	...
14	"PROLOGUE"	14	...	...	...	...	...	...	...	...	...	...	...	...	...	...	...	...	...	...
234	MISTRESS FRANKFORD ..	...	9	...	...	12	...	44	...	17	...	...	23	...	44	...	...	54	31	...
23	SISLY	...	...	3	...	7	...	...	...	...	...	...	...	8	...	...	...	3	2	...
141	SUSAN	...	..	...	23	...	...	...	9	...	28	26	...	...	...	49	...	...	6	...
18	"EPILOGUE"	...	...	...	...	...	...	...	...	...	...	...	...	...	...	...	...	..	...	18
2134		14	126	63	126	120	59	196	117	246	77	128	126	38	194	165	32	144	145	18
2044	Actual Number of Lines	14	116	63	109	113	58	189	112	240	75	125	117	38	188	156	31	141	141	18

In *British Dramatists* there is no division of Acts or Scenes. The arrangement of Scenes is obvious. It will, however, be better to let Act V. have only the last Scene.

SCHEME FOR ARRANGING THE PARTS WITH EIGHTEEN MEN.

FIFTEEN CHARACTERS SINGLY AND THREE GROUPS.

TIDY 4, CARTER 2 } 6	SANDY 5, FALCONER 1 } 6	ROGER 3, RODER 4 } 7

SUGGESTIONS FOR DISCUSSION.

1. Taking the limits within which it is to be regarded, the moral sentiment of *A Woman Killed with Kindness* is admirable.
2. Thomas Heywood's manner in domestic drama is a model for playwrights.
3. Judged by his writings, Thomas Heywood—whether looked upon as a dramatist, actor, or man—deserves the very highest respect.

LIST OF EARLIEST KNOWN EDITIONS.

Date.	*Printer.*	*Publisher.*	*Acted by*	*Present Owners.*
1607	William Iaggard	Iohn Hodgets		British Museum.
1617	Isaac Iaggard	———	The Queen's servants	British Museum.

On February 5, 1603, Henslowe "Pd unto Thomas hewode, for a womones gowne of blacke vellvett, for the playe of a womon Kylld with Kyndnes, some of vj^{li} 13^{s}." On the 12th of the same month he "Pd at the apoyntment of the company, unto Thomas Heywood, in pt of payment for his playe called A womon kylled with Kyndnes, the some of iij^{li}." On the 6th of the following month he "Pd at the apoyntment of the company, unto Thomas Hewode, in fulle payment for his playe called a womon Kyld with Kyndnes, the some of iij^{li}"; and the next day he "Pd at the apoyntment of Thomas Blackewod, unto the tayller which made the blacke satten sewt for the woman Kyld with Kyndnes, the some of x^{s}" (*Diary*, pp. 248–50).

The title of the 1607 edition is merely "A Woman kilde with Kindnesse." It is said to be "Written by Tho: Heywood."

The title of the 1617 copy, which is described as "The third Edition," is the same as that of 1607, and the author's name is given in the same form.

This play was not entered in the Stationers' Registers.

AS YOU LIKE IT.

Total Number of Lines.	CHARACTERS.	I.			II.							III.					IV.			V.			
		1	2	3	1	2	3	4	5	6	7	1	2	3	4	5	1	2	3	1	2	3	4
322	ORLANDO	68	40	...	...	...	23	...	...	16	32	...	62	...	...	...	41	...	...	...	29	...	11
66	ADAM	7	...	...	...	...	54	...	...	3	2	...	...	...	...	...	...	...	...	...	...	...	...
154	OLIVER...	62	...	...	...	...	...	...	...	...	...	2	...	...	...	...	...	...	80	...	10	...	...
3	DENNIS...	3	...	...	...	...	...	...	...	...	...	...	...	...	...	...	...	...	...	...	...	...	...
45	CHARLES	40	5	...	...	...	...	...	...	...	...	...	...	...	...	...	...	...	...	...	...	...	...
316	TOUCHSTONE	...	30	...	...	...	...	26	...	...	...	...	70	76	...	...	...	...	...	49	...	11	54
53	LE BEAU	...	53	...	...	...	...	...	...	...	...	...	...	...	...	...	...	...	...	...	...	...	...
69	DUKE FREDERICK ...	...	21	24	...	8	...	...	...	...	...	16	...	...	...	...	...	...	...	...	...	...	...
111	DUKE SENIOR	...	...	...	29	...	...	...	...	...	51	...	...	...	...	...	...	...	...	...	...	...	31
53	AMIENS...	...	...	...	3	...	...	...	30	...	20	...	...	...	...	...	...	...	...	...	...	...	...
43	1ST LORD (DUKE SENIOR)...	...	...	...	39	...	...	...	...	...	3	...	...	...	...	...	...	1	...	...	...	...	...
2	2ND LORD " ...	...	...	...	2	...	...	...	...	...	...	...	...	...	...	...	...	...	...	...	...	...	...
4	1ST LORD (DUKE FRED.)...	...	...	...	...	4	...	...	...	...	...	...	...	...	...	...	...	...	...	...	...	...	...
9	2ND LORD " ...	...	...	...	...	9	...	...	...	...	...	...	...	...	...	...	...	...	...	...	...	...	...
75	CORIN	...	...	...	...	...	...	26	...	...	...	...	37	...	10	...	...	...	...	2	...	...	...
76	SILVIUS	...	...	...	...	...	...	19	...	...	...	...	...	...	...	29	...	...	14	...	13	...	1
235	JAQUES	...	...	...	...	...	...	...	35	...	100	...	24	16	...	...	18	8	...	...	...	...	34
5	SIR OLIVER...	...	...	...	...	...	...	...	...	...	...	...	...	5	...	...	...	...	...	...	...	...	...
10	FORESTER	...	...	...	...	...	...	...	...	...	...	...	...	...	...	...	...	10	...	...	...	...	...
11	WILLIAM	...	...	...	...	...	...	...	...	...	...	...	...	...	...	...	...	...	...	11	...	...	...
24	"HYMEN"	...	...	...	...	...	...	...	...	...	...	...	...	...	...	...	...	...	...	...	...	...	24
6	"ALL" (SONG)	...	...	...	...	...	...	...	...	...	...	...	...	...	...	...	...	...	...	...	...	...	6
17	JAQUES DE BOYS	...	...	...	...	...	...	...	...	...	...	...	...	...	...	...	...	...	...	...	...	...	17
304	CELIA	...	93	66	...	...	...	7	...	...	...	...	72	...	32	...	12	...	22	...	...	...	...
749	ROSALIND	...	63	57	...	...	...	26	...	...	...	...	192	...	22	43	153	...	74	...	74	...	45
23	AUDREY	...	...	...	...	...	...	...	...	...	...	...	...	12	...	...	...	...	...	7	...	4	...
87	PHEBE	...	...	...	...	...	...	...	...	...	...	...	...	...	...	72	...	...	...	...	9	...	6
31	1ST PAGE	...	...	...	...	...	...	...	...	...	...	...	...	...	...	...	...	...	...	...	...	31	...
27	2ND PAGE	...	...	...	...	...	...	...	...	...	...	...	...	...	...	...	...	...	...	...	...	27	...
2930		180	305	147	73	21	77	104	65	19	208	18	457	109	64	144	224	19	190	69	135	73	229
2867	Actual Number of Lines	180	301	140	69	21	76	100	65	19	203	18	457	109	62	139	224	19	184	69	135	49	228

SCHEME FOR ARRANGING THE PARTS WITH EIGHTEEN MEN.

FIFTEEN CHARACTERS SINGLY AND THREE GROUPS.

SIR OLIVER 5	DENNIS 3	WILLIAM 11
2ND LORD (DUKE F.) 9	FORESTER 10	1ST LORD (DUKE F.) 4
	2ND LORD (DUKE S.) 2	
14	15	15

SUGGESTIONS FOR DISCUSSION.

1. Shakspere founded *As You Like It* upon a similar play, and not directly upon Lodge's *Rosalynde*.
2. It is a characteristic evidence of Shakspere's intention to be a moral teacher that he altered the fate of Duke Frederick.
3. From *As You Like It* much may be gathered to show the influence of poets upon one another.

THE EARLIEST KNOWN EDITION IS THE 1623 FOLIO.

On August 4, 1600, there is an entry of this play in the Stationers' Registers (see p. 99). The restriction then imposed upon its printing does not seem to have been removed, as in the case of the plays mentioned with it. The publishers of the Folio in 1623 included *As You Like It* in their entry in the Registers, evidently considering that the 1600 entry did not bring the play within the category of those which had been "formerly entred to other men."

Thomas Lodge's novel, *Rosalynde*, the first edition of which was published in 1590, should be studied in connection with this play. It is reprinted in Hazlitt's *Shakespeare's Library* and in Cassell's National Library. In the latter series, *The Tale of Gamelyn*, for some time attributed to Chaucer, is reprinted with *As You Like It*, as it is probable that Lodge was indebted to it.

THE LONDON PRODIGAL.

Total Number of Lines.	CHARACTERS.	I.		II.				III.			IV.			V.
		1	2	1	2	3	4	1	2	3	1	2	3	1
266	Flowerdale senior ...	85	...	15	...	...	15	...	60	34	...	...	12	45
124	Flowerdale junior ...	56	...	...	...	...	...	...	11	45	...	...	...	12
398	Matthew Flowerdale	92	21	20	...	...	..	...	53	47	...	29	...	136
373	Sir Lancelot	...	56	34	17	...	75	...	56	46	32	...	...	57
49	Artichoke	...	4	6	...	...	22	...	...	...	...	4	9	4
92	Weathercock	...	19	11	12	...	19	...	...	8	12	...	...	11
32	Daffodill	...	19	...	9	...	...	...	...	4	...	...	...	...
90	Civet	...	19	...	...	...	...	28	...	2	18	...	17	6
6	Drawer	...	6	...	...	...	...	...	...	...	...	...	...	...
65	Sir Arthur	...	...	13	...	16	...	...	...	20	5	2	...	9
4	Soldier	...	...	4	...	...	...	...	...	...	...	...	...	...
156	Oliver	...	...	32	...	...	37	...	...	25	14	10	...	38
9	Ralph	...	...	...	...	...	..	...	...	...	...	...	...	9
7	Ruffian	...	...	...	...	...	...	...	...	...	...	...	...	7
7	Citizen	...	...	...	...	...	...	...	..	...	...	...	...	7
53	Frances	...	4	...	...	...	...	7	...	9	11	...	13	9
122	Luce	...	4	3	4	11	...	...	...	46	...	...	18	36
69	Delia	...	...	...	...	...	...	25	...	4	2	14	12	12
12	Citizen's Wife	...	...	...	...	...	...	...	...	...	...	...	...	12
1934		233	152	138	42	27	168	60	180	290	94	59	81	410
1926	Actual Number of Lines	233	151	137	42	27	167	60	180	286	94	59	81	409

SUGGESTIONS FOR DISCUSSION.

1. As it can be shown that *Faire Em* is by Shakspere, *The London Prodigal* must also be ascribed to him (see Suggestion 1. p. 97).

2. The plot of *The London Prodigal* tells the story of a rivalship between Greene, Marlowe, and Peele for the office of poet to the Queen's servants.

3. The fact that Shakspere acted in *The London Prodigal*, and in other plays, was enough to excite the indignation of Nash and Greene at this degradation of an author's position.

EARLIEST KNOWN EDITION.

Date.	*Printer.*	*Publisher.*	*Acted by*	*Present Owners.*
1605	T. C.	Nathaniel Butter	The King's servants	British Museum. Bodleian Library. Trinity College, Cambridge. Duke of Devonshire.

The title of this edition is merely "The London Prodigall." It is said to be "By William Shakespeare."

Richard Simpson's researches (*The School of Shakspere*, Vol. II.) led him to think that *The London Prodigal* was acted before 1592. If so, the existing play is probably a revised form.

This play was not entered in the Stationers' Registers.

TWELFTH NIGHT.

Total Number of Lines.	CHARACTERS.	I.					II.					III.				IV.			V.
		1	2	3	4	5	1	2	3	4	5	1	2	3	4	1	2	3	1
221	DUKE	31	...	...	27	...	...	...	...	69	...	...	...	...	...	...	...	...	94
7	CURIO	2	...	...	...	...	...	...	...	5	...	...	...	...	...	...	...	...	...
14	VALENTINE	9	...	...	5	...	...	...	...	...	...	...	...	...	...	...	...	...	...
32	CAPTAIN	...	32	...	...	...	...	...	...	...	...	...	...	...	...	...	...	...	...
398	SIR TOBY...	..	...	67	...	7	...	...	63	...	44	7	36	...	144	10	13	...	7
183	SIR ANDREW	...	...	53	...	...	...	...	51	...	15	7	12	...	18	7	...	...	20
344	CLOWN	...	...	...	...	66	...	...	33	29	..	42	...	...	...	20	77	...	77
306	MALVOLIO	...	...	...	...	35	...	14	20	...	115	...	...	...	58	...	45	...	19
107	ANTONIO	...	...	...	...	...	13	...	...	...	...	...	...	33	33	...	...	...	28
128	SEBASTIAN	...	...	...	...	...	36	...	...	...	...	...	...	20	...	17	...	23	32
128	FABIAN	...	...	...	...	...	...	...	...	...	33	...	25	...	40	...	...	...	30
4	SERVANT	..	...	...	...	...	...	...	...	...	...	...	...	...	4	...	...	...	...
12	1ST OFFICER	...	...	...	...	...	...	...	...	...	...	...	...	...	6	...	...	...	6
4	2ND OFFICER	...	...	...	...	...	...	...	...	..	...	...	...	...	4	...	...	...	...
8	PRIEST	...	...	...	...	...	...	...	...	...	...	...	...	...	...	...	...	...	8
353	VIOLA	..	34	...	13	75	...	28	...	32	...	69	..	...	56	...	...	...	46
169	MARIA	.	...	31	...	25	...	...	41	...	20	...	17	...	29	...	6	...	...
321	OLIVIA	...	...	...	...	127	...	...	...	...	...	54	...	...	45	16	...	12	67
2739		42	66	151	45	335	49	42	208	135	227	179	90	53	437	70	141	35	434
2692	Actual No. of Lines	41	64	151	42	330	49	42	208	127	227	176	90	49	433	69	141	35	418

SUGGESTIONS FOR DISCUSSION.

1. As *Twelfth Night* is Shakspere's last play dominated by the genial spirit of Comedy, the date of its production is that of a change in his circumstances altering his view of life.

2. Shakspere in *Twelfth Night* made his grand attack on the Puritan party.

3. In *Twelfth Night*, Shakspere satirised Marston as Malvolio and Ben Jonson as Sir Toby Belch.

THE EARLIEST KNOWN EDITION IS THE 1623 FOLIO.

Under the date of February 2, 1602, John Manningham, a barrister of the Middle Temple, entered in his Diary, now amongst the Harleian MSS. in the British Museum, "At our feast wee had a play called 'Twelue Night, or What you Will,' much like the Commedy of Errores, or Menechmi in Plautus, but most like and neere to that in Italian called *Inganni*. A good practise in it to make the Steward beleeve his Lady widdowe was in love with him, by counterfeyting a letter as from his Lady in generall termes, telling him what shee liked best in him, and prescribing his gesture in smiling, his apparaile, &c., and then when he came to practise making him beleeue they tooke him to be mad." (Camden Society edition of the Diary, p. 18.)

Cunningham (*Op. cit.* p. xlv.) gives this entry from the Office Books of the Treasurers of the Chamber: "To John Heminges &c upon a warrant dated 20 April 1618 for presenting two severall Playes before his Maty, on Easter Monday Twelfte night the play soe called and on Easter Tuesday the Winter's Tale xxli." (see p. 71).

The first mention of this play in the Stationers' Registers is in the entry of the First Folio.

Commentators have written learnedly about the differences between the comedy named by Manningham and another Italian play, *Ingannati*, to which it is said *Twelfth Night* bears a yet closer resemblance. It may safely be concluded that Shakspere knew nothing about either of them. He was quite as capable as either of their authors of inventing the incidents of the story; or, at all events, he was equal to developing it after hearing it spoken about by his companions. The incident of the disguised page and her love-adventures was common enough in literature.

JULIUS CÆSAR.

Total Number of Lines.	CHARACTERS.	I.			II.				III.			IV.			V.				
		1	2	3	1	2	3	4	1	2	3	1	2	3	1	2	3	4	5
26	FLAVIUS	26	...	...	...	...	...	...	...	...	...	...	...	...	...	...	...	...	...
1	1ST COMMONER ...	1	...	...	...	...	...	...	...	...	...	...	...	...	...	...	...	...	...
33	MARCELLUS	33	...	...	...	...	...	...	...	...	...	...	...	...	...	...	...	...	...
20	2ND COMMONER ...	20	...	...	...	...	...	...	...	...	...	...	...	...	...	...	...	...	...
154	CÆSAR	...	39	...	...	72	...	...	40	...	...	...	...	3	...	...	...	...	...
136	CASCA	...	67	57	10	...	...	...	2	...	...	...	...	...	...	...	...	...	...
327	ANTONY	...	6	...	...	1	...	...	98	146	...	38	...	...	22	...	...	8	8
18	SOOTHSAYER	...	3	...	...	...	...	14	1	...	...	...	...	...	...	...	...	...	...
727	BRUTUS	...	73	...	180	3	...	...	79	55	...	...	34	204	33	6	18	3	39
507	CASSIUS	...	143	95	37	...	...	...	46	...	...	...	7	98	49	...	32	...	...
9	CICERO	...	...	9	...	...	...	...	...	...	...	...	...	...	...	...	...	...	...
18	CINNA	...	...	9	4	...	...	...	5	...	...	...	...	...	...	...	...	...	...
33	LUCIUS	..	...	...	17	...	..	6	...	...	...	...	...	10	...	...	...	...	...
44	DECIUS	...	...	...	12	25	...	...	7	...	...	...	...	...	...	...	...	...	...
17	METELLUS	...	...	...	9	...	...	...	8	...	...	...	...	...	...	...	...	...	...
8	TREBONIUS	...	...	...	3	2	...	...	3	...	...	...	...	...	...	...	...	...	...
15	LIGARIUS	...	...	...	15	...	...	...	...	...	..	...	...	...	...	...	...	...	...
30	SERVANT	...	...	...	...	5	...	..	21	4	...	...	...	...	...	...	...	...	...
2	PUBLIUS	...	...	...	...	1	...	...	1	...	...	...	...	...	...	...	...	...	...
20	ARTEMIDORUS	...	...	...	...	...	16	...	4	...	...	...	...	...	...	...	...	...	...
2	POPILIUS	...	...	...	...	...	...	...	2	...	...	...	...	...	...	...	...	...	...
15	"ALL"	...	...	...	...	...	...	...	...	14	...	...	...	...	...	...	...	...	1
23	1ST CITIZEN	...	...	...	..	...	...	...	...	18	5	...	...	...	...	...	...	...	...
24	2ND CITIZEN	...	...	...	...	...	...	...	...	18	6	...	...	...	...	...	...	...	...
23	3RD CITIZEN	...	...	...	...	...	...	...	...	16	7	...	...	...	...	...	...	...	...
23	4TH CITIZEN	...	...	...	...	...	...	...	...	14	9	...	...	...	...	...	...	...	...
16	CINNA (POET)	...	...	...	...	...	...	...	...	...	16	...	...	...	...	...	...	...	...
47	OCTAVIUS	...	...	...	...	...	...	...	...	...	...	12	...	...	25	...	...	...	10
4	LEPIDUS	...	..	...	...	...	...	...	...	...	...	4	...	...	...	...	...	...	...
26	LUCILIUS	...	...	...	...	...	...	...	...	...	...	...	10	1	1	...	...	12	2
16	PINDARUS	...	...	...	...	...	..	...	...	...	...	...	3	...	...	...	13	..	...
5	1ST SOLDIER	...	...	...	...	...	...	...	...	...	...	...	1	...	...	...	...	4	...
2	2ND SOLDIER	...	...	...	...	...	...	...	...	...	...	...	1	...	...	...	...	1	...
1	3RD SOLDIER	...	...	...	...	...	...	...	...	...	...	...	1	...	...	...	...	...	...
7	POET	...	...	...	...	...	...	...	...	...	...	...	...	7	...	...	...	...	...
39	MESSALA	...	...	...	...	...	...	...	...	...	...	...	...	14	2	...	19	...	4
32	TITINIUS	...	...	...	...	...	...	...	...	...	...	...	...	1	...	...	31	...	...
6	VARRO	...	...	...	...	...	...	...	...	...	...	...	...	6	...	...	...	..	...
4	CLAUDIUS	...	...	...	...	...	...	...	...	...	...	...	...	4	...	...	...	...	...
4	MESSENGER	...	...	...	...	...	...	...	...	...	...	...	...	...	4	...	...	...	...
8	CATO	...	...	...	...	...	...	...	...	...	...	...	...	...	...	...	3	5	...
10	CLITUS	...	...	...	...	...	...	...	...	...	...	...	...	...	...	...	...	...	10
3	DARDANIUS	...	...	...	...	...	...	...	...	...	...	...	...	...	...	...	...	...	3
3	VOLUMNIUS	...	...	...	...	...	...	...	...	...	...	...	...	...	...	...	...	...	3
7	STRATO	...	...	...	...	...	...	..	...	...	...	...	...	...	...	...	...	...	7
27	CALPURNIA	...	1	...	...	26	...	...	...	...	...	...	...	...	...	...	...	...	...
92	PORTIA	...	..	...	62	...	...	30	...	...	...	...	...	...	...	...	...	...	...
2614		80	332	170	349	135	16	50	317	285	43	54	57	348	136	6	116	33	87
2480	Actual No. of Lines	80	326	164	334	129	16	46	298	276	43	51	52	309	126	6	110	32	82

The third name in the list should be Marullus.

SCHEME FOR ARRANGING THE PARTS WITH EIGHTEEN MEN.

FIVE CHARACTERS SINGLY AND THIRTEEN GROUPS.

Popilius	2	Messala	39	1st Soldier	5	46
Artemidorus	20	1st Citizen	23	Messenger	4	47
Lepidus	4	Cinna	18	Lucilius	26	48
Trebonius	8	Marullus	33	Poet	7	48
Claudius	4	2nd Citizen	24	2nd Commoner	20	48
Octavius	47	1st Commoner	1	3rd Soldier	1	49
Cicero	9	Strato	7	Lucius	33	49
Publius	2	Ligarius	15	Titinius	32	49
Decius	44	Dardanius	3	2nd Soldier	2	49
Metellus	17	Flavius	26	Varro	6	49
Cato	8	Soothsayer	18	3rd Citizen	23	49
Volumnius	3	Cinna (Poet)	16	Servant	30	49
Clitus	10	Pindarus	16	4th Citizen	23	49

SUGGESTIONS FOR DISCUSSION.

1. *Julius Cæsar* in its present form is Ben Jonson's abridgement of Shakspere's play.
2. The unintentional result of *Julius Cæsar* is a glorification of tyrannicide.
3. The characterisation and the details of *Julius Cæsar* show Shakspere's ignorance of classical matters.

THE EARLIEST KNOWN EDITION IS THE 1623 FOLIO.

There is no earlier notice of the play either in the Stationers' Registers or (definitely) elsewhere. It would be an interesting problem for the student to endeavour to fix its date either by external or internal evidence. For this purpose references to contemporary literature have not much value, as between 1562 and 1613 many plays on the history of Julius Cæsar were published.

This may be the play described in 1613 as "Cæsars Tragedye" (see p. 103).

The passages in Plutarch's *Lives* should be carefully compared with the corresponding ones in the play. They are easily accessible in many places.

A YORKSHIRE TRAGEDY.

Total Number of Lines.	CHARACTERS.	I.									
		1	2	3	4	5	6	7	8	9	10
24	OLIVER	24	...	...	...	...	...	...	...	...	...
18	RALPH	18	...	...	...	...	...	...	...	...	...
42	SAMUEL	42	...	...	...	...	...	...	...	...	...
275	HUSBAND	...	84	20	68	26	4	...	20	7	46
13	1ST GENTLEMAN	...	7	...	...	...	...	...	1	4	1
4	2ND GENTLEMAN	...	1	...	...	...	...	...	3	...	...
1	3RD GENTLEMAN	...	1	...	...	...	...	...	...	...	...
38	SERVANT	...	3	10	...	5	...	20	...	...	...
48	4TH GENTLEMAN	...	48	...	...	...	...	...	...	...	...
64	MASTER	...	...	...	33	...	3	7	9	3	9
3	"ALL"	...	...	...	...	...	...	...	3	...	...
21	KNIGHT	...	...	...	...	...	...	...	...	21	...
1	OFFICER	...	...	...	...	...	...	...	...	...	1
163	WIFE	...	53	65	...	9	...	14	...	...	22
7	1ST SON	...	...	..	7	...	...	...	...	...	...
8	MAID	...	...	...	...	8	...	..	...	...	...
1	2ND SON	...	...	...	...	1	...	...	...	...	...
731		84	197	95	108	49	7	41	36	35	79
706	Actual Number of Lines	79	185	95	108	48	7	40	35	33	76

SUGGESTIONS FOR DISCUSSION.

1. Looked at in the light of the external evidence, Shakspere's authorship of at least the first scene of *A Yorkshire Tragedy* must be admitted, even if the rest of the play has to be given to Beaumont.
2. The brevity of *A Yorkshire Tragedy* is to be accounted for by a stage-practice of the time, of which this play is an interesting, because rare, example.
3. By inserting in *A Yorkshire Tragedy* the lines from *Pierce Penilesse*, Shakspere meant to indicate a similarity between Nash and the criminal, and thus exhibits the same unforgiving spirit that he showed towards Greene.

LIST OF EARLIEST KNOWN EDITIONS.

Date.	*Printer.*	*Publisher.*	*Acted by*	*Present Owners.*
1608	R. B.	Thomas Pauier	The King's servants	British Museum. Bodleian Library. Duke of Devonshire.
1619	T. P.	———		British Museum. Bodleian Library. Trinity College, Cambridge. Duke of Devonshire.

This play was thus entered in the Stationers' Registers:—

1608. May 2.

Master **Pavyer** Entered for his Copie vnder the handes of master WILSON and master Warden **Seton** A booke Called *A Yorkshire Tragedy* written by WYLLIAM SHAKESPERE **vjd**

The title of the 1608 edition is in the same words as in the entry, and is followed by the statement that it was "Not so new as Lamentable and true." This is an allusion to the murder which had been committed in 1605. It is stated to have been played at the Globe, and to have been "Written by W. Shakspeare."

The 1619 edition has the same words for its title. There is no reference to the acting. The author is described as "W. Shakespeare."

The outrage which forms the subject of this play is thus referred to in Stow's *Chronicle* (ed. 1631, pp. 870–1): "Walter Caluerly, of Caluerly in Yorkeshire, Esquier, murthred 2. of his yong children stabbed his wife into the body with full purpose to haue murthred her, and instantly went from his house to haue slain his yongest child at Nurse, but was preuented. For which fact at his tryall in Yorke, he stood mute, and was iudged to be prest to death, according to which iudgement he was executed at the Castell of Yorke, the fift of August." Events of the kind quickly called forth a certain sort of literature. In reference to this murder there are in the Stationers' Registers the following entries:—

1605. June 12.

Nathaniel Butter Entred for his copie vnder thandes of master HARTWELL and master **norton** warden A booke called *Twoo vnnaturall Murthers. the one practised by master* COVERLEY *a Yorkshire gent vppon his wife and happened on his children the* 23 *of Aprilis* 1605 . . . . . **vjd**

1605. July 3.

Thomas Pavyer Entred for his Copie vnder the handes of the wardens *A ballad of Lamentable Murther Donne in Yorkeshire by a gent vppon* 2 *of his owne Children sore woundinge his Wyfe and Nurse* **vjd**

1605. August 24.

Nathanael Butter Entred for his Copie vnder the hand of Master **ffeild** *The Araignement Condempnacon and Execucon of Master* CAVERLY *at Yorke in Auguste* 1605 **vjd**

HAMLET.

Total Number of Lines.	CHARACTERS.	I.					II.		III.				IV.							V.	
		1	2	3	4	5	1	2	1	2	3	4	1	2	3	4	5	6	7	1	2
38	Bernardo	34	4	...	...	...	...	...	...	...	...	...	...	...	...	...	...	...	...	...	...
10	Francisco	10	...	..	...	...	...	...	...	...	...	...	...	...	..	...	...	...	...	...	...
298	Horatio	100	50	...	26	17	...	...	...	9	...	...	...	...	...	...	2	28	...	12	54
67	Marcellus	46	6	...	7	8	..	...	...	...	...	...	...	...	...	...	...	...	...	...	...
551	King	...	93	...	...	...	...	39	40	7	50	...	34	...	44	...	67	...	141	9	27
1	Cornelius	...	1	...	...	...	...	...	...	...	...	...	...	...	...	...	...	...	...	..	...
22	Voltimand	...	1	...	...	...	...	21	...	...	...	...	...	...	...	...	...	...	...	...	...
208	Laertes	...	7	53	...	...	...	...	...	...	...	...	...	...	...	...	48	...	47	18	35
357	Polonius	...	4	68	...	...	87	146	23	13	9	7	...	...	...	...	...	...	...	...	...
1569	Hamlet	...	103	...	68	99	...	302	84	245	24	176	...	2[illegible]	26	47	...	...	...	142	230
7	"All"	...	1	...	...	...	...	...	...	1	...	...	...	...	...	...	3	...	...	1	1
95	Ghost	...	...	..	...	89	...	...	...	...	...	6	..	...	...	..	...	...	...	...	...
15	Reynaldo	...	...	...	...	...	15	...	..	...	...	...	...	...	...	...	...	...	...	...	...
105	Rosencrantz ..	...	...	...	...	...	...	50	12	15	14	...	..	9	4	1	...	...	...	...	...
57	Guildenstern ...	...	...	...	...	...	...	21	5	24	5	...	...	2	...	...	...	...	...	...	...
51	1st Player	...	...	...	...	...	...	48	...	3	...	...	...	...	...	...	...	...	...	...	..
44	Player King ...	...	...	...	...	...	...	...	...	44	...	...	...	...	...	...	...	...	...	...	...
6	Lucianus	...	...	...	...	...	...	..	...	6	...	...	...	...	...	...	...	...	...	...	...
27	Fortinbras	...	...	...	...	...	...	...	...	...	...	...	...	...	...	8	...	...	...	...	19
12	Captain	...	...	...	...	...	...	...	...	...	...	...	...	...	...	12	...	...	...	...	...
12	1st Gentleman ...	...	...	...	...	...	...	...	...	..	...	...	...	...	...	...	12	...	...	...	...
11	2nd Gentleman ...	...	...	...	...	...	...	...	...	...	...	...	...	...	...	...	11	...	...	...	...
1	Servant	...	..	...	...	...	...	...	...	...	...	...	...	..	...	...	...	1	...	...	...
5	1st Sailor	...	...	...	...	..	...	...	...	...	...	...	...	...	...	...	...	5	...	...	...
5	Messenger	...	...	...	...	...	...	...	...	...	...	...	...	...	...	...	...	...	5	...	...
107	1st Clown	...	...	...	...	...	...	...	...	...	...	...	...	...	...	...	...	...	...	107	...
19	2nd Clown	..	...	...	...	...	...	...	...	...	...	...	...	...	...	...	...	...	...	19	...
13	1st Priest	...	...	...	...	...	...	...	...	...	...	..	...	...	...	...	...	...	...	13	...
56	Osric	...	...	...	...	...	...	...	...	...	...	...	...	...	...	...	...	...	...	...	56
10	Lord	...	...	...	...	...	...	...	...	...	...	...	...	...	...	...	...	...	...	...	10
6	1st Ambassador ...	...	...	...	...	...	...	...	...	...	...	...	...	...	...	...	...	...	...	...	6
158	Queen	...	10	...	...	...	...	20	9	4	...	47	12	...	...	...	16	...	21	12	7
175	Ophelia	...	...	20	...	...	28	...	33	18	...	...	...	...	...	...	76	...	...	...	...
3	"Prologue" ...	...	...	...	...	...	...	...	...	3	...	...	...	...	...	...	...	...	...	...	...
30	Player Queen ...	...	...	...	...	...	...	...	...	30	...	...	...	...	..	...	...	...	...	...	...
4151		190	280	141	101	213	130	647	206	422	102	236	46	34	74	68	235	34	214	333	445
3930	Actual No. of Lines	175	258	136	91	191	119	633	196	417	98	217	45	33	70	66	220	34	195	322	414

THIRTEEN CHARACTERS SINGLY AND FIVE GROUPS.

Cornelius	1	
Reynaldo	15	
1st Gentleman	12	
1st Priest	13	41
Fortinbras	27	
Francisco	10	
1st Sailor	5	42
Bernardo	38	
Messenger	5	
Servant	1	44
Voltimand	22	
Lord	10	
2nd Gentleman	11	43
Captain	12	
1st Ambassador	6	
2nd Clown	19	
Lucianus	6	43

SUGGESTIONS FOR DISCUSSION.

1. The construction of *Hamlet* shows that Shakspere was a supreme theatre-poet rather than a dramatist proper.
2. It is only by looking upon Hamlet as suffering from "moral insanity" that the action of the play becomes intelligible and consistent.
3. The acting traditions of Polonius are an instance, only less forcible than those of Shylock, of the inability of the stage to represent the finer points of Shaksperian characterisation.
4. The Player's speech in *Hamlet* was originally written by Shakspere for Marlowe's *Dido*, instead of the part added by Nash.
5. Ophelia's weakness is the cause of Hamlet's failure.
6. Nearly all the characters in *Hamlet* represent persons connected with the history of Sir Philip Sidney.

LIST OF EARLIEST KNOWN EDITIONS.

Date.	*Printer.*	*Publisher.*	*Acted by*	*Present Owners.*
1603	——	N: L. and Iohn Trundell	His Highness' servants	British Museum. Duke of Devonshire.
1604	I. R.	N. L.		Duke of Devonshire. Lord Howe. Mr. A. H. Huth.
1605	I. R.	N. L.		British Museum. Trinity College, Cambridge.
——	W. S.	Iohn Smethwicke		British Museum. Bodleian Library. Trinity College, Cambridge.
1611	——	Iohn Smethwicke		British Museum. Bodleian Library. Trinity College, Cambridge. Duke of Devonshire. Mr. A. H. Huth.

In the Stationers' Registers is this entry:—

1602. July 26.
James Robertes Entred for his Copie vnder the handes of master Pasfeild and master **waterson** warden A booke called '*the Revenge of Hamlett Prince Denmarke*' *as yt was latelie Acted by the Lord Chamberleyne his servantes* vj[d]

The 1603 edition came out as "The Tragicall Historie of Hamlet Prince of Denmarke." It was declared to be by "William Shake-speare," and to have "beene diuerse times acted by his Highnesse seruants in the Cittie of London: as also in the two Vniuersities of Cambridge and Oxford, and else-where." The 1604 copy has the same title; nothing is said about its performance, but it is stated to be "Newly imprinted and enlarged to almost as much againe as it was, according to the true and perfect Coppie." A parallel-text edition of these two versions was published in 1860, with a preface by Mr. Samuel Timmins. The relation of these editions to one another and to the 1623 Folio is one of the unsettled Shakspere-questions, to which a close study should be given.

The 1605 edition is a reprint of that of 1604, and has the same title.

There is no certainty when the undated copy was issued. Some say that it could not be earlier than 1636 or 1637; others think it was published in 1607, soon after the transference of the copyright from Ling to Smethwick, which took place on November 19th of that year (see p. 79). It will be noted that there is an undated edition of *Romeo and Juliet*, the copyright of which play was transferred at the same time. All the editions after 1604 repeat the announcement about the revision and give the authorship. In the title of the undated issue and the 1611 edition, and the Folio version, "Tragedy" takes the place of "Tragicall Historie."

Shakspere was probably indebted to, and perhaps wrote part of, a play on the same subject, earlier than is now known to exist. Nash in 1589, Henslowe in 1594, and Lodge in 1596 have references to such.

In connection with Shakspere's play should be studied the translated "Hystorie of Hamblet" (reprinted in Hazlitt's *Shakespeare's Library*) and "Fratricide Punished, or Prince Hamlet of Denmark" (reprinted in German and English form in Cohn's *Shakespeare in Germany*). Both these and the 1603 version are in Furness's edition of the play. Close attention should also be given to Dr. Tanger's paper on the text of the editions in the New Shakspere Society's *Transactions*, 1880–2, Part I., and to the 1603 *Hamlet* "Harness Prize-Essays, 1880," by Mr. C. H. Herford and Mr. W. H. Widgery.

THE SILENT WOMAN.

Total Number of Lines.	CHARACTERS.	Prologues.		I.	II.				III.		IV.		V.
		1	2	1	1	2	3	4	1	2	1	2	1
505	CLERIMONT	...	...	160	...	92	...	17	80	7	36	37	76
1265	TRUEWIT	...	...	162	159	77	...	46	23	143	158	393	104
346	DAUPHINE	...	...	54	...	64	...	13	59	...	33	46	77
201	LA-FOOLE	..	...	69	...	...	...	...	21	...	9	67	35
511	MOROSE	...	...	...	82	...	150	...	...	103	13	73	90
4	MUTE	...	...	...	4	...	...	...	...	...	...	...	...
77	CUTBEARD	...	...	...	1	11	...	11	12	7	...	...	35
205	DAW	...	...	...	...	82	...	...	8	13	7	70	25
119	OTTER	...	...	...	...	...	...	...	26	5	71	...	17
5	PARSON	...	...	...	...	...	...	...	...	5	...	...	...
2	"ALL"	...	...	...	...	...	...	...	...	1	...	...	1
29	"1ST PROLOGUE"... ...	29	...	...	...	...	...	...	...	...	...	...	...
14	"2ND PROLOGUE".. ...	...	14	...	...	...	...	...	...	...	...	...	...
46	PAGE...	...	...	46	...	...	...	...	...	...	...	...	...
114	EPICŒNE	...	...	...	...	4	6	...	...	34	...	50	20
143	MISTRESS OTTER	...	...	...	...	...	...	...	105	3	17	15	3
139	HAUGHTY...	...	...	...	...	...	...	...	...	43	..	64	32
65	CENTAURE	...	...	...	...	...	...	...	...	7	...	32	26
46	MAVIS	...	...	...	...	...	...	...	...	6	...	28	12
10	TRUSTY	...	...	...	...	...	...	...	...	...	...	10	...
3846		29	14	491	246	330	156	87	334	377	344	[illegible]	[illegible]
3846	Actual Number of Lines	29	14	491	246	330	156	87	334	377	344	885	453

SCHEME FOR ARRANGING THE PARTS WITH SEVEN LADIES.

FIVE CHARACTERS SINGLY AND TWO GROUPS.

TRUSTY	10	39	PAGE	46	60
"1ST PROLOGUE"	29		"2ND PROLOGUE"	14	

SUGGESTIONS FOR DISCUSSION.

1. As the plot of *A Silent Woman* is of a kind inadmissible in comedy, the play should be looked upon as a farce.
2. Ben Jonson's "Censure of the English Poets" is not to be taken seriously.
3. Ben Jonson's greatest strength lay in the production of *Masques*, in which he left an example which Milton closely followed.

LIST OF EARLIEST KNOWN EDITIONS.

Date.	*Printer.*	*Publisher.*	*Acted by*	*Present Owners.*
1609				
1612				
1616	W. Stansby	Richard Meighen		British Museum and others. [This is the Folio] (see p. 99).
1620	William Stansby	Iohn Browne	The Children of the Revels	British Museum.

The Silent Woman at its first performance does not seem to have been well received (see *Jonson's Conversations with Drummond*, Shakespeare Society edition, p. 41).

In the Stationers' Registers are these entries:—

1610. September 20.

John Browne Entred for their Copye vnder thandes of Sir GEORGE BUCKE and master **Waterson**
John Busby for master warden **Leake**, A booke called, *Epicoene or the silent woman* by BEN: *Junior* JOHNSON **vj^d^.**

1612. September 28.

Walter. Burre Entred for his copie by assignement from **John Browne** and consent of the Wardens in full Court holden this Day. A booke called *the Commodye of 'the silent Woman'* **vj^d^**

I have not been able to find particulars about the 1609 and 1612 editions. They are not in the British Museum.

The 1620 edition (which was "to be sold by Iohn Browne," although he had transferred his copy-right in 1612 to Burre) is entitled "The Silent Woman." It states on its title-page that it is "A Comœdie," and that its author is "B. Ionson."

ALL'S WELL THAT ENDS WELL.

Total Number of Lines.	CHARACTERS.	I.			II.					III.							IV.					V.		
		1	2	3	1	2	3	4	5	1	2	3	4	5	6	7	1	2	3	4	5	1	2	3
289	BERTRAM	12	7	...	10	...	37	...	42	...	...	8	...	...	37	...	...	34	39	...	...	...	...	63
305	LAFEU...	30	...	...	32	...	103	...	32	...	...	...	...	...	...	...	..	...	...	...	53	...	22	33
411	PAROLLES	67	...	...	24	...	71	25	10	...	...	..	...	1	19	...	44	...	111	...	...	...	19	20
385	KING	...	68	...	80	...	77	...	...	...	...	...	...	...	...	...	...	...	...	...	...	...	...	160
127	1ST LORD	...	6	...	8	...	1	...	...	6	...	...	...	...	34	...	..	..	72	...	...	...	..	...
168	2ND LORD	...	5	...	5	...	1	...	...	8	...	...	...	...	37	...	42	...	70	...	...	...	...	...
44	STEWARD	...	...	26	...	...	...	...	...	...	...	...	18	...	...	...	...	...	...	...	...	...	...	...
212	CLOWN	...	...	67	...	39	...	24	...	...	24	...	...	...	...	...	...	...	...	...	40	...	18	...
3	"ALL"	...	...	...	...	...	1	...	...	...	...	...	...	...	...	...	2	...	...	...	...	...	...	...
1	4TH LORD	...	...	...	...	...	1	...	...	...	..	...	...	...	...	...	...	...	...	..	...	...	...	...
19	DUKE	...	...	...	..	...	...	...	...	13	...	6	...	...	...	...	...	...	...	...	...	...	...	...
34	1ST GENTLEMAN	...	...	...	...	...	...	...	...	...	12	...	...	...	...	...	...	...	...	...	...	10	...	12
11	2ND GENTLEMAN	...	...	...	...	...	...	...	...	...	11	...	...	...	...	...	...	...	...	...	...	...	...	...
98	1ST SOLDIER ...	...	...	...	...	...	...	...	...	...	...	...	...	...	...	...	18	...	80	...	...	...	...	...
2	2ND SOLDIER ...	...	...	...	...	...	...	...	...	...	...	...	...	...	...	...	2	...	...	...	...	...	...	...
4	SERVANT	...	...	...	...	...	...	...	...	...	...	...	...	...	...	...	...	...	4	...	...	...	..	...
306	COUNTESS	46	...	113	..	35	...	...	...	...	51	...	26	...	...	...	...	...	...	...	19	...	...	16
479	HELENA	89	...	71	68	...	32	11	20	...	42	...	...	30	...	37	...	...	...	34	...	33	...	12
1	PAGE	1	...	...	...	...	...	...	...	...	...	...	...	...	...	...	...	...	...	...	...	...	...	...
66	WIDOW	...	...	...	...	...	...	...	...	...	...	...	...	42	...	17	...	...	...	3	...	1	...	3
139	DIANA	...	...	...	...	...	...	...	...	...	...	...	...	24	...	...	...	52	..	3	...	...	...	60
23	MARIANA	..	...	...	...	...	...	...	...	...	...	...	...	23	...	...	...	...	...	...	...	...	...	...
3127		245	86	277	227	74	324	60	104	27	140	14	44	120	127	54	108	86	376	40	112	44	59	379
2966	Actual No. of Lines	244	76	262	213	74	316	57	97	23	132	11	42	104	125	48	105	76	376	36	112	38	59	340

SUGGESTIONS FOR DISCUSSION.

1. Not even Shakspere's masterly and modified treatment of the plots of the Italian novelists has been able to render their dramatic form anything but repulsive.
2. Much of *All's Well that Ends Well* is Shakspere's youthful poetry left in from an earlier draft of the play.
3. Acted by great performers, *All's Well that Ends Well* is seen as a true work of art, free from the defects which appear when the play is merely read.

THE EARLIEST KNOWN EDITION IS THE 1623 FOLIO.

This is also the date of its first entry in the Stationers' Registers.

At present there is no external evidence as to the date of its production.

It seems almost certain that Shakspere took the main part of the story from "Giletta of Narbona," which Painter, in his *Palace of Pleasure*, 1566, had translated from Boccaccio. This, which is "The Thirty-Eighth Novell" in Painter's book, is reprinted in Hazlitt's *Shakespeare's Library*.

THE ALCHEMIST.

Total Number of Lines.	CHARACTERS.	Argument.	Prologue.	I.	II.	III.		IV.				V.		
				1	1	1	2	1	2	3	4	1	2	3
1215	FACE	...	...	276	208	...	264	118	43	54	77	84	63	28
1065	SUBTLE	...	...	226	290	...	197	135	40	43	41	2	91	...
100	DAPPER	...	...	61	...	...	19	...	...	...	...	4	16	...
86	DRUGGER	...	...	33	28	...	17	...	...	...	7	...	...	1
502	MAMMON	...	...	...	284	...	...	140	..	42	..	12	...	24
230	SURLY	...	...	...	118	...	...	13	11	...	64	15	...	9
123	ANANIAS	...	...	...	27	15	18	...	...	...	26	8	...	29
91	TRIBULATION	...	...	...	...	39	45	...	...	...	...	2	...	5
132	KASTRIL	...	...	...	...	...	27	15	31	...	26	12	...	21
174	LOVEWIT	...	...	...	...	...	...	...	...	...	...	82	...	92
14	1ST NEIGHBOUR	...	...	...	...	...	...	...	...	...	...	14	...	...
14	2ND NEIGHBOUR	...	...	...	...	...	...	...	...	...	...	14	..	...
9	3RD NEIGHBOUR	...	...	...	...	...	...	...	...	...	...	9	...	...
6	4TH NEIGHBOUR	...	...	...	...	...	...	...	...	...	...	6	...	...
5	5TH NEIGHBOUR	...	...	...	...	...	...	...	...	...	...	5	..	...
9	6TH NEIGHBOUR	...	...	...	...	...	...	...	...	...	...	9	...	...
6	1ST OFFICER	...	...	..	...	...	...	...	...	...	...	...	1	5
2	2ND OFFICER	...	...	...	...	...	...	...	...	...	...	...	...	2
12	"ARGUMENT"	12	...	...	...	...	...	...	...	...	...	...	...	...
24	"PROLOGUE"	...	24	...	...	...	...	...	...	...	...	...	...	...
225	DOL	...	...	86	6	...	10	41	...	31	10	...	41	...
14	DAME PLIANT	...	...	...	...	...	...	5	8	...	1	...	...	...
4058		12	24	682	961	54	597	467	133	170	252	278	212	216
3169	Actual Number of Lines	12	24	517	770	51	492	360	98	122	189	215	152	167

SUGGESTIONS FOR DISCUSSION.

1. If, in the English drama, a model be sought of all that is regular in design and perfect in execution, it will be found in *The Alchemist*.
2. Ben Jonson's scholarship and knowledge of life enabled him to use his dramatic powers to greater advantage than any other writer of comedy.
3. As Ben Jonson fails in presenting the pathetic side of human nature, he is not entitled to take high rank among dramatists.

LIST OF EARLIEST KNOWN EDITIONS.

Date.	*Printer.*	*Publisher.*	*Acted by*	*Present Owners.*
1612	Thomas Snodham	Walter Burre		British Museum.
1616	W. Stansby	Richard Meighen		British Museum and others. [This is the Folio] (see p. 99).

The 1616 Folio says that the play was acted in 1610, when it was thus entered in the Stationers' Registers:—

1610. October 3.
Walter Burre. Entred for his Copy vnder thandes of Sir GEORGE BUCKE and Th'Wardens a Comœdy called, *The Alchymist* made by BEN: JOHNSON vj[d].

The title of the 1612 edition is simply "The Alchemist," and it is stated to be "written by Ben. Ionson."

"The Alcumist" was one of the plays acted at Court in 1613 (see p. 103).

OTHELLO.

Total Number of Lines.	CHARACTERS.	I.			II.			III.				IV.			V.	
		1	2	3	1	2	3	1	2	3	4	1	2	3	1	2
123	Roderigo	42	1	16	9	...	8	...	...	...	...	...	36	...	11	...
1117	Iago	108	27	93	156	...	218	5	1	217	9	134	62	...	75	12
139	Brabantio	46	31	62	...	...	...	...	...	...	...	...	...	...	...	..
888	Othello	...	38	115	29	...	56	..	5	201	50	109	68	6	8	203
288	Cassio	...	16	...	51	...	91	21	...	12	37	31	...	...	15	14
5	1st Officer	..	3	2	...	...	...	...	...	...	...	...	...	...	...	...
73	Duke	...	...	73	...	...	...	...	...	...	...	...	...	...	...	...
28	1st Senator	...	...	28	...	...	...	...	...	...	...	...	...	...	...	...
5	2nd Senator	...	...	5	...	...	...	...	...	...	...	...	...	...	...	...
4	Sailor	...	...	4	...	...	...	...	...	...	...	...	...	...	...	...
9	Messenger	...	...	9	...	...	...	...	...	...	..	...	...	...	...	...
61	Montano	...	...	...	21	...	33	...	...	...	...	...	...	...	..	7
4	1st Gentleman	...	...	...	3	...	...	...	1	...	...	...	...	...	...	...
14	2nd Gentleman	...	...	...	14	...	...	...	...	...	..	...	...	...	...	...
17	3rd Gentleman	...	...	...	17	...	...	...	...	...	...	...	...	...	...	...
5	"All"	...	...	...	2	...	2	...	...	...	...	...	...	...	...	1
2	4th Gentleman	...	...	...	2	...	...	...	...	...	...	...	...	...	...	...
13	Herald	...	...	...	...	13	...	...	...	...	...	...	...	...	...	...
30	Clown	...	...	...	...	...	...	18	...	...	12	...	...	...	...	...
5	1st Musician...	...	...	...	...	...	...	5	...	...	...	...	..	...	...	...
76	Lodovico...	...	...	...	...	...	...	...	...	...	...	25	...	2	9	40
26	Gratiano	...	...	...	...	...	...	...	...	...	...	...	...	...	9	17
389	Desdemona	...	..	28	30	...	1	...	...	72	81	14	64	57	...	42
245	Emilia	...	...	...	3	...	...	13	...	28	18	...	44	49	4	86
36	Bianca	...	...	...	...	...	...	...	...	...	17	12	...	...	7	...
3602		196	116	435	337	13	409	62	7	530	224	325	274	114	138	422
3316	Actual Number of Lines	184	99	410	321	13	394	58	6	479	201	293	252	106	129	371

In III. 4 Desdemona's lines should be 80, and in V. 1 Cassio's 16. The total lines should be 3317, as the total of II. 3 should be 395.

SCHEME FOR ARRANGING THE PARTS WITH EIGHTEEN MEN.

FIFTEEN CHARACTERS SINGLY AND THREE GROUPS.

1st Officer	5	7	2nd Senator	5	9	Sailor	4	9
4th Gentleman	2		1st Gentleman	4		1st Musician	5	

SUGGESTIONS FOR DISCUSSION.

1. From the close resemblance of *Othello* to the story in Giraldi's *Hecatommithi*, it must be inferred that Shakspere knew Italian.
2. The point of Othello's passion is not Jealousy, but agony at the loss of his ideal.
3. It requires a thorough-bred gentleman to play Othello.

EARLIEST KNOWN EDITION.

Date.	*Printer.*	*Publisher.*	*Acted by*	*Present Owners.*
1622	N. O.	Thomas Walkley	The King's servants	British Museum. Bodleian Library. Trinity College, Cambridge. Mr. A. H. Huth.

In *The Egerton Papers* (p. 343) edited by Collier for the Camden Society, the following is quoted in Mainwaring's account of expenses in connection with Queen Elizabeth's visit to Lord Ellesmere at Harefield:

6 August, 1602. Rewardes to the vaulters, players, and dauncers.. Of this x[li] to Burbidge's players for Othello.

This is said to be one of Collier's forgeries.

It has been stated that in 1604 there was on "Hallamas Day being the first of Nouembar A play in the Banketinge house att Whithall called The Moor of Venis" performed "By the kings Ma[tis] plaiers" (Cunningham, *Op. cit.* See p. 71).

On April 30, 1610, the Secretary to the German Embassy in London recorded that at the Globe "y fut representé l'histoire du More de Venise."

Before a party at Court the play, under the title of "The Moor of Venice," was acted in 1613 (see p. 103).

In the Stationers' Registers is this entry:—

1621. October 6.

Thomas Walkley Entred for his copie vnder the handes of Sir George Buck, and Master **Swinhowe** warden, *The Tragedie of Othello, the moore of Venice.* **vj[d]**

As "The Tragœdy of Othello, The Moore of Venice," the edition of 1622 was issued with the statement that it had "beene diuerse times acted at the Globe, and at the Black-Friers," and that it was "Written by William Shakespeare." In the 1623 Folio the title is the same.

The tale from Giraldi, alluded to above, is given with an English translation in Hazlitt's *Shakespeare's Library*.

MEASURE FOR MEASURE.

Total Number of Lines.	CHARACTERS.	I.				II.				III.		IV.						V.
		1	2	3	4	1	2	3	4	1	2	1	2	3	4	5	6	1
880	DUKE...	67	...	51	...	...	...	25	...	141	114	38	91	83	...	13	...	257
205	ESCALUS	11	...	...	...	109	...	...	...	...	32	...	...	...	8	...	...	45
321	ANGELO	12	...	...	...	35	85	...	117	...	...	...	...	...	29	...	...	43
321	LUCIO	...	54	...	63	...	15	...	...	...	101	...	...	25	...	...	...	63
27	1ST GENTLEMAN ...	...	27	...	...	...	...	...	...	...	...	...	...	...	...	...	...	...
11	2ND GENTLEMAN ...	...	11	...	...	...	...	...	...	...	...	...	...	...	...	...	...	...
176	POMPEY	...	19	...	...	83	...	...	...	...	16	...	25	33	...	...	...	...
115	CLAUDIO	...	58	...	...	...	...	...	...	54	...	...	3	...	...	...	...	...
171	PROVOST	...	3	...	...	1	19	12	...	5	5	...	96	17	...	...	...	13
6	FRIAR THOMAS ...	...	...	6	...	...	...	...	...	...	...	...	...	...	...	...	...	...
81	ELBOW	...	...	...	...	62	...	...	...	...	19	...	...	...	...	...	...	...
11	FROTH	...	...	...	...	11	...	...	...	...	...	...	...	...	...	...	...	...
3	JUSTICE	...	...	...	...	3	...	...	...	...	...	...	...	...	...	...	...	...
6	SERVANT	...	...	...	...	...	4	...	2	...	...	...	...	...	...	...	...	...
23	ABHORSON	...	...	...	...	...	...	...	...	...	...	...	12	11	...	...	...	...
5	MESSENGER	...	...	...	...	...	...	...	...	...	...	...	5	...	...	...	...	...
17	BARNARDINE	...	...	...	...	...	...	...	...	...	...	...	...	17	...	...	...	...
36	FRIAR PETER	...	...	...	...	...	...	...	...	...	...	...	...	...	...	1	6	29
37	MISTRESS OVERDONE	...	28	...	...	...	...	...	...	...	9	...	...	...	...	...	...	...
426	ISABELLA	...	...	...	27	...	94	...	78	97	...	25	...	9	...	...	9	87
9	FRANCISCA	...	...	...	9	...	...	...	...	...	...	...	...	...	...	...	...	...
10	JULIET	...	...	...	...	...	...	10	...	...	...	...	...	...	...	...	...	...
6	BOY	...	...	...	...	...	...	...	...	...	...	6	...	...	...	...	...	...
68	MARIANA	...	...	...	...	...	...	...	...	...	...	13	...	...	...	...	2	53
2971		90	200	57	99	304	217	47	197	297	296	82	232	195	37	14	17	590
2821	Actual No. of Lines	84	198	54	90	300	187	42	188	280	296	76	226	190	37	13	15	545

In Scheme for arranging the parts with seven ladies omit MISTRESS OVERDONE.

SUGGESTIONS FOR DISCUSSION.

1. Shakspere's main purpose in *Measure for Measure*, written on behalf of his fellow Roman Catholics, was to exalt the ascetic ideal.
2. Without *Measure for Measure*, Shakspere's analysis of human character would be incomplete.
3. The carelessness of the plot of *Measure for Measure* is inexcusable.

THE EARLIEST KNOWN EDITION IS THE 1623 FOLIO.

Mr. Halliwell-Phillipps (*Outlines*, Vol. I. p. 197) says, "On the evening of December the 26th, 1604, the comedy of Measure for Measure was performed before the Court at Whitehall." The authority for this statement is a document among the Malone papers in the Bodleian Library. The same performance is quoted by Cunningham (*Op. cit.* p. 204) thus: "By his Matis plaiers. On St. Stiuens Night in the Hall A Play called Mesur for Mesur. Shaxberd" (see p. 71).

The subject of this play had been dealt with by George Whetstone in dramatic form in 1578, and as a narrative in 1582. With Whetstone's version, called *The History of Promos and Cassandra*, Shakspere was doubtless familiar, although *Measure for Measure* shows considerable departures from it. Whetstone's play and tale are both reprinted in Hazlitt's *Shakespeare's Library*, where also may be seen the story from Giraldi to which Whetstone may have been indebted; but the main incident was a very common one in literature (see Douce's *Illustrations of Shakspeare*, ed. 1839, pp. 94-99).

This play is not mentioned in the Stationers' Registers till the Folio entry on November 8, 1623.

PHILASTER.

Total Number of Lines.	CHARACTERS.	I.		II.				III.		IV.				V.				
		1	2	1	2	3	4	1	2	1	2	3	4	1	2	3	4	5
91	CLEREMONT	21	...	...	...	..	10	15	...	20	10	...	5	3	...	5	...	2
380	DION	113	...	...	...	...	40	59	...	20	32	2	13	5	...	63	...	33
39	THRASILINE	11	...	...	...	...	5	8	...	8	...	...	...	3	...	4	...	...
322	KING	59	...	...	...	...	67	...	22	8	44	...	11	...	...	54	...	57
236	PHARAMOND	41	28	...	85	...	21	...	...	...	9	16	14	...	...	...	20	2
769	PHILASTER	95	102	30	...	...	...	179	61	...	31	62	63	...	29	39	21	57
31	1ST WOODMAN ...	...	...	...	...	...	...	...	...	...	31	...	...	...	...	...	...	...
9	2ND WOODMAN ...	...	...	...	...	...	...	...	...	...	8	1	...	...	...	...	...	...
34	COUNTRY FELLOW ..	...	...	...	...	...	...	...	...	...	...	34	...	...	...	...	...	...
4	"ALL"	...	...	...	...	...	...	...	...	...	...	...	1	...	...	...	3	...
5	1ST MESSENGER ..	...	...	...	...	...	...	...	...	...	...	...	...	...	...	5	...	...
4	2ND MESSENGER ...	...	...	...	...	...	..	...	...	...	...	...	...	...	...	4	...	...
87	CAPTAIN	...	...	...	...	..	...	...	...	...	...	...	...	...	...	...	87	...
7	1ST CITIZEN	...	...	...	...	...	...	...	...	...	...	...	...	...	...	...	7	...
3	2ND CITIZEN	...	...	...	...	...	...	...	...	...	...	...	...	...	...	...	3	...
4	3RD CITIZEN	...	...	...	...	...	...	...	...	...	...	...	...	...	...	...	4	...
2	4TH CITIZEN	...	...	..	...	...	...	...	...	...	...	...	...	...	...	...	2	...
1	5TH CITIZEN	...	...	...	...	...	...	...	...	...	...	...	...	...	...	...	1	...
133	MEGRA	25	...	...	32	...	60	...	...	...	1	...	...	...	...	...	...	15
74	GALATEA	12	...	...	45	10	4	...	...	...	3	...	...	...	...	...	...	...
25	LADY	7	11	...	...	5	...	...	2	...	...	...	...	...	...	...	...	...
311	ARETHUSA	...	92	...	...	38	7	...	93	1	...	34	9	...	10	12	...	15
357	BELLARIO	...	...	34	...	18	...	84	16	...	18	14	55	...	17	26	...	75
2928		384	233	64	162	71	214	345	194	57	187	163	171	11	56	212	148	256
2743	Actual No. of Lines	372	206	61	159	69	206	302	188	57	178	156	156	11	52	202	147	221

SUGGESTIONS FOR DISCUSSION.

1. In the plays of Beaumont and Fletcher, the respective shares of the writers can be determined by metrical tests.
2. In his own day Fletcher's popularity exceeded that of Shakspere, because he was a greater master in the delineation of the softer passions.
3. The nonsense that Dryden wrote about Ben Jonson and Beaumont should be a warning to loose critics.

LIST OF EARLIEST KNOWN EDITIONS.

Date.	*Printer.*	*Publisher.*	*Acted by*	*Present Owners.*
1620	———	Thomas Walkley	The King's servants	British Museum.
1622	———	Thomas Walkley	The King's servants	British Museum.

The date of the first performance of *Philaster* is uncertain. It is usually set down somewhere about 1608 (see 1821 *Variorum*, Vol. II. p. 453). It was acted more than once at the Court festivities in 1613 (see p. 103).

The play was thus entered in the Stationers' Registers :—

1620. January 10.

Thomas Walkley Entred for his copie vndèr the handes of Master TAUERNOR and Master **Jaggard** warden A Play Called *PHILASTER* **vjd**

The first of the editions named above is called "Phylaster . Or, Loue lyes a Bleeding." It is said to be "written by { Francis Baymont and Iohn Fletcher } Gent." and the statement is given that it was "acted at the Globe." The title of the 1622 edition differs only in spelling. The edition is described as "The second Impression, corrected, and amended." The name of the first author is given as "Beaumont," and it is recorded that the play had been "Acted, at the Globe, and Blacke-Friers."

In the consideration of the plays by Beaumont and Fletcher, it will be useful to consult the papers by Mr. Fleay and by Mr. Boyle in the New Shakspere Society's *Transactions*, 1874, Part I., and 1880-6, Part III.

LEAR.

Total Number of Lines.	CHARACTERS.	I. 1	2	3	4	5	II. 1	2	3	4	III. 1	2	3	4	5	6	7	IV. 1	2	3	4	5	6	7	V. 1	2	3
379	KENT	44	...	...	37	2	...	104	...	32	41	17	...	18	...	15	...	...	...	29	...	...	...	16	...	...	24
344	GLOUCESTER ...	25	61	...	...	...	30	15	...	12	...	..	20	23	...	15	33	44	...	...	...	...	63	...	...	3	...
323	EDMUND	3	128	.	...	...	63	1	...	...	...	...	6	...	14	...	...	...	1	...	...	...	...	...	31	...	76
770	LEAR	122	...	...	131	22	...	..	..	161	..	43	...	68	...	31	...	...	...	...	...	...	106	32	...	...	54
156	ALBANY	1	...	..	11	...	...	...	...	...	...	...	...	...	...	...	...	..	43	...	...	...	...	...	14	...	87
109	CORNWALL	1	...	...	...	...	14	32	...	12	...	..	...	...	12	...	38	...	...	...	...	...	...	...	...	...	...
12	BURGUNDY	12	...	...	...	...	...	...	...	...	...	...	...	...	.	...	...	...	...	...	...	...	...	...	...	...	...
32	FRANCE	32	...	...	...	...	...	..	...	...	...	...	...	...	...	...	...	..	...	...	...	...	...	...	...	...	...
406	EDGAR	...	11	...	...	...	1	...	21	...	...	...	...	74	...	47	...	33	...	...	...	...	119	...	12	10	78
80	OSWALD	...	...	3	6	...	...	27	...	...	...	...	...	...	...	...	6	...	10	...	...	12	16	...	...	...	...
16	KNIGHT	...	...	...	16	...	...	...	...	...	...	...	...	...	...	...	...	...	...	...	..	...	...	...	...	...	...
252	FOOL	..	...	...	109	31	...	...	...	43	...	40	...	13	...	16	...	...	...	...	...	...	...	...	...	...	...
87	GENTLEMAN ...	...	...	...	...	1	...	...	...	5	17	...	...	...	...	...	...	...	...	34	...	...	16	9	...	...	5
11	CURAN	...	...	...	...	...	11	...	...	...	...	...	...	...	...	...	...	...	...	...	...	...	...	...	...	...	...
9	1ST SERVANT ...	...	...	...	...	...	...	...	..	...	...	...	...	...	...	...	9	...	...	...	...	...	...	...	...	...	...
5	2ND SERVANT ...	...	...	...	...	...	...	...	...	...	...	...	...	...	...	...	5	...	...	...	...	...	...	...	...	...	...
5	3RD SERVANT ...	...	...	...	...	...	...	...	...	...	...	...	...	...	...	...	5	...	...	...	...	...	...	...	...	...	...
12	OLD MAN	...	...	..	...	...	...	...	...	...	...	...	...	...	...	...	...	12	...	..	...	...	...	...	...	...	...
19	MESSENGER... ...	...	...	...	...	...	...	...	...	...	...	...	...	...	...	...	...	...	17	...	2	...	...	...	...	..	...
18	DOCTOR	...	...	...	...	...	...	...	...	...	...	...	...	...	...	...	...	...	...	...	5	...	...	13	...	...	...
6	CAPTAIN	...	...	...	...	...	...	...	...	...	...	...	...	...	...	...	...	...	...	...	...	...	...	...	...	..	6
10	HERALD	...	...	...	...	...	...	...	...	...	...	...	...	...	...	...	...	...	...	...	...	...	...	...	...	...	10
201	GONERIL	31	...	25	66	...	...	...	...	15	...	...	...	...	...	...	2	...	39	...	...	...	...	...	7	...	16
115	CORDELIA	46	...	...	...	...	...	...	...	...	...	...	...	...	...	...	...	...	..	...	24	...	...	40	...	...	5
191	REGAN	17	...	...	...	...	23	8	..	59	...	...	...	...	...	...	19	...	...	...	...	33	...	...	14	...	18
3568		334	200	28	376	56	142	187	21	339	58	100	26	196	26	124	117	89	110	63	31	45	320	110	78	13	379
3336	Actual No. of Lines	312	200	27	371	56	131	180	21	312	55	97	26	189	26	122	108	82	98	57	29	40	293	98	69	11	326

In II. 4 Lear's lines should be 162.

FOURTEEN CHARACTERS SINGLY AND FOUR GROUPS.

BURGUNDY 12, 3RD SERVANT 5 } 17	CURAN 11, CAPTAIN 6 } 17	OLD MAN 12, 2ND SERVANT 5 } 17	HERALD 10, 1ST SERVANT 9 } 19

SUGGESTIONS FOR DISCUSSION.

1. The Folio-text of *Lear* is Shakspere's revision of his own work.
2. Our estimate of *Lear*, as a whole, depends upon the view we take of the Fool.
3. A study of *Lear* shows that the language of poetry is more forcible than the language of painting.

LIST OF EARLIEST KNOWN EDITIONS.

Date.	*Printer.*	*Publisher.*	*Acted by*	*Present Owners.*
1608	———	Nathaniel Butter	The King's servants	British Museum. Bodleian Library. Trinity College, Cambridge. Duke of Devonshire, and eight others.
1608	———	Nathaniel Butter	The King's servants	British Museum. Bodleian Library. Trinity College, Cambridge. Duke of Devonshire.

On April 6 and 8, 1594, Henslowe notes performances of "Kinge leare" by "the Quenes men and my lord of Susex to geather."

In the Stationers' Registers are these entries. In that of 1594 Adam Islip's name was first entered and then struck out:

1594. May 14.

Edward White. Entred alsoe for his Copie vnder thandes of bothe the wardens a booke entituled *The moste famous Chronicle historye of* LEIRE *kinge of England and his Three Daughters* **vj[d] C.**

1605. May 8.

Simon Stafford Entred for his Copie vnder thandes of the Wardens A booke called '*the Tragecall historie of kinge* LEIR *and his Three Daughters &c.*' *As it was latelie Acted* **vj[d]**

John Wright Entred for his Copie by assignement from **Simon Stafford** and by consent of Master **Leake**, *The Tragicall history of kinge* LEIRE *and his Three Daughters* PROVIDED that **Simon Stafford** shall haue the printinge of this booke **vj[d]**

Mr. Arber adds this note: "It is evident that *King* LEAR was printed by **S. Stafford** before the 8th May, 1605, though not entered until it was assigned on that date. See a similar case of *The merry wives of Windsor* . . . ." (But see p. 113). Of the book entered in 1594 no copy is known. There is a copy of the 1605 book in the British Museum entitled "The True Chronicle History of King Leir, and his three daughters, Gonorill, Ragan, and Cordella." It is said to have "been diuers and sundry times lately acted"; but the place of acting is not named. The play is reprinted in Hazlitt's *Shakespeare's Library*.

Shakspere's play was thus entered in the Registers:—

1607. November 26.

Nathanael Butter
John Busby Entred for their copie vnder thandes of Sir GEORGE BUCK knight and Thwardens A booke called . Master WILLIAM SHAKESPEARE *his* '*historye of Kinge* LEAR' *as yt was played before the kinges maiestie at Whitehall vppon Sainct Stephens night at Christmas Last by his maiesties servantes playinge vsually at the* '*Globe*' *on the Banksyde* **vj[d]**

One of the editions published in the following year bears the title "M. William Shak-speare: His True Chronicle Historie of the life and death of King Lear and his three Daughters. With the vnfortunate life of Edgar, sonne and heire to the Earle of Gloster, and his sullen and assumed humor of Tom of Bedlam." The fact of the performance recorded in the entry is stated. The only variations in the title of the other edition are in the spelling of some words. The author's name is given as "Shake-speare." But in the texts of the two editions and in copies of the same edition there are many variations (see 'Cambridge' *Shakespeare* and Furness's edition of the play). A comparison of these two editions with one another and with the Folio should be made by the enquiring student (see a paper by Delius in the New Shakspere Society's *Transactions*, 1875-6, Part I.). In the Folio the play is called "The Tragedie of King Lear."

An investigation into the sources of the plot will be of much interest. The historical versions of the story, passages in Sidney's *Arcadia* (1598), many poetical forms of the incidents, the 1605 play, should all be looked at. Hazlitt and Furness supply all that is necessary. The more critically disposed searcher may trace the course of the story through writers other than English (see Mr. C. H. Herford's paper on "Some Variants of the Lear-story," in *Owens College Magazine*, June, 1883).

TIMON OF ATHENS.

Total Number of Lines.	CHARACTERS.	I.		II.		III.						IV.			V.			
		1	2	1	2	1	2	3	4	5	6	1	2	3	1	2	3	4
111	Poet	77	...	...	...	...	...	...	...	...	...	...	...	...	34	...	...	...
75	Painter	31	...	...	...	...	...	...	...	...	...	...	...	...	44	...	...	...
11	Merchant	11	...	...	...	...	...	...	...	...	...	...	...	...	...	...	...	...
12	Jeweller	12	...	...	...	...	...	...	...	...	...	...	...	...	...	...	...	...
863	Timon	69	106	...	73	...	...	...	21	...	56	41	...	378	119	...	...	...
20	Messenger	9	...	...	...	...	...	...	...	...	...	...	...	...	...	11	...	...
29	Old Athenian	29	...	...	...	...	...	...	...	...	...	...	...	...	...	...	...	...
5	Lucilius	5	...	...	...	...	...	...	...	...	...	...	...	...	...	...	...	...
264	Apemantus	59	80	...	30	...	...	...	...	...	...	...	...	95	...	...	...	...
160	Alcibiades	2	6	...	...	...	...	...	...	80	...	...	...	32	...	...	...	40
51	1st Lord	9	13	...	...	...	...	...	...	...	29	...	...	...	...	...	...	...
50	2nd Lord	12	8	...	...	...	...	...	...	...	30	...	...	...	...	...	...	...
9	Ventidius	...	9	...	...	...	...	...	...	...	...	...	...	...	...	...	...	...
7	"All"	...	1	...	...	...	...	...	...	...	2	...	...	4	...	...	...	...
15	3rd Lord	...	3	...	...	...	...	...	...	...	12	...	...	...	...	...	...	...
37	1st Servant	...	8	...	1	3	...	19	...	...	...	...	6	...	...	...	...	...
204	Flavius	...	25	...	77	...	...	...	21	...	...	...	33	37	11	...	...	...
11	2nd Servant	...	3	...	...	...	...	...	...	...	...	...	8	...	...	...	...	...
10	3rd Servant	...	4	...	...	...	...	...	...	...	...	...	6	...	...	...	...	...
122	1st Senator	...	...	35	...	...	...	...	...	31	...	...	...	...	27	3	...	26
21	Caphis	...	...	3	18	...	...	...	...	...	...	...	...	...	...	...	...	...
28	1st Varro's Servant	...	...	...	19	...	...	...	9	...	...	...	...	...	...	...	...	...
16	Isidore's Servant	...	...	...	16	...	...	...	...	...	...	...	...	...	...	...	...	...
25	Fool	...	...	...	25	...	...	...	...	...	...	...	...	...	...	...	...	...
30	Flaminius	...	...	...	1	25	...	...	4	...	...	...	...	...	...	...	...	...
38	Lucullus	...	...	...	...	38	...	...	...	...	...	...	...	...	...	...	...	...
44	Lucius	...	...	...	...	...	44	...	...	...	...	...	...	...	...	...	...	...
31	1st Stranger	...	...	...	...	...	31	...	...	...	...	...	...	...	...	...	...	...
7	2nd Stranger	...	...	...	...	...	7	...	...	...	...	...	...	...	...	...	...	...
20	Servilius	...	...	...	...	...	13	...	7	...	...	...	...	...	...	...	...	...
1	3rd Stranger	...	...	...	...	...	1	...	...	...	...	...	...	...	...	...	...	...
25	Sempronius	...	...	...	...	...	...	25	...	...	...	...	...	...	...	...	...	...
16	Titus	...	...	...	...	...	...	...	16	...	...	...	...	...	...	...	...	...
11	Hortensius	...	...	...	...	...	...	...	11	...	...	...	...	...	...	...	...	...
32	Lucius' Servant	...	...	...	...	...	...	...	32	...	...	...	...	...	...	...	...	...
6	Philotus	...	...	...	...	...	...	...	6	...	...	...	...	...	...	...	...	...
7	2nd Varro's Servant	...	...	...	...	...	...	...	7	...	...	...	...	...	...	...	...	...
63	2nd Senator	...	...	...	...	...	...	...	...	11	...	...	...	...	26	1	...	25
5	3rd Senator	...	...	...	...	...	...	...	...	1	...	...	...	...	...	4	...	...
3	4th Lord	...	...	...	...	...	...	...	...	...	3	...	...	...	...	...	...	...
14	1st Bandit	...	...	...	...	...	...	...	...	...	...	...	...	14	...	...	...	...
6	2nd Bandit	...	...	...	...	...	...	...	...	...	...	...	...	6	...	...	...	...
6	3rd Bandit	...	...	...	...	...	...	...	...	...	...	...	...	6	...	...	...	...
15	Soldier	...	...	...	...	...	...	...	...	...	...	...	...	...	...	...	10	5
6	"Cupid"	...	6	...	...	...	...	...	...	...	...	...	...	...	...	...	...	...
2	1st Lady	...	2	...	...	...	...	...	...	...	...	...	...	...	...	...	...	...
10	Page	...	...	...	10	...	...	...	...	...	...	...	...	...	...	...	...	...
5	Phrynia	...	...	...	...	...	...	...	...	...	...	...	...	5	...	...	...	...
8	Timandra	...	...	...	...	...	...	...	...	...	...	...	...	8	...	...	...	...
2567		325	274	38	270	66	96	44	134	123	132	41	53	585	261	19	10	96
2372	Actual No. of Lines	294	257	35	242	66	94	42	119	117	130	41	50	542	231	17	10	85

The total lines should be 2373, as the total of I. 2 should be 258.

SCHEME FOR ARRANGING THE PARTS WITH EIGHTEEN MEN AND SEVEN LADIES.

Men's Parts.

SEVEN CHARACTERS SINGLY AND ELEVEN GROUPS.

Lucilius 5 ⎫	Ventidius 9 ⎫	Lucius' Servant 32 ⎫
Caphis 21 ⎪	Flaminius 30 ⎪	Isidore's Servant 16 ⎪
1st Stranger 31 ⎬ 64	Messenger 20 ⎬ 65	2nd Servant 11 ⎬ 65
2nd Varro's Servant 7 ⎭	2nd Bandit 6 ⎭	3rd Bandit 6 ⎭
Lucullus 38 ⎫	Lucius 44 ⎫	Sempronius 25 ⎫	2nd Senator 63 ⎫
Titus 16 ⎬ 64	Philotus 6 ⎬ 65	Jeweller 12 ⎬ 65	3rd Stranger 1 ⎬ 67
3rd Servant 10 ⎭	3rd Lord 15 ⎭	1st Varro's Servant 28 ⎭	4th Lord 3 ⎭
Merchant 11 ⎫	Old Athenian 29 ⎫	Hortensius 11 ⎫	1st Bandit 14 ⎫
Servilius 20 ⎬ 68	Fool 25 ⎬ 69	1st Lord 51 ⎬ 69	2nd Lord 50 ⎬ 69
1st Servant 37 ⎭	Soldier 15 ⎭	2nd Stranger 7 ⎭	3rd Senator 5 ⎭

Ladies' Parts.

Omit PHRYNIA and TIMANDRA.

SUGGESTIONS FOR DISCUSSION.

1. *Timon of Athens*, in its present form, is a fragment of Shakspere's work added to by Cyril Tourneur.
2. The "light ending" test shows that the undoubted Shakspere-part of *Timon of Athens* was written in 1607.
3. The misanthropy of Timon is the representation of the state of mind by which Shakspere was agitated when he wrote his Sonnets.

THE EARLIEST KNOWN EDITION IS THE 1623 FOLIO.

This is also the date of its first mention in the Stationers' Registers.

There is in existence a manuscript play on the subject of Timon probably written about 1600. There is no evidence that it was printed in Shakspere's time, and it is not likely that he knew anything about it. It can be investigated by the student, as it was reprinted by the Shakespeare Society in 1842 and again by Hazlitt in *Shakespeare's Library*.

In Painter's *Palace of Pleasure*, 1566, "The Twenty-eighth Nouell" is "Of the strange and beastlie nature of Timon of Athens, enemie to mankinde, with his death, buriall, and epitaphe." Shakspere would be familiar with it, and with some passages in the translated *Plutarch*, where, in the Lives of Antony and Alcibiades, mention is made of Timon. But all these are too fragmentary to be in any real sense the foundation of the play. Shakspere, doubtless, knew the story as a popular one, and there is no need to think, with most editors, that he derived inspiration from Lucian's *Dialogues*, a book in a tongue he could not read, and to which some parts of the play are nearer than to the other alleged sources. If the double authorship of *Timon of Athens* is conceded, there may be no difficulty in reference to Lucian.

Mr. Fleay has endeavoured to isolate the part of this play that he considers to have been written by Shakspere. This, with his paper on the authorship and the discussion thereon, can be studied in the New Shakspere Society's *Transactions*, 1874, Part I.

A KING AND NO KING.

Total Number of Lines.	CHARACTERS.	I.		II.		III.			IV.				V.			
		1	2	1	2	1	2	3	1	2	3	4	1	2	3	4
406	MARDONIUS	154	...	...	1	19	...	76	...	55	...	...	63	...	...	38
428	BESSUS	64	10	86	...	2	133	24	...	...	47	...	32	...	23	7
1129	ARBACES	307	...	...	53	208	...	113	...	67	...	121	...	...	...	260
190	TIGRANES	26	28	...	6	47	...	...	...	51	...	...	...	28	...	4
9	1ST GENTLEMAN	5	...	...	...	4	...	...	...	...	...	...	...	...	...	...
8	2ND GENTLEMAN	4	...	...	...	1	...	...	...	...	...	...	...	..	...	3
3	MESSENGER	3	...	...	...	...	...	...	...	...	...	...	...	...	...	...
268	GOBRIAS	...	...	78	...	56	...	...	25	20	...	1	...	...	...	88
143	BACURIUS	...	...	23	...	3	33	...	...	17	...	...	...	5	62	...
11	1ST MAN	...	...	...	11	...	...	...	...	...	..	...	...	...	..	...
12	2ND MAN	...	...	...	12	...	...	...	...	...	...	...	...	...	..	...
14	3RD MAN	...	...	...	14	...	...	...	...	...	...	...	...	...	...	...
7	PHILIP	...	...	...	7	...	...	...	...	...	...	...	...	...	...	...
2	4TH MAN	...	...	...	2	...	...	...	...	...	...	...	...	...	...	...
6	"ALL"	...	...	...	6	...	...	...	...	...	...	...	...	...	...	...
17	3RD GENTLEMAN	...	...	...	...	...	17	...	...	...	...	..	...	...	...	...
86	1ST SWORDMAN	...	...	...	...	...	...	...	...	...	70	...	5	...	11	...
82	2ND SWORDMAN	...	...	...	...	...	...	...	...	...	53	...	4	...	25	...
108	LYGONES	..	...	...	...	...	..	...	...	...	...	...	47	55	...	6
3	SERVANT	...	...	...	...	...	...	...	..	...	...	...	...	...	3	...
183	SPACONIA	...	30	64	...	10	...	...	23	45	...	...	...	11	...	...
46	ARANE	...	...	17	...	10	...	...	...	...	...	...	...	...	...	19
255	PANTHEA	...	...	101	...	52	...	...	41	...	...	55	...	..	...	6
7	WOMAN	...	...	...	7	...	...	...	...	...	...	...	...	...	...	...
37	1ST CITIZEN'S WIFE ...	...	...	...	37	...	...	...	...	...	...	...	...	...	...	...
18	2ND CITIZEN'S WIFE ...	...	...	...	18	...	...	...	...	...	...	..	...	...	...	...
3478		563	68	369	174	412	183	213	89	255	170	177	151	99	124	431
3207	Actual Number of Lines	537	63	342	173	345	183	202	80	252	162	154	146	86	124	358

SCHEME FOR ARRANGING THE PARTS WITH EIGHTEEN MEN.

SEVENTEEN CHARACTERS SINGLY AND ONE GROUP.

SERVANT 3 }
4TH MAN 2 } 5

SUGGESTIONS FOR DISCUSSION.

1. The mode of clearing up the difficulties of the plot in *A King and No King* should be dramatically inadmissible.
2. For certain kinds of dramatic writing the free metrical style of Beaumont and Fletcher is more suitable than the strict Shaksperian rhythm.
3. Beaumont and Fletcher degraded Woman by representing her as the recipient of a soulless homage.

EARLIEST KNOWN EDITION.

Date.	*Printer.*	*Publisher.*	*Acted by*	*Present Owner.*
1619	——	Thomas Walkley	The King's servants	British Museum.

This play was licensed in 1611.

Cunningham (*Op. cit.* p. 211) prints a record of the performance of *A King and No King* on December 26, 1611. The authenticity of this, said to be taken from a MS. in the Audit Office, is doubted. (But see Halliwell-Phillipps's *Outlines*, Vol. II., p. 309). The play was one of those acted before the Court in 1613 (see p. 103).

Beaumont died in 1616.

The earliest notice of the play in the Stationers' Registers is in

1618. August 7.

Master **Blounte** Entred for his Copie vnder the handes of Sir GEORGE BUCKE and Master **Adames** warden A play Called *A king and noe kinge* **vj**[d]

The edition published in the following year has no mention of Blount in the title-page, and has merely the short title of the entry. It is said to be by "Francis Beamont, and Iohn Fletcher," and to have been "Acted at the Globe."

MACBETH.

Total Number of Lines.	CHARACTERS.	I.							II.				III.						IV.			V.							
		1	2	3	4	5	6	7	1	2	3	4	1	2	3	4	5	6	1	2	3	1	2	3	4	5	6	7	8
69	DUNCAN	...	15	...	36	...	18	...	...	...	...	...	...	...	...	...	...	...	...	...	...	...	...	...	...	...	...	...	...
210	MALCOLM	...	6	...	10	...	...	...	...	...	14	...	...	...	...	...	...	...	...	...	141	...	...	...	11	...	6	2	20
35	SERGEANT	...	35	...	...	...	...	...	...	...	...	...	...	...	...	...	...	...	...	...	...	...	...	...	...	...	...	...	...
72	LENNOX...	...	2	...	...	...	...	...	...	...	20	...	...	...	...	5	...	32	6	...	...	...	7	...	...	...	...	...	...
134	ROSS	...	18	16	...	...	...	...	...	...	...	26	...	...	...	5	...	...	...	19	41	...	...	...	...	...	...	...	9
705	MACBETH	...	...	50	16	4	...	48	45	39	33	...	114	41	...	105	...	...	75	...	...	...	...	55	...	44	...	10	26
112	BANQUO...	...	...	42	2	...	8	...	24	...	11	...	21	...	4	...	...	...	...	...	...	...	...	...	...	...	...	...	...
21	ANGUS	...	...	12	...	...	...	...	...	...	...	...	...	...	...	...	...	...	...	...	...	...	9	...	...	...	...	...	...
23	MESSENGER... ...	...	...	...	...	5	...	...	...	...	...	...	...	...	...	...	...	...	...	9	...	...	...	...	...	9	...	...	...
40	PORTER...	...	...	...	...	...	...	...	...	...	40	...	...	...	...	...	...	...	...	...	...	...	...	...	...	...	...	...	...
179	MACDUFF	...	...	...	...	...	...	...	...	...	40	14	...	...	...	...	...	...	...	...	91	...	...	...	3	...	2	10	19
9	DONALBAIN	...	...	...	...	...	...	...	...	...	9	...	...	...	...	...	...	...	...	...	...	...	...	...	...	...	...	...	...
5	"ALL"	...	...	...	...	...	...	...	...	...	2	...	...	...	...	...	1	...	...	...	...	...	...	...	1	...	...	...	1
11	OLD MAN	...	...	...	...	...	...	...	...	...	...	11	...	...	...	...	...	...	...	...	...	...	...	...	...	...	...	...	...
1	ATTENDANT... ...	...	...	...	...	...	...	...	...	...	...	...	1	...	...	...	...	...	...	...	...	...	...	...	...	...	...	...	...
32	1ST MURDERER ...	...	...	...	...	...	...	...	...	...	...	...	10	...	11	7	...	...	...	4	...	...	...	...	...	...	...	...	...
17	2ND MURDERER ...	...	...	...	...	...	...	...	...	...	...	...	8	...	9	...	...	...	...	...	...	...	...	...	...	...	...	...	...
5	SERVANT	...	...	...	...	...	...	...	...	...	...	...	...	2	...	...	...	...	...	...	...	...	...	3	...	...	...	...	...
8	3RD MURDERER ...	...	...	...	...	...	...	...	...	...	...	...	...	...	8	...	...	...	...	...	...	...	...	...	...	...	...	...	...
24	LORD	...	...	...	...	...	...	...	...	...	...	...	...	...	...	3	...	21	...	...	...	...	...	...	...	...	...	...	...
2	1ST APPARITION ...	...	...	...	...	...	...	...	...	...	...	...	...	...	...	...	...	...	2	...	...	...	...	...	...	...	...	...	...
5	ENGLISH DOCTOR	...	...	...	...	...	...	...	...	...	...	...	...	...	...	...	...	...	...	...	5	...	...	...	...	...	...	...	...
47	SCOTCH DOCTOR	...	...	...	...	...	...	...	...	...	...	...	...	...	...	...	...	...	...	...	...	38	...	9	...	...	...	...	...
12	MENTEITH	...	...	...	...	...	...	...	...	...	...	...	...	...	...	...	...	...	...	...	...	...	10	...	2	...	...	...	...
11	CAITHNESS	...	...	...	...	...	...	...	...	...	...	...	...	...	...	...	...	...	...	...	...	...	11	...	...	...	...	...	...
5	SEYTON...	...	...	...	...	...	...	...	...	...	...	...	...	...	...	...	...	...	...	...	...	...	...	3	...	2	...	...	...
30	OLD SIWARD ...	...	...	...	...	...	...	...	...	...	...	...	...	...	...	...	...	...	...	...	...	...	...	...	10	...	3	6	11
7	YOUNG SIWARD ...	...	...	...	...	...	...	...	...	...	...	...	...	...	...	...	...	...	...	...	...	...	...	...	...	...	...	7	...
82	1ST WITCH	6	...	34	...	...	...	...	...	...	...	...	...	...	...	...	2	...	40	...	...	...	...	...	...	...	...	...	...
48	2ND WITCH	6	...	12	...	...	...	...	...	...	...	...	...	...	...	...	...	...	30	...	...	...	...	...	...	...	...	...	...
48	3RD WITCH	5	...	14	...	...	...	...	...	...	...	...	...	...	...	...	...	...	29	...	...	...	...	...	...	...	...	...	...
261	LADY MACBETH ...	...	...	...	...	71	11	43	...	46	6	...	3	18	...	40	...	...	...	...	...	23	...	...	...	...	...	...	...
2	FLEANCE	...	...	...	...	...	...	...	2	...	...	...	...	...	...	...	...	...	...	...	...	...	...	...	...	...	...	...	...
39	HECATE	...	...	...	...	...	...	...	...	...	...	...	...	...	...	...	34	...	5	...	...	...	...	...	...	...	...	...	...
4	2ND APPARITION ...	...	...	...	...	...	...	...	...	...	...	...	...	...	...	...	...	...	4	...	...	...	...	...	...	...	...	...	...
5	3RD APPARITION ...	...	...	...	...	...	...	...	...	...	...	...	...	...	...	...	...	...	5	...	...	...	...	...	...	...	...	...	...
42	LADY MACDUFF ...	...	...	...	...	...	...	...	...	...	...	...	...	...	...	...	...	...	...	42	...	...	...	...	...	...	...	...	...
21	SON...	...	...	...	...	...	...	...	...	...	...	...	...	...	...	...	...	...	...	21	...	...	...	...	...	...	...	...	...
27	GENTLEWOMAN ...	...	...	...	...	...	...	...	...	...	...	...	...	...	...	...	...	...	...	...	...	27	...	...	...	...	...	...	...
2410		17	76	180	64	80	37	91	71	85	175	51	157	61	32	165	37	53	196	95	278	88	37	70	27	55	11	35	86
2108	Actual No. of Lines	12	67	156	58	74	31	82	64	73	152	41	142	56	22	144	37	49	156	85	240	87	31	62	21	52	10	29	75

The total lines should be 2109, as 86 is the total of IV. 2, in which Lady Macduff's lines should be 43.

SCHEME FOR ARRANGING THE PARTS WITH EIGHTEEN MEN AND SEVEN LADIES.

Men's Parts.

TWELVE CHARACTERS SINGLY AND SIX GROUPS.

Lord	24	25	Angus	21	26	Messenger	23	28
Attendant	1		English Doctor	5		Servant	5	
Menteith	12	27	Caithness	11	27	Donalbain	9	28
Young Siward	7		Seyton	5		1st Apparition	2	
3rd Murderer	8		Old Man	11		2nd Murderer	17	

Ladies' Parts.

FOUR CHARACTERS SINGLY AND THREE GROUPS.

Hecate	39	41	Gentlewoman	27	52	Lady Macduff	43	48
Fleance	2		Son	21		3rd Apparition	5	
			2nd Apparition	4				

SUGGESTIONS FOR DISCUSSION.

1. *Macbeth* in its present state is the original drama altered by Middleton.
2. Shakspere wrote *Macbeth* to show his belief in the influence that beings of the spirit-world have upon every man and woman.
3. The internal evidence of *Macbeth* and contemporary records prove that Shakspere had been to Scotland.

THE EARLIEST KNOWN EDITION IS THE 1623 FOLIO.

In the Stationers' Registers is this record: "27 die Augusti 1596. Tho. Millington—Thomas Millington is likewyse fyned at ijs vjd for printinge of a ballad contrarye to order, which he also presently paid. Md. the ballad entituled The taming of a shrew. Also one other Ballad of Macdobeth." Coming in a part of the Registers, permission to print which was not granted to Mr. Arber, this extract is taken from Furness's edition of *Macbeth*, p. 387.

In *Kemps nine daies wonder*, 1600, there is an allusion to "a penny Poet, whose first making was the miserable stolne story of Macdoel, or Macdobeth, or Macsomewhat" (ed. Camden Society, p. 21). It has been thought that this ballad, of which no copy exists, may have furnished Shakspere with hints.

There was a play on this subject before the King at Oxford in 1605.

But these and other sources (see Furness, *Op. cit.*) are very improbable ones for Shakspere, who, taking an outline of the facts from Holinshed, filled it in according to his own ideas.

Amongst the Ashmolean MSS. in the Bodleian there is one by Dr. Simon Forman, in which he gives an account of the performances of some of Shakspere's plays. He saw *Macbeth* acted at the Globe on April 20, 1610. His "Booke of Plaies and Notes thereof" was printed in the New Shakspere Society's *Transactions*, 1875-6, Part II.

Any near approach to the date of the composition of *Macbeth* must, within certain limits, be determined by internal evidence.

THE KNIGHT OF THE BURNING PESTLE.

Total Number of Lines.	CHARACTERS.	Prologue.	Induction.	I.			II.					III.					IV.					V.			Epilogue.
				1	2	3	1	2	3	4	5	1	2	3	4	5	1	2	3	4	5	1	2	3	
292	CITIZEN	...	64	12	11	14	6	30	9	4	13	6	13	8	12	7	18	8	...	...	19	21	5	11	1
458	RALPH	...	6	...	71	...	...	59	16	...	...	...	49	...	52	...	...	41	...	...	36	5	72	51	...
176	VENTERWELS	...	...	38	...	...	16	...	...	8	15	5	...	...	...	...	...	...	47	9	...	13	...	25	...
242	JASPER	...	...	35	...	14	...	38	...	...	...	80	...	...	...	...	11	...	...	26	...	27	...	11	...
181	HUMPHREY	...	...	76	...	...	31	37	...	8	...	5	...	...	...	...	...	...	14	...	...	10	...	...	...
12	TIM	...	...	...	3	...	...	5	2	...	...	...	...	...	2	...	...	...	...	...	...	...	...	...	...
35	GEORGE	...	...	...	3	...	...	7	20	...	...	...	...	...	5	...	...	...	...	...	...	...	...	...	...
267	MERRYTHOUGHT	...	...	...	...	41	...	...	...	...	71	...	...	...	...	38	...	...	...	...	48	...	...	69	...
7	TAPSTER	...	...	...	...	...	...	...	4	...	...	...	3	...	...	...	...	...	...	...	...	...	...	...	...
51	HOST	...	...	...	...	...	...	...	...	...	...	...	46	...	5	...	...	...	...	...	...	...	...	...	...
18	BARBER	...	...	...	...	...	...	...	...	...	...	...	...	...	18	...	...	...	...	...	...	...	...	...	...
12	1ST KNIGHT	...	...	...	...	...	...	...	...	...	...	...	...	...	12	...	...	...	...	...	...	...	...	...	...
12	2ND KNIGHT	...	...	...	...	...	...	...	...	...	...	...	...	...	12	...	...	...	...	...	...	...	...	...	...
2	MAN	...	...	...	...	...	...	...	...	...	...	...	...	...	2	...	...	...	...	...	...	...	...	...	...
16	3RD KNIGHT	...	...	...	...	...	...	...	...	...	...	...	...	...	16	...	...	...	...	...	...	...	...	...	...
7	SERVANT	...	...	...	...	...	...	...	...	...	...	...	...	...	...	...	...	...	3	4	...	...	...	...	...
2	SERGEANT	...	...	...	...	...	...	...	...	...	...	...	...	...	...	...	...	...	...	...	...	...	2	...	...
2	HAMERTON	...	...	...	...	...	...	...	...	...	...	...	...	...	...	...	...	...	...	...	...	...	2	...	...
6	GREENGOOSE	...	...	...	...	...	...	...	...	...	...	...	...	...	...	...	...	...	...	...	...	...	6	...	...
2	1ST SOLDIER	...	...	...	...	...	...	...	...	...	...	...	...	...	...	...	...	...	...	...	...	...	2	...	...
2	2ND SOLDIER	...	...	...	...	...	...	...	...	...	...	...	...	...	...	...	...	...	...	...	...	...	2	...	...
1	"ALL"	...	...	...	...	...	...	...	...	...	...	...	...	...	...	...	...	...	...	...	...	...	1	...	...
63	"PROLOGUE"	26	37	...	...	...	...	...	...	...	...	...	...	...	...	...	...	...	...	...	...	...	...	...	...
511	WIFE	...	41	33	23	26	18	76	22	18	21	16	38	18	35	49	19	7	...	...	5	24	3	6	13
161	LUCE	...	...	48	...	...	...	13	...	...	...	38	...	...	...	...	...	...	...	62	...	...	...	...	...
74	BOY	...	...	1	...	...	...	5	...	...	...	...	...	6	...	2	19	...	10	13	7	...	...	11	...
185	MISTRESS MERRYTHOUGHT	...	...	...	...	64	...	36	2	...	...	...	9	...	...	43	...	...	19	...	...	...	...	12	...
20	MICHAEL	...	...	...	...	5	...	7	2	...	...	...	2	...	...	1	...	...	...	...	...	...	...	3	...
6	WOMAN	...	...	...	...	...	...	...	...	...	...	...	...	...	6	...	...	...	...	...	...	...	...	...	...
25	POMPIONA	...	...	...	...	...	...	...	...	...	...	...	...	...	...	...	...	25	...	...	...	...	...	...	...
5	2ND BOY	...	...	...	...	...	...	...	...	...	...	...	...	...	...	...	...	...	...	...	5	...	...	...	...
2853		26	148	243	111	164	71	313	77	38	120	150	160	32	177	140	67	81	93	114	120	100	95	199	14
2771	Actual Number of Lines	26	148	217	111	164	69	295	77	38	120	141	160	32	174	140	64	80	91	105	116	98	95	196	14

SCHEME FOR ARRANGING THE PARTS WITH EIGHTEEN MEN AND SEVEN LADIES.

Men's Parts.

FIFTEEN CHARACTERS SINGLY AND THREE GROUPS.

MAN	2	4	SERGEANT	2	9	TAPSTER	7	9
1ST SOLDIER	2		SERVANT	7		2ND SOLDIER	2	

Ladies' Parts.

FIVE CHARACTERS SINGLY AND TWO GROUPS.

MICHAEL	20	25	POMPIONA	25	31
2ND BOY	5		WOMAN	6	

SUGGESTIONS FOR DISCUSSION.

1. There is a definite connection between *Don Quixote*, *The Knight of the Burning* Pestle, and *Hudibras*.
2. The popularity of Beaumont and Fletcher was owing to the fact that they suited themselves to the gross tastes of the Court and age, thus showing a marked contrast to Shakspere, who elevated the public to himself.
3. *The Faithful Shepherdess*, possessing only beauties of detail, does not rank so high as Ben Jonson's *Sad Shepherd*, while compared with Milton's *Comus* it is a miserable failure.

EARLIEST KNOWN EDITION.

Date.	*Printer.*	*Publisher.*	*Acted by*	*Present Owner.*
1613	——	Walter Burre		British Museum.

This edition had merely "The Knight of the Burning Pestle" for its title. "W. B.," the publisher, dedicating it to Master Robert Keysar in a smartly-written letter, alludes to its rejection two years before by the theatre-going public, who did not understand "the privy mark of irony about it." He refers to its likeness to *Don Quixote*, the first English translation of which appeared in 1612, but part of which dated from 1605.

The play was not entered in the Stationers' Registers.

PERICLES.

Total Number of Lines.	CHARACTERS.	I.					II.						III.					IV.							V.			
		Chorus.	1	2	3	4	Chorus.	1	2	3	4	5	Chorus.	1	2	3	4	Chorus.	1	2	3	4	5	6	Chorus.	1	2	3
307	"GOWER"	42					40						60					52				51			24		20	18
67	ANTIOCHUS		67																									
603	PERICLES		98	94		17		79		25		33		59		28										115		55
28	THALIARD		6		22																							
1	MESSENGER		1																									
33	1ST LORD			1		7			6		16															3		
11	2ND LORD			2					2		7																	
122	HELICANUS			31	19						32															39		1
110	CLEON					74										14					22							
4	"ALL"					2			1		1																	
43	1ST FISHERMAN							43																				
31	2ND FISHERMAN							31																				
20	3RD FISHERMAN							20																				
153	SIMONIDES								28	67		58																
3	3RD LORD								2		1																	
7	1ST KNIGHT									6		1																
1	MARSHAL									1																		
2	ESCANES										2																	
1	2ND KNIGHT											1																
1	3RD KNIGHT											1																
10	1ST SAILOR													10														
6	2ND SAILOR													6														
109	CERIMON														84		8											17
3	PHILEMON														3													
6	SERVANT														6													
25	1ST GENTLEMAN														18								6			1		
18	2ND GENTLEMAN														14								4					
23	LEONINE																		23									
2	1ST PIRATE																		1	1								
1	2ND PIRATE																		1									
2	3RD PIRATE																		2									
32	PANDAR																			28				4				
99	BOULT																			44				55				
107	LYSIMACHUS																							52		55		
9	TYRIAN SAILOR																									9		
2	DAUGHTER		2																									
89	DIONYZA					9										6			38		36							
82	THAISA								22	22		4			2		10											22
11	LYCHORIDA													11														
190	MARINA																		46	16				61		65		2
117	BAWD																			74				43				
10	"DIANA"																									10		
2501		42	174	128	41	109	40	173	61	121	59	98	60	86	127	48	18	52	111	163	58	51	10	215	24	297	20	115
2391	Actual No. of Lines	42	171	124	40	108	40	173	60	116	58	93	60	82	111	41	18	52	103	163	51	51	10	212	24	265	20	103

SCHEME FOR ARRANGING THE PARTS WITH EIGHTEEN MEN AND SEVEN LADIES.

Men's Parts.

Omit PANDAR and BOULT.

TWELVE CHARACTERS SINGLY AND SIX GROUPS.

Part	Lines	Group total
1ST PIRATE	2	24
2ND GENTLEMAN	18	
2ND KNIGHT	1	
3RD LORD	3	
PHILEMON	3	26
3RD PIRATE	2	
3RD FISHERMAN	20	
3RD KNIGHT	1	
1ST KNIGHT	7	24
2ND LORD	11	
2ND SAILOR	6	
1ST SAILOR	10	25
TYRIAN SAILOR	9	
SERVANT	6	
ESCANES	2	26
LEONINE	23	
MESSENGER	1	
MARSHAL	1	27
1ST GENTLEMAN	25	
2ND PIRATE	1	

Ladies' Parts: Omit BAWD.

SUGGESTIONS FOR DISCUSSION.

1. The stage-management of *Pericles* and the slavish reproduction of the romance of Apollonius show that the whole play could not have been written by Shakspere.
2. The story of Marina as an artistic whole written by Shakspere can be separated from *Pericles*, showing the rest of the play to be parts added by Wilkins and Rowley.
3. Cerimon is Dr. John Hall.

LIST OF EARLIEST KNOWN EDITIONS.

Date.	*Printer.*	*Publisher.*	*Acted by*	*Present Owners.*
1609	——	Henry Gosson	The King's servants	British Museum. Bodleian Library. Trinity College, Cambridge.
1609	——	Henry Gosson	The King's servants	British Museum. Hamburg Public Library. Duke of Devonshire.
1611	S. S.	——	The King's servants	British Museum.
1619	——	T. P.		British Museum. Bodleian Library. Trinity College, Cambridge.

In the Stationers' Registers are the following entries:—

1576. July 17.
William Howe. Receyued of him for his licence to ymprint a booke intituled *the most excellent pleasant and variable historie of the strange adventures of prince* APOLLONIUS LUCINA *his wife and* THARSA *his daughter* viij[d]
This booke is sett foorth in print with this title *The patterne of peynfull aduentures.*

1608. May 20.
Edward Blount. Entred for his copie vnder thandes of Sir GEORGE BUCK knight and Master Warden **Seton** A booke called. *The booke of* PERICLES *prynce of Tyre* vj[d]
Edward Blunt Entred also for his copie by the lyke Aucthoritie. A booke Called. ANTHONY. *and* CLEOPATRA vj[d]

In 1608 T. P. printed for Nat. Butter a novel by George Wilkins called "The Painfull Aduentures of Pericles Prince of Tyre. Being The true History of the Play of *Pericles*, as it was lately presented by the worthy and ancient Poet, Iohn Gower." Copies are in the British Museum and the Zurich Public Library.

The 1609 copies are two distinct editions. In each and in the 1611 version the title is "The Late, And much admired Play, Called Pericles, Prince of Tyre. With the true Relation of the whole Historie, aduentures, and fortunes of the said Prince: As also, The no lesse strange, and worthy accidents, in the Birth and Life, of his Daughter Mariana." The play is said to have "been diuers and sundry times acted by his Maiesties Seruants, at the Globe on the Banck-side," and to have been written "By William Shakespeare." In the 1619 edition, which was issued with *The Whole Contention* in one volume (see p. 65). the latter part of the title and the allusion to the acting are omitted. The author is described as "W. Shakespeare."

Notwithstanding its evident popularity and its clear statement of authorship, the play was not included in the 1623 Folio, and was not printed with Shakspere's works till 1664. It looks as if there had been some barrier to its inclusion, other than a literary one.

The story of *Pericles* is met with in various forms (see Douce's *Illustrations of Shakspeare*, ed. 1839, pp. 398–403). Hazlitt, in *Shakespeare's Library*, reprints "The Story of Apollonius of Tyre" from Gower's *Confessio Amantis*, from which probably the authors of *Pericles* drew their inspiration. Hazlitt also prints Twine's novel, the entry of which in the Stationers' Registers is recorded above. The earliest known edition is one without date, "Imprinted at London by Valentine Simmes for the Widow Newman."

The story of Marina referred to in the second suggestion has been extracted by Mr. Fleay. It is printed in the New Shakspere Society's *Transactions*, 1874, Part I. The student should consult his paper accompanying it, and also Mr. Boyle's paper on the authorship of the play in the *Transactions* for 1880–5, Part II.

Total Number of Lines.	CHARACTERS.	I.					II.							III.							
		1	2	3	4	5	1	2	3	4	5	6	7	1	2	3	4	5	6	7	8
16	Philo	16	...	...	...	...	...	...	...	...	...	...	...	...	...	...	...	...	...	...	...
829	Antony	25	59	47	...	...	...	86	25	...	...	16	28	...	19	...	25	...	...	21	...
6	1st Attendant ...	1	1	...	...	...	...	...	...	...	1	...	...	...	...	...	...	...	...	...	...
5	Demetrius...	5	...	...	...	...	...	...	...	...	...	...	...	...	...	...	...	...	...	...	...
32	Alexas...	...	11	...	...	17	...	...	...	...	...	...	...	...	...	4	...	...	...	...	...
32	Soothsayer	...	13	...	...	...	...	...	19	...	...	...	...	...	...	...	...	...	...	...	...
356	Enobarbus...	...	47	...	...	...	...	79	...	...	...	44	18	...	22	...	...	9	...	30	...
79	1st Messenger ...	...	15	...	16	...	...	...	...	...	25	...	...	...	...	18	...	...	...	3	...
1	2nd Attendant ...	...	1	...	...	...	...	...	...	...	...	...	...	...	...	...	...	...	...	...	...
4	2nd Messenger ...	...	4	...	...	...	...	...	...	...	...	...	...	...	...	...	...	...	...	...	...
420	Cæsar	...	...	...	62	...	...	56	1	...	...	16	15	...	21	...	...	...	83	...	5
70	Lepidus	...	...	...	15	...	...	27	...	8	...	6	12	...	2	...	...	...	...	...	...
19	Mardian	...	...	...	...	6	...	...	...	...	1	...	...	...	...	...	...	...	...	...	...
136	Pompey...	...	...	...	...	...	42	...	...	...	...	64	30	...	...	...	...	...	...	...	...
6	Menecrates	...	...	...	...	...	6	...	...	...	...	...	...	...	...	...	...	...	...	...	...
68	Menas	...	...	...	...	...	8	...	...	...	...	27	33	...	...	...	...	...	...	...	...
4	Varrius	...	...	...	...	...	4	...	...	...	...	...	...	...	...	...	...	...	...	...	...
40	Mecænas	...	...	...	...	...	...	17	...	4	...	...	...	...	...	...	...	...	10	...	...
61	Agrippa	...	...	...	...	...	...	30	...	3	...	...	...	...	13	...	...	...	5	...	...
11	1st Servant	...	...	...	...	...	...	...	...	...	...	...	11	...	...	...	...	...	...	...	...
8	2nd Servant	...	...	...	...	...	...	...	...	...	...	...	8	...	...	...	...	...	...	...	...
30	Ventidius	...	...	...	...	...	...	...	...	...	...	...	...	30	...	...	...	...	...	...	...
11	Silius	...	...	...	...	...	...	...	...	...	...	...	...	11	...	...	...	...	...	...	...
49	Eros	...	...	...	...	...	...	...	...	...	...	...	...	...	...	...	...	18	...	...	...
25	Canidius	...	...	...	...	...	...	...	...	...	...	...	...	...	...	...	...	...	...	16	...
63	1st Soldier	...	...	...	...	...	...	...	...	...	...	...	...	...	...	...	...	...	...	13	...
1	Taurus...	...	...	...	...	...	...	...	...	...	...	...	...	...	...	...	...	...	...	...	1
40	Scarus...	...	...	...	...	...	...	...	...	...	...	...	...	...	...	...	...	...	...	...	...
12	"All"	...	...	...	...	...	...	...	...	...	...	...	...	...	...	...	...	...	...	...	...
48	Dolabella...	...	...	...	...	...	...	...	...	...	...	...	...	...	...	...	...	...	...	...	...
16	Euphronius	...	...	...	...	...	...	...	...	...	...	...	...	...	...	...	...	...	...	...	...
31	Thyreus	...	...	...	...	...	...	...	...	...	...	...	...	...	...	...	...	...	...	...	...
15	2nd Soldier	...	...	...	...	...	...	...	...	...	...	...	...	...	...	...	...	...	...	...	...
13	3rd Soldier	...	...	...	...	...	...	...	...	...	...	...	...	...	...	...	...	...	...	...	...
5	4th Soldier	...	...	...	...	...	...	...	...	...	...	...	...	...	...	...	...	...	...	...	...
1	Captain	...	...	...	...	...	...	...	...	...	...	...	...	...	...	...	...	...	...	...	...
23	1st Guard...	...	...	...	...	...	...	...	...	...	...	...	...	...	...	...	...	...	...	...	...
4	2nd Guard...	...	...	...	...	...	...	...	...	...	...	...	...	...	...	...	...	...	...	...	...
1	3rd Guard...	...	...	...	...	...	...	...	...	...	...	...	...	...	...	...	...	...	...	...	...
21	Dercetas	...	...	...	...	...	...	...	...	...	...	...	...	...	...	...	...	...	...	...	...
19	Diomedes	...	...	...	...	...	...	...	...	...	...	...	...	...	...	...	...	...	...	...	...
6	Egyptian	...	...	...	...	...	...	...	...	...	...	...	...	...	...	...	...	...	...	...	...
32	Proculeius	...	...	...	...	...	...	...	...	...	...	...	...	...	...	...	...	...	...	...	...
2	Gallus	...	...	...	...	...	...	...	...	...	...	...	...	...	...	...	...	...	...	...	...
5	Seleucus	...	...	...	...	...	...	...	...	...	...	...	...	...	...	...	...	...	...	...	...
31	Clown	...	...	...	...	...	...	...	...	...	...	...	...	...	...	...	...	...	...	...	...
670	Cleopatra	21	6	70	...	60	...	...	...	...	106	...	...	...	...	34	...	...	...	15	...
109	Charmian	...	43	8	...	8	...	...	...	...	10	...	...	...	...	9	...	...	...	...	...
3[illegible]	Iras	...	15	...	...	...	...	...	...	...	...	...	...	...	...	...	...	...	...	...	...
36	Octavia	...	...	...	...	...	...	...	3	...	...	...	...	...	3	...	16	...	14	...	...
6	Boy	...	...	...	...	...	...	...	...	...	...	...	6	...	...	...	...	...	...	...	...
3558		68	215	125	93	91	60	295	48	15	143	173	161	41	80	65	41	27	112	98	6
3063	Actual No. of Lines	62	204	105	84	78	52	250	42	10	119	145	141	37	66	51	38	25	98	81	6

CLEOPATRA.

						IV.															V.	
	9	10	11	12	13	1	2	3	4	5	6	7	8	9	10	11	12	13	14	15	1	2
...	...	...	...	...	...	...	...	...	...	...	...	...	...	...	...	...	...	...	...	...	...	...
ANTONY	4	...	58	...	110	...	41	...	31	11	...	5	37	...	9	...	43	...	106	23	...	...
1ST ATTENDANT	...	...	...	...	3	...	...	...	...	...	...	...	...	...	...	...	...	...	...	...	...	...
...	...	...	...	...	...	...	...	...	...	...	...	...	...	...	...	...	...	...	...	...	...	...
...	...	...	...	...	...	...	...	...	...	...	...	...	...	...	...	...	...	...	...	...	...	...
...	...	...	...	...	...	...	...	...	...	...	...	...	...	...	...	...	...	...	...	...	...	...
ENOBARBUS	...	15	...	...	44	...	11	...	...	...	20	...	...	17	...	...	...	...	...	...	...	...
1ST MESSENGER	...	...	...	...	...	...	...	...	...	...	2	...	...	...	...	...	...	...	...	...	...	...
...	...	...	...	...	...	...	...	...	...	...	...	...	...	...	...	...	...	...	...	...	...	...
...	...	...	...	...	...	...	...	...	...	...	...	...	...	...	...	...	...	...	...	...	...	...
CÆSAR	...	...	...	22	...	13	...	...	...	...	10	...	...	...	...	4	...	...	...	...	54	58
...	...	...	...	...	...	...	...	...	...	...	...	...	...	...	...	...	...	...	...	...	...	...
MARDIAN	...	...	...	...	...	...	...	...	...	...	...	...	...	...	...	...	...	...	12	...	...	...
...	...	...	...	...	...	...	...	...	...	...	...	...	...	...	...	...	...	...	...	...	...	...
...	...	...	...	...	...	...	...	...	...	...	...	...	...	...	...	...	...	...	...	...	...	...
...	...	...	...	...	...	...	...	...	...	...	...	...	...	...	...	...	...	...	...	...	...	...
...	...	...	...	...	...	...	...	...	...	...	...	...	...	...	...	...	...	...	...	...	...	...
MECÆNAS	...	...	...	...	...	5	...	...	...	...	...	...	...	...	...	...	...	...	...	...	4	...
AGRIPPA	...	...	...	...	...	...	...	...	...	...	1	3	...	...	...	...	...	...	...	...	6	...
...	...	...	...	...	...	...	...	...	...	...	...	...	...	...	...	...	...	...	...	...	...	...
...	...	...	...	...	...	...	...	...	...	...	...	...	...	...	...	...	...	...	...	...	...	...
...	...	...	...	...	...	...	...	...	...	...	...	...	...	...	...	...	...	...	...	...	...	...
...	...	...	...	...	...	...	...	...	...	...	...	...	...	...	...	...	...	...	...	...	...	...
EROS	...	...	8	...	...	...	...	...	1	2	...	2	...	...	...	...	...	...	18	...	...	...
CANIDIUS	...	9	...	...	...	...	...	...	...	...	...	...	...	...	...	...	...	...	...	...	...	...
1ST SOLDIER	...	...	...	...	...	...	...	12	3	12	10	...	...	13	...	...	...	...	...	...	...	...
...	...	...	...	...	...	...	...	...	...	...	...	...	...	...	...	...	...	...	...	...	...	...
SCARUS	...	21	...	...	...	...	...	...	...	...	...	11	...	...	1	...	7	...	...	...	...	...
"ALL"	...	...	1	...	...	...	1	3	1	...	...	...	...	...	...	...	...	...	2	1	1	2
DOLABELLA	...	...	...	5	...	...	...	...	...	...	...	...	...	...	...	...	...	...	...	...	1	42
EUPHRONIUS	...	...	...	14	2	...	...	...	...	...	...	...	...	...	...	...	...	...	...	...	...	...
THYREUS	...	...	...	2	29	...	...	...	...	...	...	...	...	...	...	...	...	...	...	...	...	...
2ND SOLDIER	...	...	...	...	...	...	...	8	...	...	...	...	...	7	...	...	...	...	...	...	...	...
3RD SOLDIER	...	...	...	...	...	...	...	6	...	...	...	...	...	7	...	...	...	...	...	...	...	...
4TH SOLDIER	...	...	...	...	...	...	...	5	...	...	...	...	...	...	...	...	...	...	...	...	...	...
CAPTAIN	...	...	...	...	...	...	...	...	1	...	...	...	...	...	...	...	...	...	...	...	...	...
1ST GUARD	...	...	...	...	...	...	...	...	...	...	...	...	...	...	...	...	...	...	5	...	...	18
2ND GUARD	...	...	...	...	...	...	...	...	...	...	...	...	...	...	...	...	...	...	2	...	...	2
3RD GUARD	...	...	...	...	...	...	...	...	...	...	...	...	...	...	...	...	...	...	1	...	...	...
DERCETAS	...	...	...	...	...	...	...	...	...	...	...	...	...	...	...	...	...	...	4	...	17	...
DIOMEDES	...	...	...	...	...	...	...	...	...	...	...	...	...	...	...	...	...	...	16	3	...	...
EGYPTIAN	...	...	...	...	...	...	...	...	...	...	...	...	...	...	...	...	...	...	...	...	6	...
PROCULEIUS	...	...	...	...	...	...	...	...	...	...	...	...	...	...	...	...	...	...	...	...	1	31
GALLUS	...	...	...	...	...	...	...	...	...	...	...	...	...	...	...	...	...	...	...	...	...	2
SELEUCUS	...	...	...	...	...	...	...	...	...	...	...	...	...	...	...	...	...	...	...	...	...	5
CLOWN	...	...	...	...	...	...	...	...	...	...	...	...	...	...	...	...	...	...	...	...	...	31
CLEOPATRA	...	...	8	...	46	...	2	...	9	...	...	...	5	...	...	...	1	8	...	68	...	211
CHARMIAN	...	...	2	...	...	...	...	...	1	...	...	...	...	...	...	...	...	4	...	5	...	19
IRAS	...	...	4	...	...	...	...	...	...	...	...	...	...	...	...	...	...	...	...	4	...	7
...	...	...	...	...	...	...	...	...	...	...	...	...	...	...	...	...	...	...	...	...	...	...
...	...	...	...	...	...	...	...	...	...	...	...	...	...	...	...	...	...	...	...	...	...	...
	4	45	81	43	234	18	55	34	47	25	43	21	42	44	10	4	51	12	166	104	90	428
Actual No. of Lines	4	37	74	36	201	16	45	23	38	17	39	16	39	35	9	4	49	10	140	91	77	369

ANTONY AND CLEOPATRA.

SCHEME FOR ARRANGING THE PARTS WITH EIGHTEEN MEN.

SEVEN CHARACTERS SINGLY AND ELEVEN GROUPS.

Ventidius 30 ⎫ Thyreus 31 ⎬ 67 Taurus 1 ⎪ 4th Soldier 5 ⎭	Eros 49 ⎫ Demetrius 5 ⎬ 67 3rd Soldier 13 ⎭	Scarus 40 ⎫ Philo 16 ⎬ 67 Silius 11 ⎭	Dercetas 21 ⎫ Menecrates 6 ⎬ 67 Soothsayer 32 ⎪ 2nd Servant 8 ⎭
	Mecænas 40 ⎫ 1st Guard 23 ⎬ 67 2nd Messenger 4 ⎭	Agrippa 61 ⎫ Seleucus 5 ⎬ 67 Captain 1 ⎭	
Gallus 2 ⎫ 1st Soldier 63 ⎬ 67 2nd Attendant 1 ⎪ 3rd Guard 1 ⎭	Canidius 25 ⎫ Alexas 32 ⎬ 67 Egyptian 6 ⎪ 2nd Guard 4 ⎭	Diomedes 19 ⎫ Clown 31 ⎬ 67 1st Attendant 6 ⎪ 1st Servant 11 ⎭	
	Dolabella 48 ⎫ Varrius 4 ⎬ 67 2nd Soldier 15 ⎭	Proculeius 32 ⎫ Euphronius 16 ⎬ 67 Mardian 19 ⎭	

SUGGESTIONS FOR DISCUSSION.

1. Blount's entry unaccompanied by any edition of the play proves that Shakspere did not sanction the printing of any of his works after 1604.
2. A comparison of *Antony and Cleopatra* with *Samson Agonistes* shows that Shakspere teaches the same moral lesson as Milton, but with incomparably greater art.
3. The abundance of incident and detail in *Antony and Cleopatra* greatly detracts from the excellence of the play.

THE EARLIEST KNOWN EDITION IS THE 1623 FOLIO.

In the Stationers' Registers is this entry :—

1593. October 19.

Symond waterson.	Entred for his Copie vnder thandes of both the wardens a booke intituled *The Tragedye of* CLEOPATRA	vj[d]

This is Daniel's play which was published in the following year.

On May 20, 1608, "Anthony and Cleopatra" was entered in the Registers by Edward Blount (see p. 159), who was one of those by whom the first Folio was brought out, and by whom, with Jaggard, the play was again entered on November 8, 1623. In the Folio the play is entitled "The Tragedie of Anthonie, and Cleopatra." In the Folio's Table of Contents, called the "Catalogve," it is described as "Anthony and Cleopater."

There is no need to consider that either Daniel's play, or any other dramatic form, furnished Shakspere with hints, as for the facts, and sometimes the words, it is clear that he went to North's English translation of Amyot's French version of Plutarch's *Lives*.

THE DUCHESS OF MALFI.

Total Number of Lines.	CHARACTERS.	I.		II.					III.					IV.		V.				
		1	2	1	2	3	4	5	1	2	3	4	5	1	2	1	2	3	4	5
191	DELIO	10	15	14	13	...	25	...	14	...	29	...	...	...	...	29	...	29	...	13
462	ANTONIO	35	123	28	28	37	...	...	30	65	...	...	37	...	...	24	...	32	23	...
798	BOSOLA	43	41	123	30	57	...	...	16	61	1	...	26	54	167	...	100	...	29	50
287	CARDINAL	3	25	...	...	...	39	35	...	...	7	...	...	...	...	...	118	...	25	35
533	FERDINAND	...	126	...	...	...	...	68	46	101	19	...	...	55	57	...	34	...	5	22
24	SILVIO	...	8	...	...	...	...	...	...	...	16	...	...	...	...	...	...	...	...	...
30	CASTRUCCIO	...	23	7	...	...	...	...	...	...	...	...	...	...	...	...	...	...	...	...
13	RODERIGO	...	2	...	3	...	...	...	...	...	...	...	...	...	...	...	...	...	1	7
6	GRISOLAN	...	2	...	1	...	...	...	...	...	...	...	...	...	...	...	...	...	1	2
53	1ST SERVANT ...	...	...	...	14	...	8	...	...	...	...	...	...	1	23	...	1	...	6	...
8	2ND SERVANT ...	...	...	...	8	...	...	...	...	...	...	...	...	...	...	...	...	...	...	...
5	2ND OFFICER ...	...	...	...	...	...	...	...	...	5	...	...	...	...	...	...	...	...	...	...
2	3RD OFFICER ...	...	...	...	...	...	...	...	...	2	...	...	...	...	...	...	...	...	...	...
3	4TH OFFICER ...	...	...	...	...	...	...	...	...	3	...	...	...	...	...	...	...	...	...	...
5	1ST OFFICER ...	...	...	...	...	...	...	...	...	5	...	...	...	...	...	...	...	...	...	...
29	MALATESTI	...	...	...	...	...	...	...	...	...	8	...	...	...	...	...	7	...	6	8
68	PESCARA	...	...	...	...	...	...	...	...	...	12	...	...	...	...	30	13	...	2	11
18	1ST PILGRIM ...	...	...	...	...	...	...	...	...	...	...	18	...	...	...	...	...	...	...	...
15	2ND PILGRIM ...	...	...	...	...	...	...	...	...	...	...	15	...	...	...	...	...	...	...	...
16	"ALL"	...	...	...	...	...	...	...	...	...	...	16	...	...	...	...	...	...	...	...
24	1ST MADMAN ...	...	...	...	...	...	...	...	...	...	...	...	...	...	24	...	...	...	...	...
10	2ND MADMAN ...	...	...	...	...	...	...	...	...	...	...	...	...	...	10	...	...	...	...	...
12	3RD MADMAN ...	...	...	...	...	...	...	...	...	...	...	...	...	...	12	...	...	...	...	...
14	4TH MADMAN ...	...	...	...	...	...	...	...	...	...	...	...	...	...	14	...	...	...	...	...
4	1ST EXECUTIONER	...	...	...	...	...	...	...	...	...	...	...	...	...	4	...	...	...	...	...
42	DOCTOR	...	...	...	...	...	...	...	...	...	...	...	...	...	...	...	42	...	...	...
69	CARIOLA	...	10	...	2	...	...	...	...	21	...	...	2	...	34	...	...	...	...	...
577	DUCHESS	...	142	37	...	...	...	...	10	121	...	...	106	65	96	...	...	...	...	...
9	OLD LADY	...	...	4	5	...	...	...	...	...	...	...	...	...	...	...	...	...	...	...
143	JULIA	...	...	...	...	...	36	...	...	...	...	...	...	...	...	9	98	...	...	...
10	"ECHO"	...	...	...	...	...	...	...	...	...	...	...	...	...	...	...	...	10	...	...
3480		91	517	213	104	94	108	103	116	384	92	49	171	175	441	92	413	71	98	148
3143	Actual No. of Lines	89	440	200	93	79	83	80	100	345	81	43	150	161	423	83	393	64	95	141

SCHEME FOR ARRANGING THE PARTS WITH EIGHTEEN MEN.

TWELVE CHARACTERS SINGLY AND SIX GROUPS.

Roderigo	13	18	2nd Officer	5	19	1st Executioner	4	19
1st Officer	5		4th Madman	14		2nd Pilgrim	15	
1st Pilgrim	18	20	Grisolan	6	19	2nd Servant	8	20
3rd Officer	2		2nd Madman	10		3rd Madman	12	
			4th Officer	3				

SUGGESTIONS FOR DISCUSSION.

1. Parts of *The Duchess of Malfi* exceed the Just bounds of poetry and tragedy.
2. In flashes of genius which suddenly light up a wide horizon of emotions, Webster alone among English dramatists can be said to equal Shakspere.
3. In his references to the play-writers of his time, Webster showed that he failed to appreciate Shakspere's merits.

EARLIEST KNOWN EDITION.

Date.	*Printer.*	*Publisher.*	*Acted by*	*Present Owner.*
1623	Nicholas Okes	Iohn Waterson	The King's servants	British Museum.

There is no previous entry of the play in the Stationers' Registers.

In the Bodleian there is a MS. note by Malone recording his opinion "that the *Dutchess of Malfy* was produced about the year 1612." Dyce says (*The Works of John Webster*, ed. 1877, p. 54): "We are certain that the *Duchess of Malfi* was performed before March, 1618-19, when Burbadge, who originally played Ferdinand, died; and we may conclude that it was first produced about 1616."

The title of the 1623 edition is "The Tragedy of the dvtchesse of Malfy." It is said to have been "Presented priuatly at the Black-Friers; and publiquely at the Globe," and to be "The perfect and exact Coppy, with diuerse things Printed, that the length of the Play would not beare in the Presentment. Written by John Webster."

The story is to be found in Painter's *Palace of Pleasure*, 1566, and other places (see Dyce, *loc. cit.*).

TROILUS AND CRESSIDA.

Total Number of Lines.	CHARACTERS.	Prologue.	I.			II.			III.			IV.					V.									
			1	2	3	1	2	3	1	2	3	1	2	3	4	5	1	2	3	4	5	6	7	8	9	10
541	TROILUS	...	74	...	...	...	85	...	...	90	...	...	21	5	92	11	1	90	32	2	...	8	...	...	...	30
453	PANDARUS	...	42	172	...	...	...	...	91	61	...	...	36	...	18	...	...	...	9	...	...	...	...	...	...	24
143	ÆNEAS	...	5	...	58	...	...	...	...	...	...	20	20	...	9	25	...	3	...	...	...	...	...	...	...	3
35	ALEXANDER	...	...	35	...	...	...	...	...	...	...	...	...	...	...	...	...	...	...	...	...	...	...	...	...	...
195	AGAMEMNON... ...	...	...	...	66	...	...	59	...	...	14	...	...	...	...	36	4	...	...	...	11	...	...	...	5	...
158	NESTOR	...	...	...	93	...	...	20	...	...	2	...	...	...	...	28	...	...	...	...	14	...	...	...	1	...
488	ULYSSES	...	...	...	179	...	...	81	...	...	122	...	...	...	...	62	3	28	...	...	13	...	...	...	...	...
12	MENELAUS	...	...	...	1	...	...	...	...	...	1	...	...	...	...	9	1	...	...	...	...	...	...	...	...	...
89	AJAX	...	...	...	...	26	...	28	...	...	3	...	...	...	...	21	3	...	...	...	1	5	...	...	2	...
321	THERSITES	...	...	...	...	85	...	61	...	...	48	...	...	...	...	...	61	23	...	30	...	...	13	...	...	...
195	ACHILLES	...	...	...	...	28	...	11	...	...	74	...	...	...	...	25	23	...	...	...	4	6	8	16	...	...
70	PATROCLUS	...	...	...	...	3	...	19	...	...	31	...	...	...	...	7	10	...	...	...	...	...	...	...	...	...
20	PRIAM	...	...	...	...	...	12	...	...	...	...	...	...	...	...	...	...	...	8	...	...	...	...	...	...	...
212	HECTOR	...	...	...	...	...	75	...	...	...	...	...	...	...	...	79	5	...	35	3	...	10	...	5	...	...
4	HELENUS	...	...	...	...	...	4	...	...	...	...	...	...	...	...	...	...	...	...	...	...	...	...	...	...	...
103	PARIS	...	...	...	...	...	30	...	31	...	...	31	...	8	3	...	...	...	...	...	...	...	...	...	...	...
103	DIOMEDES	...	...	...	...	...	...	5	...	...	2	32	...	...	12	6	2	29	...	4	6	4	...	...	1	...
21	SERVANT	...	...	...	...	...	...	...	20	...	...	...	...	...	...	...	...	...	...	...	1	...	...	...	...	...
31	CALCHAS	...	...	...	...	...	...	...	...	...	29	...	...	...	...	...	...	2	...	...	...	...	...	...	...	...
2	DEIPHOBUS	...	...	...	...	...	...	...	...	...	...	1	...	...	1	...	...	...	...	...	...	...	...	...	...	...
3	"ALL"	...	...	...	...	...	...	...	...	...	...	...	...	...	...	1	...	...	...	...	...	...	...	...	1	1
3	MARGARELON ...	...	...	...	...	...	...	...	...	...	...	...	...	...	...	...	...	...	...	...	...	...	3	...	...	...
1	MYRMIDON	...	...	...	...	...	...	...	...	...	...	...	...	...	...	...	...	...	...	...	...	...	...	1	...	...
31	"PROLOGUE" ...	31	...	...	...	...	...	...	...	...	...	...	...	...	...	...	...	...	...	...	...	...	...	...	...	...
312	CRESSIDA	...	...	115	...	...	...	...	...	71	...	...	44	...	25	11	...	46	...	...	...	...	...	...	...	...
5	BOY	...	...	3	...	...	...	...	...	2	...	...	...	...	...	...	...	...	...	...	...	...	...	...	...	...
37	CASSANDRA	...	...	...	...	...	13	...	...	...	...	...	...	...	...	...	...	...	24	...	...	...	...	...	...	...
30	HELEN	...	...	...	...	...	...	...	30	...	...	...	...	...	...	...	...	...	...	...	...	...	...	...	...	...
15	ANDROMACHE ...	...	...	...	...	...	...	...	...	...	...	...	...	...	...	...	...	...	15	...	...	...	...	...	...	...
3633		31	121	325	397	142	219	284	172	224	326	84	121	13	160	321	113	221	123	39	50	33	24	22	10	58
3496	Actual No. of Lines	31	119	321	392	142	213	277	172	220	316	79	115	12	150	293	106	197	112	38	47	31	24	22	10	57

SCHEME FOR ARRANGING THE PARTS WITH EIGHTEEN MEN.

SIXTEEN CHARACTERS SINGLY AND TWO GROUPS.

HELENUS	4		DEIPHOBUS	2	
MENELAUS	12	19	SERVANT	21	24
MARGARELON	3		MYRMIDON	1	

SUGGESTIONS FOR DISCUSSION.

1. The Rhyme-test confirms the theory that *Troilus and Cressida* was written in three sections at different periods of Shakspere's life.
2. The military allusions in *Troilus and Cressida*, together with contemporary records, prove that Shakspere served under Leicester in the Low Countries.
3. *Troilus and Cressida* was Shakspere's last attempt at comedy when he was no longer capable of it.

LIST OF EARLIEST KNOWN EDITIONS.

Date.	*Printer.*	*Publishers.*	*Acted by*	*Present Owners.*
1609	G. Eld	R. Bonian and H. Walley		British Museum. Bodleian Library. Trinity College, Cambridge. Duke of Devonshire.
1609	G. Eld	R. Bonian and H. Walley	The King's servants	

The following entries occur in the Stationers' Registers:—

1565. July 22—1566. July 22.
Purfoote Recevyd of **Thomas purfoote** for his lycense for pryntinge of a ballett intituled *the history of* TROILVS *Whose throtes hath Well bene tryed* iiijd

Warton conjectured that "throtes" was a miswriting for "troth."

1581. June 23.
Edwarde white Lycenced vnto him vnder thandes of the wardens *A proper ballad Dialoge wise betwene* TROYLVS *and* CRESSIDA iiijd

On April 7, 1599, Henslowe "Lent unto Thomas Downton, to lende unto Mr Dickers and harey cheattell, in earneste of ther boocke called Troyeles and creasse daye the some of iijli" (*Diary*, p. 147). On the 16th of the same month he "Lent unto harey cheattell and Mr Dickers, in pte of payment of ther boocke called Troyelles and cresseda xxs" (*Diary*, p. 148). At p. 149 of the *Diary*, "Troyeles and creasseday" occurs as an entry without further comment. This book seems to have been ultimately called "The tragedie of Agamemnon" (see *Diary*, p. 153), and further payments to the amount of £4 15s. were made for it in May, 1599.

The following entries are also in the Registers:—

1603. February 7.
Master **Robertes** Entred for his copie in full Court holden this day to print when he hath gotten sufficient aucthority for yt, The booke of '*TROILVS and CRESSEDA*' *as yt is acted by my lord Chamberlens Men* vjd

1609. January 28.
Richard Bonion
Henry Walleys Entred for their Copy vnder thandes of Master SEGAR deputy to Sir GEORGE BUCKE and master warden **Lownes** a booke called *the history of* TROYLVS *and* CRESSIDA vjd

Nothing is known of any book in connection with Roberts's entry.

The first mentioned of the 1609 editions is called "The Famous Historie of Troylus and Cresseid. Excellently expressing the beginning of their loues, with the conceited wooing of Pandarus Prince of Licia." It is said to be "Written by William Shakespeare." It has a preface in which it is described as "a new play, never staled with the stage." The title of the other edition is simply "The Historie of Troylus and Cresseida." The statement is added that "it was acted by the Kings Maiesties seruants at the Globe." The author's name is given in the same form as in the other edition. By some critics it is held that there is really only one 1609 edition, which was issued with different title-pages, and that the one accompanied by the Preface is the later of the two. The student should form an independent opinion on this question.

In the 1623 Folio the play, which there has a whole-page Prologue, is called "The Tragedie of Troylus and Cressida." Its name is not given in the "Catalogve," and it has two only of its pages numbered.

Commentators, of course, have been very dogmatic about the materials Shakspere used for this play. There is no need to cite definite authorities, as through Chaucer and Chapman and others the Elizabethans were familiar enough with the incidents in dramatic and other forms.

To the critical student the literary character and chronological position of *Troilus and Cressida* are each a puzzle. In an attempted solution, the facts mentioned above and an allusion in (Marston's) *Histrio-Mastix* must be taken into consideration.

CORIOLANUS.

Total Number of Lines.	CHARACTERS.	I.										II.			III.			IV.							V.					
		1	2	3	4	5	6	7	8	9	10	1	2	3	1	2	3	1	2	3	4	5	6	7	1	2	3	4	5	6
96	1st Citizen	72	...	...	...	...	...	...	...	...	...	...	...	10	3	...	...	...	...	...	4	...	7	...	...	...	...	...	...	...
45	"All"	8	2	...	2	...	...	...	...	1	...	1	...	6	9	...	7	...	...	...	...	...	3	...	...	...	...	...	2	4
30	2nd Citizen	11	...	...	...	...	...	...	...	...	...	...	...	17	...	...	...	...	...	...	...	...	2	...	...	...	...	...	...	...
598	Menenius	92	...	...	...	...	...	...	...	...	...	130	39	13	88	20	14	5	5	...	...	...	56	...	40	58	...	38	...	...
886	Marcius	75	...	...	34	18	50	...	9	45	...	20	24	67	147	58	50	45	...	...	25	64	...	...	...	14	106	...	...	35
38	1st Messenger ...	2	...	...	2	...	9	...	...	...	...	9	...	...	...	...	...	...	...	...	...	...	11	...	...	...	...	5	...	...
62	1st Senator... ...	7	7	...	8	...	...	...	...	...	...	...	13	...	17	3	1	...	...	...	...	...	...	...	...	...	...	...	6	...
281	Cominius	3	...	...	...	...	44	...	...	55	...	3	47	...	30	10	11	7	...	...	...	...	40	...	31	...	...	...	...	...
60	Titus Lartius ...	6	...	...	19	11	...	7	...	5	...	...	...	...	12	...	...	...	...	...	...	...	...	...	...	...	...	...	...	...
313	Sicinius...	16	...	...	...	...	...	...	...	...	...	34	10	54	61	...	54	...	16	...	...	...	43	...	11	...	...	14	...	...
255	Brutus	19	...	...	...	...	...	...	...	...	...	61	14	56	44	...	25	...	10	...	...	...	22	...	4	...	...	...	...	...
274	Aufidius	...	30	...	...	...	...	...	10	...	32	...	...	...	...	...	...	...	...	...	...	56	...	48	...	1	9	...	...	88
13	2nd Senator ...	...	7	...	...	...	...	...	...	...	...	...	...	...	6	...	...	...	...	...	...	...	...	...	...	...	...	...	...	...
11	1st Soldier... ...	...	...	...	7	...	...	...	...	...	4	...	...	...	...	...	...	...	...	...	...	...	...	...	...	...	...	...	...	...
1	2nd Soldier ...	...	...	...	1	...	...	...	...	...	...	...	...	...	...	...	...	...	...	...	...	...	...	...	...	...	...	...	...	...
34	1st Roman	...	...	...	...	1	...	...	...	...	...	...	...	...	...	...	...	...	...	33	...	...	...	...	...	...	...	...	...	...
1	2nd Roman	...	...	...	...	1	...	...	...	...	...	...	...	...	...	...	...	...	...	...	...	...	...	...	...	...	...	...	...	...
2	3rd Roman	...	...	...	...	2	...	...	...	...	...	...	...	...	...	...	...	...	...	...	...	...	...	...	...	...	...	...	...	...
12	Lieutenant... ...	...	...	...	...	...	...	1	...	...	...	...	...	...	...	...	...	...	...	...	...	...	...	11	...	...	...	...	...	...
6	Herald	...	...	...	...	...	...	...	...	...	...	6	...	...	...	...	...	...	...	...	...	...	...	...	...	...	...	...	...	...
17	1st Officer... ...	...	...	...	...	...	...	...	...	...	...	...	17	...	...	...	...	...	...	...	...	...	...	...	...	...	...	...	...	...
24	2nd Officer... ...	...	...	...	...	...	...	...	...	...	...	...	24	...	...	...	...	...	...	...	...	...	...	...	...	...	...	...	...	...
62	3rd Citizen... ...	...	...	...	...	...	...	...	...	...	...	...	...	57	...	...	...	...	...	...	...	...	5	...	...	...	...	...	...	...
7	4th Citizen... ...	...	...	...	...	...	...	...	...	...	...	...	...	7	...	...	...	...	...	...	...	...	...	...	...	...	...	...	...	...
2	5th Citizen... ...	...	...	...	...	...	...	...	...	...	...	...	...	2	...	...	...	...	...	...	...	...	...	...	...	...	...	...	...	...
2	6th Citizen... ...	...	...	...	...	...	...	...	...	...	...	...	...	2	...	...	...	...	...	...	...	...	...	...	...	...	...	...	...	...
3	7th Citizen... ...	...	...	...	...	...	...	...	...	...	...	...	...	3	...	...	...	...	...	...	...	...	...	...	...	...	...	...	...	...
16	Ædile	...	...	...	...	...	...	...	...	...	...	...	...	...	1	...	9	...	...	...	...	...	6	...	...	...	...	...	...	...
3	1st Patrician ...	...	...	...	...	...	...	...	...	...	...	...	...	...	1	2	...	...	...	...	...	...	...	...	...	...	...	...	...	...
1	2nd Patrician ...	...	...	...	...	...	...	...	...	...	...	...	...	...	1	...	...	...	...	...	...	...	...	...	...	...	...	...	...	...
24	Volsce	...	...	...	...	...	...	...	...	...	...	...	...	...	...	...	...	...	...	24	...	...	...	...	...	...	...	...	...	...
41	1st Servingman...	...	...	...	...	...	...	...	...	...	...	...	...	...	...	...	...	...	...	...	...	41	...	...	...	...	...	...	...	...
42	2nd Servingman...	...	...	...	...	...	...	...	...	...	...	...	...	...	...	...	...	...	...	...	...	42	...	...	...	...	...	...	...	...
57	3rd Servingman...	...	...	...	...	...	...	...	...	...	...	...	...	...	...	...	...	...	...	...	...	57	...	...	...	...	...	...	...	...
20	2nd Messenger ...	...	...	...	...	...	...	...	...	...	...	...	...	...	...	...	...	...	...	...	...	...	6	...	...	...	...	14	...	...
35	1st Sentinel ...	...	...	...	...	...	...	...	...	...	...	...	...	...	...	...	...	...	...	...	...	...	...	...	...	35	...	...	...	...
14	2nd Sentinel ...	...	...	...	...	...	...	...	...	...	...	...	...	...	...	...	...	...	...	...	...	...	...	...	...	14	...	...	...	...
10	1st Conspirator	...	...	...	...	...	...	...	...	...	...	...	...	...	...	...	...	...	...	...	...	...	...	...	...	...	...	...	...	10
9	2nd Conspirator	...	...	...	...	...	...	...	...	...	...	...	...	...	...	...	...	...	...	...	...	...	...	...	...	...	...	...	...	9
14	3rd Conspirator	...	...	...	...	...	...	...	...	...	...	...	...	...	...	...	...	...	...	...	...	...	...	...	...	...	...	...	...	14
15	1st Lord	...	...	...	...	...	...	...	...	...	...	...	...	...	...	...	...	...	...	...	...	...	...	...	...	...	...	...	...	15
11	2nd Lord	...	...	...	...	...	...	...	...	...	...	...	...	...	...	...	...	...	...	...	...	...	...	...	...	...	...	...	...	11
4	3rd Lord	...	...	...	...	...	...	...	...	...	...	...	...	...	...	...	...	...	...	...	...	...	...	...	...	...	...	...	...	4
315	Volumnia	...	...	52	...	...	...	...	...	...	...	42	...	...	...	77	...	7	34	...	...	...	...	...	...	...	103	...	...	...
41	Virgilia	...	...	25	...	...	...	...	...	...	...	5	...	...	...	...	...	1	4	...	...	...	...	...	...	...	6	...	...	...
1	Gentlewoman ...	...	...	1	...	...	...	...	...	...	...	...	...	...	...	...	...	...	...	...	...	...	...	...	...	...	...	...	...	...
48	Valeria	...	...	46	...	...	...	...	...	...	...	2	...	...	...	...	...	...	...	...	...	...	...	...	...	...	...	...	...	...
2	Young Marcius ...	...	...	...	...	...	...	...	...	...	...	...	...	...	...	...	...	...	...	...	...	...	...	...	...	...	2	...	...	...
3858		311	46	124	73	33	103	8	19	106	36	313	188	294	420	170	171	65	69	57	29	260	201	59	86	122	226	71	8	190
3410	Actual No. of Lines	283	38	124	63	29	87	7	15	94	33	286	164	271	336	145	143	58	54	57	26	251	161	57	74	117	209	65	7	156

SCHEME FOR ARRANGING THE PARTS WITH EIGHTEEN MEN.

SEVEN CHARACTERS SINGLY AND ELEVEN GROUPS.

HERALD	6	63
VOLSCE	24	
1ST PATRICIAN	3	
2ND CITIZEN	30	
1ST SOLDIER	11	62
1ST SERVINGMAN	41	
1ST CONSPIRATOR	10	
3RD ROMAN	2	62
3RD SERVINGMAN	57	
7TH CITIZEN	3	
2ND SENATOR	13	64
2ND OFFICER	24	
2ND MESSENGER	20	
4TH CITIZEN	7	
1ST LORD	15	63
1ST ROMAN	34	
2ND SENTINEL	14	
2ND PATRICIAN	1	64
2ND SOLDIER	1	
3RD CITIZEN	62	
1ST OFFICER	17	64
1ST MESSENGER	38	
2ND CONSPIRATOR	9	
LIEUTENANT	12	65
2ND LORD	11	
2ND SERVINGMAN	42	
ÆDILE	16	65
1ST SENTINEL	35	
3RD CONSPIRATOR	14	
1ST SENATOR	62	65
2ND ROMAN	1	
5TH CITIZEN	2	
TITUS LARTIUS	60	66
3RD LORD	4	
6TH CITIZEN	2	

SUGGESTIONS FOR DISCUSSION.

1. Although *Coriolanus* shows that home-ties are stronger than the brute forces of the world, it fails to interest because it is mainly a delineation of social and personal pride.
2. *Coriolanus*, containing so much of the very words of Plutarch, goes far towards earning for him the title of "the biographical Shakespeare of universal history."
3. Shakspere's social and political views can be gathered from *Coriolanus*.

THE EARLIEST KNOWN EDITION IS THE 1623 FOLIO.

Coriolanus was not entered in the Stationers' Registers till 1623, when in the Folio the play was called "The Tragedy of Coriolanus."

There is no external evidence for determining the date of its composition, which must be conjectured from its literary style, including its metrical characteristics.

Nothing is known of any earlier dramatic version of the apocryphal story of Coriolanus, and it is plain enough that here Plutarch was Shakspere's sole authority.

THE VIRGIN-MARTYR.

Total Number of Lines.	CHARACTERS.	I.	II.			III.			IV.			V.	
		1	1	2	3	1	2	3	1	2	3	1	2
614	THEOPHILUS	88	...	46	29	22	83	...	8	26	55	139	118
284	HARPAX	54	...	48	...	...	10	87	...	43	8	29	5
11	PRIEST	5	...	...	...	6	...	...	...	...	...	...	...
236	SAPRITIUS	69	...	...	18	24	10	...	81	11	13	...	10
11	SEMPRONIUS	6	...	...	...	...	5	...	...	...	...	...	...
175	DIOCLESIAN	97	...	...	...	..	...	...	...	...	...	...	78
16	KING OF EPIRE	16	...	...	...	...	...	...	...	...	...	...	...
11	KING OF PONTUS	8	...	...	...	...	...	...	...	...	...	...	3
19	KING OF MACEDON ...	19	...	...	...	...	...	...	...	...	...	...	...
125	MACRINUS	38	...	7	31	...	...	...	26	...	18	...	5
257	ANTONINUS	90	...	...	55	...	...	...	53	...	59	...	...
268	SPUNGIUS...	...	97	...	50	...	...	89	...	32	...	...	...
239	HIRCIUS	...	70	...	51	...	...	84	...	34	...	...	...
11	1ST DOCTOR	...	...	...	...	...	..	...	11	...	...	...	...
23	SLAVE	...	...	...	...	...	...	...	23	...	...	...	...
9	GETA	...	...	...	...	...	...	...	...	...	...	9	...
2	JULIANUS...	...	...	...	...	...	...	...	...	...	...	2	...
19	MAXIMINUS	...	...	...	...	...	...	...	...	...	...	...	19
63	CALISTA	2	...	...	...	50	11	...	...	...	...	...	...
23	CHRISTETA	2	...	...	...	16	5	...	...	...	...	...	...
152	ARTEMIA	63	...	...	26	...	27	...	...	...	...	...	36
153	ANGELO	...	52	...	30	2	3	12	3	6	21	21	3
329	DOROTHEA	...	40	...	47	131	16	...	22	17	56	...	...
3050		557	259	101	337	251	170	272	227	169	230	200	277
2689	Actual Number of Lines	474	253	87	304	213	134	270	185	157	194	177	241

SUGGESTIONS FOR DISCUSSION.

1. All the prose in *The Virgin-Martyr* was written by Dekker.
2. Massinger's plays furnish confirmation of the supposition that he had become a Roman Catholic.
3. Massinger's excellent metre is a better model for dramatists in general to imitate than Shakspere's.

EARLIEST KNOWN EDITION.

Date.	*Printer.*	*Publisher.*	*Acted by*	*Present Owner.*
1622	B. A.	Thomas Iones	The servants of his MaJesty's Revels	British Museum.

In the Office-book of Sir George Bucke, Master of the Revels (1610–1622) is this entry: "1620. Oct. 6—For new reforming *The Virgin-Martyr* for the Red Bull, 40s."

The play was thus entered in the Stationers' Registers:—

1621. December 7.
Thomas Jones. Entred for his copie vnder the hands of Sir George Bucke, and Master **Swinhowe** warden A Tragedy called *The Virgin Martir.* **vjd**

On the title-page of the 1622 edition the play is called "The Virgin Martir, a tragedie." It is said to have "bin divers times publickely Acted with great Applause," and to have been "written by Phillip Messenger and Thomas Deker."

The papers by Mr. Fleay and Mr. Boyle referred to on p. 147 take Massinger into consideration.

As an instance of the modern method of determining the respective shares of the writers of a play in which there is a composite authorship, the student should refer to Mr. Fleay's paper, "Who Wrote our Old Plays?" (*Macmillan's Magazine*, September, 1874).

CYMBELINE.

Total Number of Lines.	CHARACTERS.	I.						II.					III.							IV.				V.				
		1	2	3	4	5	6	1	2	3	4	5	1	2	3	4	5	6	7	1	2	3	4	1	2	3	4	5
66	1st Gentleman	66																										
13	2nd Gentleman	13																										
448	Posthumus	29			57						96	35												33		85	69	44
291	Cymbeline	20								15			30				29					21						176
217	Pisanio	10		13		3	4			1				27		86	28					16						29
52	1st Lord		15					7		7			1									15				7		
275	Cloten		10					31		72			24				88			27	23							
52	2nd Lord		18					32		1			1															
436	Iachimo				83		154		41		73														11			74
44	Philario				20						24																	
25	Frenchman				25																							
73	Cornelius					25																						48
9	Musician									9																		
4	Messenger									2																	2	
104	Lucius												19				10				43				5			27
336	Belarius														90			30			109	26			3			78
169	Guiderius														11			10			113	19			1			15
143	Arviragus														11			13			90	19			1			9
3	Attendant																3											
15	1st Senator																		15									
3	1st Tribune																		3									
1	2nd Senator																		1									
15	Captain																				11					4		
43	Soothsayer																				7							36
6	2nd Captain																									6		
1	"All"																										1	
51	1st Gaoler																										51	
1	2nd Gaoler																										1	
40	Sicilius																										40	
14	1st Brother																										14	
8	2nd Brother																										8	
21	"Jupiter"																										21	
166	Queen	33				67				10			22				34											
596	Imogen	45		33			83		10	54				59		134		57			85							36
15	Lady			2		1			2	9																		1
12	Mother																										12	
3768		216	43	48	185	96	241	70	53	180	193	35	97	86	112	220	192	110	19	27	481	52	64	33	21	102	219	573
3340	Actual No. of Lines	178	43	40	185	87	210	70	51	160	152	35	87	84	107	196	168	96	16	27	403	46	54	33	18	94	215	485

The total lines should be 3341, as the total of IV. 2 should be 404.

SCHEME FOR ARRANGING THE PARTS WITH EIGHTEEN MEN.

ELEVEN CHARACTERS SINGLY AND SEVEN GROUPS.

Character	Lines	Total
Philario	44	58
1st Brother	14	
1st Tribune	3	59
2nd Lord	52	
2nd Gaoler	1	
Attendant	3	
Musician	51	60
1st Gaoler	9	
Soothsayer	43	60
Messenger	4	
2nd Gentleman	13	
Sicilius	40	61
1st Senator	15	
2nd Captain	6	
Captain	15	61
Frenchman	25	
"Jupiter"	21	
1st Lord	52	61
2nd Senator	1	
2nd Brother	8	

SUGGESTIONS FOR DISCUSSION.

1. The tone of *Cymbeline* shows that the play was written when Shakspere, having passed through his life-gloom into a time of serenity and repose, had finally returned to Stratford.

2. The moral beauty of womanhood is the all-pervading idea of *Cymbeline*.

3. The non-essential parts of *Cymbeline* show great carelessness in their treatment.

THE EARLIEST KNOWN EDITION IS THE 1623 FOLIO.

At that time its first mention occurs in the Stationers' Registers.

In the Folio the play is called "The Tragedie of Cymbeline."

Cymbeline is one of the plays about which Dr. Forman (see p. 155), who died in September, 1611, has left notes. At present there is no other external evidence by which its date can be ascertained.

Some of the incidents Shakspere would have met with in *Holinshed*. The slander-story was often told in early foreign literature. It is in one of Boccaccio's novels. Shakspere's indebtedness to this is by no means clear, as it is not known that there was in his time any English version of the *Decameron*. From early writers Hazlitt (*Shakespeare's Library*) gives passages to which parts of the play bear a resemblance.

THE DUKE OF MILAN.

Total Number of Lines.	CHARACTERS.	I.			II.	III.			IV.			V.	
		1	2	3	1	1	2	3	1	2	3	1	2
239	GRACCHO	33	...	...	50	...	43	6	50	...	4	47	6
21	JULIO	6	...	...	...	...	15	...	...	...	...	...	...
111	STEPHANO	31	...	...	24	...	...	2	...	13	28	...	13
174	TIBERIO	78	...	4	53	...	...	5	...	11	12	...	11
683	FRANCISCO	...	31	56	152	...	17	67	75	33	63	110	79
10	1ST GENTLEMAN	...	...	8	...	...	...	...	...	...	2	...	...
5	2ND GENTLEMAN	...	...	3	...	...	...	...	...	...	2	...	...
5	3RD GENTLEMAN	...	...	3	...	...	...	...	...	...	2	...	...
715	SFORZA	...	...	269	...	119	...	51	...	..	168	...	108
2	1ST COURIER	...	...	2	...	...	...	...	...	...	...	...	...
4	2ND COURIER	...	...	4	...	...	...	...	...	...	...	...	...
141	PESCARA	...	...	30	...	9	...	2	...	...	35	...	65
7	1ST FIDDLER	...	...	...	7	...	...	...	...	...	...	...	...
43	MEDINA	...	...	...	...	43	...	...	...	...	...	...	...
74	HERNANDO	...	...	...	...	74	..	...	...	...	...	...	...
16	ALPHONSO	...	...	...	...	16	...	...	...	...	...	...	...
51	CHARLES	...	...	...	...	51	...	...	...	...	...	...	...
57	OFFICER	...	...	...	...	...	57	...	...	...	...	...	...
7	GIOVANNI	...	...	...	...	...	7	...	...	...	...	...	...
18	SERVANT	...	...	...	...	...	3	...	...	...	1	5	9
13	1ST DOCTOR	...	...	...	...	...	...	...	...	...	...	...	13
5	2ND DOCTOR	...	...	...	...	...	...	...	...	...	...	...	5
1	"ALL"	...	...	...	...	...	...	...	...	...	...	...	1
117	MARIANA	...	7	4	71	...	...	3	...	...	30	...	2
54	ISABELLA	...	8	3	32	...	...	...	...	...	6	...	5
346	MARCELIA	...	...	69	143	...	...	53	...	40	41	...	...
9	GENTLEWOMAN	...	...	...	...	...	9	...	...	...	...	...	...
67	EUGENIA	...	...	...	...	...	...	...	...	...	...	60	7
2995		148	46	455	532	312	151	189	125	97	394	222	324
2500	Actual Number of Lines	126	38	382	433	269	120	162	116	79	316	187	272

SCHEME FOR ARRANGING THE PARTS WITH EIGHTEEN MEN.

FOURTEEN CHARACTERS SINGLY AND FOUR GROUPS.

2ND DOCTOR	5	9	GIOVANNI	7	12	1ST FIDDLER	7	12	1ST DOCTOR	13	15
2ND COURIER	4		3RD GENTLEMAN	5		2ND GENTLEMAN	5		1ST COURIER	2	

SUGGESTIONS FOR DISCUSSION.

1. No author reflects the social corruption of the latter half of the reign of James I. so much as Massinger.
2. Massinger's characters act from single motives and become what they are in spite of events; thus differing from Shakspere's, who act from mixed motives and are made what they are by various circumstances.
3. Nearly all Massinger's plays teem with political allusions from the standpoint of the Herberts.

EARLIEST KNOWN EDITION.

Date.	*Printer.*	*Publisher.*	*Acted by*	*Present Owner.*
1623	B. A.	Edward Blackmore	The King's servants	British Museum.

Cunningham (see p. 71) has, in a list of the performances before the Queen in 1579-80, a record of "A History of the Duke of Millayn and the Marques of Mantua shewed at Whitehall on St. Stephens daie at nighte enacted by the Lord Chamberlaynes srvants" (p. 154). There is nothing more than the similarity of title to show that this was an earlier play on the same subject as Massinger's.

In the Stationers' Registers are these entries :—

1623. January 20.

Edward Blackmore George Norton.	Entred for their Copie vnder the handes of Sir JOHN ASHLEY knight Master of the Reuelles and Master **Gilmyn** warden, A play called *SFORZA, Duke of Millaine,* made by Master. MESSENGER vjd

1623. May 5.

Edward Blackmore.	Assigned ouer vnto him by **George Norton** and consent of a full court holden this Daie all the estate, right and title the said **George** hath in the play called, *The Duke of Millan* vjd

In 1623 the play was issued as "The Dvke of Millaine. A Tragædie." The title-page says it had "beene often acted by his Maiesties seruants, at the blacke Friers," and had been "Written by Philip Massinger gent."

THE WINTER'S TALE.

Total Number of Lines.	CHARACTERS.	I.		II.			III.			IV.				V.		
		1	2	1	2	3	1	2	3	1	2	3	4	1	2	3
24	ARCHIDAMUS	24	...	...	...	...	...	...	...	...	...	...	...	...	...	...
305	CAMILLO	26	123	...	...	...	...	...	...	...	18	...	131	...	...	7
277	POLIXENES	...	129	...	...	...	...	...	...	...	44	...	94	...	...	10
681	LEONTES	...	210	108	...	109	...	73	...	...	...	...	...	105	...	76
63	1ST LORD...	...	...	18	...	12	...	9	...	...	...	...	...	24	...	...
110	ANTIGONUS	...	...	30	...	29	...	...	51	...	...	...	...	...	...	...
13	GAOLER	...	...	...	13	...	...	...	...	...	...	...	...	...	...	...
52	1ST SERVANT	...	...	...	...	8	...	5	...	...	...	...	39	...	...	...
2	2ND SERVANT	...	...	...	...	2	...	...	...	...	...	...	...	...	...	...
24	CLEOMENES	...	...	...	...	...	11	1	...	...	...	...	...	12	...	...
28	DION...	...	...	...	...	...	16	1	...	...	...	...	...	11	...	...
27	OFFICER	...	...	...	...	...	...	27	...	...	...	...	...	...	...	...
11	MARINER	...	...	...	...	...	...	...	11	...	...	...	...	...	...	...
144	SHEPHERD	...	...	...	...	...	...	...	47	...	...	...	89	...	8	...
209	CLOWN	...	...	...	...	...	...	...	38	...	...	48	86	...	37	...
32	"TIME"	...	...	...	...	...	...	...	...	32	...	...	...	...	...	...
319	AUTOLYCUS	...	...	...	...	...	...	...	...	...	...	87	207	...	25	...
205	FLORIZEL...	...	...	...	...	...	...	...	...	...	...	...	167	38	...	...
48	1ST GENTLEMAN	...	...	...	...	...	...	...	...	...	...	...	...	18	30	...
17	2ND GENTLEMAN	...	...	...	...	...	...	...	...	...	...	...	...	...	17	...
71	3RD GENTLEMAN	...	...	...	...	...	...	...	...	...	...	...	...	...	71	...
211	HERMIONE	...	68	46	...	...	...	89	...	...	...	...	...	...	...	8
22	MAMILLIUS	...	4	18	...	...	...	...	...	...	...	...	...	...	...	...
9	1ST LADY...	...	...	9	...	...	...	...	...	...	...	...	...	...	...	...
4	2ND LADY	...	...	4	...	...	...	...	...	...	...	...	...	...	...	...
331	PAULINA	...	...	...	44	84	...	60	...	...	...	...	...	67	...	76
20	EMILIA	...	...	...	20	...	...	...	...	...	...	...	...	...	...	...
128	PERDITA	...	...	...	...	...	...	...	...	...	...	...	118	3	...	7
13	DORCAS	...	...	...	...	...	...	...	...	...	...	...	13	...	...	...
21	MOPSA	...	...	...	...	...	...	...	...	...	...	...	21	...	...	...
3421		50	534	233	77	244	27	265	147	32	62	135	965	278	188	184
3074	Actual Number of Lines	50	465	199	66	207	22	244	143	32	62	135	873	233	188	155

SCHEME FOR ARRANGING THE PARTS WITH EIGHTEEN MEN AND SEVEN LADIES.

Men's Parts.

FIFTEEN CHARACTERS SINGLY AND THREE GROUPS.

ARCHIDAMUS	24	26	GAOLER	13	30	CLEOMENES	24	35
2ND SERVANT	2		2ND GENTLEMAN	17		MARINER	11	

Ladies' Parts.

FIVE CHARACTERS SINGLY AND TWO GROUPS.

DORCAS	13	22	EMILIA	20	24
1ST LADY	9		2ND LADY	4	

SUGGESTIONS FOR DISCUSSION.

1. The freedom with which Shakspere used the incidents of *Pandosto* shows that he did not hesitate to profit by the work of an author whom he despised.
2. Shakspere wrote *The Winter's Tale* to enforce the lesson of forgiveness of wrongs.
3. The anachronisms which abound in *The Winter's Tale* seriously detract from the enjoyment of the play.

THE EARLIEST KNOWN EDITION IS THE 1623 FOLIO.

Dr. Forman (see p. 155) has left a MS. note about a performance of "the Winters Talle at the glob" which he saw on May 15, 1611.

Cunningham (*Op. cit.* p. 210) says that amongst the plays acted before the King in 1611 there was performed by the King's players on "The 5th of Nouember; A play called ye winters nights Tayle" (see p. 71).

In 1613 "The Winters Tale" was one of the plays acted at Court at the wedding of the Princess Elizabeth (see p. 103).

According to Cunningham "the Winter's Tale" was acted before James I. on Easter Tuesday, 1618 (see p. 129).

Sir Henry Herbert, who in 1623 became Deputy Master of the Revels, made in that year the following entry in his Office-book: "For the kings players;—an olde playe called Winters Tale, formerly allowed of by Sir George Bucke, and likewyse by mee on Mr. Hemmings his worde that there was nothing prophane added or reformed, thogh the allowed booke was missinge; and therefore I returned itt without a fee, this 19 of August, 1623" (see 1821 *Variorum*, Vol. II., pp. 462-3, and Halliwell-Phillipps's *Outlines*, Vol. II., p. 300). Sir George Bucke succeeded to the Mastership of the Revels upon the death of Tylney in October, 1610; but he had in 1603 obtained the reversion of the office and had acted as Master, granting licences, for some time before Tylney's death. Sir George licensed *Lear* (see p. 149) in 1607, *Pericles* (see p. 159), *Antony and Cleopatra* (see p. 159), and Heywood's *Lucrece* (see p. 119) in 1608, and *Troilus and Cressida*, by deputy (see p. 167), in 1609.

The earliest mention of the play in the Stationers' Registers is on November 8, 1623, with other plays of the Folio, in which its title is "The Winters Tale."

Greene's *Pandosto*, first published in 1588, is reprinted in Hazlitt's *Shakespeare's Library*.

THE TEMPEST.

Total Number of Lines.	CHARACTERS.	I.		II.		III.			IV.	V.	Epilogue.
		1	2	1	2	1	2	3	1	1	
4	MASTER	4	...	...	...	...	...	...	...	...	...
46	BOATSWAIN	29	...	...	...	...	...	...	...	17	...
110	ALONSO	2	...	26	...	...	...	26	...	56	..
148	ANTONIO	8	...	126	...	...	...	12	...	2	...
165	GONZALO	22	...	90	...	...	..	28	...	25	...
122	SEBASTIAN	4	...	98	...	...	...	12	...	8	...
8	"ALL"	5	3	...	...	...	...	...	...	...	...
665	PROSPERO	...	339	...	...	10	...	15	98	183	20
179	CALIBAN...	...	30	...	55	...	66	...	20	8	...
140	FERDINAND	...	45	...	...	59	...	...	23	13	...
12	ADRIAN	...	...	11	...	...	...	1	...	...	..
11	FRANCISCO	...	...	10	...	...	...	1	...	...	...
112	TRINCULO	...	...	...	58	...	33		16	5	...
174	STEPHANO	...	...	...	80	...	63	...	26	5	...
142	MIRANDA	...	87	...	...	45	...	...	3	7	...
190	ARIEL	...	87	11	...	...	4	30	29	29	...
41	"IRIS"	...	...	...	...	...	...	...	41	...	...
24	"CERES"	...	...	...	...	...	...	...	24	...	...
7	"JUNO"...	...	...	...	...	...	...	...	7	...	...
2300		74	591	372	193	114	166	125	287	358	20
2065	Actual Number of Lines	72	500	327	193	96	163	109	267	318	20

SUGGESTIONS FOR DISCUSSION.

1. Shakspere's observance of the Unities in *The Tempest* entitles it to special commendation.
2. Shakspere's object in writing *The Tempest* was to bring forward the question of the relationship of civilised and uncivilised races.
3. The various allegorical interpretations of *The Tempest* show that as a play it is uninteresting, and that it was written when Shakspere's powers were failing.

THE EARLIEST KNOWN EDITION IS THE 1623 FOLIO.

Before this date the play was not entered in the Stationers' Registers. In the edition the play is called merely "The Tempest."

Cunningham (*Op. cit.* p. 210) says that in 1611 on "Hallomas nyght was presented att Whithall before ye Kings Matie a play called the Tempest". "By the Kings Players" (see p. 71).

The play was one of those acted at Court in 1613 (see p. 103).

In connection with *The Tempest* should be read Jacob Ayrer's "Comedia von der schönen Sidea," reprinted with an English translation in Cohn's *Shakespeare in Germany*. This play is one of those acted by English players in Germany about the year 1600 (see p. 75). Ayrer was a notary in Nuremburg, where he died in 1605. It has been thought that some lost English play supplied a common source to Ayrer and Shakspere.

THE BIRTH OF MERLIN.

Total Number of Lines.	CHARACTERS.	I.		II.		III.						IV.					V.	
		1	2	1	2	1	2	3	4	5	6	1	2	3	4	5	1	2
75	Cador	12	3	...	18	...	7	...	...	...	3	...	1	...	4	17	...	10
152	Donobert	27	35	...	22	10	30	...	...	...	3	..	...	...	...	...	...	25
28	Gloster	4	5	...	10	...	1	...	...	...	1	...	...	...	...	...	...	7
74	Edwin	15	3	...	12	9	16	...	...	...	8	...	1	...	3	3	...	4
44	Toclio	26	...	13	4	1	...	...	...	...	...	...	...	...	...	...	...	...
214	Aurelius	...	129	...	64	...	...	...	...	...	21	...	...	...	...	...	...	...
18	Oswald	...	4	14	...	...	...	...	...	...	...	...	...	...	...	...	...	.
65	Hermit	...	31	...	23	...	10	...	...	...	...	...	...	...	...	...	...	1
1	1st Lord	...	1	...	...	...	...	...	...	...	...	...	...	...	...	...	...	...
2	2nd Lord	...	2	...	...	...	...	...	...	...	...	..	...	...	...	...	...	...
336	Clown	...	...	84	...	90	...	...	71	...	...	73	..	...	...	17	...	1
273	Prince	...	...	51	86	...	...	...	...	...	27	...	14	16	9	42	...	28
3	"All"	...	...	...	1	...	1	...	...	...	1	...	...	...	...	...	...	...
149	Edol	...	...	...	63	...	...	...	...	...	32	...	26	4	...	14	...	10
2	Captain	...	...	...	1	...	...	...	...	...	...	...	1	...	...	...	...	...
49	Ostorius	...	...	...	19	...	...	...	...	24	6	...	...	...	...	...	...	...
18	Octa	...	...	...	5	...	...	...	...	8	5	...	...	...	...	...	...	...
39	Proximus	...	...	...	25	...	...	...	...	2	...	12	...	...	...	...	...	...
47	Sir Nicodemus ..	...	...	...	...	47	...	...	...	...	...	...	...	...	...	...	...	...
92	Devil	...	...	...	...	10	...	27	20	...	...	...	...	...	...	...	35	...
3	Bishop	...	...	..	...	...	3	...	...	...	...	...	...	...	...	...	...	...
266	Merlin	...	...	...	...	...	...	...	21	...	...	103	...	..	...	69	53	20
14	1st Gentleman ...	...	...	...	...	...	...	...	...	...	...	14	...	...	...	...	..	...
13	2nd Gentleman ...	...	...	...	...	...	...	...	...	...	...	13	...	...	...	...	...	...
45	Vortiger	...	...	...	...	...	...	...	...	...	...	38	...	7	...	...	...	...
3	Messenger	...	..	...	...	...	...	...	...	...	...	3	...	...	...	...	...	...
39	Constantia	8	...	...	...	...	31	...	...	...	...	...	...	...	...	...	...	...
130	Modestia	37	28	...	...	...	65	...	...	...	...	...	...	...	...	...	...	...
103	Artesia	...	29	...	14	...	...	...	...	...	52	...	...	...	...	...	...	8
113	Joan	...	...	34	...	19	...	...	16	..	...	21	...	...	...	...	23	...
5	Spirit	...	...	...	1	...	...	...	...	...	...	4	...	...	...	...	...	...
1	Armel	...	...	...	1	...	...	...	...	...	...	...	...	...	...	...	...	...
2	Plesgetii	...	...	...	2	...	...	...	...	...	...	...	...	...	...	...	...	...
20	Gentlewoman ...	...	...	...	20	...	...	...	...	...	...	...	...	...	...	...	...	...
12	Lucina	...	...	...	...	...	...	12	...	...	...	...	...	...	...	...	...	...
2450		129	270	196	391	186	164	39	128	34	159	281	43	27	16	162	111	114
2384	Actual No. of Lines	127	256	195	381	186	160	39	127	33	148	276	42	24	15	159	104	112

SCHEME FOR ARRANGING THE PARTS WITH EIGHTEEN MEN AND SEVEN LADIES.

Men's Parts.

FOURTEEN CHARACTERS SINGLY AND FOUR GROUPS.

			GLOSTER	28	31			
			MESSENGER	3				
OCTA	18	33	OSWALD	18	34	PROXIMUS	39	43
2ND LORD	2		CAPTAIN	2		BISHOP	3	
2ND GENTLEMAN	13		1ST GENTLEMAN	14		1ST LORD	1	

Ladies' Parts.

FIVE CHARACTERS SINGLY AND TWO GROUPS.

LUCINA	12	14	CONSTANTIA	39	40
PLESGETH	2		ARMEL	1	

SUGGESTIONS FOR DISCUSSION.

1. As parts of *The Birth of Merlin* are far above the level of Rowley's other work and of most other dramatists, it is almost certain that the play contains fragments of Shakspere's writing.
2. The separate conduct of the plots contained in *The Birth of Merlin* is definite proof that Shakspere could have had no hand in the present form of the play.
3. It is inconceivable that Shakspere could have presented any part of the Arthurian legend for the mere amusement of the groundlings.

EARLIEST KNOWN EDITION.

Date.	*Printer.*	*Publisher.*	*Acted by*	*Present Owners.*
1662	Tho: Johnson	Francis Kirkman and Henry Marsh		British Museum. Bodleian Library. Trinity College, Cambridge.

The title of this edition is "The Birth of Merlin: or The Childe hath found his Father." It is said to have "been seueral times Acted with great Applause," and to have been "Written by William Shakespear, and William Rowley." In the most recent edition (1887), edited by Drs. Warnke and Proescheldt, the Introduction says that the "grammar and versification bear distinctly the stamp of the age of Queen Elizabeth or King James I." It was not included with the other doubtful plays in the 1664 Folio.

In 1597 Henslowe has several entries (*Diary*, pp. 87–9) of a play which he describes as "Uterpendragon" and "Pendragon." It was a new play on April 29th of that year, and was acted by "the lord admerall players."

In 1596–7 Henslowe has many notes about the purchase of properties for, and the receipts at the performances of, a play which he calls "Valteger" (*Diary*, pp. 76–86, 273). This has been supposed to be identical with the play which elsewhere (p. 204) he calls "Vortiger," and to have some connection with part of the story of *The Birth of Merlin*.

HENRY VIII.

Total Number of Lines.	CHARACTERS.	Prologue.	I.				II.				III.		IV.		V.					Epilogue.
			1	2	3	4	1	2	3	4	1	2	1	2	1	2	3	4	5	
192	BUCKINGHAM	...	118	...	...	...	74	...	...	...	...	...	...	...	...	...	...	...	...	...
211	NORFOLK	...	105	9	...	...	...	39	...	...	...	54	...	...	...	...	4	...	...	...
18	ABERGAVENNY... ..	...	18	...	...	...	...	...	...	...	...	...	...	...	...	...	...	...	...	...
436	WOLSEY	...	5	42	...	42	...	32	...	48	40	227	...	..	...	...	...	...	...	...
2	1ST SECRETARY ..	...	2	...	...	...	...	...	...	...	...	...	...	...	...	...	...	...	...	...
14	BRANDON	...	14	...	...	...	...	...	...	...	...	...	...	...	...	...	...	...	...	...
5	SERGEANT	...	5	...	..	...	...	...	...	...	...	...	...	...	...	...	...	...	...	...
457	KING	...	...	79	...	19	...	32	...	95	...	61	...	...	85	13	50	...	23	...
2	"ALL"	...	...	1	...	...	...	...	...	...	...	...	...	...	...	...	1	...	...	...
61	SURVEYOR	...	...	61	...	...	...	...	...	...	...	...	...	...	...	...	...	...	...	...
150	CHAMBERLAIN	...	...	...	34	28	...	28	22	...	...	19	...	...	...	...	1	18	...	...
48	SANDS	...	...	...	21	27	...	...	...	...	...	...	...	...	...	...	...	...	...	...
68	LOVELL	...	...	...	27	4	6	...	...	...	...	...	...	...	31	...	...	...	...	...
9	GUILDFORD	...	...	...	...	9	...	...	...	...	...	...	...	...	...	...	...	...	...	...
4	SERVANT	...	...	...	...	4	...	...	...	...	...	...	...	...	...	...	...	...	...	...
112	1ST GENTLEMAN ...	...	...	...	...	...	67	...	...	...	3	...	41	...	1	...	...	...	...	..
88	2ND GENTLEMAN ...	...	...	...	...	..	44	..	...	..	...	...	44	...	...	...	...	...	...	...
4	VAUX	...	...	...	...	...	4	...	...	...	...	..	...	...	...	...	...	...	...	...
93	SUFFOLK	...	...	...	...	...	...	17	...	...	..	63	...	...	7	...	6	...	...	...
53	CAMPEIUS...	...	...	...	...	...	..	15	...	15	23	...	...	...	...	...	...	...	...	.
91	GARDINER...	...	...	...	...	...	..	2	...	...	...	...	...	...	42	...	47	...	...	...
4	SCRIBE	...	...	...	...	...	...	...	...	4	...	...	...	...	...	...	...	...	...	...
3	CRIER	...	...	...	...	...	...	...	...	3	...	...	...	...	...	...	...	...	...	...
59	GRIFFITH	...	...	...	...	...	...	...	...	1	...	...	...	58	...	...	...	...	...	...
8	LINCOLN	...	...	...	..	...	...	...	...	8	...	...	..	...	...	...	...	...	...	...
81	SURREY	...	...	...	...	...	...	...	...	...	...	79	...	...	...	...	2	...	...	...
49	CROMWELL	...	...	...	...	...	...	...	...	...	...	29	...	...	...	..	20	...	..	...
57	3RD GENTLEMAN ...	...	...	...	...	...	...	...	...	...	...	...	57	...	...	...	...	...	...	...
4	MESSENGER	...	...	...	...	...	...	...	...	...	...	...	...	4	...	...	...	...	...	..
11	CAPUCIUS	...	...	...	...	...	...	...	...	...	...	...	...	11	...	...	...	...	...	...
4	DENNY	...	...	...	...	...	...	...	...	...	...	...	...	...	4	...	...	...	...	...
134	CRANMER	...	...	...	...	...	...	...	...	...	...	...	...	...	19	16	43	...	56	...
7	KEEPER	...	...	...	...	...	...	...	...	...	...	...	...	...	...	3	4	...	...	...
9	BUTTS	...	...	...	...	...	...	...	...	...	...	...	...	...	...	9	...	...	...	...
32	CHANCELLOR	...	...	...	...	...	...	...	...	...	...	...	...	...	...	...	32	...	...	...
36	PORTER	...	...	...	...	...	...	...	...	...	...	...	...	...	...	...	...	36	...	...
3	"WITHIN"	...	...	...	...	...	...	...	...	...	...	...	...	...	...	...	...	3	...	...
41	MAN	...	...	...	...	...	...	...	...	...	...	...	...	...	...	...	...	41	...	...
4	GARTER	...	...	...	...	...	...	...	...	...	...	...	...	...	...	...	...	...	4	...
32	"PROLOGUE"	32	...	...	...	...	...	...	...	...	...	...	...	...	..	...	...	...	...	..
374	QUEEN KATHARINE	...	...	53	...	...	...	...	..	86	121	...	...	114	...	...	...	...	...	...
58	ANNE	...	...	...	...	4	...	...	54	...	...	...	...	...	...	...	...	...	...	...
68	OLD LADY	...	...	...	...	...	...	...	51	...	...	...	...	...	17	...	...	...	...	...
18	PATIENCE	...	...	...	...	...	...	...	...	...	12	...	...	6	...	...	...	...	...	...
1	BOY	...	...	...	...	...	...	...	...	...	...	...	...	...	1	...	...	...	...	...
14	"EPILOGUE"	...	...	..	...	...	...	...	...	...	...	...	...	...	...	...	...	...	...	14
3229		32	268	244	82	137	195	165	127	260	199	532	142	193	207	41	210	98	83	14
2821	Actual No. of Lines	32	226	214	67	108	169	144	107	241	184	460	117	173	177	35	182	94	77	14

In I. 1 268 should be 267. In I. 2 the totals should be 245 and 215. The total lines should be 2822.

Character	Lines	Total
Surrey	81	87
1st Secretary	2	
Servant	4	
Cromwell	49	88
Porter	36	
Crier	3	
Campeius	53	89
Chancellor	32	
Vaux	4	
Capucius	11	85
Denny	4	
Butts	9	
Surveyor	61	
Lincoln	8	85
Lovell	68	
Sergeant	5	
Messenger	4	
Sands	48	89
Man	41	
Abergavenny	18	86
3rd Gentleman	57	
Keeper	7	
Scribe	4	
Guildford	9	86
Griffith	59	
Brandon	14	
Garter	4	

SUGGESTIONS FOR DISCUSSION.

1. *Henry VIII.* was written in 1603, then set aside for political reasons and, altered by Fletcher, was brought out in 1613 as a rival to Rowley's play on the same subject.
2. The grandeur of England resulting from the establishment of the Reformation is the governing thought of *Henry VIII.*
3. The only Shakspere-parts left in *Henry VIII.* are the scenes in which Katharine appears.

THE EARLIEST KNOWN EDITION IS THE 1623 FOLIO.

The play was there called "The Famous History of the Life of King Henry the Eight."

In the Stationers' Registers is this entry :—

1599. September 7.

master **Dawson** Entred for his copie vnder the handes of master Sonybanck and the Wardens. A Booke or poeme called *The life and Deathe of Thomas Woolsey Cardinall* vj^d

Henslowe notes (*Diary*, p. 189) that he "Lent unto Samwell Rowlye 1601, to paye unto harye Chettell, for writtinge the Boocke of carnalle Wolseye lyfe, the 5 of June, some of xx^s," and (p. 193) that he "Layd owt at the apoyntment of my sonne and the companye unto harey cheattell for the altrynge of the booke of carnowlle Wollsey, the 28 of June 1601 xx^s," and on July 14th there is the note of a payment in full to Chettle of xxxx^s for the same play. For properties in it xx^s were paid on July 17th; xxxvij^s on August 7th; xxj^li and iij^li x^s on the 10th; xx^s on the 11th; xx^s and x^s on the 12th; viij^li 4^s on the 13th; xiiij^d on the 14th. On the 18th Chettle was paid xx^s more. On the 20th x^s and on the 21st xx^s were spent on a dress for it. On the 24th Chettle received xx^s "in earneste called the j pt of carnall Wollsay." On September 3rd the Master of the Revels was paid for licensing "the remainder of Carnowlle Wollseye." The last two references seem to be to a second play on the subject, which is probably that mentioned in the following note, stating that Henslowe "Lent unto Robarte shawe, to lend unto hary Chettell, and antonye Mondaye, and mihell Drayton, in earneste of a boocke called the Rissenge of carnowlle Wolsey, the 10 of octobr . 1601 xxxx^s." Further payments to authors, to whom "Smythe" was then added, were made on November 6th, 9th, and 12th. On the 15th of May in the following year Chettle received xx^s "for the mendynge of the fyrste pte of carnowlle Wollsey," and in May and June various sums were paid for dresses "for the 2 pte of Wollsey" (pp. 220-2).

The following entry is in the Registers :—

1605. February 12.

Nathanaell Butter yf he gett good alowance for the enterlude of *King Henry the 8th* before he begyn to print it, And then procure the wardens handes to yt for the entrance of yt : He is to haue the same for his copy

When the Globe was burned down in 1613, there was a play being acted which dealt with the events of the reign of Henry VIII. Authorities are not agreed that it was Shakspere's play. Stokes (*Chronological Order*, p. 166) says "there cannot be a doubt that the piece . . . . was Shakespeare's *Henry VIII.*' Halliwell-Phillipps (*Outlines*, Vol. II., p. 292) says there is "decisive proof that it was not Shakespeare's Henry the Eighth."

This very interesting question, however, fades into insignificance in comparison with that modern development of criticism which, by the application of mechanical tests, attributes many cherished passages in the play to Fletcher instead of Shakspere. The student should make himself conversant with Fletcher's acknowledged works, and then come to his own conclusion. Reference should be made to Mr. Spedding's paper (*Gentleman's Magazine*, August, 1850), reprinted with other matter bearing on the subject in the New Shakspere Society's *Transactions*, 1874, Part I., and to a paper by Mr. Boyle in the *Transactions* for 1880-6, Part III., in which he divides the play between Massinger and Fletcher.

THE TWO NOBLE KINSMEN.

Total Number of Lines.	CHARACTERS.	Prologue.	I. 1	I. 2	I. 3	I. 4	I. 5	II. 1	II. 2	II. 3	II. 4	II. 5	II. 6	III. 1	III. 2	III. 3	III. 4	III. 5	III. 6	IV. 1	IV. 2	IV. 3	V. 1	V. 2	V. 3	V. 4	Epilogue.
331	THESEUS		65			44						26						10	62		20		17		50	37	
125	PIRITHOUS		3		10							14						4	11		34		2		3	44	
514	ARCITE			47					117	39		25		79		47			107				43		4	6	
593	PALAMON			73					165					62		36			131				80			46	
12	VALERIUS			12																							
5	HERALD					5																					
124	GAOLER							31	21											33		12		24		3	
105	WOOER							5												63		4		33			
15	1ST COUNTRYMAN									11								4									
30	2ND COUNTRYMAN									21								9									
25	3RD COUNTRYMAN									16								9									
17	4TH COUNTRYMAN									12								5									
106	GERROLD																	106									
1	TABORER																	1									
1	BAVIAN																	1									
27	1ST FRIEND																			27							
22	2ND FRIEND																			22							
10	BROTHER																			10							
7	"ALL"																			3					4		
4	GENTLEMAN																				4						
49	MESSENGER																				44			4		1	
92	DOCTOR																					48		44			
13	1ST SERVANT																								13		
9	1ST KNIGHT																									9	
6	2ND KNIGHT																									6	
3	3RD KNIGHT																									3	
32	"PROLOGUE"	32																									
24	BOY		24																								
77	1ST QUEEN		64			1	12																				
53	2ND QUEEN		40			2	11																				
50	3RD QUEEN		34			2	4																				
102	HIPPOLYTA		21		44							6						1	15		6				9		
368	EMILIA		22		56				28			13						2	50		69		37		88	3	
327	DAUGHTER							26			33		39		38		26	25		43		40		57			
14	WOMAN								14																		
1	NELL																	1									
18	"EPILOGUE"																										18
3312		32	273	132	110	54	37	62	345	99	33	84	39	141	38	83	26	178	376	201	177	104	179	162	171	158	18
2821	Actual No. of Lines	32	234	116	97	49	16	62	281	83	33	64	39	123	38	53	26	162	309	154	156	104	173	112	150	137	18

SCHEME FOR ARRANGING THE PARTS WITH EIGHTEEN MEN AND SEVEN LADIES.

Men's Parts.

THIRTEEN CHARACTERS SINGLY AND FIVE GROUPS.

Valerius 12, Herald 5, Taborer 1	18	Brother 10, Bavian 1, 1st Knight 9	20
Gentleman 4, 1st Countryman 15	19	1st Servant 13, 2nd Knight 6	19
3rd Knight 3, 4th Countryman 17	20		

Ladies' Parts.

THREE CHARACTERS SINGLY AND FOUR GROUPS.

Boy 24, "Epilogue" 18	42	Woman 14, 2nd Queen 53	67
Nell 1, 1st Queen 77	78	"Prologue" 32, 3rd Queen 50	82

SUGGESTIONS FOR DISCUSSION.

1. Most, if not all, of *The Two Noble Kinsmen* was written by Fletcher and Massinger.
2. In *The Two Noble Kinsmen* the degradation of Shakspere's work by Fletcher's underplot is painful and almost intolerable.
3. The departures from Chaucer which are made in *The Two Noble Kinsmen* are in accordance with Shakspere's mode of treating originals.

EARLIEST KNOWN EDITION.

Date.	*Printer.*	*Publisher.*	*Acted by*	*Present Owners.*
1634	Tho. Cotes	Iohn Waterson	The King's servants	British Museum. Bodleian Library. Trinity College, Cambridge. Trinity College, Dublin. Mr. P. A. Daniel.

In the Stationers' Registers is this entry :—

1634. April 8.
Master John Waterson Entred for his Copy vnder the hands of Sir Henry Herbert and master **Aspley** warden a TragiComedy called *the two noble kinsmen* by John ffletcher and William Shakespeare **vjd.**

On the title-page, where the play is called simply "The Two Noble Kinsmen," it is said to have been "Presented at the Blackfriers . . . . with great applause" and to have been "Written by the memorable Worthies of their time; {Mr. John Fletcher, and Mr. William Shakspeare.} Gent." This is the only external evidence connecting the play with Shakspere.

Much has been written on the conclusions to be derived from an examination of the play itself (see Spalding's "Letter on Shakspeare's Authorship of The Two Noble Kinsmen," first printed in 1833, and republished by the New Shakspere Society in 1876; Hickson's paper in 1847, reprinted in the New Shakspere Society's *Transactions*, 1874, Part I.; Furnivall's Introduction to the 'Leopold' *Shakspere*; Littledale's Introduction to the play edited by him for the New Shakspere Society, Part II., 1885; and Boyle's paper on "Massinger and *The Two Noble Kinsmen*" in the New Shakspere Society's *Transactions*, 1880-5, Part II.). Prepared by a study of Fletcher's style, the student will be in a position to form an independent opinion on this difficult question of authorship.

The story of Palamon and Arcite had been frequently dramatised and acted. A play by Edwards with that title was performed before Queen Elizabeth in 1566. A new play called "palamon and arsett" was brought out on September 17, 1594, by Henslowe for "my Lord Admeralle and my Lorde chamberlen men" at Newington, and repeated in the following two months (*Diary*, pp. 41, 43-4). No copy of either of these plays is known to exist.

The literary consideration of this play must include a comparison with Chaucer's *Knightes Tale.*

A NEW WAY TO PAY OLD DEBTS.

Total Number of Lines.	CHARACTERS.	I.			II.			III.			IV.			V.
		1	2	3	1	2	3	1	2	3	1	2	3	1
411	WELLBORN	104	...	67	29	24	26	...	4	10	...	40	...	107
100	TAPWELL	72	...	...	...	...	...	...	...	...	...	28	...	...
227	ALLWORTH	39	27	2	...	17	...	76	3	1	8	...	42	12
50	ORDER	...	16	13	...	18	...	...	...	...	...	2	...	1
38	AMBLE	...	9	6	...	20	...	...	...	...	2	...	...	1
119	FURNACE	...	43	19	...	51	...	...	...	...	...	4	...	2
10	WATCHALL	...	2	3	...	5	...	...	...	...	...	...	...	...
150	GREEDY	...	...	21	...	...	...	...	67	...	24	28	...	10
702	OVERREACH	...	...	14	73	...	46	...	176	60	106	...	54	173
298	MARRALL	...	...	2	75	30	76	...	28	4	5	28	...	50
251	LOVELL	...	...	...	...	...	...	43	42	6	87	...	...	73
1	"ALL"	...	...	...	...	...	...	...	...	...	...	1	...	...
7	1ST CREDITOR	...	...	...	...	...	...	...	...	...	...	7	...	...
6	2ND CREDITOR	...	...	...	...	...	...	...	...	...	...	6	...	...
1	3RD CREDITOR	...	...	...	...	...	...	...	...	...	...	1	...	...
12	WILLDO	...	...	...	...	...	...	...	...	...	...	...	...	12
25	FROTH	9	...	...	...	...	...	...	...	...	...	16	...	...
265	LADY ALLWORTH	...	65	19	..	25	...	...	29	12	55	...	...	60
17	WOMAN	...	...	3	...	13	...	...	...	...	1	...	...	...
14	CHAMBERMAID	...	...	7	...	7	...	...	...	...	...	...	...	...
118	MARGARET	...	...	...	...	...	...	...	48	1	...	...	61	8
2822		224	162	176	177	210	148	119	397	94	288	161	157	509
2479	Actual Number of Lines	210	145	141	148	210	148	104	329	77	251	160	141	415

SUGGESTIONS FOR DISCUSSION.

1. Fletcher wrote in July–August, 1625, nearly all the first two acts of *A New Way to Pay Old Debts.*

2. Massinger meant the character of Sir Giles Overreach to be a true picture for all time of that wilful selfishness which mistakes the inveteracy of its purposes for their rectitude.

3. In tragedy Massinger was second only to Shakspere, and in the higher comedy not inferior to Ben Jonson.

EARLIEST KNOWN EDITION.

Date.	*Printer.*	*Publisher.*	*Acted by*	*Present Owner.*
1633	E. P.	Henry Seyle	The Queen's servants	British Museum.

The following entry occurs in the Stationers' Registers:—

1632. November 10.

Master **Seile** Entred for his Copy vnder the hands of Sir HENRY HERBERT and Master **Aspley** warden . . . .

Idem. Entred for his Copy vnder the same handes a Comedy called *A new way to pay old Debtes* by PHILLIP MASSINGER vjd.

There is no external evidence to determine the date of this play. On the title-page of the 1633 edition it is said to have "beene often acted at the Phœnix in Drury-Lane." Sir Henry Herbert's term of office began in 1623. If it is true that Fletcher wrote part of it, the date of its composition must be not later than 1625, the year of Fletcher's death.

CHAPTER X.

The Elizabethan Dramatists.

"The web of our life is of a mingled yarn, good and ill together."
All's Well that Ends Well, IV. iii. 83-4.

IN the previous pages reference has so often been made to personal incidents in connection with the Elizabethan dramatists, that it is desirable to have at hand some record of the story of their lives. This chapter, however, pretends to afford neither new facts nor re-arrangement of old ones; the reader who seeks for full information is referred to the Introductions to the editions of the various authors' works and to other well-known biographical sources.[1] I give only a bare outline sufficient to show the student the main facts in the life of each of the writers whose work has been brought under consideration.

In writing about these authors, it is impossible to be correct, as often their history is shrouded in impenetrable obscurity: identification, even, is not always possible. In such cases I have been obliged to give the least improbable theory. The orthography of their names presents another difficulty. In the period in which they lived spelling was not a fixed science. In Chapter IX. may be

[1] For information about the Oxford men reference should be made to Bliss's 1813-20 edition of Wood's *Athenæ Oxonienses* and *Fasti Oxonienses*. Full details concerning the Cambridge men who died before 1609 will be found in *Athenae Cantabrigienses* by C. H. and T. Cooper, 1858, 1861. The 1812 *Biographia Dramatica* is very useful. The *Dictionary of National Biography*, at present only in the letter F, is invaluable.

seen many instances of the variety of ways in which it was permissible to spell proper names.

Concerning the name of the greatest figure in the drama of that time, the literary world has now and then been greatly disturbed, and occasionally controversy about it has raged hotly. Although I have adopted the poet's own form, I think that those who are not satisfied with that should, considering the latitude allowed in his day, be allowed to indulge their fancy unmolested. I will go so far as to admit that those who represent the name otherwise than as I have given it are not necessarily devoid of all moral principles, and that one may write "Shakspeare," or even "Shakespeare," or any other erratic form, and yet be an affectionate parent, a dutiful child, a loving partner, a faithful friend—in fact, may fulfil all the other duties of citizenship in a most exemplary manner.

In reference to the five authentic signatures of the poet it has been said by one[1] who is an unsurpassed authority on all points connected with Shakspere's history that the signature on the deed in the Guildhall, London, "is unquestionably Shakspere" (p. 20); that on the mortgage deed now in the British Museum "the form of Shakspere cannot in this instance be admitted with anything like certainty" (p. 22). Of the first signature on the will it is said "that it was originally Shakspere may be safely concluded" (p. 22). Of the second it is declared "that here we should read Shakspere" (p. 23); and in reference to the third it is said "that the character

[1] J. O. Halliwell-Phillipps. *New Lamps or Old? A few additional Words on the Momentous Question respecting the E and the A in the name of our National Dramatist.* Second Edition. 1880.

The world of letters has now to lament the loss of this loving student of Shakspere. His laborious investigations recorded in many a volume form a perpetual monument to his worth. He died on January 3rd, 1889.

following the letter *k* is the then well-known and accepted contraction for *es*" (p. 24). But it is added that "its situation in this signature is peculiar and difficult of explanation." On the monument over his grave the name is "Shakspeare." In the Church Registers[1] the birth- and death-records of the poet and his family have the form "Shakspere." In the light of these statements it is important for those students who believe in the personality of the man of Stratford to adopt the spelling which he himself favoured rather than introduce that which has been called "the important central *e*," but which is really nothing more than a printer's device, especially as upon the highest authority we are told that "the choice of the pronunciation of Shakespeare's name is of course a question independent of the form in which it should be printed. The general instinct seems to be adverse to the ancient orthoepy of Shaxpere, and the main reason against the prudence of adopting the short form is that it might encourage the name to be so spoken. There can be little doubt that the poet was generally called Shaxpere or Shaxper in the provinces, but certainly not always. In the earliest known document respecting any member of the poet's family, one which refers to property at Snitterfield near Stratford-on-Avon, the name of his grandfather is given as Shakespere, showing the first syllable to be long."[2] But students who wish to be accurate will not be influenced by any question of supposed euphony or of prettiness of appearance, and instead of following a popular delusion, they will accept the way in which the poet wrote it rather than the fashion in which somebody else printed it.

If early printed copies are allowed to be authorities for the

[1] The entries are not contemporaneous with the events, but are copies made some few years afterwards.

[2] Halliwell-Phillipps, *Op. cit.* pp. 13, 14.

spelling of personal names "Rare Ben's" surname must be written "Johnson," for thus it appears in the 1601 *Every Man in his Humour*. The name of the literary partner of Fletcher is given as "Baymont" in the earliest known edition of *Philaster*, and afterwards it appears as "Beamont." The author of *The Virgin-Martyr* is described on the title-page of the 1622 edition as "Messenger." In short, printers' spelling of that period is the most uncertain guide that can be taken. The various ways in which the names of many of the Elizabethan dramatists have come down to us are familiar to students of the literature of the age.

The names that follow are given in the order in which their work is considered in Chapter IX.

William Shakspere.

The day of William Shakspere's birth is unknown. On the 26th of April, 1564, he was baptized in the Church of the Holy Trinity, Stratford-on-Avon, and from the fact that it was then common to baptize children when only a few days old, and in deference to the tradition that he died on the anniversary of his birth, it has been generally agreed to look upon the 23rd of April as his birth-day. This was the date according to the Old Style; if transferred into modern reckoning, it would be May 3rd. It is matter of conjecture only that he was born in the house in Henley Street, which is now pointed out as the birth-place. In 1556 the present block consisted of two separate houses. The easternmost, that which now contains the Museum and Library, was bought in that year by John Shakspere, who was living and carrying on business, as a glover and sort of general dealer, somewhere in Henley Street at least as early as 1552. It may have been in 1557 that

John Shakspere married Mary Arden, of Wilmecote, near Stratford. In 1558 Joan was born, and probably died soon after.[1] In 1562 Margaret was born; she died in 1563. In 1564 William was born.

In 1575 his father bought other property in Stratford, part of which was, almost certainly, the other portion of the block referred to. After tradition had fixed upon the house, it of course took the largest upstair apartment and called it the room where William first saw light. There is positive evidence that in 1597 John Shakspere had the land on the western side of the block.[2]

It seems that it was the custom for boys to begin school-life at the age of seven. Probably therefore, although there is no direct evidence on the matter, William went to the Stratford Free Grammar School in 1571, the year in which his father, having for three years previously served the office of High Bailiff or Mayor, was elected Chief Alderman. The course of instruction at such a school is shown in Professor Baynes's papers on "What Shakespeare learnt at School."[3]

About 1578 John Shakspere began to get into money-difficulties.[4] At this period many plays were acted at Stratford by various companies of actors, who performed in the hall under the schoolroom of the Grammar School. The boy Shakspere doubtless saw some of

[1] The fifth child born in 1569 was also named Joan.

[2] Much information in detail about all these matters is given in Mr. Halliwell-Phillipps's *Outlines* and in Mr. Joseph Hill's *Shakespeare's Birthplace and Adjoining Properties*. 1885.

[3] *Fraser's Magazine*, November, 1879; January and May, 1880.

[4] In 1592 "Mr. John Shackespere" is amongst those reported to the Council by the Commissioners for the county of Warwick "for not comminge monethlie to the Chürche according to hir MaJesties lawes," and that he had absented himself "for feare of processe for debtte." *Calendar of State Papers*. Domestic. 1591—1594. p. 290; and Halliwell-Phillipps's *Outlines*, Vol. II., pp. 245—6. The latter gives very full "Annals" of the poet's father, which are of great interest.

them. But nothing is known of what he did as a lad or when he left school.

In 1582 he married (it is surmised) Anne Hathaway of Shottery, near Stratford. But there is no conclusive proof of this. Shakspere's grand-daughter, Elizabeth, whose second husband was Sir John Barnard, mentions in her will "the daughters of her kinsman Thomas Hathaway;" and it is known that some Hathaways lived at Shottery. It was not till 1836 that the marriage-bond was discovered in the Worcester Registry by Sir Thomas Phillipps. In the words of this deed, the contracting parties were "William Shagspere one thone partie, and Anne Hathwey, of Stratford in the dioces of Worcester." The omission of Shottery in this document is of no import, as it would be included in the general title of Stratford. But the difficulty of identifying Shakspere's wife has been increased by the Rev. T. P. Wadley's recent discovery in the Bishop's Register at Worcester, of an entry, dated 1582, which refers to a marriage-license being granted "inter Willielmum Shaxpere et Annam Whateley de Temple Grafton."[1] Their first child, Susanna, was baptized on May 26th, 1583; and on February 2nd, 1585, their twin children, Hamnet and Judith, were baptized.

Guesses have been plentiful in reference to Shakspere's movements about this period.[2] As he was afterwards so mixed up with the

[1] Whateley might easily be a miscopying of Hathaway. The *crux* in the case is Temple Grafton, a village some few miles from Stratford.

[2] In *The Contemporary Review* for April, 1889, Dean Plumptre has revived the almost forgotten idea that about this time Shakspere was one of a company of players that the Earl of Leicester had taken to the Netherlands, and that he was the "Will, my lord of Lesters Jesting plaier," by whom Sir Philip Sidney sent a letter in 1586 to his father-in-law, Secretary Walsingham. (See the Shakespeare Society's *Papers*, Vol. I., 1844, and "Was Shakespeare a Soldier?" in Thoms's *Three Notelets on Shakespeare*, 1865.)

In the 'Cambridge Bible' *Ecclesiastes*, the Dean has a very interesting essay on the parallelism between the thoughts expressed by the writer of the Sacred Book and those which may be assumed to be the outpouring of Shakspere's own soul.

Burbages, the most plausible theory is, that in a subordinate capacity he became attached in 1587 to the Queen's servants, then acting at Stratford,[1] having as their leader James Burbage, who had been one of the Earl of Leicester's players, and that with them he travelled to London.

By 1592 he had, either as writer or actor, or both, excited the wrathful jealousy of Robert Greene.[2] In 1593 *Venus and Adonis* was printed by Richard Field, a former townsman of Stratford, whom Shakspere knew and, on that account probably, employed.

In December, 1594, he was acting with the Lord Chamberlain's servants before the Queen at Greenwich, and in the entry of payments his name comes between those of Kemp and Richard Burbage. This is the earliest record of his association with a company of actors. His histrionic connections before this date are all guesswork. Mr. Halliwell-Phillipps says *(Outlines*, Vol. I. p. 110) "it would appear not altogether unlikely that the poet was one of Lord Strange's actors in March, 1592;[3] one of Lord Pembroke's[4] a few months later; and that he had joined the company of the Earl of Sussex, in or before January, 1594."[4]

In 1596 Shakspere's only son, Hamnet, died when eleven and a half years old, and was buried at Stratford on the 11th of August.

In the same year, no doubt through his son's influence, John Shakspere received a grant of arms from the Heralds' College.

By 1597 William must have been in flourishing circumstances, as

[1] See 1821 *Variorum*, Vol. II., p. 151.

[2] See *Green's Groats-worth of Wit, bought with a Million of Repauntance*, 1596. This is the earliest copy known. It was reprinted in 1813 by Sir Egerton Brydges, and in 1874 by the New Shakspere Society in *Shakspere Allusion-Books*. Greene died in September, 1592.

[3] This is because they played *Henry VI.* (see p. 63).

[4] This is because they played *Titus Andronicus* (see p. 59).

in that year he became the possessor of the largest house in Stratford, the "Great House" that had belonged to the Clopton[1] family for a long period, and which had become known as "New Place" some time before it came into the possession of Shakspere, who bought it, in bad condition, from William Underhill for "sixty pounds sterling."[2] Mere fragments of the foundations of the original house now remain. It has been thought incredible that, by the unaided results of his everyday calling, he could have raised himself to the social position he enjoyed at that time. There is a tradition, to which however it is not necessary to attach much credence, that Lord Southampton, to whom he had dedicated *Venus and Adonis* and *Lucrece*, had given him £1000, a gift which in those days would have been extraordinarily munificent. From this period there is evidence that in the midst of his literary successes he was not unmindful of his duty to his family, for from time to time he invoked the aid of the law to recover small sums of money due to him for various reasons.

In 1599 heraldic impalement of arms for his mother with those granted to his father was allowed. When the Globe theatre was built in that year Shakspere, as shown by a document of later date, was one of "the partners in the profittes" of that house.

In 1601 Shakspere's father died at Stratford, and was buried on the 8th September.

[1] See Stow's *Survey of London*, ed. 1633, pp. 89, 292, 573—4, for notice of Sir Hugh Clopton, the builder of "the great stone arched Bridge at Stratford upon Avon," who was Sheriff of London in 1486 and Lord Mayor in 1491.

[2] It came again to the Cloptons through Sir Edward Walker, who bought it in 1675 from the trustee of Lady Barnard, Shakspere's grand-daughter. Sir Edward's daughter married Sir John Clopton, who about the year 1700 pulled down the house and erected another building on its site, which in its turn was destroyed in 1759 by the Rev. Francis Gastrell, into whose possession it had passed in 1756, and who, annoyed by the visits of pilgrims to the poet's death-place, left Stratford and pulled down the house to avoid paying rates for it.

In *The Return from Parnassus*, a University play written in 1601,[1] Shakspere's superiority as a dramatic writer is fully recognised,[2] and in 1603 his name occurs in a license granted by James I. to certain actors to play at the Globe and elsewhere. His means were now increasing fast, and he added to his estate much real property at Stratford.

On June 5th, 1607, his eldest daughter, Susanna, now twenty-four years of age, married Dr. John Hall, a medical practitioner in the town.[3]

As a result of this alliance Shakspere became a grandfather in 1608, the year in which his mother died. She was buried at Stratford on September 9th.

In December, 1609, when the Children of the Chapel left the Blackfriars Theatre, it is said that their places were taken by "men players," among whose names occurs that of "Shakspeare."[4] It is difficult, however, to believe that at that time he was really engaged in acting.

After this, except in connection with Stratford affairs, but little is known about him till 1616, when he executed his will a short time before his death at New Place on April 23rd in that year. He was buried in the chancel of his parish church.

[1] See Arber's Reprint.

[2] Act IV. Scene 5. "Few of the vniuersity pen plaies well, they smell too much of that writer *Ouid*, and that writer *Metamorphosis*, and talke too much of *Proserpina* and *Iuppiter*. Why heres our fellow *Shakespeare* puts them all downe, I and *Ben Ionson* too. O that *Ben Ionson* is a pestilent fellow, he brought vp *Horace* giuing the Poets a pill, but our fellow *Shakespeare* hath giuen him a purge that made him beray his credit."

[3] He kept detailed accounts of his cases; and after his death some of these, translated from the Latin, were published under the title of *Select Observations on English Bodies, or Cures both Empericall and Historicall performed upon very eminent Persons in desperate Diseases*. He records the symptoms and treatment of illnesses of himself, his wife, his daughter, the poet Drayton and other well-known people.

[4] For a copy of the document see Halliwell-Phillipps's *Outlines*, Vol. I. p. 291.

WILLIAM SHAKSPERE'S DESCENDANTS AND NEAR RELATIVES.

Dates about which there is a little doubt are in *Italic*.

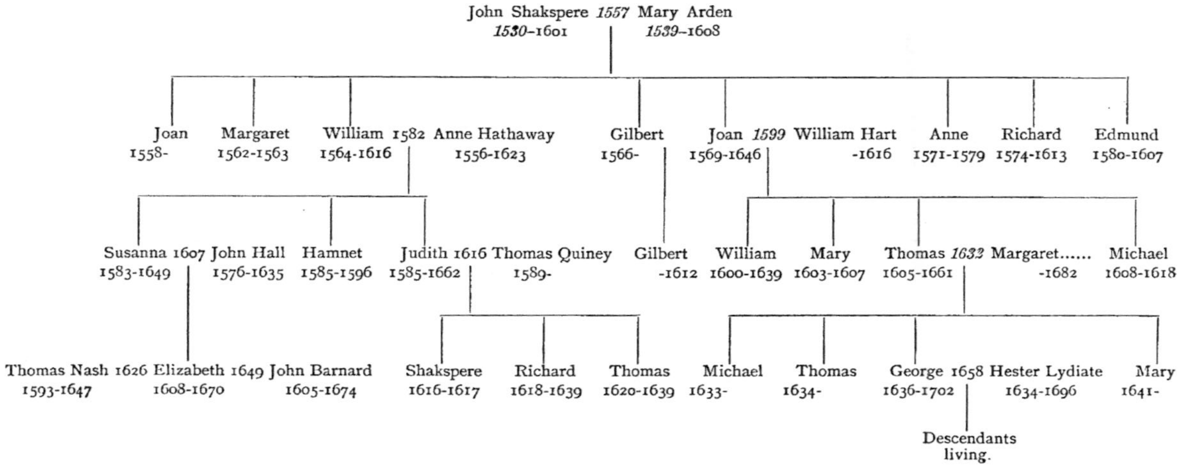

In his will he mentions by name his daughter Judith, his daughter Susanna Hall, his grand-daughter ("neece") Elizabeth, his sister Joan Hart and her three sons, his son-in-law Dr. Hall, and several persons outside his family.

In 1670 in the person of his grand-daughter, then Lady Barnard, Shakspere's lineal descendants came to an end.

John Lyly.

From indirect evidence it is thought that Lyly, "*plebeii filius*," was born in 1554, in Kent. He went to Magdalen College, Oxford, in 1569, and took his B.A. in 1573 and M.A. in 1575. The first part of his great work, *Euphues*,[1] was published in 1579. In that year he was incorporated M.A. of Cambridge. He seems to have expected to have been made Master of the Revels upon the death of Sir Thomas Benger in 1577. But Edmund Tylney was appointed in 1579, and held the office till 1610 (see p. 177). Probably about 1583 Lyly began writing comedies. All his early plays were acted by the choir-boys in their schoolroom at St. Paul's. In 1589 he was taking part in the Marprelate controversy. In *Athenae Cantabrigienses* it is said that upon different occasions between 1593 and 1601 Lyly represented Aylesbury and Appleby in parliament. In December, 1597, he wrote a pathetic letter to Secretary Cecil expressing his disappointment at not receiving the posts to which he had been looking forward.[2]

In 1598, as one of the leaders of comedy, he is described in

[1] This popular work is now easily accessible to the student, as it is in Arber's excellent series of Reprints.

[2] See *Calendar of State Papers*, Domestic. 1595—1597, p. 551. Lyly's earlier communications on the same subject are given by Fairholt and by Arber.

Meres's comprehensive list as "eloquent and wittie Iohn Lilly" (see p. 9).

In 1599 "John Lilly" was committed to the Tower "on suspicion of helping Gerard, the Jesuit, out of the Tower."[1]

The date of his marriage is unknown. He had three children: John, born in 1596, died in the following year; John, born in 1600; and Frances, born in 1603.

Lyly died in 1606, and was buried at St. Bartholomew-the-Less, London.

Lyly's plays are *The Woman in the Moon* (*1583*); *Campaspe* (1584); *Sapho and Phao* (1584); *Endymion* (*1585*); *Gallathea* (1585); *Midas* (1592); *Mother Bombie* (1594); *Love's Metamorphosis* (1601). These were all published separately. Blount, in 1632, issued all but the first and the last in one volume. From then no collected edition appeared till Fairholt's two volumes in 1858.

Henry Morley's article on "Euphuism" (*Quarterly Review*, April, 1861) should be studied in connection with Lyly's work.

Fleay gives "Annals of the Career of John Lyly" in *Shakespeariana*, Vol. IV., 1887.

Christopher Marlowe.

Kit Marlowe, the son of a shoemaker, was born in 1564. He was baptized in the Church of St. George-the-Martyr, Canterbury, on the 26th February in that year. In 1578 he was at the King's School in that city. This he left in 1579 and went to Corpus Christi College,[2] Cambridge, becoming B.A. in 1583 and M.A. in 1587.

[1] *Calendar of State Papers*. Domestic. 1598—1601, pp. 253-4.

[2] Then called Bene't College.

It is possible that *Tamburlaine*, which at once brought him fame, was written before he left the University. At first he wrote for the Lord Admiral's company,[1] by whom *Faustus* was acted (see p. 67); but when in 1589 they were ordered "to forbere playinge," he wrote for the Earl of Pembroke's servants,[2] who played *Edward II.* (see p. 77).

In 1593 he came to an untimely end, being killed in a quarrel.[3] He was buried at Deptford on June 1st.

Meres says that "our tragicall poet Marlow for his Epicurisme and Atheisme had a tragicall death" (see p. 9). This charge, corroborated by Greene's references[4] and the unsupported testimony of a man hanged at Tyburn in 1594, was frequently repeated by Marlowe's contemporaries; but it is inconsistent with the not irreverent spirit of *Faustus*.

Marlowe's plays are *Tamburlaine*, in two parts (*1586-7*)[5]; *Faustus*[6]

[1] Known also as the Earl of Nottingham's servants.

[2] They also acted *The True Tragedy* (see p. 69) and *The Taming of a Shrew* (see p. 97). These facts must be borne in mind in an endeavour to fix the authorship of these plays. (See Fleay's edition of *Edward II.*, pp. 12–13.)

[3] This is usually described as a tavern-brawl, and, very much to Marlowe's disadvantage, is looked at from the point of view of to-day. But here, and in the careers of some of Marlowe's associates, allowance must be made for the differences in social life then existing.

[4] *Groats-worth of Wit* (see p. 194), p. 29, and Epistle to *Perimedes*.

[5] See Nash's Preface to Greene's *Menaphon*, 1589. This, of which there was an edition in 1587, forms one of Arber's Reprints.

Henslowe has various entries of a confusing character concerning "Tamber came," "tamberlen," &c. (see *Diary*, pp. 25-82).

[6] This play has been edited by Dr. W. Wagner (1877) in "The London Series of English Classics," and (with Greene's *Friar Bacon*) in the "Clarendon Press Series" by Professor A. W. Ward (1878). It is almost needless to say that both editions are indispensable to the student (see p. 67). It is said that the note given on p. 67 recording "adycyons to Fostus" in 1597 is a forgery (see Mr. Henry B. Wheatley's *Notes on the Life of John Payne Collier*, 1884, p. 61).

(1588); *Jew of Malta*[1] *(1589)*; *Edward II.*[2] *(1592)*; *Massacre at Paris*[3] *(1592)*. With the exception of *Edward II.*, played by Lord Pembroke's servants, all these were probably often acted by the Lord Admiral's men.[4]

Dido, acted by the Chapel children, was left incomplete, and was finished by Nash. The poem *Hero and Leander* was written only in part by Marlowe, and continued by Chapman.

Marlowe also wrote other poems. His works in collected form were published by Pickering in three volumes in 1826. They were edited by Dyce in three volumes in 1850, and a one-volume edition was published by Routledge in 1858, and reprinted since. There is also a cheap undated volume under the editorship of Colonel Cunningham. Mr. A. H. Bullen's three-volume edition was published in 1885.

[1] The earliest known edition is 1633. Henslowe has many notes about the performance of a play with this title. The first is on February 26th, 1592, by "my lord Stranges mene."

[2] Very useful and most desirable helps in the study of this play, and other parts of Marlowe's work, are to be found in the editions by Mr. F. G. Fleay in "Collins' Series" (1877), and by Mr. O. W. Tancock in the "Clarendon Press Series" (1880).

Whilst thankful for the editions mentioned in the foregoing notes, students have a right to grumble at not receiving more. Not reckoning Shakspere, the Elizabethan drama, of which the literary world professes to be so proud, is represented in the Clarendon Press Series by three plays, and in the Pitt Press Series by *The Two Noble Kinsmen* alone. This is not a creditable record for great English Universities.

In this department of literature the Clarendon Press has given us nothing since 1880 (except the *Parnassus* plays and the second edition of Prof. Ward's book in 1887), and the London Series nothing since 1877, the year in which the only one of these plays was published in Collins' Series. The only play issued by the Pitt Press was in 1875.

[3] It has been supposed that this is referred to by Henslowe first under the name of "the guyes" (*Diary*, p. 30), then as "the Gwies" (p. 36), and afterwards as "the masacer" (p. 36 *et seq.*).

[4] See title-pages of 1590 *Tamburlaine*, 1604 *Faustus*, and the undated *Massacre at Paris*.

"Annals of the Career of Christopher Marlowe," compiled by Mr. Fleay, may be found in *Shakespeariana*, Vol. II., 1885.

Marlowe and Shakspere were born in the same year. In 1593, when Marlowe died, Shakspere's work was insignificant. If a comparison of the two writers should be made this fact must be put in the forefront of the consideration.

A movement is now on foot to commemorate Marlowe's service to dramatic literature.

Robert Greene.

The date of Greene's birth, which took place at Norwich, is unknown. As he went to St. John's College, Cambridge, in 1575, and took his B.A. in 1579, it may be set down about 1560. Before taking his M.A., in 1583, he travelled much on the Continent. He was incorporated M.A. at Oxford in 1588. The idea that he was the Robert Greene appointed one of the Queen's chaplains in 1576 may, of course, be dismissed. Indeed, there is no authority for believing that he was ever ordained. In one of his works, dated 1585, he is called a "student in Phisicke."[1] It is thought that he married Elizabeth Taylor in 1586. It is quite certain that he early deserted his wife and that he led an unusually wild life. He met with a most miserable death in London "in a shoemakers house neere Dow-gate," on September 3rd, 1592, and was buried the following day "in the New-churchyard[2] neere Bedlam," which was

[1] Title-page of *Planetomachia*.

[2] For a notice of this ground, given by Sir Thomas Rowe in 1569 "to be a place for buriall of the dead, to such Parishes in London as wanted Churchyards," see Stow's *Survey of London*, ed. 1633, pp. 92, 175, 587.

then situated in Moorfields. He left a very touching and repentant letter addressed to his wife.

Meres, in 1598, refers to Greene's merits as a poet, places him amongst "the best for comedy," and also alludes to the manner of his death (see pp. 8, 9).

Greene's known plays are *Orlando Furioso,* said to have been acted by Lord Strange's men in 1592 (see Henslowe's *Diary,* p. 21), and, as an instance of Greene's bad faith, to have been sold by the author first to the Queen's servants and then to the Lord Admiral's company; *Friar Bacon,* acted by Lord Strange's men (see p. 73) and by the Queen's servants (see title-page of 1594 edition); *James IV.*; *Alphonsus.* The exact dates of these are not known. *A Looking Glass for London and England* was written in conjunction with Lodge, and acted by Lord Strange's men in 1592 (see Henslowe's *Diary,* p. 23). *George-a-Green, the Pinner of Wakefield,* acted by the servants of the Earl of Sussex,[1] was once thought, on slender evidence, to have been written by Greene, but there is now considerable doubt about its authorship.

Greene's dramatic works and poems were edited by Dyce in 1831 in two volumes. A one-volume edition (with Peele's works) containing Dyce's editorial matter was first published by Routledge in 1861.

Greene wrote many prose-works,[2] the best known of which are the *Groats-worth of Wit* (see p. 194) and *Pandosto* or *The Hystorie of Dorastus and Fawnia,* which supplied Shakspere with the story of *The Winter's Tale* (see p. 177). In some of them he has left much that is autobiographical.

[1] See title-page of 1599 edition and Henslowe's *Diary,* pp. 31–3, where it is entered under each section of its title.

[2] Dyce gives a full list.

Greene's works were collected by Dyce in 1828 in two volumes. Other editions were published in 1829 and 1839.

The student of biography will find many interesting things about Greene's personal characteristics recorded by Chettle, Harvey,[1] and Nash. Much of it is quoted by Dyce.

Greene has been greatly blamed for his disparaging references to Shakspere, but in his justification it must be remembered that in 1592 Shakspere had done nothing worthy of note, and there was scarcely any promise of the rich harvest that was to come. Greene's treatment of Shakspere was undoubtedly illiberal, but he could not be expected to look onwards with prophetic eye and, although there should be no palliation of his general immoral record, it is wrong to condemn him for the thought, not unreasonable then, that University men had a monopoly of dramatic writing, or for the failure to comprehend that the literary attainments of himself and fellows would be of indifferent service in their own field of work when compared with native genius aided by the keen observation of ever watchful intelligence.

Greene's career, ending with death at the age of 32, is a most saddening instance of a life of great literary possibilities frittered away by the wildest debauchery.

George Peele.

From an allusion in a MS. at Oxford it appears that George Peele, son of James Peele,[2] Clerk at Christ's Hospital, was born in

[1] Collier reprinted Harvey's "Foure Letters" in *Miscellaneous Tracts* 1870. The Third Letter is in the New Shakspere Society's *Shakspere Allusion-Books*, 1874.

[2] See note by Mr. John H. Ingram in *The Athenæum*, July 2nd, 1881.

1558.[1] The place of his birth[2] and the details of his life are uncertain. In 1572 he entered at Pembroke College,[3] Oxford, going afterwards to Christ Church, and took his B.A. in 1577 and M.A. in 1579. Thence he went to London, and became one of the well-known literary set of whom it was said they "spend their wits in making plaies." In 1583 he makes an allusion to his wife, but her identity has not been discovered. Peele was about this time much engaged in the production of plays and pageants for festive and public occasions. Some of these doubtless were of his own composition. After a time he was presumably leading as abandoned a life, and thereby reduced to the same straits, as Greene, whose appeal[4] to him seems to have been without any good influence. As a poet and as one of "our best for Tragedie" Meres (see pp. 8, 9) in 1598 has reference to Peele, whose death, which he records, took place about 1596.

Peele's plays are *The Arraignment of Paris* (printed in 1584 and acted by the Children of the Chapel); possibly *The Battle of Alcazar*[5] (1592), acted by the Lord Admiral's servants; *Edward I.*[6] (1593); *The Old Wives' Tale* (printed in 1595, had been acted by the Queen's servants); *King David* (see p. 83). *Sir Clyomon and Sir Clamydes*

[1] See *Plays and Poems of Greene and Peele*, ed. Dyce, 1883, p. 324.

[2] Some elaborate theories have been founded upon the assumption that he was a native of Devonshire.

[3] Then called Broadgates Hall.

[4] See *Groats-worth of Wit*. New Shakspere Society Reprint, p. 30.

[5] It is supposed that this play is mentioned by Henslowe under such titles as "mulomorco," "mulamulluco," &c. (*Diary*, p. 21), and "Stewtley" (p. 83). With this play should be read *The Famous History of the Life and Death of Captain Thomas Stukely*, 1605, reprinted in Simpson's *School of Shakspere*, and which Simpson thought belonged to the Lord Chamberlain's Company.

[6] Henslowe (*Diary*, p. 55) has, on August 29th, 1595, an entry of a new play, which he calls "longe shanke."

(acted by the Queen's servants and printed in 1599) has been attributed to Peele. There are also extant several poems by Peele covering the period from 1585 to 1595.

Editions of his collected works were issued by Dyce in 1828 in two volumes, of which there was a second edition in 1829, with a third volume added in 1839. The works of Greene and Peele have also been issued together (see p. 203). There is a two-volume edition of Peele's works edited by Mr. A. H. Bullen in 1888.

Ben Jonson.

It is almost certain that Ben Jonson was born in London in January, 1573, a month after the death of his father, who was a minister. Upon very insufficient evidence it has been concluded that, after being nearly three years a widow, his mother married a master-bricklayer.[1] After receiving a small amount of private teaching, the boy was sent to Westminster School at the time when Camden was one of the masters. It is doubtful if Jonson was ever at College.[2] In early life he served with the English forces in the

[1] From many later references it is known that in some way Ben was mixed up with the trade of his reputed step-father. See Henslowe's letter in *Memoirs of Edward Alleyn*, Shakespeare Society edition, pp. 50-1; allusions in Dekker's *Satiro-mastix*, pp. 108, 159, 189, in Hawkins's reprint in *The Origin of the English Drama*, Vol. III.; *The Return from Parnassus*, ed. Arber, p. 13; *Calendar of State Papers*. Domestic. 1611-1618, p. 512 (January 10, 1618).

[2] Drummond says ("Conversations," Section XIII.) "He was Master of Arts in both the Universities, by their favour, not his studie." But there must be some mistake about this. His Oxford M.A. in 1619 was by creation, not incorporation, thus showing that at that date he had no other degree, and there is no record of his afterwards receiving a degree from Cambridge. Jonson after his visit to Drummond was back in London in April, 1619. The Oxford degree was conferred on July 19th. Jonson, in his dedication of *The Fox* (1607), addressing the two Universities, speaks of "the bounty of your act." This, which has been thought to be an acknowledgement of the bestowal of

Netherlands, but apparently only for a short time. He married probably about 1592, but it was not a happy union. In his poems he refers to his wife and children.

There is great uncertainty about his movements till 1597, when he was engaged with Henslowe (*Diary*, pp. 80, 106, 116, 255-6).

In 1598 Meres included " Beniamin Iohnson " in the list of those who are "our best for Tragedie"[1] (see p. 9). This was probably in reference to his literary powers, but in the same year he killed Gabriel Spencer, one of the actors in Henslowe's company (see *Diary*, p. 111). For this he was tried[2] at the Old Bailey, found guilty, and, escaping capital punishment by virtue of "benefit of clergy,"[3] was branded as a felon and sent to prison, where he became a Roman Catholic.[4] In 1599 he was again working for Henslowe[5] (*Diary*, pp. 155-6) in conjunction with Dekker and Chettle and "other gentellman."[6] Soon after this he quarrelled with Marston and Dekker, when much fierce recriminatory writing

[1] He must have earned this position through the patchwork he had done for Henslowe. In this year he was working with Porter and Chettle (*Diary*, p. 131) at *Hot Anger soon Cold*, a play now lost.

[2] See *The Athenæum*, March 6, 27, June 19, 26, 1886.

[3] This is referred to by Dekker (*Op. cit.* p. 107), where Asinius says to Horace (Ben Jonson) "thou . . . read'st as legibly as some that have been sav'd by their neck-verse."

[4] "Thereafter he was 12 yeares a Papist."

[5] *Page of Plymouth*, the play then written by Jonson and Dekker, is lost. Its story is known (see Shakespeare Society's *Papers*, Vol. II., 1845).

[6] Probably Marston. This was on *Robert II.*

degrees, refers to the performances of the play at Oxford and Cambridge and his gratitude to "the two famous Universities for their love and acceptance shown to this poem in the presentation."

Perhaps Ben, who was not deficient in self-assurance, thought the degrees should have been his *de jure*, like the student in Arts who, having failed to get a degree, requested the editors of *Crockford*, 1888, to insert his name with "B.A.d.j." after it.

followed. In 1601 Henslowe paid Jonson 40*s*. for additions to *The Spanish Tragedy*[1] (*Diary*, p. 201), and in 1602 there was another payment for further additions, and for a play about Richard III., concerning which nothing is now known.

From 1603 Ben, well qualified by previous experience,[2] was the leading spirit of those "merry Meetings at the Mermaid,"[3] in Cheapside, which had been established about then by Sir Walter Raleigh, and which gathered together all the wits of the time in the social prototype of the modern club.

In 1605 Jonson voluntarily joined Chapman and Marston, who were in prison for writing a play[4] which gave offence at Court, because it was supposed to contain "something against the Scots." Soon after this he was concerned, as a loyal Roman Catholic, in laying bare the intentions of the Guy Fawkes conspirators.[5]

For many years little is known of his personal movements. About 1610 "he was reconciled with the Church, and left of to be a recusant." For part of the time that Sir Walter Raleigh was imprisoned in the Tower, Jonson acted as his secretary, and in 1613 went to France in charge of Sir Walter's eldest son. In June, 1616, when the king was entertained by the "new Company of Merchant Adventurers,"[6] representatives of trades were presented

[1] The play is printed in Hazlitt's *Dodsley*, with the added parts indicated.

[2] "The Mermaid" is mentioned in the 1601 *Every Man in his Humour*. Although Jonson did not limit his patronage to that establishment (see an ode in Herrick's *Hesperides* and *Calendar of State Papers*. Domestic. Addenda. 1623-1625, p. 278) he never sank to the low life of Greene and Peele.

[3] See "Mr. Francis Beaumont's Letter to Ben Jonson" (*The Works of Beaumont and Fletcher*, ed. Darley, Vol. II., p. 710).

[4] *Eastward Ho!* acted by the Children of the Revels.

[5] See *Calendar of State Papers*. Domestic. 1603-1610, p. 245.

[6] In Stow's *Survey of London*, ed. 1633, p. 618, these are called "New French Merchants Adventurers." The old Merchants Adventurers were incorporated by Edward IV.

to his Majesty "and spake such language as Ben Jonson putt in theyre mouthes" (*Calendar of State Papers.* Domestic. 1611-1618, p. 373). James I. now granted him a life-pension of 100 marks. In the same year Jonson brought out the first volume of his "Works," an unusual title to be then applied to plays, and one of which much fun was made. In 1618 he walked to Scotland, and amongst many visits paid one to William Drummond, who has left notes[1] of their conversations. In 1621 there is a record that "Ben Jonson's pension is increased from 100 marks to 200*l.*"[2]; but after-events seem to show that the order was not carried into effect. It is said that at this time he was offered a knighthood, which he declined; but he accepted as more remunerative the reversion of the Mastership of the Revels after Sir George Bucke and Sir John Astley.[3] He never held it, however, as Sir John outlived him.

It was probably about this time that his library, containing many books and MSS., was destroyed by fire. In 1625 he had an attack of paralysis, from which he never quite recovered, although he was well enough to write and to receive, upon the death of Middleton in 1628, the appointment of historian to the City of London, with which was a salary of 100 nobles. In this year he was unjustly accused of being the author of some political verses which gave great offence.[4] In 1631 Charles I. granted his petition

1 Reprinted by the Shakespeare Society in 1842, and in Vol. III. of Jonson's Works, 1870, edited by Cunningham (see p. 211).

2 See *Calendar of State Papers.* Domestic. 1619-1623, p. 303. In this volume there are several other interesting references to Jonson.

3 There were at a time several potential holders of this office. In 1622 the next reversion was granted to William Painter.

4 See *Calendar of State Papers.* Domestic. 1628-1629, p. 360. From his examination on this charge, we learn that he ordinarily wore at his girdle a dagger with a white haft.

to have his pension turned from marks into pounds,[1] and for some time he was still busy with his pen, often in preparing public pageants. But when "Jonson was old in years, feeble in body, and poor in purse"[2] he offended Inigo Jones, the architect and surveyor of the king's works, with whom he had been engaged in producing various gorgeous masques represented at Court. There had been an earlier quarrel with Jones, whose influence now was sufficient to get others appointed in the place of Jonson, who satirised his opponent in a play[3] in 1633, but who wrote nothing more of importance. He died on August 17th, 1637, and three days after was buried in Westminster Abbey.

Ben Jonson's plays are *Every Man in his Humour*[4] (acted by the Lord Chamberlain's servants in 1598); *Every Man out of his Humour* (by same in 1599); *The Case is Altered* (by the Children of the Chapel in 1599); *Cynthia's Revels* (by same in 1600); *The Poetaster*[5] (by same in 1601); *Sejanus* (by the Lord Chamberlain's servants in 1603); *The Fox* (by the King's servants in 1605); *The Silent Woman* (by the Children of the Revels in 1609); *The Alchemist* (entered in the Stationers' Registers in 1610); *Catiline* (acted by the King's servants in 1611); *Bartholomew Fair* (by the Lady Elizabeth's servants in 1614); *The Devil is an Ass* (by the King's servants in 1616); *The Staple of News* (by the same in 1625); *The New Inn*

[1] The order is printed in full by Whalley, *The Works of Ben Jonson*, 1756, Vol. I., pp. lviii.-lxi.

[2] Notwithstanding his pension, he was applying to persons for money-help. His salary as "the Citties Chronologer" had been stopped in November, 1631. It was renewed in 1634.

[3] *A Tale of a Tub.*

[4] At p. 99 it should have been stated that on the title-page of the 1601 edition the author's name is given as "Ben. Johnson." An excellent edition of this play has been edited by Mr. Henry B. Wheatley in the "London Series of English Classics."

[5] Written to ridicule Marston and Dekker.

("never acted, but most negligently played" by the same in 1629); *The Magnetic Lady* (acted at Blackfriars in 1632); *A Tale of a Tub* (acted at the same place in 1633). *The Sad Shepherd* is unfinished.

Besides these plays, Jonson wrote many masques[1] and poems of various sorts, and some prose, including his *Discoveries*[2] and an *English Grammar.*

Collected editions of Ben Jonson's works were published in 1616 (Vol. I.) and 1631 (Vol. II.), 1640 (2 vols.), 1641 (2 vols.), 1692, 1716 (6 vols.), 1756 (Whalley's in 7 vols.), 1811 (Coleman's edition, published by Stockdale in 4 vols., including plays of Beaumont and Fletcher), 1816 (Gifford's in 9 vols.), 1838 (Barry Cornwall's), reissued by Routledge in 1861, 1875 (new edition of Gifford's by Cunningham in 9 vols.), 1870 (three-volume edition of latter).

"Ben Jonson; Annals of his Career," by Mr. F. G. Fleay, in *Shakespeariana*, Vol. I., 1883-4, should be studied.

The student should consult Mr. J. A. Symonds' book on Ben Jonson in the 'English Worthies' series, 1886.

In *The Nineteenth Century* for April and May, 1888, Mr. Swinburne has articles on Ben Jonson.

John Marston.

As there is considerable doubt about the identity of Marston the dramatist, the date of his birth is entirely a matter of speculation. Most probably he is the John Marston who was born at Coventry about 1575, who took his B.A. at Oxford in 1594, and married a daughter of the Rev. William Wilkes, chaplain to James I.

[1] Special study should be given to these. See a Note by Prof. C. H. Herford (*Academy*, June 29, 1889, pp. 452-3).

[2] See an article by Mr. Swinburne in *The Fortnightly Review*, October, 1888.

In 1607 "he retired to prepare for clerical life. He was appointed to the living of Christchurch [in Hampshire]. He resigned his living in 1631 and died in 1634"[1] in Aldermanbury, London, and was buried in the Temple Church.

In literary circles Marston was first known by the name of William Kinsayder.[2] His earliest productions were some Satires, published in 1598. These excited the admiration of that general literary idolater, Meres, who refers to Marston, "the Author of Pigmalions Image, and certain Satyres," as being "very profitable" (see pp. 7, 8). It is supposed that in 1599 Marston had negotiations with Henslowe (*Diary*, p. 156). If it is correct that the entry of September 28th of that year refers to Marston, it is probable that he was the "other gentellman" (see p. 207) working in the same month[3] with Dekker, Jonson, and Chettle at "a playe calld Robart the Second, Kinge of Scottes tragedie." Soon after with Dekker, he was quarrelling with Jonson. A reconciliation took place a little later on, for in 1604 Marston dedicated *The Malcontent* to Ben, and when in 1603 Marston and Chapman were in prison for writing *Eastward Ho!*, Jonson chose to go into confinement with them. Not long after this Marston changed his profession.

Some of the plays attributed to Marston are conjoint productions. Most, if not all, of his own plays were written for the Children's Companies. The plays with which he has been credited are *Antonio and Mellida* (1602); *Antonio's Revenge* (1602); *The Mal-*

[1] Miss Emma Phipson in *The Academy*, June 16, 1888, p. 417.

[2] See Dedication to *The Scourge of Villainy* and *The Return from Parnassus* (ed. Arber, p. 12), where there are also "censures" of the following dramatists: Lodge, Marlowe, Jonson, Shakspere (see p. 196), and Nash.

[3] On the later date there was great confusion about the name of "the new poete."

content (1604, written partly by Webster and acted by the King's servants); *Eastward Ho!* (1605, with Chapman and Jonson); *The Dutch Courtezan* (1605); *Parasitaster* (1606); *Sophonisba* (1606); *What You Will* (1607) and (?) *The Insatiate Countess* (1613).

The 1633 edition of his plays does not include *The Malcontent, Eastward Ho!*, or *The Insatiate Countess.* In the case of the first two the reason is clear. The last is probably not by him.

In 1856 Marston's works were issued in three volumes with an introduction by J. O. Halliwell [Phillipps]. In 1887 Mr. A. H. Bullen edited an edition in three volumes.

There are some points of interest in Mr. Fleay's two articles on "Shakespeare and Marston" in *Shakespeariana*, Vol. I., 1883-4.

Thomas Heywood.

Of the non-dramatic life of all the Elizabethan dramatists there is perhaps most uncertainty about that of Thomas Heywood; yet he seems to have been the most prolific writer[1] and the most enthusiastic actor[2] of them all. He was a native of Lincolnshire, but the dates of his birth and death are unknown; they may be put down at 1576 and 1648. He speaks of "the time of my residence in Cambridge," but he did not take any degree. In 1596 he was connected as a writer with Henslowe (see *Diary*, p. 78) to whom in 1598 he bound himself as a covenant-servant,[3] and by the

[1] Some years before he had finished writing he said that he had had "either an entire hand, or at the least a main finger" in two hundred and twenty plays.

[2] His *Apology for Actors*, first published in 1612 and reprinted by the Shakespeare Society in 1841, is an eloquent defence of the calling.

[3] Henslowe (*Diary*, p. 260) thus notes the transaction, similar ones to which he recorded at pp. 256-9. In one of these the actor was to receive 5/- a week for one year

following February he had also written two plays[1] for the company (*Diary*, pp. 140, 143-5), both of which are lost, as are also *The London Florentine* and *Like quits Like*, which he wrote with Chettle in 1602 and 1603 (*Diary*, pp. 229-30). In 1602 he was writing with Wentworth Smith[2] and also doing a little patchwork for Henslowe (*Diary*, pp. 238-40). In the same year he was also writing with Dekker and Webster[3] (*Diary*, pp. 242-3) and alone[4] (*Diary*, pp. 244, 246). These plays are not now known. In 1603, after writing with Chettle and by himself (*Diary*, pp. 247, 249), his name is found as one of nine "servants to the Queen" receiving a theatrical license (*Calendar of State Papers*. Domestic. Addenda. 1623-1625, p. 530).

Heywood's extant plays,[5] which number about twenty, date from

[1] *War without Blows and Love without Strife* and *Joan as good as my Lady.*

[2] "*alberte galles.*"

[3] *Lady Jane*, in which they were assisted by Chettle and Smith. *Christmas comes but once a Year* was written by the four dramatists without the help of Smith. These plays were for "my Lorde of Worsters players."

[4] *The Blind Eats many a Fly*, written also for the Earl of Worcester's servants.

[5] The 1607 *Fair Maid of the Exchange* gives its *dramatis personæ* in groups in the way in which the characters are arranged in Chapter IX. of this book, showing how sets of parts may be taken by the performers. See also Fulwell's *Like Will to Like* 1568, Preston's *Cambyses* 1570, Woodes' *Conflict of Conscience* 1581, and *Mucedorus* 1598 (foolishly attributed by some to Shakspere). These are all reprinted in Hazlitt's *Dodsley.*

---

and 6/8 for the other. This was about the usual payment for those thus hiring themselves.

> Md. that this 25 of marche 1598, Thomas Hawoode came and hiered hime seallfe with me as a covenante searvante for ij yeares, by the Recevinge of ij syngell pence, acordinge to the statute of winchester, and to begine at the daye above written, and not to playe any wher publicke abowt London not whille thes ij yeares be exspired, but in my howsse: yf he do, then he dothe forfette unto me, by the Recevinge of thes ij[d], fortie powndes, and wittnes to this
>
> | | |
> |---|---|
> | Antony Monday | W^M. Borne |
> | Gabrell Spencer | Thoms Dowton |
> | Robart Shawe | Richard Jonnes |
> | Richard Alleyn. | |

Edward IV. in 1600 to perhaps *The Wise Woman of Hogsdon* in 1638. *Edward IV.* states on its title-page that it had been "played by the Right Honorable the Earle of Derbie his seruants." The 1611 *Golden Age*, the 1617 *Woman Killed with Kindness*, the 1631 *Fair Maid of the West*, the 1637 *Royal King and Loyal Subject*, and the 1655 *Fortune by Land and Sea* (written with William Rowley) all mention performances by the Queen's servants,[1] but it is not known to what particular companies these allude, as the references may be to the first performances, and the dates of these are uncertain.

Heywood also worked with Richard Brome,[2] and wrote many poems.[3] Some of his plays were issued by the Shakespeare Society (1842-1851), and a complete edition was published by Pearson in six volumes in 1874.

Francis Beaumont and John Fletcher.

Of the family history of these two writers, whose names have an inseparable literary union, more is known than about that of most of their fellows.

Beaumont, the third son of Francis Beaumont, a judge of the Common Pleas, was born, probably at Grace Dieu in Leicestershire, in 1584.[4] In 1597 he went to Pembroke College,[5] Oxford. As he took no degree it is presumed that he left Oxford on account of his father's death in 1598, although his departure could not have been

[1] These were the actors previously under the patronage of the Earl of Worcester.

[2] *The Late Lancashire Witches.* Brome's works were published in 3 vols. in 1873.

[3] See p. 120 for a reference to some.

[4] In this year a Government Commission recommended that Beaumont's paternal grandmother "should be restrained of her liberty, as a recusant and great favourer of Papists" (*Calendar of State Papers.* Domestic. 1581-1590, p. 185).

[5] Then called Broadgates Hall.

on account of money-difficulties. In 1600 Beaumont became a student of the Inner Temple. Upon his entrance to literary life he became very intimate with Ben Jonson,[1] and wrote a few things before the literary partnership with Fletcher began about 1607. In 1613 he married Ursula Isley of Sundridge in Kent, by whom he had two daughters. Soon after his marriage he seems to have given up writing. He died on March 6th, 1616, and was buried in Westminster Abbey.

Fletcher was born in December, 1579. His father, who then held the living of Rye in Sussex, became Dean of Peterborough in 1583, Bishop of Bristol in 1589, Bishop of Worcester in 1593, and Bishop of London in 1595. From the latter position he was suspended by Queen Elizabeth because he married a second time. He died in 1596.

It is thought that the son John went to Cambridge at the age of twelve, but there is no record of any degree having been conferred upon him. There is no reason for thinking that the Fletcher mentioned by Henslowe in 1596 (*Diary*, p. 78) was the poet. In addition to his work with Beaumont he wrote with some other dramatists.[2] The nature of the partnership of Beaumont and Fletcher is an interesting subject for investigation.

After Beaumont's death Fletcher wrote many plays to which special attention should be given by those who, guided by considerations of style, wish to form an estimate of the extent to which he may have been concerned in the plays of which he has been

[1] See Poems upon *The Fox* and others.

[2] After his death some of his work received additions from other hands. His literary connections with Shakspere, William Rowley, Middleton, Massinger, and Shirley would form the subject of a curious and, perhaps, profitable enquiry.

thought to have been part-author.[1] He died in 1625, and was buried at St. Saviour's, Southwark, on the 29th of August.

Very few early copies of the plays of Beaumont and Fletcher exist. About fifty plays are usually ascribed to them. Of these there are only four editions known anterior to Beaumont's death,[2] and four others that were printed between that time and the date of Fletcher's death.[3] There is evidence, however, that other plays had been licensed or acted before the death of Beaumont.[4] It is, therefore, exceedingly difficult, if not impossible, to arrive at a final conclusion about those plays that should be allotted to them separately and those in which they were jointly concerned.

The plays of Beaumont and Fletcher were published in collected form in 1647, 1679, 1711 (7 vols.), 1750 (10 vols.), 1778 (10 vols.), 1812 (14 vols., edited by Weber), 1839 (2 vols., edited by Darley), 1843 (11 vols., edited by Dyce), and in 1859, and after, Darley's edition was issued by Routledge.

John Webster.

About the details of Webster's life there is great uncertainty.

[1] John was not the only literary member of the family. His uncle and his cousins, Phineas and Giles, were all able writers.

[2] The 1607 *Woman-Hater* (acted by the Children of Paul's), the 1613 *Knight of the Burning Pestle* (see p. 157), the 1615 *Cupid's Revenge* (acted by the Children of the Revels), and the 1616 *Scornful Lady* (acted at Blackfriars).

[3] The 1619 *King and No King* (acted by the King's servants at the Globe, see p. 153), the 1619 *Maid's Tragedy* (acted at Blackfriars), the 1620 and 1622 *Philaster* (acted by the King's servants at the Globe and at Blackfriars, see p. 147), and the 1621 *Thierry and Theodoret* (acted at the Blackfriars).

[4] Mention of the performance of two of these (*The Maid's Tragedy* and *The Captain*) will be found on p. 103. In reference to the others much information, extracted from the Office-book of Sir Henry Herbert, Deputy Master of the Revels, is given in the 1821 *Variorum*, Vol. III., pp. 224-34.

It has been surmised that he was born about 1575. In 1598 (?) and 1601 Henslowe has entries about a now lost play[1] by Webster (*Diary*, pp. 110, 202-4). In 1602 he was working at a play[2] with Munday, Drayton, Middleton "and the Rest" (*Diary*, p. 221), and at another[3] with Dekker, Drayton, Middleton, and Munday (*Diary*, p. 222). Both these are lost. With Chettle, Dekker, Heywood, and Smith he was also engaged in the same year (see p. 214).

Nothing is known in detail of Webster's movements or mode of life. 1650 has been set down as about the time of his death.

Webster's known plays are *The White Devil* (1612, acted by the Queen's, previously the Earl of Worcester's, servants); *The Duchess of Malfi* (acted by the King's servants, see p. 165); *The Devil's Law-case* (1623, acted by the Queen's servants); *Appius and Virginia* (acted before 1639 at the Cockpit). With Dekker he wrote *Westward Ho!* (acted before 1605 by the Children of Paul's); *Northward Ho!* (acted by the Children of Paul's and printed in 1607); *Sir Thomas Wyatt*[4] (acted by the Queen's servants and printed in 1607); *A Cure for a Cuckold* and *The Thracian Wonder* (first printed in 1661) were attributed to him and William Rowley. Webster's part in *The Malcontent* has already been referred to in connection with Marston (see p. 213).

Much of Webster's writing must have been lost, for little has come down to the present time except the few plays mentioned. These were edited by Dyce in 1830 (4 vols.) and by Hazlitt in

[1] *The Guise* (see the Dedication of *The Devil's Law-case*).

[2] *Cæsar's Fall*. The inclusion of Webster in this entry is suspected to be a forgery See p. 61 of Mr. Wheatley's book mentioned at p. 200.

[3] "too harpes." The two plays were for the Lord Admiral's servants.

[4] A later form of *Lady Jane* (see p. 214).

1857 (4 vols.). Dyce's edition in a single volume was published by Routledge in 1861, and reprinted since.

Mr. Fleay, in *Shakespeariana*, Vol. I., 1883-4, writes on "John Webster; Annals of his Career;" and in *The Nineteenth Century*, June, 1886, there is an article on Webster by Mr. Swinburne.

Philip Massinger.

Arthur Massinger, the poet's father, was in high and confidential service[1] in "the noble family of the Herberts."[2] Philip was born at Salisbury in 1584. In 1602 he went to Oxford, which he left in 1606 without a degree and came to London. If he then began writing for the stage, amongst the MS. plays which ended their existence in Warburton's kitchen-oven must have been all Massinger's early ones, as the first existing dramatic reference to any is in 1620. It seems that this is very likely, for about 1613-5 he was in money-difficulties, and was, with others, borrowing small sums from Henslowe.[3] Nothing more is known of the details of Massinger's life. Some of his literary work was done in alliance with Dekker and some with Fletcher. In 1639 he died, and was buried at St. Saviour's, Southwark, probably in the same grave with Fletcher.

There is no edition known of any play by Massinger of an earlier date than 1622, when *The Virgin-Martyr* (acted by the servants of the Revels) was printed (see p. 171). In writing this he had the assistance of Dekker. The plays of which he seems to have been sole

[1] See *Calendar of State Papers*. Domestic. 1595-1597, pp. 489, 497, for references to negotiations carried on by him between the Earl of Pembroke and Lord Burghley.

[2] See Dedication of *The Bondman*.

[3] *Massinger*, ed. Cunningham, n.d., pp., xi., xii.

author are *The Duke of Milan* (1623, acted by the King's servants); *The Bondman* (acted at the Cockpit 1623); *The Renegado* (acted at the Cockpit 1624); *The Parliament of Love* (acted at the Cockpit 1624); *The Spanish Viceroy*[1] (acted in 1624); *The Roman Actor* (acted by the King's servants in 1626); *The Great Duke of Florence* (acted by the Queen's servants in 1627); *The Maid of Honour* (printed in 1632, but supposed to have been acted in 1628); *The Picture* (acted by the King's servants in 1629); *Minerva's Sacrifice*[1] (acted by the King's servants in 1629); *The Emperor of the East* (acted by the King's servants in 1631); *Believe as you List*[2] (acted by the King's servants in 1631); *The Unfortunate Piety*[1] (acted by the King's servants in 1631); *The City Madam* (acted by the King's servants in 1632); *A New Way to Pay Old Debts*[3] (printed in 1633); *The Guardian* (acted by the King's servants in 1633); *Cleander*[1] (acted by the King's servants in 1634); *A Very Woman* (acted by the King's servants in 1634); *The Orator*[1] (acted by the King's servants in 1635); *The Bashful Lover* (acted by the King's servants in 1636); *The Unnatural Combat*[3] (printed in 1639); *The King and the Subject*[1] (acted by the King's servants in 1638); *Alexius*[1] (acted by the King's servants in 1639); *The Fair Anchoress of Pausilippo* (acted by the Kings servants 1640). Besides some of those mentioned above as lost, it is known[4] that Warburton's cook destroyed *The Forced Lady, The Noble Choice, The Wandering Lovers, Philenzo and Hippolita, Antonio and Vallia, The Tyrant, Fast and Welcome, The Woman's Plot.* These must have been all early plays.

[1] Now lost. The titles of these lost plays are obtained from Sir Henry Herbert's Office-book (see p. 217).

[2] The only known copy of this 1631 edition was found in 1844.

[3] Perhaps it would be right to put this amongst Massinger's early plays, or at all events before 1623, as it is not mentioned in Sir Henry Herbert's book.

[4] Gifford's *Massinger*, Vol. I. p. clxvii.

The Fatal Dowry (of which Field was part-author) and *The Old Law* (written partly by Middleton and William Rowley) were both written before 1622.

Massinger's plays were edited in 1751 (4 vols.), 1761 (4 vols. edited by Coxeter), 1779 (4 vols. edited by Monck Mason), 1805 (4 vols.), 1813 (4 vols. edited by Gifford) and in 1840 in a one-volume edition, with Ford's works and containing Gifford's notes, of which there have been later reprints. An edition in one volume, edited by Col. Cunningham, was issued about 1872.

In *The Fortnightly Review*, July 1889, there is an article on Massinger by Mr. Swinburne.

In the plan of work presented in this book there is no opportunity afforded for the separate reading and study of the plays of any writers except those of whose lives I have given a sketch. But as considerable attention should be given to many other workers, I append a few biographical notes about them, and also add some information concerning all those who may fairly be counted as contributors to the Elizabethan Drama. The term is used to include many works written years after the death of the queen whose name is employed to designate this particular branch of literature. This must be so, or many of Shakspere's plays would fall outside the expressive phrase. But there should be some limit to the time it should cover. The dramatic authors of whom I give notes were all alive in Elizabeth's reign, although in some cases their writing was over when she was on the throne, and in others their work had not begun.

At first sight it will seem strange that only the names of many Elizabethan plays have survived, and this will occur most prominently in connection with the plays referred to in Henslowe s *Diary*. But in explanation, it is merely necessary to remember that the actors thought it opposed to their interests that the plays should be printed because they desired to retain a stage-monopoly in them, and also wished that those who wanted to become acquainted with the plays should do so only at the theatre. It may, perhaps, be taken for granted that when a play in course of performance appeared in printed form, the issue was an evidence of its popularity and of the smartness of a printer or publisher to profit by the prevailing taste. In self-defence an author would afterwards sanction, and perhaps superintend, the publication of an edition in order to correct the errors of a former issue.

John Bale.	Samuel Daniel.
John Heywood.	Henry Chettle.
Richard Edwards.	Michael Drayton.
Thomas Legge.	Thomas Nash.
Thomas Sackville.	Thomas Middleton.
Anthony Munday.	Thomas Dekker.
Thomas Lodge.	John Ford.
George Chapman.	James Shirley.

Some study should be given to the work of JOHN BALE, the author of *Kyng Johan*,[1] which is a link between the moralities and that form of historical play which, worthily attempted by Marlowe, found its most able exponent in Shakspere.

John Bale was born in 1495 at Cove in Suffolk. He went to Jesus College, Cambridge, and became B.D. in 1529. Edward VI. made him Bishop of Ossory in Ireland. In Mary's reign he retired

[1] Printed by the Camden Society in 1838.

to the Continent; but returning upon Elizabeth's accession, was made Canon of Canterbury in 1560. He died in 1563, the year before Shakspere was born. He wrote several dramatic pieces.[1]

The works of JOHN HEYWOOD, who was born about 1497,[2] deserve a place in a Shakspere Society's scheme of study, because his interludes are the bridge between the Moralities and that style of English Comedy which found a crude expression in *Ralph Roister Doister*[3] and its advanced development in the work of John Lyly.

It seems that John Heywood went to Oxford entering at Pembroke College (see p. 205), but there is no record of his degree. He became a great favourite at Court in the reigns of Henry VIII. and Mary. On November 10th, 1558, there was a "grant of lease for 40 years to John Heywood, of the Manor of Bolmer and other lands in Yorkshire, at the rent of 30*l.* for his life, and 51*l.* 10*s.* for the rest of the term." (*Calendar of State Papers.* Domestic. 1547—1580, p. 112). When Elizabeth came to the throne, Heywood went abroad and did not return to England. His works were very popular and were often printed. The first collected form was issued in

[1] *God's Promises* is reprinted in Hazlitt's *Dodsley*. There is a full list of Bale's works in *Athenae Cantabrigienses*.

[2] There is a letter from John Heywood to Lord Burghley, in which he calls attention to his age as 78, in 1575 (*Calendar of State Papers.* Domestic. Addenda. 1566–1579, p. 482). The date of his death is unknown; but this shows that it has been usually placed too early.

[3] The discovery of this play in 1818 dislodged *Gammer Gurton's Needle* from the place of honour as the first regular English Comedy. It was reprinted in 1818, 1821, in 1830 in *The Old English Drama*, by the Shakespeare Society in 1847, in Hazlitt's *Dodsley*, and in Arber's series. It was written by Nicholas Udall, an Oxford man, who became head-master of Eton and of Westminster. Its date of composition is 1551 at the latest. It was thus entered in the Stationers' Registers:

1566. July 22—1567. July 22.

hackett Recevyd of **Thomas hackett** for his lycense for pryntinge of a play intituled *RAUF RUYSTER DUSTER &c.* iiijd

1562. The British Museum has a copy of the 1566 edition. His best known Interlude is *The Four P.P.*,[1] a rhymed controversy between a Palmer, a Pardoner, a 'Pothecary, and a Pedlar. Heywood wrote other plays and many epigrams. His *Proverbs* are a very interesting collection of familiar expressions woven in verse. They were much used by Shakspere and other later writers. Mr. Julian Sharman edited them in a pleasant volume in 1874.

RICHARD EDWARDS, born in 1523, went to Oxford in 1540, entering at Corpus Christi College. He took his B.A. in 1544 and M.A. in 1547. In 1561 he was master of the children or singing-boys of the Chapel Royal. It is not unlikely that his play acted in 1565 by the children of the Chapel was his *Damon and Pythias*,[1] the only play which has survived. In September, 1566, his *Palamon and Arcite*, (see p. 185) was played before the Queen upon her visit to Oxford.[2] Edwards died in the following month. His poetical merits, recognised by Elizabethan writers, were not overlooked by Meres, who classed him among "the best for comedy" (see p. 9).

THOMAS LEGGE is included in this list as the author of *Richardus Tertius* (see p. 87). He was born in Norwich about 1536. He entered at Corpus Christi College, Cambridge, in 1552, but in 1555 went to Trinity. He took his B.A. in 1557 and M.A. in 1560. He was a distinguished member of the University, and was created LL.D. in 1575. In the *Calendar of State Papers*. Domestic. 1547—1580, pp. 625, 635; 1581—1590, pp. 26, 43, 72, there are records of Legge in connection with University-matters in 1579, 1581, 1582. About this time Legge was much harassed on account of his religious

[1] Reprinted in Hazlitt's *Dodsley*.
[2] See Stow's *Chronicle*, ed. 1631, p. 660.

opinions, and was even imprisoned. Some of the charges brought against him are curiously absurd (see *Athenae Cantabrigienses*, Vol. II. p. 455). He was Vice-Chancellor in 1587 and 1593.

He wrote also a dramatic version of the Destruction of Jerusalem (see p. 59) no copy of which exists. This was probably in Latin. It is not known if he wrote any plays in English. The watchful Meres found out his merits, and placed him amongst those "best for Tragedie" (see p. 9). He died in 1607, and was buried in Caius College Chapel.

In the course of study, it will not be right to ignore the dramatic position of THOMAS SACKVILLE, who is known as the author of the first English Tragedy. He was born in 1536, in Sussex. His paternal grandmother was great-aunt to Queen Elizabeth. When about fifteen, he went to Oxford, which he soon left for Cambridge, where however he took no degree. In 1558 he was an active member of the House of Commons. His tragedy of *Gorboduc*,[1] sometimes known as *Ferrex and Porrex*, was first published in 1565; but had been acted some years previously. After writing this he gave but little time to literature, and devoted himself to the public service. Only a little of his verse has come down to us. In 1567 he was created Lord Buckhurst. Having served the State in various capacities,[2] he

[1] Hawkins included this in *The Origin of the English Drama*, 1772. It was also reprinted by the Shakespeare Society in 1847. The first edition erroneously stated that Norton was part-author. It was thus entered in the Stationers' Registers:

1565. July 22—1566. July 22.

greffeth Receved of **Wylliam greffeth** for his lycense for pryntinge of *a Tragdie of* GORBODUC *where iij actes were Wretten by* THOMAS NORTON *and the laste by* THOMAS SACKVYLE, *&c.* iiij[d]

[2] He was deputed to convey to Mary Stuart the sentence of her death, a message which he bore with consummate delicacy.

was sent, in 1587, on a diplomatic mission to the Netherlands, when the Earl of Leicester was there commanding the English forces.

If it is true that Shakspere was there at the time (see p. 193), the visit of Lord Buckhurst becomes one of peculiar interest, as then in companionship with Leicester would be the mature statesman who had written a dignified tragedy—the first of its kind in the English language—and the young man of three-and-twenty who, destitute then of all literary promise, attained a place unrivalled in the world's history as the creator of dramas in which the brightest humour, the most tender pathos, and the deepest tragedy were alike to find a delineator who could present them in language for which no fitting adjective has yet been found.

In 1591 Lord Buckhurst was elected Chancellor of the University of Oxford, of which he was then incorporated M.A. In 1594 he was one of the Commissioners at the trial of Dr. Lopez,[1] "the Original of Shylock" (see p. 101), who was hanged at Tyburn for supposed complicity in the plot to poison the queen. Meres, of course, included him amongst "our best for Tragedie" (see p. 9). In 1599 Lord Buckhurst, after the death of Lord Burghley, was made Lord High Treasurer, and as such was the president of the tribunal before which Essex and Southampton were tried in 1600. After James's accession, Lord Buckhurst, who was then created Earl of Dorset, continued to serve his country in high office. He died in 1608 "while sitting at the Council Table in Whitehall."[2]

ANTHONY MUNDAY, the son of a London draper, was born in

[1] In the *Calendar of State Papers*. Domestic. 1591-1594 there is much in reference to Lopez, who, having been chief physician to Leicester (see Lodge's *Illustrations of British History, &c., in the Reign of Elizabeth*, Vol. II., p. 224), became in 1586 domestic physician to Elizabeth.

[2] The edition of his works published in 1859 is accompanied by a full memoir.

1553.[1] In October, 1576, he was apprenticed to John Aldee, a stationer,[2] but soon showed a disinclination for settling down in quiet business-ways. To see life he took the usual Continental travel. He came back to England in 1581, and was actively engaged in giving evidence in the trials of English Jesuits, who were soon after executed. Upon this subject he wrote some pamphlets. The very miscellaneous character of his writings shows that he was one of the most versatile of the Elizabethan authors. His *John a Kent and John a Cumber*,[3] written in 1595, should be read in connection with Greene's *Friar Bacon*. In December, 1597, and January, 1598, with Drayton he was paid for writing *Mother Redcap*[4] (Henslowe's *Diary*, pp. 106-7, 117), of which nothing is now known. In February, 1598, he wrote by himself *The First Part of Robin Hood*[5] (*Diary*, p. 118), which was acted by the Lord Admiral's servants, and printed in 1601. In the composition of *The Second Part of Robin Hood*,[6] written in the same month, he was assisted by Chettle (*Diary*, p. 119). In June, 1598, he was working with Wilson, Chettle, and

[1] This is gathered from the statement over his tomb (see Stow's *Survey of London*, ed. 1633, p. 869).

[2] This was the title given to those who were engaged in issuing books either by printing or selling. The term, applied now only to "the dealer in the raw material of books," has an interesting etymology.

[3] Printed by the Shakespeare Society in 1851. It is prefaced by a memoir of the writer and a full list of his works. The tract about the 1582 execution is included in the volume.

[4] Collier is in error in saying that "Henslowe's Diary is the only source of information respecting any such piece." Creede was licensed to print it on March 10, 1595, and it was entered to Pavier on August 14, 1600.

[5] Known also as *The Downfall of Robert, Earl of Huntington*. In November, 1598, Chettle was paid for making additions to it (*Diary*, p. 139). It is reprinted in Hazlitt's *Dodsley*.

[6] Acted by the Lord Admiral's servants, it was printed in 1601 as *The Death of Robert, Earl of Huntington*. It is in Hazlitt's *Dodsley*.

Drayton at *The Funeral of Richard Cœur de Lion* (*Diary*, pp. 124-5), a play now lost. In July, 1598, with Hathway he wrote *Valentine and Orson* (*Diary*, p. 128). This has not come down to us. In August, 1598, he began "a comodey for the corte" (*Diary*, p. 131), but it seems not to have been finished; but in the same month he wrote *Chance Medley* in conjunction with Wilson, Chettle or Dekker, and Drayton (*Diary*, p. 132). The name only of this play is at present known. In this very busy year, when he was also deviser of the city-pageants, Meres endorsed contemporary opinion by placing him amongst "the best for comedy," adding that he is "our best plotter"[1] (see p. 9). In October, 1599, he was engaged upon *Sir John Oldcastle*[2] with Drayton, Wilson, and Hathway (*Diary*, p. 158). In January, 1600, he and the same writers produced *Owen Tudor* (*Diary*, p. 163), now lost. In June, 1600, with Drayton, Hathway, and Dekker, he wrote another lost play, *Fair Constance of Rome* (*Diary*, pp. 171-2). In October and November, 1601, as mentioned at p. 183, he was concerned with Chettle, Drayton, and Smith upon a lost play or plays dealing with events of the reign of Henry VIII.[3] (*Diary*, pp. 202-4). In May, 1602, he and Dekker were engaged on another lost play, which Henslowe calls "Jeffte" or "Jeffa" (*Diary* pp. 220-4). In the same month it is recorded that it took Munday,

[1] This excited the ridicule of Ben Jonson (see *The Case is Altered*, I., i. Gifford has an interesting note about this satirical passage).

[2] Acted by the Lord Admiral's servants, printed in 1600, and ascribed to Shakspere as some copies had his name on the title-page. In 1602 Dekker made some additions to a play with this title (*Diary*, pp. 237, 239), but it is uncertain whether they were to this or to a second part which was in contemplation when this was written. It was included in the 1664 Shakspere Folio. Sir Walter Scott reprinted it in *Ancient British Drama*, 1810.

[3] *Thomas, Lord Cromwell* (see p. 105), attributed to Shakspere belonged to the Lord Chamberlain's servants.

Drayton, Webster,[1] Middleton, "and the Rest," to write a play on *Cæsar's Fall* (*Diary*, pp. 221-2), and his services were required, with those of Dekker, Drayton, Middleton, and Webster for a play, which appears in the *Diary* (p. 222) as "too harpes." Both these plays are now unknown. From July to September, 1602, Antony the poet, who probably was Munday, was writing a play called *The Widow's Charm* [2] (*Diary*, pp. 224-6). Henslowe's last note about Munday is in December, 1602, when he seems to have been sole author of a play which is called "the seeat at tenes" (*Diary*, p. 228). The alterations in the 1618 edition of Stow's *Survey of London*, bringing it up to date, were made by Munday. He died in August, 1633.

The dates of the birth and death of THOMAS LODGE are said to be 1556 and 1625. His father became Lord Mayor of London. The son went to Oxford, entering at Trinity College about 1573. He took his B.A. in 1577. One of his earliest services to the Drama was his *Defence of Poetry, Music, and Stage Plays*,[3] which was suppressed directly it was issued. It was written in reply to Gosson's *School of Abuse*,[4] 1579. Lodge wrote other prose-works, the best known of which is *Rosalynde*,[5] printed in 1590, and containing the story which Shakspere used in *As You Like It*. Lodge's only

[1] The insertion of Webster's name is said to be a forgery. At least, I presume this is the entry to which Mr. Henry B. Wheatley refers at p. 61 of *Notes on the Life of John Payne Collier*, 1884.

[2] This has been thought to be *The Puritan*, ascribed to Shakspere in the 1664 Folio. It was first printed in 1607, and had been acted by the children of Paul's. Its author was stated to have been W.S. It was reprinted in *Ancient British Drama*, 1810.

[3] Reprinted by the Shakespeare Society in 1853. The edition includes his *Alarum against Usurers*, which contains a further contribution to the controversy.

[4] Reprinted by the Shakespeare Society in 1841, and in Arber's series.

[5] Reprinted in Hazlitt's *Shakespeare's Library*.

known plays are *A Looking Glass for London and England,*[1] written with Greene (see p. 203), and *The Wounds of Civil War,*[2] of which he is the sole author. He wrote much other verse, both lyrical and satirical. Lodge's reference to a play of *Hamlet,* mentioned at p. 135, is in *Wit's Misery,* 1596. In 1598 Meres considered him one of "the best for Comedy (see p. 9). Later on he took a foreign medical degree, and through this was incorporated M.D. at Oxford in 1602. He not only practised medicine, but wrote one or two works thereon. Dated March 9th, 1606, there is a note in reference to Lodge in the *Calendar of State Papers.* Domestic. 1603—1610, p. 298.

GEORGE CHAPMAN was born near Hitchin, in 1559. It is very doubtful if he was at either University. At all events, he took no degree. His earliest published poems are of the year 1594. On February 12th, 1596, his *Blind Beggar of Alexandria*[3] was brought out by Henslowe (*Diary,* p. 64). In May, 1598, Chapman was engaged upon a play, the name of which is not given (D*iary,* pp. 123-4). In June he began *The Will of a Woman,* of which nothing is now known. In the autumn of the same year he wrote *The Fountain of New Fashions* (D*iary,* pp. 135-6), now lost. At p. 137 of the D*iary* there is an entry which seems to connect him about this time with Ben Jonson. Meres, in 1598, not only placed him amongst the best for Tragedy and Comedy, but gave him a special position with Marlowe, on

[1] Acted in 1592 (see Henslowe's *Diary,* p. 23).

[2] Reprinted in Hazlitt's *Dodsley.* It was acted by the Lord Admiral's servants.

[3] Acted by the Lord Admiral's servants. Printed in 1598. It has recently come into prominent notice, as Mr. P. A. Daniel's familiarity with Elizabethan literature enabled him at once to say that some extracts, said to come from an unknown play by Shakspere, were from this play. (See *Academy,* September 22, 1888, p. 187, and October 6, p. 224).

account of the excellence of his poetry. In January, 1599, he wrote a tragedy (*Diary*, p. 141), of which not even the name has survived. From January to July, 1599, he was at work upon *The World Runs on Wheels* (*Diary*, pp. 143, 145, 153-4). This has not come down to the present time, unless it is that now known as *All Fools.*[1] In the latter month there is a note about "a pastrall tragedie" he was writing (*Diary*, p. 154). Then he seems to have given himself for a time to his celebrated translation of Homer. In 1605 he was in prison with Marston and Jonson for writing *Eastward Ho!*[2] (see p. 208.) After this period his plays followed one another with great rapidity. In some of his dramatic writing he was associated with Shirley. Some of his plays were destroyed by Warburton's cook (see pp. 219-20). Chapman also wrote many poems and translations. Recent critics consider him to be the poet referred to by Shakspere in the Sonnets[3] (lxxviii—lxxxvi.) Chapman died in London in 1634, and was buried in St. Giles's.

Chapman's plays were issued in three volumes in 1873. There is a cheap edition of his complete works (1874-5), edited by Mr. R. H. Shepherd, and with an essay by Mr. Swinburne.

Samuel Daniel, who was born near Taunton in 1562, went to Oxford in 1579, entering at Magdalen Hall, but took no degree. He issued some excellent sonnets in 1592. About this time he became the tutor of William Herbert,[4] whose name is so intimately

[1] Printed in 1605, when it was said to have been "Presented at the Black Fryers, And lately before his Maiestie."

[2] He seems also to have been in trouble about his *Byron's Conspiracy*.

[3] But see under Daniel.

[4] Born April 8, 1580. His father, the Earl of Pembroke, having married, as his first wife, Catherine, sister of Lady Jane Grey, was thus allied to the royal houses of both

associated with that of Shakspere. In 1593 Daniel wrote *Cleopatra*[1] (see p. 163). His only other drama, *Philotas*, was published in 1605. From 1594 to 1611 he wrote many historical poems (see p. 63), and from 1604 to 1615, several Court Masques. On January 30th, 1604, when the King issued a warrant authorising the formation of a company to be called the Children of the Revels to the Queen, Daniel was appointed to superintend the presentation of their pieces, and none were to be performed without his approbation and allowance.[2] On the occasion of the marriage of Lord Roxburgh to Mrs. Drummond in 1614 Daniel "wrote a pastoral, solemn and dull" (*Calendar of State Papers*. Domestic. 1611-1618, p. 223). In the following year he was instrumental in procuring Royal sanction to the appointment of "a company of youths to perform comedies and tragedies at Bristol, under the name of the Youths of Her Majesty's Royal Chamber of Bristol" (*Op. cit.* pp. 294, 549). In Daniel's case the complimentary expressions which Meres used in 1598 (see pp. 8, 9) were the echo of the views of many critics of the time. Daniel died near Beckington in Wiltshire, in 1619.

Daniel's collected works were published in 1602, and his complete

[1] Dedicated to the Countess of Pembroke.
[2] See *English Drama and Stage*, p. 41.

England and France. His mother, the Earl's third wife, was Sir Philip Sidney's sister. She translated from the French a play on the subject of Cleopatra. William Herbert who "became a nobleman of New coll. in Lent Term 1592," succeeded to the Earldom in 1601. He was then in disgrace and was imprisoned by the Queen. (For full references to this, see Mr. Thomas Tyler's Introduction to the 1885 Facsimile of Shakspere's Sonnets.) On August 30, 1605, during the King's visit, William and his brother Philip were "created Masters of Arts" at Oxford. The 1623 Folio was dedicated to them. William was elected Chancellor of the University in 1626. On April 10, 1630, "Wm. Earl of Pembrok died of an Apoplexie at Baynard's Castle" (*The Obituary of Richard Smith*, issued by the Camden Society in 1849).

works in 1623, and in two volumes in 1718, and privately printed in three volumes in 1885, edited by the Rev. Dr. Grosart.

Notwithstanding the claims of Chapman to be considered the rival poet of Shakspere (see p. 231), I think a strong case might be made out for Daniel. His connection with William Herbert, the W.H. of the Sonnets; his great contemporary reputation; "the proud full sail of his great verse;" the close resemblances in style which Daniel's Sonnets bear to Shakspere's own; and the 1604 appointment, [1] are all points that cannot be lightly ignored.

HENRY CHETTLE, the son of Robert Chettle, a London dyer, was born probably in 1561. He was first brought into contact with the world of letters by being apprenticed to Thomas East, a stationer,[2] in 1577. He took up his freedom of the Stationers' Company on October 6th, 1584. He then probably worked as a journeyman-printer. About 1587-8 he was sent to Cambridge on the business of the Company, and received six shillings for his expenses. (Arber's *Transcript*, I., 528.) In 1591 with William Hoskins he printed, for Nicholas Ling and John Busby, a sermon by Henry Smith, minister of St. Clement Danes, and "The bayting of Dyogenes" was licensed to him alone on September 17th of that year. But he soon gave up this part of book-production, and in 1592 he edited *Green's Groats-worth of Wit*,[3] and in the same year he wrote *Kind-Harts Dreame*[4] which has a reference to it. Soon afterwards he became mixed up

[1] This has been made the subject of one of those detestable literary forgeries which so harass the Shakspere student (see Collier's *Shakespeare*, ed. 1858, Vol. I., p. 173; Shakespeare Society's *Papers*, Vol. IV., pp. 157-8; and Mr. Wheatley's *John Payne Collier*, p. 56).

[2] See p. 227. At p. 150 of Henslowe's *Diary* is an entry of the year 1599, in which he called himself stationer.

[3] See p. 194.

[4] Reprinted by the Percy Society, and in 1874 by the New Shakspere Society.

with the Harvey and Nash controversy. In February, 1598, he was helping Munday in *The Second Part of Robin Hood* (see p. 227). In March with Drayton, he was working at a play the name of which Henslowe gives very imperfectly, and during the next few months with Drayton and Dekker at a play concerning the reign of Henry I., with Drayton, Dekker, and Wilson at plays which we may call *Earl Godwin and his Three Sons*, *Sir Pierce of Exton*, and *The Black Batman of the North* (*Diary*, pp. 120-6). Nothing is now known of these. In June with Wilson, Munday, and Drayton he was writing *The Funeral of Richard Cœur de Lion* (see p. 228). In July he seems to have been engaged single-handed at *A Woman's Tragedy*, now lost (*Diary*, p. 127). In August his co-workers were Porter and Ben Jonson (see p. 207), and in the same month with Wilson he was writing *Catiline's Conspiracy*, also lost (*Diary*, pp. 132-3), which has to be said of a play apparently on the subject of Brute the mythical king of Britain and his descendant Bladud; while in August, September, and October he was writing with Day's assistance (*Diary*, pp. 131, 133-4, 136-2). In November he gave some extra touches to a play by Munday (see p. 227), and by himself began a lost comedy called *'Tis No Deceit to Deceive the Deceiver* (*Diary*, pp. 139-40). In this year the easily-satisfied Meres considered him to be one of "the best for Comedy amongst us" (see p. 9). In February, 1599 he wrote "Troyes Revenge, with the tragedy of polefeme" (*Diary*, pp. 145-9). In March he was working with Porter at a play which Henslowe calls "the Spensers" (*Diary*, pp. 146-9). On April 7th occurs the first entry about a play in which he was engaged on the subject of Troilus and Cressida (see p. 167). In the same month he was working upon *Sir Placidas* (*Diary*, pp. 149-50). In August he was writing with Dekker *The Stepmother's Tragedy* (*Diary*, pp. 154-5, 157).

Nothing is now known of any of these plays written in this part of 1599. In September he was at work with Dekker, Ben Jonson, and perhaps Marston (see p. 207). *Patient Grissil,*[1] written with Dekker and Haughton was begun at the end of the year (*Diary*, pp. 158, 96, 162), when alone Chettle wrote *The Orphan's Tragedy* (*Diary*, pp. 93, 160, 201), and *The Arcadian Virgin* with Haughton (*Diary*, p. 161). The last two plays are lost. In February, March, and April, 1600, he was at work upon *Damon and Pythias*[2] (*Diary*, pp. 93, 165-6, 168-9). In March also he was engaged with Dekker, Haughton, and Day upon *The Seven Wise Masters* (*Diary*, pp. 165-6). These plays are unknown. About the same time, alone, he was writing *The Wooing of Death* (*Diary*, p. 169) and, with Dekker and Day, *The Golden Ass, Cupid and Psyche* (*Diary*, p. 170). These works have not survived. In May he was part-author with Day in *The Blind Beggar of Bethnal Green*[3] (*Diary*, p. 171). In March, 1601, he was sole author of *All is not Gold that Glisters* (*Diary*, p. 185), and in April and May with Dekker he was writing *King Sebastian of Portugal*[4] (*Diary*, pp. 186-8). Both are lost. In June of the same year we meet with the first of the entries connecting Chettle with a play or plays on some incidents in the reign of Henry VIII. (see p. 183). In November he began *Too Good to be True*, which he finished in the January following with Hathway and Smith (*Diary*, pp. 204, 206-7), and in the latter month (*Diary*, p. 218) he was "mendinge" *The Proud Woman of Antwerp*, which had been written by Day and Haughton (*Diary*, p. 193).

[1] Printed in 1603, and reprinted by the Shakespeare Society in 1841.

[2] There is extant an earlier play with this title (see p. 224),

[3] Printed in 1659, and now included in Day's works.

[4] Sir Henry Herbert in 1630 refused to license Massinger's play on this subject, "because itt did contain dangerous matter." He adds "I had my fee notwithstandinge, which belongs to me for reading itt over, and ought to be brought always with the booke" (1821 *Variorum*, Vol. III., pp. 229-31).

In March, 1602, he undertook to write only for the Lord Admiral's Company (*Diary*, p. 219). In May he was working with Smith on *Love Parts Friendship* (*Diary*, p. 220) and by himself on *Tobias* (*Diary*, pp. 220, 222-3). In July he began *A Danish Tragedy* (*Diary*, p. 224). The last five plays are not extant. In September, 1602, he was writing a now lost play, *Robin Goodfellow*, for "my Lorde of Worsters players" (*Diary*, p. 239). In this there was no breach of the undertaking of the previous March, as both the companies were under the management of Henslowe. Also in September, Henslowe notes (*Diary*, pp. 225-6) that Chettle was working with Robinson at a tragedy called "Femelanco." But nothing is known either of play or coadjutor. In October and November he was working with Dekker, Heywood, Smith, and Webster (see p. 214). At the end of the year and in the beginning of 1603 Chettle was at work upon his play *Hoffman*[1] (*Diary*, p. 229), and engaged in writing with Heywood[2] (see p. 214). In May he seems to have been engaged with others in a play "wherein Shores wiffe is writen" (see p. 87). Notwithstanding this prolific work, Chettle was always in needy circumstances. This may be seen from various entries in Henslowe's *Diary*. He was dead before 1607.

MICHAEL DRAYTON was born at Hartshill in Warwickshire in 1563, It has been thought that he went to Oxford, but he took no degree. He was the author of much well-known historical verse (see pp. 40, 77, 89). In most laudatory terms he is mentioned several times by Meres, who in this case was expressing the opinion of his contemporaries. Meres also considered him to be one of "the best for

[1] Printed in 1631. Reprinted in 1853, with an introduction by H. B. L.

[2] See also *Diary*, pp. 230-1.

Tragedie" (see p. 9). It is unfortunate that none of the plays of which he was sole author have come down to the present time. We know from Henslowe that at least from 1597 to 1602 he was busily engaged in dramatic writing. In December, 1597, and January, 1598, he was working with Munday at *Mother Redcap* (see p. 227). In the following months he was writing with Chettle and Dekker and Wilson and Munday (see pp. 234, 228). In June, July, and August, with Wilson and Dekker he wrote three plays, now lost: "the made manes mores," "haneball and hermes, other wisse called worsse feared then hurte," and "perce of winschester" (*Diary*, pp. 126-9, 131, 133). He was also engaged in August with others upon *Chance Medley* (see p. 228). Towards the end of the year he wrote with Dekker *The First Civil Wars in France* and "Connan prince cornwell," both of which are lost (*Diary*, pp. 134, 136-7, 141). In January, 1599, he wrote by himself "Willm Longsword" or "Wm longberd" (*Diary*, pp. 95, 142). These plays are unknown. In October and December, 1599, and January, 1600, he was writing with Munday, Wilson, and Hathway[1] (see p. 228). In June they were joined by Dekker (see p. 228). In 1601 Drayton was concerned in the Cardinal Wolsey plays (see p. 183). In May, 1602, he was at work with several others at plays called *Cæsar's Fall* and "too harpes" (see p. 218). Professor Ward (*English Dramatic Literature*, Vol. I., p. 463) says that *The Merry Devil of Edmonton*[2] attributed to Shakspere has also been ascribed to Drayton. Drayton died in 1631, and was buried in Westminster Abbey. His works in complete form were published in folio in

[1] Part of this work was on *Sir John Oldcastle*.

[2] Published anonymously in 1608. It had been acted by the King's servants at the Globe. It is reprinted in Hazlitt's *Dodsley*.

1748, and in four volumes in 1753. It is of interest to know that Drayton when "labouring of a Tertian" was under the medical care of Shakspere's son-in-law, Dr. Hall, who cured him by a far less liberal administration of drugs than he commonly used.

THOMAS NASH, the son of a minister, was born at Lowestoft in 1567. He took his B.A. at Cambridge in 1586. In the Public Record Office there is a collection of Latin poems on *Ecclesiasticus*, xli. One of these is by Nash. These were written by scholars of St. John's (see *Calendar of State Papers*. Domestic. Addenda. 1580-1625, p. 166).

Probably in 1587 he wrote the preface to Greene's *Menaphon*,[1] making special reference to Marlowe's *Tamburlaine*. About this time he was an active contributor to the Marprelate controversy, to which he brought the full force of his literary powers, and aided by the dislike of Puritanism which the dissipation of, at all events, his early life encouraged, his writings were of an exceedingly vigorous character. In 1592 he issued his *Pierce Penilesse*,[2] which became exceedingly popular as a clever picture of the manners of the time and as an appeal for a more general and liberal recognition of scholarship.

Nash's only known dramatic production is *Summer's Last Will and Testament*,[3] which, containing disparaging references to *Greene's Groatsworth of Wit*, shows that the friendly relations which existed between him and Greene in 1587 had ceased. The converse had

[1] The earliest known edition is 1589 (see p. 200).

[2] Reprinted by the Shakespeare Society in 1842, and by Collier in *Miscellaneous Tracts*. It is supposed to contain a reference to Shakspere's 1 *Henry VI*. Its connecting link with *A Yorkshire Tragedy* is referred to at p. 133.

[3] Reprinted in Hazlitt's *Dodsley*. It was acted by one of the Children's companies.

happened, at least on Nash's part, in his quarrel with Harvey, to whom he apologised in 1593 for the attack made upon him in the Marprelate discussion.[1] Nash finished *Dido,* which Marlowe had left incomplete at his death in 1592. *The Isle of Dogs*, a lost play, which Nash wrote in 1597 for the Lord Admiral's servants, brought both actors and author into trouble. The players were suppressed and the writer imprisoned (see Henslowe's *Diary,* pp. 94, 98-9, 258-9). Nash is one of those whom Meres thought to be "the best for Comedy"[2] (see p. 9). He was dead by 1601.

It is conjectured that THOMAS MIDDLETON was born in 1570, and that he went to Cambridge. He wrote a large number of plays and pageants.[3] In May, 1602, he was working with several other dramatists at *Cæsar's Fall* and at "too harpes" (see p. 218). In October and November he was writing for Henslowe (*Diary,* pp. 241, 227-8,) a play, which is now lost, in which Henslowe thought the Earl of Chester[4] was a prominent person. In December he added a prologue and epilogue to Greene's *Friar Bacon* (see p. 73). In 1604 he was writing with Dekker (*Diary,* p. 232). He wrote a large number of plays, in some of which he was helped by William Rowley. His earlier plays were acted by the Children of Paul's and the Children of the Revels. Middleton's possible connection

[1] In Harvey's *Third Letter* (see p. 204) there is much referring to Nash.

[2] Meres has also references to Nash in connection with the Harvey dispute and with *The Isle of Dogs* (see *Shakspere Allusion-Books,* p. 164). The latter is of great interest, as it fixes the identity of Nash as Greene's "Young Juvenal" in the *Groatsworth of Wit* (*Op. cit.* p. 30).

[3] A musical allegory for a civic feast in 1622 is preserved in MS. in the Public Record Office (see *Calendar of State Papers.* Domestic. 1619-1623, p. 379).

[4] But not unlikely this is Middleton's play, *The Mayor of Quinborough*, in which Rainulph, monk of Chester, presents the dumb-show.

with *Macbeth* (see p. 155) should be investigated. In 1620 he was appointed Chronologer to the City of London, a post in which he was succeeded by Ben Jonson (see p. 209). Middleton's political references in *A Game of Chess*, 1624, will form an interesting subject of study (see *Calendar of State Papers*. Domestic. Addenda. 1623-1625, p. 329). He died in 1627.

Middleton's works were edited by Dyce in five volumes in 1840, and by Mr. A. H. Bullen in 1885 in eight volumes. "Thomas Middleton: Annals of his Career," by Mr. Fleay, is to be found in *Shakespeariana*, Vol. I., 1883-4. Mr. Swinburne had an article on Middleton in *The Nineteenth Century*, January, 1886.

It has been thought that THOMAS DEKKER was born about 1570. Beyond the fact that he was born in London, nothing is known of his early life. The note in Henslowe's *Diary* (p. 71) that he was paid on December 20th, 1597, for "adycyons to Fostus" is a forgery (see p. 200). In January, 1598, he was writing a play for Henslowe called *Phaeton*[1] (*Diary*, pp. 117-8). In February Henslowe advanced money to get Dekker out of the Counter[2] (*Diary*, p. 118). In March Dekker supplied Henslowe with a piece called "the treplesetie of cockowlles" (*Diary*, p. 119), and with Drayton and Chettle wrote *Henry I.* (see p. 234). Shortly afterwards, with Drayton, Chettle, and Wilson, he was at work at the plays mentioned on p. 234. In June, July, and August he was engaged with Wilson and Drayton

[1] Now lost. On December 14, 1600 (*Diary*, pp. 173-4), further payment was made for it. Part of this play may have been used by Dekker in *The Sun's Darling*, a masque which he wrote with Ford about 1624.

[2] There were three debtors' prisons of this name. That with which Dekker was familiar was in the Poultry. Another was in Wood Street. The third was in Southwark. a part of the Parish Church of St. Margaret (see Stow's *Survey of London*, ed, 1633, p. 454).

(see p. 237). In the latter month he was, perhaps, at work with Wilson and Munday (see p. 228). In the last four months of the year he was working with Drayton (see p. 237). The foregoing work excited the admiration of Meres, who in that year placed Dekker amongst the "best for Tragedie" (see p. 9). In January, 1599, he wrote a play intended to be an introduction to *The First Civil Wars in France* (*Diary*, p. 142). A few days after he had been paid for this he was arrested at the instance of the Lord Chamberlain's servants, when Henslowe lent money for his release (*Diary*, p. 143). On April 7th he received the first payment for plays about Troilus and Cressida (see p. 167). In May he wrote by himself *Orestes' Furies* (*Diary*, p. 151), but it is now lost. His play *The Shoemaker's Holiday* was written in July, 1599, when it was mentioned by Henslowe (*Diary*, p. 154) under the name of *The Gentle Craft*, the second part of its title.[1] About the same time he wrote a play with Chettle (see p. 234), and in August he seems to have been sole author of a lost play known as *Bear a Brain* (*Diary*, p. 155). In the same month he was writing with Ben Jonson (see p. 207) and others. In November and December he received payments for "the hole history of Fortunatus"[2] (*Diary*, pp. 159-61). In December, with Chettle and Haughton, he was working at *Patient Grissil* (see p. 235). Nothing is known of *Truth's Supplication to Candlelight* (*Diary*, pp. 95, 163), which was the unaided production of Dekker in January, 1600, or of "the Spaneshe Mores tragedie," which in February he wrote with Haughton and Day (*Diary*, p. 165). In March he was at work with Chettle, Haughton, and Day (see

[1] It was printed in 1600.

[2] Dekker's *Old Fortunatus* was printed in 1600. Its relation to the play with a somewhat similar name acted in 1596 (see *Diary*, p. 64) is uncertain. Extra payment for it may have been made on September 6, 1600 (*Diary*, p. 173).

p. 235). A little later he was writing with Day and Chettle (see p. 235), and in June with Drayton, Hathway, and Munday (see p. 228). In April and May, 1601, he was at work with Chettle (see p. 235). *Satiro-mastix,* acted in 1601 by the Lord Chamberlain's servants at the Globe, is of great interest in connection with his quarrel with Jonson (see p. 206). In January, 1602, he did some patchwork for Henslowe (*Diary,* p. 207). In May he and Munday were working together (see p. 228), and both of them with Drayton, Middleton, and Webster (see p. 218). Dekker's play *A Medicine for a Curst Wife,* begun in July (*Diary,* pp. 224-5, 238, 240), has been lost. In August, September, November, and December he did a little "mendinge" (*Diary,* pp. 236, 239, 227, 39). In October and November he had been engaged with Chettle, Heywood, Smith, and Webster (see p. 214). In 1604 he was writing with Middleton (*Diary,* p. 232). In addition to these coadjutors mentioned by Henslowe, Dekker wrote with Massinger (see p. 219). He was certainly one of the most fluent of the Elizabethan writers. Besides his many plays he wrote much other prose and verse. He died probably about 1638.

His own extant plays, edited by Mr. R. H. Shepherd, were published in four volumes in 1873. Mr. Fleay has compiled lengthy "Annals of the Career of Thomas Dekker" (*Shakespeariana,* Vol. II. 1885). Mr. Swinburne has an article on Dekker in *The Nineteenth Century,* January, 1887.

John Ford, the son of a magistrate, was born in 1586, at Ilsington in Devonshire. He entered at the Middle Temple in 1602, and may thus have seen the performance of *Twelfth Night* which took place there in that year. (see p. 129). His earliest literary productions were not of a dramatic character. His first plays, written with Dekker and Webster, are lost. The plays of which he was sole author date from 1628 to 1638. It is supposed that he died in 1640.

Ford's plays were edited by Weber in 1811 in two volumes, by Gifford in 1827 in two volumes, and by Dyce in three volumes in 1869. A one-volume edition (with Massinger's works) was published in Moxon's series, and afterwards by Routledge in 1865. Mr. Swinburne has an article on Ford in *The Fortnightly Review*, July, 1871.

JAMES SHIRLEY was born in London in 1596. He went to Oxford, and afterwards to Cambridge, and was ordained, holding for a short time a living in Hertfordshire. This he soon gave up, as he became a Roman Catholic. He then devoted himself to teaching, and wrote some books on English and Latin Grammar. His first play was published in 1625. From that time to the closing of the theatres in 1642 he wrote many plays. As an author he seems to have been slightly connected with Fletcher and Chapman. He died in 1666.

Shirley's works were edited in six volumes by Dyce (with Gifford's notes) in 1833. This edition was reviewed in *The Quarterly Review* for April, 1833. There is an article on Shirley in *The Gentleman's Magazine*, May, 1880.

For convenience of reference, some of the foregoing information is summarised in the following table.

	Born.	*University.*	*B.A.*	*M.A.*	*Died.*	*Aged.*
Bale, John	1495	Cambridge[1]	——	——	1563	68
Heywood, John	1497	Oxford	——	——	*1576*	*79*
Edwards, Richard ...	1523	Oxford	1544	1547	1566	43
Legge, Thomas	1536	Cambridge	1557	1560[2]	1607	71
Sackville, Thomas ...	1536	Cambridge[3]	——	1571	1608	72
Munday, Anthony... ...	1553	——	——	——	1633	80
Lyly, John	1554	Oxford	1573	1575	1606	*52*
Lodge, Thomas	*1556*	Oxford[4]	1577	——	*1625*	*69*
Peele, George	1558	Oxford	1577	1579	*1596*	*38*
Chapman, George... ...	1559	——	——	——	1634	75
Greene, Robert	*1560*	Cambridge	1579	1583[5]	1592	*32*
Chettle, Henry	1561	——	——	——	*1606*	*45*
Daniel, Samuel	1562	Oxford	——	——	1619	57
Drayton, Michael	1563	*Oxford*	——	——	1631	68
Marlowe, Christopher ...	1564	Cambridge	1583	1587	1593	29
Shakspere, William ...	1564	——	——	——	1616	52
Nash, Thomas	1567	Cambridge	1586	——	*1600*	*33*
Middleton, Thomas ...	*1570*	*Cambridge*	——	——	1627	*57*
Dekker, Thomas	*1570*	——	——	——	*1638*	*68*
Jonson, Ben	1573	——	——	1619[6]	1637	64
Marston, John	*1575*	*Oxford*	*1594*	——	*1634*	*59*
Webster, John	*1575*	——	——	——	*1650*	*75*
Heywood, Thomas ...	*1576*	——	——	——	*1648*	*72*
Fletcher, John	1579	*Cambridge*	——	——	1625	45
Beaumont, Francis ...	1584	Oxford	——	——	1616	32
Massinger, Philip... ...	1584	Oxford	——	——	1639	55
Ford, John	1586	——	——	——	*1640*	54
Shirley, James	1596	Cambridge[7]	——	——	1666	70

The *Italics* in the above table indicate some considerable degree of uncertainty.

1 Became B.D. in 1529.
2 Created LL.D. in 1575.
3 Created M.A. of Cambridge on the visit of the French Ambassador in reference to the Queen's talked of marriage with the Duc d'Anjou. Sackville entered first at Oxford, of which he was incorporated M.A. in 1592, after his election as Chancellor in 1591, when his opponent was the Earl of Essex.
4 Incorporated M.D. in 1602.
5 Also M.A. of Oxford by incorporation in 1588.
6 By creation at Oxford.
7 Was at Oxford first.

Fragments only are known of the lives of **Ulpian Fulwell, George Whetstone, Thomas Kyd, Henry Porter, William Haughton, Robert Wilson, Richard Hathway, John Day, Samuel Rowley, William Rowley, George Wilkins, Cyril Tourneur, Nathaniel Field.** But something of the unassisted dramatic writing of each[1] has survived to the present time.

ULPIAN FULWELL was born in 1546. In 1578 he entered at St. Mary's Hall, Oxford, but took no degree. His interlude *Like Will to Like* was published in 1568 and again in 1587. It is reprinted in Hazlitt's *Dodsley*.

The only known play by GEORGE WHETSTONE is *Promos and Cassandra*, printed in 1578 (see p. 145). In 1584 he took part in the controversy about dramatic performances by writing a short work objecting to "the use of stage-plays on the Sabbath-day, and the abuse of them at all times." He wrote an elegy on the death of Sir Philip Sidney, which is preserved in the Public Record Office (see *Calendar of State Papers*. Domestic. 1581-1590, pp. 387-8).

Nothing is known of the dates of the birth and death of THOMAS KYD. It has been thought that he died about 1594. There is no evidence as to his career. Thomas Heywood refers[2] to him as the author of *The Spanish Tragedy*, which was entered in the Stationers' Registers on October 6th, 1592. This play, which was sometimes called *Jeronimo*, was often referred to by contemporary writers, and it was often acted (see Henslowe's *Diary*, p. 21 *et seq.*) and printed.

[1] Except Hathway. I have included him because he was not only very busy for Henslowe, but is mentioned by Meres.

[2] *Apology for Actors*, 1612. Shakespeare Society edition, p. 45.

Henslowe notes (pp. 201, 223) that Ben Jonson made additions to it in 1601-2. There is also *The First Part of Jeronimo*, published anonymously, of which Kyd is supposed to be the author. His other known play is *Cornelia*.[1] Malone (1821 *Variorum*, Vol. II., pp. 316, 372) would bring Kyd into close connection with Shakspere, for, prompted by Farmer, he thought that Kyd wrote *The Taming of a Shrew* (see p. 97), and suspected him to be the author of the lost *Hamlet* (see p. 135) and of the 1594 *Leir* (see p. 149). Meres has an extra good word for Kyd, whom he not only ranks amongst the masters of tragedy (see p. 9), but whom he seems to have thought the English counterpart of Tasso (see p. 8).

Of HENRY PORTER nothing definite is known. In December, 1596, he was working for Henslowe (*Diary*, p. 77). In May, 1598, he wrote a play called *Love Prevented* (*Diary*, p. 124), of which nothing is now known. In August he was writing with Chettle and Ben Jonson (see p. 207). In December and in the following February he received payments for the second part of *The Two Angry Women of Abington*[2] (*Diary*, pp. 141, 145-6). In the latter month he undertook to write for Henslowe only. In March he was writing with Chettle (see p. 234). At p. 94 of the *Diary* are some vague records of money-transactions between Porter and Henslowe in 1599, and at p. 261 is a curious note about the indebtedness of the writer to the manager.

In *Shakespeariana*, Vol. III., 1886, Mr. Fleay, under the title of

[1] The three plays are reprinted in Hazlitt's *Dodsley*.

[2] Henslowe has no entry of a first part. The only play known by this name was printed twice in 1599. Its title-page says it had been acted by the Lord Admiral's servants. It was reprinted by the Percy Society and in Hazlitt's *Dodsley*, and is in a recently-issued volume of the 'Mermaid' Series of old plays.

"Annals of the Career of Henry Porter," gives a chronicle of the entries which refer to him in Henslowe's *Diary*.

William Haughton was working for Henslowe in November, 1597 (*Diary*, p. 104). In the early part of 1598 he wrote *A Woman will have her Will*,[1] the only extant play of which it is certain that he was sole author (*Diary*, pp. 119, 122). In 1599 he seems to have written a lost play, *The Poor Man's Paradise* (*Diary*, p. 155). Towards the end of the year he was engaged with Dekker and Chettle upon *Patient Grissil* (see p. 235), with Day upon *John Cox* and *Thomas Merry* (*Diary*, pp. 95, 158-9; 92-3, 160-1), and with Chettle alone (see p. 235). In February, 1600, he was working with Dekker and Day (see p. 241), and in March the three were joined by Chettle (see p. 235). Part of this month Haughton spent in the Clink prison, said by Stow to be "for such as should brabble, fray, or breake the peace" (*Survey of London*, ed. 1633, p. 449). In the latter half of the month he was engaged upon a play that had the title at least of Sackville's tragedy (*Diary*, pp. 166-7). In April he was writing *The English Fugitives* (*Diary*, p. 168), now lost. In May he received a small advance for a play which never got much beyond its title of *The Devil and his Dam* (*Diary*, p. 169), but in the same month Henslowe paid £7 to Haughton and "Mr Pett" for *Strange News out of Poland* (*Diary*, p. 170). This is all that is known either of play or joint-author. About the same time Haughton began another play, of which the name is uncertain (*Diary*, p. 171). In December, 1600, and January, 1601, he had something to do with a play concerning Robin Hood (*Diary*, pp. 174-5). In January,

[1] Known also as *Englishmen for my Money*. Editions were issued in 1616, 1626, and 1631. It is reprinted in *The Old English Drama*, 1830, and in Hazlitt's *Dodsley*.

February, March, and July he was associated with Day in the series of plays connected with *The Blind Beggar of Bethnal Green* (*Diary*, pp. 180, 183-4, 186, 188, 194-5), of which only the first part, written by Chettle and Day, is now known (see p. 235). In April, May, August, and September, with Day and Smith, he was writing a lost play, *The Conquest of the West Indies* (*Diary*, pp. 185-6, 196-7, 199). From May to November, with Day, he wrote *The Six Yeomen of the West* (*Diary*, pp. 188-9), and a play in which The Proud Woman of Antwerp and Friar Rush were conspicuous (*Diary*, pp. 193-4, 201, 203-4). In July and September (*Diary*, pp. 195, 199, 200) Henslowe paid Day and Haughton for a play which is called "the 2 pte of Thome Dowghe," but it is not known to what this refers. In October Haughton was associated with Hathway and Smith in a play or plays called *The Six Clothiers* (*Diary*, pp. 202-3, 213), and in September, 1602, he was at work upon "a playe called Cartwryght" (*Diary*, p. 225); but these plays are lost.

In *Shakespeariana*, Vol. III., 1886, Mr. Fleay gives "Annals of the Careers of W. Houghton, *(sic)* Wadeson and Pett," in which are some ingenious suggestions about some of Haughton's plays having been printed with titles other than those given to them by Henslowe.

There is considerable uncertainty about the identity of ROBERT WILSON, who, in conjunction with Drayton, Dekker, and Chettle, was working for Henslowe from March to August, 1598 (see pp. 234, 237), and with Munday, Drayton, and Hathway on *Sir John Oldcastle* and *Owen Tudor* in 1599 and 1600 (see p. 228). He seems to have been the sole author in 1599 of a play about Henry Richmond. *The Cobbler's Prophecy*, printed in 1594, was written by Robert

Wilson. In 1598 Meres included Wilson among "the best for comedie" (see p. 9) and spoke of him as "our wittie Wilson, who, for learning and extemporall witte in this facultie [extemporall verse], is without compare or compeere" (*Shakspere Allusion-Books*, p. 164). He may have been the "R. W." the author of *The Three Ladies of London*, 1584 and 1592, and that "plesant and statelie morrall" *The Three Lords and Three Ladies of London*, 1590, which were reprinted by the Roxburghe Club in 1851 and in Hazlitt's *Dodsley*. But when the earliest date of the plays is compared with the date at which Wilson began writing for Henslowe, this looks doubtful. There was another "R.W." amongst the dramatists: Robert Wilmot, in 1591, altered *Tancred and Gismunda*,[1] a play which having been written by Gentlemen of the Inner Temple was acted by them before Queen Elizabeth in 1568. Wilmot, as a poet, is highly spoken of by Edward Webbe in *A Discourse of English Poetrie*, 1586 (ed. Arber, p. 35). It has been sought to show that the dramatist who wrote for Henslowe was Robert Wilson, one of the leaders of the Queen's players in 1583. But of this there is no evidence.

Richard Hathway, whom Meres in 1598 considered to be one of "the best for comedy" (see p. 9), wrote for Henslowe in that year (*Diary*, pp. 122-3). He worked with Munday, Drayton, and Wilson (see p. 228), with Smith and Haughton (see p. 248), with Smith and Chettle (see p. 235), with Day and Smith (*Diary*, pp. 228, 230-1, 245-8), with Rankins (*Diary*, pp. 97, 174-5, 183-6). None of his individual writing has come down to the present time, nor any dramatic production of his last-named helper, although

[1] Reprinted in Hazlitt's *Dodsley*.

there is extant a volume of Satires by Rankins dated 1587, a form of literature for which Meres gave him praise (see p. 8). In the book (*The Mirror of Monsters*) Rankins had written against the stage.

JOHN DAY is said to have been some time at Caius College, Cambridge, but he took no degree. In 1598 he was working with Chettle for Henslowe (see p. 234). In 1599 he was writing with Haughton (see p. 247). In January, 1600, he was at work upon a play which Henslowe describes insufficiently as "the etalyan tragedie of " (*Diary*, p. 163). In February he was associated in authorship with Dekker and Haughton (see p. 241), and in March with Chettle, Dekker, and Haughton (see p. 235), and soon after with Dekker and Chettle (see p. 235), and with Chettle only in May and June (see p. 235). During nearly the whole of 1601 he was working with Haughton (see p. 248); part of the time they were joined by Smith. In 1602 *The Bristol Tragedy*[1] was "written by hime selffe" (*Diary*, pp. 220-2). From November to the following March he was working with Smith and Hathway (see p. 249), and in May, 1603, he was writing with Chettle (see p. 87). After this Day left Henslowe, and wrote for other companies.[2] His works were privately printed by Mr. Bullen in 1880. Mr. Fleay's "Annals of the Career of John Day" (*Shakespeariana*, Vol. II., 1885) should be consulted.

If the titular distinction was not a necessary qualification in the recipient of the bounty, it may be to this writer that a grant in reversion "of a Poor Knight's room in Windsor" was made on

[1] This has been supposed to be the same as *The Fair Maid of Bristol*, printed in 1605.

[2] His *Parliament of Bees* is printed in a volume of the 'Mermaid' Series of old plays.

November 25th, 1611 (*Calendar of State Papers*. Domestic. 1611-1618, p. 93).

The earliest notice of Samuel Rowley is in 1598, when he was one of the Lord Admiral's men acting for Henslowe (*Diary*, p. 120). Many of the entries in the *Diary* show that when he had gained Henslowe's confidence, he was the intermediary for payment between manager and author. In November, 1599, he engaged himself as a covenant-servant (see p. 213) to Henslowe (*Diary*, p. 260). By December, 1601, Henslowe thought the actor might be trusted to write, first of all in conjunction with another[1] (*Diary*, p. 205) and then by himself (*Diary*, p. 226), for payments were made to him as an author. But of these plays nothing is now known. *The Noble Soldier*, an extant play credited to Samuel Rowley, was entered in the Stationers' Registers as a production by Dekker. No part-authorship has been alleged in *When You See Me You Know Me*,[2] of interest in connection with Shakspere's *Henry VIII*. (see Suggestion 1 on p. 183) and the burning of the Globe Theatre.

As nothing is known of the unaided work of the other writers who were engaged for Henslowe, it is not necessary to say anything about either of them except Wentworth Smith, who has been frequently mentioned in the preceding pages. He may have been the reviser of *Locrine* (see p. 89) and the author of *Thomas, Lord Cromwell* (see p. 105) and of *The Puritan* (see p. 229).

William Rowley, to whom, with Shakspere, *The Birth of Merlin* was attributed (see p. 181), is known as the sole author of a

[1] He was also a conjoint author in other plays. It is said (see p. 67) that he and William Bird were paid for "adicyones in Docter Fostes" on November 22, 1602.

[2] First printed in 1605. Edited by Karl Elze in 1874.

few plays,[1] and also to have been concerned with several other dramatists. 1607 is the earliest date of a play in which he was concerned, when *The Travels of Three English Brothers* was written with Day and Wilkins. He wrote also with Thomas Heywood (see p. 215), with Fletcher (see p. 216), with Webster (see p. 218), with Middleton (see p. 239), and perhaps with Dekker and Ford. Some of his plays in MS. were destroyed by Warburton's servant (see p. 219). Nothing certain is known about his life. Rowley referred to by Meres (see p. 9) was Ralph Rowley (see *Athenae Cantabrigienses*, Vol. II.). William Rowley, the dramatist, may have been the actor of that name who was connected with the Prince's servants, formerly the Lord Admiral's men.

The connections of GEORGE WILKINS with *Pericles* are referred to at p. 159. *The Miseries of Enforced Marriage*, the only play that he is known to have written, is reprinted in Hazlitt's *Dodsley*. The earliest edition, 1607, states that it was acted by the King's servants.

CYRIL TOURNEUR, whose problematical share in *Timon of Athens* is mentioned at p. 151, has had the honour of having his small contributions to dramatic literature edited in two volumes by Churton Collins (1878), included with the slight quantity of his other poetical matter. *The Revenger's Tragedy*, acted by the King's servants and printed in 1607, is also to be found in Hazlitt's *Dodsley*.

Mr. Swinburne wrote an article on Tourneur in *The Nineteenth Century*, March, 1887.

NATHANIEL FIELD, born in 1587, was the son of a London minister. He became one of the Children of the Chapel, and was

[1] Two are reprinted in Hazlitt's *Dodsley*.

also an author.[1] He helped Massinger in writing *The Fatal Dowry*, and was in money-difficulties with him (see p. 219). Two plays—*A Woman is a Weathercock*, acted by the Children of the Revels and printed in 1612, and *Amends for Ladies*, acted by the Prince's servants and the Lady Elizabeth's, published in 1618—are known to have been written by Field.[2] There is extant a letter which he wrote to the Preacher at St. Mary Overy's in 1616, in which he "remonstrates against his condemnations from the pulpit of all players. Though, like other trades, that of actors has many corruptions, it is not condemned in Scripture, and being patronized by the King, it is disloyal to preach against it" (*Calendar of State Papers.* Domestic. 1611-1618, p. 419). In 1619 he is associated with the King's servants in a theatrical license.

Field's name occurs in the 1623 Folio as one of the principal actors in the plays therein given. He died in 1632, aged about 45.

[1] There was a Nathaniel Field, Fellow of New College, Oxford, known to have written Latin verses (see Hazlitt's *Dodsley*, Vol. XV., p. 417).

[2] Both are reprinted in Hazlitt's *Dodsley*, and in a volume in the 'Mermaid' Series.

CHAPTER XI.

The Editions of Shakspere's Works.

> "Small have continual plodders ever won
> Save base authority from others' books."
>
> *Love's Labour's Lost*, I. i. 86–7.

FROM the lists in Chapter IX. it will be seen that much of Shakspere's work was printed separately before the collected edition of the plays appeared in 1623. I give the information here in another form, that the student may see conveniently the order of publication and what plays were printed in any particular year. A separate list is given of the poems,[1] and of the foundation-plays of 2[2] and 3 *Henry VI.*,[3] *John*,[4] and *The Taming of the Shrew*,[5] as contemporary opinion seems to have credited him with some share in their authorship.

[1] *Venus and Adonis*		1593	1594		1596		1599		1602 (2)					1617		1620	
**Lucrece*			1594			1598		1600		1607			1616				
The Sonnets											1609						
[2] *The Contention*			1594					1600							1619 } †		
[3] *The True Tragedy*				1595				1600							1619 } †		
[4] *The Troublesome Raigne*	1591											1611					1622
[5] *The Taming of a Shrew*			1594		1596					1607							

* Taking the British Museum *Catalogue of Early Printed Books* as my authority, I stated on p. 119 that there were two 1616 editions of *Lucrece*. But the entry in the Catalogue giving one of that year with the imprint of J. G. for John Stafford is a mistake. That was published in 1655. The British Museum 1616 copy is the same as that in the Bodleian.

† With *Pericles* in one volume.

Titus Andronicus				1600							1611					
Love's Labour's Lost		1598														
Richard II.	1597	1598							1608 (2)					1615		
A Midsummer-Night's Dream				1600 (2)												
Richard III.	1597	1598			1602			1605				1612				1622
Romeo and Juliet[1]	1597		1599							1609						
The Merchant of Venice				1600 (2)												
Much Ado about Nothing				1600												
1 *Henry IV.*		1598	1599				1604		1608				1613			1622
2 *Henry IV.*				1600												
The Merry Wives of Windsor					1602										1619	
Henry V.				1600	1602				1608							
Hamlet[1]						1603	1604	1605			1611					
Othello																1622
Lear									1608 (2)							
Pericles										(2) 1609	1611				1619[2]	
Troilus and Cressida										1609 (2)						

[1] There is also an undated Quarto (see p. 91 and p. 135).
[2] With *The Contention* and *The True Tragedy* in one volume.

Mr. Fleay's tables of the Quartos[1] should also be consulted. The *Othello* is the only one in which there is any attempt at division of acts or scenes.

As it is of interest to see how these early editions set forth their authorship, they are here arranged in that way. Of the plays that have a suspicion of Shakspere's part-authorship I have included those which are put forward in this book for study. The two syllables of the full surname were often hyphenated.

(1) Anonymous.

1591 *Troublesome Raigne.*
1594 *Contention.*
1594 *A Shrew.*
1595 *True Tragedy.*
1596 *Edward III.*
1596 *A Shrew.*
1597 *Richard II.*
1597 *Richard III.*
1597 *Romeo and Juliet.*
1598 1 *Henry IV.*
1599 *Romeo and Juliet.*
1599 *Edward III.*
1600 *Titus Andronicus.*
1600 *Contention.*
1600 *True Tragedy.*
1600 *Henry V.*
1602 *Henry V.*
1607 *A Shrew.*
N.D. *Romeo and Juliet.*[2]
1608 *Henry V.*
1609 *Romeo and Juliet.*
1611 *Titus Andronicus.*

(2) W. S.

1595 *Locrine.*
1602 *Thomas, Lord Cromwell.*
1613 *Thomas, Lord Cromwell.*

(3) W. Sh.

1611 *Troublesome Raigne.*

[1] New Shakspere Society's *Transactions*, Part I., 1874, and *Shakespeare Manual*, pp. 139-50. He confuses the businesses of printer and publisher. These were almost invariably quite distinct. Publishers not owning printing-plant did not of course print books, but occasionally a printer sold retail the book he had printed, *e.g.* Eld printed and sold Tourneur's *Revenger's Tragedy*.

[2] Some copies have "W. Shakespeare."

(4) W. Shakspeare.
1608 *Yorkshire Tragedy.*

(5) William Shakspeare.
1608 *Lear* ("Pide Bull").

(6) W. Shakespere.
1598 *Love's Labour's Lost.*

(7) W. Shakespeare.

1599 1 *Henry IV.*
1600 *Merchant of Venice* (Roberts).
1604 1 *Henry IV.*
N.D. *Romeo and Juliet.*[1]
1608 1 *Henry IV.*
1613 1 *Henry IV.*
1619 *Merry Wives.*
1619 *Yorkshire Tragedy.*
1619 *Pericles.*
1622 *Troublesome Raigne.*
1622 1 *Henry IV.*

(8) William Shakespeare.

1598 *Richard II.*
1598 *Richard III.*
1600 *Midsummer-Night's Dream* (2).
1600 *Merchant of Venice* (Heyes).
1600 *Much Ado about Nothing.*
1600 2 *Henry IV.*
1602 *Richard III.*
1602 *Merry Wives.*
1603 *Hamlet.*
1604 *Hamlet.*
1605 *Richard III.*
1605 *London Prodigal.*
1605 *Hamlet.*
N.D. *Hamlet.*
1608 *Richard II.* (2).
1608 *Lear.*
1609 *Pericles* (2).
1609 *Troilus and Cressida* (2).
1611 *Hamlet.*
1611 *Pericles.*
1612 *Richard III.*
1615 *Richard II.*
1619 *Whole Contention.*
1622 *Richard III.*
1622 *Othello.*

[1] Some copies are anonymous.

(9) John Fletcher and William Shakspeare.
1634 *Two Noble Kinsmen.*

(10) William Shakespear and William Rowley.
1662 *Birth of Merlin.*

In the First Folio it is said that readers had been "abus'd with diuerse stolne, and surreptitious copies, maimed, and deformed by the frauds and stealthes of iniurious impostors, that expos'd them." It is clear that this refers to only some of the earlier editions,[1] as for some of the plays the editors of the Folio printed from the Quartos. Probably we shall never know the exact relation of the Quarto and Folio versions in the cases where there is a discrepancy of text. In some of these cases, notwithstanding the statement of the Folio-editors, the Quarto-readings are obviously better. The question is further complicated by the way in which it is known that unauthorised copies were often obtained. An imperfect form of shorthand was in existence,[2] and those who practised it were employed by enterprising printers or publishers to take notes of a popular play during its performance. But with the system, crude as it then was, it would not be possible to accurately record the spoken words.[3] Further divergence from the author's expressions

[1] Probably all of them were sold at sixpence each (see Preface to *Troilus and Cressida*). The Sonnets sold at fivepence. Nowadays the original Quartos vary much in price. Lately 2 *Henry IV.* fetched £225.

[2] In 1558 Dr. Timothy Bright published his "Charactery. An Arte of Shorte, Swift, and Secrete Writing by Character." Peter Bales's book, *The Writing Schoolemaster*, was entered in the Stationers' Registers on December 1, 1589, and published the following year. It consists of three parts, the first of which is "The arte of Brachygraphie; that is to write as fast as a man speaketh, treatably writing but one letter for a word, &c." *The Art of Stenographie* was entered on April 19, 1602.

[3] In contemporary literature there are allusions to the wrongs which the Elizabethan playwrights suffered from this practice (see Webster's *Devil's Law-case*, IV., ii., and a note by Collier to a passage about Bales's system in Nash's *Summer's Last Will and Testament* in Hazlitt's *Dodsley*, Vol. VIII., p. 41).

would take place through this mode of procuring a play, as doubtless, then as now, the actors often deviated in small ways from the written copy with which they had been provided.

The literary value of the Quartos is often estimated by the reputation of their printers and publishers.[1] I give such notes about them as I have been able to obtain. These notes will prove of further interest to the Shakspere-student, who will be glad to know as much as possible about those who had the responsibility of mechanically presenting the author's thoughts to after-generations and who have in too many instances by their careless work provided us with puzzles of interpretation which unfortunately are often insoluble, but for which, perhaps, we ought not to be unthankful, considering the occupation they have afforded to many, with the consequent result of directing a close attention to the text. The biographical notes, such as they are, will be welcomed for the third reason that they throw light on that absorbingly interesting history of book-publication, with which every Englishman should be familiar, and in connection with which he should closely study Milton's *Areopagitica*.

[1] Occasionally the name of printer or publisher is absent from the title-page. In non-dramatic books the printer's name in some cases was stated for the first time, and sometimes repeated, in the colophon. This I have not always had the opportunity of examining.

With all their vices, the Stationers were often modest enough to obscure their identity under the guise of initials, which, well known no doubt to their contemporaries, not seldom prove harassing to nineteenth-century searchers. Even Mr. P. Z. Round in his Introduction (1886) to the Facsimile of the First Quarto of *Pericles* suggests that T. P., the printer of Wilkins's novel, was Pavier, whereas it was Thomas Purfoot. Following Collier's hint, Mr. Fleay in the Tables referred to at p. 256 calls W. W. (the printer of *Love's Labour's Lost* and other Quartos), Waterson instead of White. There were stationers of the name of Waterson, but not with W. as an initial. Richard Waterson was made free on December 7, 1555. "Sim. Waterson, bookseller, died" March 16, 1635. "John Waterson, once a bookseller, died" February 10, 1656. Simon (see p. 63) had been made free on August 14, 1583; John (see p. 165) on June 27, 1620.

My authorities have been Herbert's edition of Ames's *Typographical Antiquities*, Arber's *Transcript of the Stationers' Registers*, and the British Museum *Catalogue of Early Printed Books.*[1]

An examination of the "devices" on the title-pages will reveal much that is both curious and attractive. In the absence of specified names they are unfortunately useless for determining by what printers or publishers books with deficient imprints were issued. Looking no further than the Facsimile Quartos published by Mr. Quaritch under the superintendence of Dr. Furnivall, it will be seen that the same device is on the 'Roberts' *Merchant of Venice* in 1600, the 1608 *Henry V.*, the second 1608 *Lear*, and *The Whole Contention* in 1619.[2] No more can be said than that at a particular date a printer or publisher was in possession of a certain device.[3] Some interesting observations on devices will be found in Dr. Furness's edition of *Lear*, p. 357, and in Mr. P. A. Daniel's Introduction to the Facsimile "Pide Bull" *Lear*, pp. iv., v.[4]

This is the place where I should repair an injustice I did to Mr. Arber at p. 11 in reference to the varieties of type in which he

[1] Since this chapter was written I have seen an announcement of *The Earlier History of English Bookselling*, with a chapter on "Bookselling in the Time of Shakespeare." The book itself I have not seen.

[2] Having been Richard Jones's, this device may have belonged to Roberts (who had the reverse initials of its former possessor) in 1600 (in which case the device on *A Midsummer-Night's Dream* of that year must be that of its unnamed publisher), but considering the course of his career it could not have been his in 1619, when with the business it might have passed to William Jaggard. It, however, points to Roberts as the printer of the editions of *Henry V.* and *Lear* referred to above.

[3] The same device was used for *Skialetheia* printed by Roberts for Ling in 1598, for the earlier 1608 *Richard II.* printed by White for Lawe, for Hannay's *Songs and Sonnets* printed by Haviland for Butter in 1622, and for the 1630 *Othello* printed by Matthews for Hawkins.

[4] Anyone interested in the question of printers' devices will be well repaid by a careful investigation of Vol. II. of the Rev. T. F. Dibdin's *Bibliographical Decameron*.

printed the entries from the Stationers' Registers. I had overlooked a statement, placed in Volume I. between matter quoted from the Company's Records, in which he explains various points in the typography of his *Transcript*. Here it will be sufficient to say that in the entries which are to be found in Chapter IX. all contractions are printed in full and the names of all members of the Stationers' Company are printed in **Clarendon** type. I ought also to have said that he has many cross-references which are most helpful, and also very useful but incomplete alphabetical lists of printers and publishers, and that a fifth (the index) volume "is [October 15th, 1888] far advanced." In its absence I have had from the *Transcript* to make my own index of the Shakspere-stationers. This, which involved a considerable expenditure of time, I shall be happy to place at the disposal of anyone who wishes to pursue the interesting enquiry with more detail. A few general observations will render many of the statements in the notes much clearer.[1]

Before the Royal Charter of Incorporation was granted to the Stationers' Company in 1556 there had been, with a continuous history from 1545, an association of those engaged in the work of producing books, who had formed themselves,[2] with the sanction of the civic authorities, into a guild, the members of which paid a groat quarterly as a subscription. In the time of Edward VI. the Booksellers (Publishers), who bought the books from the printers in

[1] Those who are desirous to know more I refer to Mr. Arber's lucid Introductions, and to many documents he has printed in the volumes mentioned.

[2] At various periods there are indications that the craft was an organised body long before this. Arber (Vol. I., p. xxiii.) quotes a petition in 1403 to the Mayor and Aldermen of the City of London from "the Craft of Writers of Text-letter, those commonly called 'Limners,' and other good folks, citizens of London, who were wont to bind and to sell books" and (Vol. IV., p. xxiv.) other documentary evidence in reference to the earlier fraternity.

sheets, were able to exact such terms that the printers had difficulty in making a bare living. The Charter, which was necessary in order that there should be a central control over the issue of books, placed the publishers in a still better position. A successful effort, however, was made by which, from 1558 to 1582, Royal Patents were issued to certain printers for the issue of defined classes of books,[1] but this of course inflicted a grievance upon those who were unprivileged, and gave rise to much dissatisfaction amongst many of the London printers.

When the Company received its Charter the management was vested in a Master and two Wardens. The Mastership was a post of honour, to which it does not seem that any particular duties were attached. The Wardens were the responsible and representative officers of the Company. Through them its transactions were accomplished.[2]

In 1559, on account of the number of "vnfrutefull, vayne and infamous bokes and papers," Elizabeth ordered that nothing should be printed without special permission, in which episcopal sanction was to be a prominent feature, and the entry of publications, which at first was only a cash-receipt, as stated at p. 12, became a concession of copyright,[3] and the names in the entries so freely quoted in Chapter IX. are commonly those of the representative of the Bishop of London or of the Master of the Revels with one or both of the Wardens.[4] This mode of sanction con-

[1] It seems that there was no necessity to have these entered in the Registers. The Patents were gradually absorbed by the Company.

[2] The Court of Assistants was not defined in the Charter. It seems to have been formed later as an executive body.

[3] Sometimes the authority was granted by the full Court of Assistants. The changes in the amount paid for entering books will have been noticed in Chapter IX.

[4] In some classes of books special licensers were required.

tinued till the Long Parliament in 1640, when the Star-Chamber, which exercised a considerable jurisdiction in matters concerning book-production, was abolished. Then it came to be recognised that the merits of a book were to be judged after its issue.

In 1560 the Stationers' Company had obtained such a reputation that the Lord Mayor included it amongst the Livery Companies of the City of London,[1] some of its members being thereby permitted to wear a certain dress on all state-occasions, and its order of precedence in all civic functions was allotted.

The Freedom of the Company, without which its exclusive rights could not be exercised, was conferred (1) by Apprenticeship,[2] (2) by Patrimony,[3] (3) by Redemption.[4] At the discretion of the authorities other persons were admitted as Brethren, and these enjoyed only a small part of the Freemen's privileges. As by a general order of 1556 it was required that apprentices should be at least twenty-four years of age upon the receipt of the freedom, it will be possible to estimate the ages of many of the Elizabethan stationers.[5] Certain of the Freemen were admitted into a small

[1] This seems to have been a restitution of ancient rights.

[2] The fee then payable was three shillings and fourpence. The earliest record of apprenticeship is in January, 1555, and the latest in June, 1605. Some were apprenticed merely to obtain the freedom. An express stipulation was often made that the apprentice was not to be taught any of the work connected with the issue of books. Up to 1578 a master receiving an apprentice had to pay sixpence upon presenting him to the Court of Managers. After that date the fee was half-a-crown. Many employers were fined for not presenting an apprentice at the time of his entering.

[3] Some who were entitled to their freedom by patrimony qualified also by apprenticeship.

[4] This was at the discretion of the governing body, who varied the fee, which in some cases was not much higher than that payable after apprenticeship. Peter Short, the printer of the 1598 *1 Henry IV.* and other quarto plays, became free by redemption.

[5] This cannot be done in all cases, as some were apprenticed at an age when this rule would not apply. Munday (see p. 227) was 23 when he was apprenticed. In no case could the apprenticeship be for less than seven years.

inner set called the Livery. The Company also from their own number appointed a Renter and an Assistant-Renter (who acted somewhat as sub-treasurers under the Wardens) and a Court of Assistants, forming with the Master and Wardens the governing body of the Company. A Star-Chamber decree in 1566 directed the Company to choose certain of their members to be known as Searchers, who amongst other duties had to discover books of which the Chamber disapproved. The decree defined the destination of such books and the punishments to be awarded to their producers.[1] The records of the Company from 1571 to 1576 are lost.

In the few years succeeding 1577 there was great trouble in the printing-trade. There were too many engaged in the work for it to be profitable,[2] and efforts were made to control by Act of Parliament the number of books issued, and of the apprentices by whom the ranks of the workmen were recruited. The Patents which had been in force for nearly twenty years were felt to be a great hardship, and the unprivileged printers, to defend themselves, issued pirated editions with the name of the patentee upon them.[3] The consideration of the grievance was referred to a Commission, which introduced reforms; some of the results of which were that the patentees gave up their profits in certain books[4] "for the

[1] Fines inflicted for various forms of "breaking of orders" were imposed with the strictest impartiality. Scarcely a member of the Company escaped. It is only fair to the later Stationers to say that if the entry of the fines had been continued in detail they would probably have had a record equal to their predecessors.

[2] In 1577 the London printers, Journeymen and all, numbered about 175.

[3] Roger Ward in 1582 printed 10,000 copies of a school-book which had been licensed to John Day. The proceedings of the Star-Chamber in this matter are given by Mr. Arber in Vol. II., pp. 753-69. It is interesting to note that to favour the Journeymen-printers no edition of a book except a few school-books and others was allowed to exceed 1250. In most instances the issue was smaller.

[4] Amongst others Tottell, who had the monopoly of the Law-books, gave up "Romea and Julietta" (see p. 91).

reliefe of the poore of the saide Companie," and the unprivileged printers were allowed to print books of which the original owner did not care to issue another edition, and on paying sixpence in the pound on the cost of production they were permitted to print books which had been long out of print.[1] The number of apprentices was also limited by authority. The existence of secret presses was another difficulty.[2] To prevent recourse to these, official lists of the number of authorised presses in London were issued from time to time.[3] Much in reference to the customs of the journeymen-printers is quoted by Mr. Arber in Vol. III., pp. 21-25, and in Vol. IV., pp. 13-20, and concerning those engaged in the book-trade generally, will be found most interesting extracts from *The Schollers Purgatory*, written and printed by Wither in 1625.

In 1637 the Star-Chamber decreed that no printing should be done except in London and at the Universities. More than fifty years before, the Stationers' Company, desiring to monopolise the whole of English printing, had endeavoured to prevent Cambridge taking any part in the work. But the days of restriction were over, for although the 1637 edict was re-affirmed in the order of the Lords and Commons of the 14th June, 1643, the following year heard the trumpet-blast of Milton, in which he was careful to avoid the charge of "introducing license, while he opposed licensing," and which settled for ever that only over the *circulation* of books

[1] This will explain a note made to many an entry in the Registers. A note was often added to the effect that the concession was granted for one edition only.

[2] A few of these were engaged about this time in bringing out some of the Mar-prelate pamphlets (see pp. 198 and 238).

[3] Arber prints lists that were made in 1583, 1615, and 1636. That of 1615 allotted the number of presses (in 14 cases two, in 5 one) that the master-printers were allowed. The last gives the succession of the master-printers from an early time, but, compiled long after the events which it chronicles, its dates are often inaccurate.

could supervision be tolerated by a free and enlightened people. Englishmen of to-day owe much of their literary freedom to Milton's manly, outspoken plea for a diversity of reading which cannot be cramped by a fear of meeting with unaccepted views, and for his eloquent and cogent argument that literature would be brought low and perhaps be lost sight of altogether if great thinkers, with either actual or potential reputations, were to have their works subjected to the censorship of a small body of paid licensers, whose caprices would be readily aroused and whose judgements might be easily warped. Milton's magnificent appeal still has force to kindle into enthusiasm all who read it.

This outline of the constitution of the Stationers' Company and of some of the incidents of its history will, if borne in mind, make the following notes[1] intelligible without repetition of many details that would otherwise be necessary.

The figures in brackets after the names of the plays refer to the lists on pp. 256-7, and thus show the way in which the editions of each printer and publisher had their authorship described. The books I mention as having been issued by these members of the Company are nearly always limited to those to which reference has been made in the foregoing pages. I have not as a rule said in the notes anything about the Register-entries of the Quartos. All these can be seen in Chapter IX. To facilitate reference the pages are given after the figures in brackets.

[1] I have not encumbered these notes with frequent references to authorities. Those who wish to verify the statements can easily do so, as the information in *Typographical Antiquities* is given under the names of the Stationers, and the full Tables of Contents in the volumes of Mr. Arber's *Transcript* group the references according to years, and an almost trustworthy alphabetical list of Printers and Publishers is given in the British Museum Catalogue.

PRINTERS.

James Roberts.

1600 *Titus Andronicus* (1), p. 59.
1600 *A Midsummer-Night's Dream* (8), p. 85.
1600 *The Merchant of Venice* (two), (7 and 8), p. 101.
1604 *Hamlet* (8), p. 135.
1605 *Hamlet* (8).

There is no record of James Roberts's apprenticeship. His freedom was obtained on June 27th, 1564.

He received apprentices from 1567 to 1602. His first was not made free till 1596. The last, whom he promised "to putt to schole till he can wryte and reade," was "dismissed out of the Company" "for disobedience and takinge wages within his prentiship." Some of them had been passed over to Roberts to serve the last part of their time which had been begun with other Stationers.

Many publications were entered to him from 1569 to 1606. Amongst the earliest was "The Death of Lucryssia" (see p. 119). In 1589 he and Richard Watkins received a twenty-one years' patent for printing "Almanacks and Prognostications," because they had bestowed much care on this kind of publication. In 1594 Charlwood's copyright of thirty or forty books of a very general character was transferred to Roberts, who in the following year was ordered to desist from printing a school-book, and then entered his first play. In 1599 he, a privileged printer, availed himself of the "sixpence in the £" arrangement. *Troilus and Cressida*, with a deferred order, appears against his name in 1603 (see p. 167). One of his books in 1604 had this proviso: if it "shalbe thought fytt to be printed Then Master **Robertes** shall haue the Woork-

PUBLISHERS.

John Harrison.

1594 *Lucrece*, p. 119.
1596 *Venus and Adonis*, p. 118.
1598 *Lucrece*.
1600 *Lucrece*.
1607 *Lucrece*.

When John Harrison received his freedom on August 19th, 1556, he paid three shillings and fourpence in lieu of giving a breakfast to the other members of the Company, which had been the earlier custom.

He received many apprentices between 1559 and 1604, less than half of whom passed to their freedom. One bound in 1576 for nine years was to "serue the first vj yeres of his apprentiship with **Jhon Symon** bookebynder in consideracon that the same **Jhon** shall teache him his occupacon." One in 1579 was "neuer to be made free for he hath runne awaye iij. tymes"; and in 1592 one was transferred to another stationer, having served four and a half years out of ten, two of which were then remitted.

From 1556 to 1610 many books, in which were included Latin and Greek works, were entered to him. In 1579, as one of the officers of the Company and in conjunction with the Queen's printer, he received license to issue a Latin translation of the Bible and commentary. The translation had been made by Emanuel Tremillius, an English version of one of the Psalms from which was included by King James in his *Essayes in Poesie*, reprinted in Arber's series. It is interesting to note that he and Bishop in 1580 had the copyright of of Calvin's *Commentaries*, a book which Mary had placed in the Royal Interdict of 1555, and that they passed over the

PRINTERS.

James Roberts *(Continued).*

manship of the printing for the Company and be paid for his woork."

When he became a master-printer is uncertain. He was not the possessor of a press in 1583. In 1578 he was one of six who apologised to the Wardens and Assistants for having made complaints; they promised not to offend again. Before August, 1594, he had married Charlwood's widow. He was fined two shillings and eightpence "as appereth 27 *Augusti* 1596. *inter ordinancones huius libri.*" This comes in the part which Mr. Arber did not receive permission to print. In the same year Roberts was taken into the Livery with a fee of twenty shillings. In 1597 he was one of the three "chozen to goo to dynner to my lord Maiours feast," which then and for many years after was held on October 29th. In 1602 he paid £5 to escape serving the office of Renter. In 1608 his business was sold to William Jaggard, to whom in 1615 the copyright of several books that had belonged to Roberts was transferred.

The 1600 *Titus Andronicus* Roberts printed for Edward White, one of the editions of *The Merchant of Venice* (conditionally entered to him in 1598) for Heyes in 1600, *Hamlet* (which had been entered to him in 1602) in 1604 and 1605 for Ling. He also printed for Simon Waterson Daniel's *Cleopatra* in 1594 with Edward Aldee, Kyd's *Cornelia* in 1594 for Ling and Busby, in 1595 a poem by Chapman for Richard Smith, Drayton's *Mortimeriados* for Matthew Lownes in 1596, *Euphues* in 1597 for Gabriel Cawood, for Edmond Mattes in 1598 Marston's *Pygmalion's Image* and his *Scourge of Villainy* in 1599 for Busby, the well-known antho-

PUBLISHERS.

John Harrison *(Continued).*

part on *Galatians* to Thomas Purfoot senior in 1581.

Soon after his enfranchisement Harrison's name appears in a list of the members who had to bear their share of the expenses of the Bridewell, and also in a subscription-list of "The benevolence gyven towardes our corperation." In 1558 he was fined for printing a ballad without license, and also in 1560 for opening his shop on Sunday. In 1562 he was fined a shilling because "he Revyled **Brodehed** with vnsemely Wordes." His adversary was fined three shillings. About this period he was one of twenty who were fined for selling the works of Nostradamus. With a fee of fifteen shillings he was received into the Livery in 1564, and in the same year with eighteen other booksellers, of whom the Senior Warden was one, he was fined for keeping his shop open on St. Luke's Day. In 1565 he was fined with several others "for Stechen of bookes which ys contrary to the orders of this howse, &c." In 1568 and 1570 he served the offices of Junior and Senior Renter. In 1573 he was Junior Warden. After this he often acted as one of the auditors of the Company's accounts, and in 1576 and at other times he was one of the Searchers. In 1577 he signed the complaint about privileged printers. In 1578 and 1580 he was Senior Warden, and was appointed to the Mastership in 1583, filling the post again in 1588 and 1596. Between 1584 and 1594 his name often appears as one of the Court of Assistants. In 1586 one of the members was fined five shillings "for diuerse vndecent speches by him vsed

PRINTERS.

James Roberts (*Continued*).

logy, *England's Helicon*, in 1600 for John Flasket, and Drayton's *Barons' Wars* for Ling in 1603. In 1605 he printed one of Greene's prose-works for Ling. He printed, probably in 1593, *Peirs Gaveston* (see p. 77) for Ling and Busby.

Roberts's work was done "at his house in Barbican," probably at the "signe of the Haulfe Eagle & Keye," which had been Charlwood's place of business. This device is on Roberts's 1600 *Midsummer-Night's Dream*.

Thomas Creede.

1594 *The Contention* (1), p. 65.
1595 *Locrine* (2), p. 89.
1598 *Richard III.* (8), p. 87.
1599 *Romeo and Juliet* (1), p. 91.
1600 *Henry V.* (1), p. 117.
1602 *Richard III.* (8).
1602 *The Merry Wives of Windsor* (8), p. 113.
1602 *Henry V.* (1).
1605 *Richard III.* (8).
1605 *The London Prodigal* (8), p. 127.
1612 *Richard III.* (8).

On October 7th, 1578, Thomas Creede was admitted to the freedom of the Company by Thomas East, to whom he was probably apprenticed in the time of which the Registers are lost.

From 1594 to 1602 he received a few apprentices, concerning one of whom in 1595 it is said "Thomas Creede promiseth the to enter into bond in xlli not to teache **John Wilkynson** the arte of pryntinge and to bring in his Indenture, to make the bonde by." In the same year he was fined half-a-crown for breaking the order concerning the presentation of apprentices at the time of enrolment.

PUBLISHERS.

John Harrison (*Continued*).

against master **harrison** assistant of this cumpanye."

Venus and Adonis and the 1594 *Lucrece* were printed by Field; but Harrison employed Short in 1598, his son in 1600, and Okes in 1607 for his other editions of *Lucrece*. Harrison published the 1577 edition of Holinshed's *Chronicles*, and with others the 1587 edition.

His place of business was "at the signe of the white Greyhound in Paules Church-yard," where the 1593 *Venus and Adonis* was to be sold, although Harrison's name does not appear in the imprint.

Edward White.

1600 *Titus Andronicus* (1), p. 59.
1611 *Titus Andronicus* (1).

Edward White, the son of a mercer of St. Edmundsbury, was apprenticed to William Loble for seven years from Michaelmas, 1565. The record of his freedom is lost.

From 1576 to 1604 he received many apprentices, the first of whom was his brother Andrew, who was made free in 1584. Another of his apprentices was John Wright, who was concerned in the publication of Shakspere's *Sonnets*. Not many of the others took up their freedom. White was fined in 1589 for not presenting one of them. After the record of one enrolment it is said: "This apprentise must serue this terme with Edmond Holland haberdasher vsinge the trade of bookbinding. and not to be accoumpted for any of master **White** number of prentises that he may haue by the ordonnances."

PRINTERS.

Thomas Creede (*Continued*).

After his enfranchisement the earliest notice about him in the Registers is in 1593. From then to 1609 many books were entered to him, for several of which from 1596 to 1600 he took advantage of the "sixpence in the £" concession. *Mother Redcap* (see p. 227) was licensed to him in 1595. In 1596 he received the copyright of *Kind-Harts Dreame* (see p. 233), which had been licensed to William Wright in 1592. Of one book in 1597 it was said: "This copie to be alwaies printed for **Nicholas Linge** by the seid **Thomas Creede** as often as it shalbe printed." Of a book that had been licensed to John Wolfe in 1597, Creede in 1598 was to have "the alowance thereof, leavinge out *the discourse touchinge the quene of Scottes* by him crossd out." To one of Creede's entries this note was added: "This cannot be alowed to hym because it is in Controuersye"; and on some other occasions the entry was made conditionally upon authority being obtained before the work was printed.

Creede probably worked as a Journeyman for some time. He was not owning a printing-press in 1583. In 1599 he was one of fourteen unprivileged printers who received notice that books which they had issued were to be burned in Stationers' Hall. Marston's *Pygmalion* and *The Scourge of Villainy* were amongst those marked for destruction. In the 1615 allotment of presses Creede was permitted to have one. Between this and 1620 he sold his business to Bernard Alsop and Thomas Fosset.

Creede printed the 1594 *Contention* for Millington, *Richard III.* in 1598 and 1602 for Wise, and in 1605 and 1612 for Lawe,

PUBLISHERS.

Edward White (*Continued*).

Many books were licensed to Edward White between 1577 and 1612, the year in which he died. In 1578-9 and again in 1594 he sinned, and was sinned against, in the matter of appropriation of ballads. On one of the occasions his offence is described as "without lycence and yt being an vndecent ballat." In 1580-1 the usual form of license is varied by the expression "Tollerated vnto him." In 1581 he entered a ballad about *Troilus and Cressida* (see p. 167). In 1582, in the case of a medical book by Peter Levens, the entry has the addendum, "And the said **Edward** hathe vndertaken to beare and discharge all troubles that maie arise for the printinge thereof." In 1584 one of his licenses had this note: "PROVIDED ALWAIES that yf yt belonge alreadye to anie other man or be collected out of anie book alredy extante in printe in English That then this licence to be voyd"; and in 1586 a similar notice is appended to the entries of some ballads and books, forty-eight of which he entered in one month. In 1592 he appropriated *The Spanish Tragedy* (see p. 245), which belonged to Abel Jeffes, having been entered to him on October 6th but not paid for at the time, and Jeffes had taken *Arden of Feversham* (attributed to Shakspere and several times reprinted, edited in 1887 by Mr. Bullen, and in 1888 by Drs. Warnke and Proescholdt), which was the property of White, who had entered it on April 8th. It was therefore decided that the copies of both should be forfeited for the benefit of the poor, and a fine of ten shillings in each case was inflicted. In 1594 White entered the unknown *Leire* Chronicle (see p. 149)

PRINTERS.

Thomas Creede *(Continued).*

the 1599 *Romeo and Juliet* for Burby, *Henry V.* in 1600 for Millington and Busby and in 1602 for Pavier, the 1602 *Merry Wives* for Johnson, and the 1605 *London Prodigal* for Butter. In 1593 he printed one of Greene's prose-works for William Ponsonby. In 1594 for William Barley he printed Lodge's *Looking Glass*, and reprinted it in 1598 for Barley and in 1602 for Pavier. In 1594 he also printed *The True Tragedy of Richard the Third* for Barley, in 1595 an edition of Nash's *Pierce Penilesse* (see p. 133) for Ling and W. W.'s translation of *Menæchmi* (see p. 71), in 1598 Lyly's *Mother Bombie* for Burby and Greene's *James IV.* and *The Famous Victories* (see p. 117) for both of which he had received licenses in 1594, in 1599 *Sir Clyomon* (see p. 205) and Greene's *Alphonsus*, in 1604 two editions of Marston's *Malcontent* for Aspley, in 1606 Chapman's *Monsieur D'Olive* for William Holmes, and in 1612 *The Merry Devil of Edmonton* for Johnson.

In 1595 Creede was "dwelling in Thames streete, at the signe of the Katheren-wheele, neare the olde Swanne." In 1600 he was "in the Old Chaunge, at the Eagle & Childe, neare Old Fish-streete."

William White.

1598 *Love's Labour's Lost* (6), p. 79.
1600 *The True Tragedy* (1), p. 69.
1608 *Richard II.* (Two), (8), p. 81.
1613 1 *Henry IV.* (2), p. 107.

The date of William White's apprenticeship is lost. As his freedom on April 10th, 1583, was obtained through Mis-

PUBLISHERS.

Edward White *(Continued).*

and Peele's *King David* (see p. 83); in 1596 a ballad about *Romeo and Juliet* (see p. 91). On June 25th, 1600, is this entry: "YT IS ORDERED touchinge a Disorderly ballad of *the wife of Bathe.* printed by **Edward aldee** and **william white** and sold by **Edward white**: That all the same ballates shalbe brought in and burnt And that either of the printers for theire Disorders in printinge yt shall pay **v**s. A pece for a fine. And that master **white** for his offence and Disorder in sellinge it shall pay **x**s. for a fine .**xx**s. And ther imprisonment is respited till another tyme." In 1603, as appears by the following note, a heavy fine was inflicted upon him: "YT IS ORDERED that master **Edward White** shall pay **vj**li. **xiij**s. **iiij**d. for a fine for that he had. **v**c. of the bookes of *basilicon Doron* of the second ympression Disorderly printed by **Edward Aldee** and hath sold the same number so that they cannot be taken beinge forfayted by thordonnances. **vj**li. **xiij**s. **iiij**d. And being to indure imprisonment for the same by thordonnances . his ymprisonment is respyted to the further order of the Company." This was about King James's book on the attributes of Kings, of which the first edition, consisting of only seven copies, had been printed in Edinburgh in 1599. The second was printed in London in 1603. Edward White was with others fined concerning it in April, 1603.

In 1585 Edward White and five others petitioned the Queen to deter and punish those who had printed the books for which John Day had received a patent, and to which, after Day's death, White

PRINTERS.

William White *(Continued).*

tress Jugge, he was doubtless apprenticed to John Jugge, who died before White's time was out.

He has a record of only three apprentices. Of the first in 1595 it is said: "PROVIDED ALWAIES, and yt is ordered and the said **william white** agreeth that this apprentize at any time duringe his apprentiship shall not be put to learne the arte of printinge." In 1603 the last, Bernard Alsop, was a transfer who afterwards succeeded to Creede's business.

From 1588 to 1615 many books were licensed to him, the earlier ones in conjunction with Gabriel Simpson, a fellow-apprentice with whom he was in partnership and who had received his freedom on the same day. In 1599 he received *The Spanish Tragedy* from Jeffes (see p. 270). On October 16th, 1600, White entered "A booke Called *the lettinge of Humours blood in the head vayne with a newe morisco Daunced by Seven Satyres vppon the bottome of DIOGENES tubbe,*" for buying which many booksellers were fined in the following March. In 1600 and 1603 he took advantage of the "six-pence in the £" arrangement.

On August 18th, 1595, White and Simpson were "fined at **Ten Shillinges** for printinge part of a book of master BROUGHTONS without aucthoritie. And they are ordered to bringe the leaues printed into the hall and not to procede with the printinge of the Residue till they have aucthoritie for it. Also their Imprisonment is Referred over till further order be taken. They agree to pay this fine the next court daie. **x**s. paid **vj**s. **viij**d. and the rest remitted."

In 1599 White was included with

PUBLISHERS.

Edward White *(Continued).*

and his co-signatories considered they were entitled. In 1588 he was elected into the Livery, the fee for which had then become twenty shillings. Afterwards he was one of the Court of Assistants. In 1589 he was fined one shilling "for none attendance on my Lord maiour vpon Allhallowen day." Some of his transactions soon after are thus chronicled: "*Item* Receaued by thhandes of **John wolf** for a quaterne of the *shorte Dyctyonaryes* menconed in the last Accoumpte, whiche quarterne he soulde to **Edwarde white xij**s. **iiij**d." and "*Item*, Receaued of **Edwarde White** for half a C of *shorte Dictionaries* **xxiiij**s. **viij**d." In 1593 he and Abel Jeffes had to pay £3 10s. for confiscated books. In 1594 he was one of the three "chosen to goo to my lord Maiours feast." In 1599 he was fined one shilling for being late on the day for election of the Company's officers. He was made Junior Warden in 1600. On February 22nd, 1604, his son was admitted to the freedom by patrimony, and on June 11th the father was fined one shilling "for beinge absent this Day at the Court . beinge reasonably warned thereunto." About this time he paid £10 "for his Dispensacon from the second vnderwardenship." In 1606 he became Senior Warden. After his death in 1612 his widow retained some interest in the business till 1624, when she transferred some copyrights to Edward Aldee. Her son had received some previously and had assigned them to Pavier and Wright in 1620.

White's edition of *Titus Andronicus* in 1600 was printed by Roberts. In 1582 and 1588 White published some of Munday's pamphlets, all of which perhaps

PRINTERS.

William White *(Continued).*

Creede and the other twelve printers whose books were then destroyed (see p. 270). In 1600 he was in trouble about printing the ballad of *The Wife of Bath* (see p. 271), in 1603 he offended by printing a book belonging to John Harrison, and in 1607 he entered a book which was soon discovered to belong to somebody else. William White seems not only to have been a partner with Simpson, but about the time of Simpson's death to have bought the business that had belonged to Richard Jones and William Hill; and soon after 1615, when he had received permission to work one press, to have passed the business on to his son John, who was made free on May 17th, 1614.

William White printed *Love's Labour's Lost* for Burby, the 1600 *True Tragedy* for Millington, the two 1608 editions of *Richard II.* and the 1613 1 *Henry IV.* for Lawe. After printing *The Spanish Tragedy* in 1599 without a publisher's name, he printed it in 1602 for Pavier. In 1616 he printed *Englishmen for my Money* (see p. 247), which had been entered to him in 1601.

Whilst White was in partnership with Simpson they were "at the White Horse in Fleet Lane, over against Sea-coal-lane." Afterwards, when working by himself, he was "dwelling in Cow-lane."

PUBLISHERS.

Edward White *(Continued).*

were printed by Charlwood, the predecessor of Roberts. In 1584, 1587, 1588, 1599, he issued some of Greene's prose-works, most of which were printed by John Wolfe. His 1594 edition of *Friar Bacon* was probably printed by Adam Islip (see p. 73). Edward Aldee printed for him the undated editions of Marlowe's *Massacre at Paris* and of Kyd's *Spanish Tragedy*. In 1592 and 1608 he published the English Faustus-history printed respectively by Thomas Orwin and John Windet, and in 1596 Edward Aldee printed for him an edition of that popular anthology, *The Paradise of Dainty Devices*, collected by Richard Edwards (see p. 224). He probably published the 1599 *King David* (see p. 83). With Ling he issued a medical work for Lodge in 1603 and a poem by Drayton in 1604, which latter Aldee printed.

Edward White had "his shoppe at the little North doore of S. Paules Church, at the signe of the gunne."

Nicholas Ling.

1603 *Hamlet* (with Trundell) (8), p. 135.
1604 *Hamlet* (8).
1605 *Hamlet* (8).
1607 *The Taming of a Shrew* (1), p. 97.

Nicholas Ling, the son of a parchment-maker of Norwich, was apprenticed to Henry Bynneman for eight years from Michaelmas, 1570. He received his freedom on January 19th, 1579.

From 1582 to 1604 he had several apprentices. Concerning one in 1585 it is said: "PROVIDED ALWAIES and yt is agreed that yf the said **nicholas linge** shall Departe with Any of his shoppes

PRINTERS.

Valentine Simmes.

1597 *Richard II.* (1), p. 81.
1597 *Richard III.* (1), p. 87.
1598 *Richard II.* (8).
1600 *The Contention* (1), p. 65.
1600 *Much Ado about Nothing* (8), p. 103.
1600 2 *Henry IV.* (8), p. 111.
1604 1 *Henry IV.* (7), p. 107.
1607 *The Taming of A Shrew* (1), p. 97.
1611 *The Troublesome Raigne* (3), p. 95.

Valentine Simmes, the son of an Oxford "sherman" (see 2 *Henry VI.*, IV. ii. 141), was apprenticed to Henry Sutton for eight years from Christmas, 1576. Sutton died before the time was up, and Simmes was made free on March 8th, 1585, by Joan Sutton, the widow.

There is a record of only four apprentices for him between 1594 and 1604.

In 1594, the date of his first book-entry, he had "Graunted vnto him the printinge of master LATYMERS *sermons* but yt is referred to the consent of most voyces, whether he shall print yt for the stock, or generally for the parteners, or for the wholle companye that will laye on paper PROUIDED that he is to paie vj^{d} in the li to thuse of the poore accordinge to the order." Between that date and 1610 he had several books licensed to him, of which five were by the "sixpence in the £" arrangement. In the early part of 1596, Bynneman's widow gave Simmes the residue of the copyrights which had belonged to her husband, Ling's master.

In 1595, for printing a school-book to which he was not entitled, Creede had his press and the sheets seized. He was fined one shilling in 1598 "for printinge a thinge disorderly," and in the following

PUBLISHERS.

Nicholas Ling *(Continued).*

That then he shall putt out this Apprentice to some of ye cumpanie at ye Discretion and appointment of the master and Wardens for the tyme beinge." One entered in 1597 was "putt away for vntruth and mysbehavior and neuer to be made free." It was said of one in 1602 that he was "never bound gone away and neuer to be free." One of his apprentices was John Helme.

Between 1582 and 1607 many books were entered to Ling. His first was in a conJoint entry with Charlwood, the predecessor of Roberts, with whom Ling was associated in the production of *Hamlet.* In 1584, on the same day that Calvin's Commentary on the Epistle to the Philippians (see p. 267) was licensed to him, he was fined for printing it without order. It is possible that for a short time Ling may have had a press, perhaps on hire from Mistress Bynneman; for not only is there this reference—which by itself need not be taken literally,—but he is said to have printed the 1598 *Rosalynde* and the 1600 *Every Man out of his Humour.* In 1590 *Rosalynde* (see p. 125) was entered to him and Busby. Ling and Millington on May 17th, 1594, entered *The Rich Jew of Malta*, a ballad on which had been entered by Danter in the same month. In 1597 he entered, and afterwards edited and enlarged, the book of which Meres's *Wits Treasury* (see p. 9) is the second part.

In 1594 Ling was fined three shillings and fourpence "for offendinge in buyinge and dispersinge of *psalmes* Disorderly printed." He and Creede were associated by authority in 1597 (see p. 270). Ling was received into the Livery in 1598, when the fee had become £2. In

PRINTERS.

Valentine Simmes *(Continued)*.

year he was in trouble with Creede and others (see p. 270). In 1601 he had to pay three shillings and fourpence "for pryntinge *A proclamacon* formerly printed for the Crowne office whiche he hathe nowe this tyme printed without Alowance or entrance;" and in 1603 for printing "a ballad belonginge to mistres **aldee**" he was fined thirteen shillings and fourpence; and in the same year, perhaps alluding to this ballad, is this note: "YT IS ORDERED that he shall presently bring into the hall to be vsed according to the ordonance in yat behalf . Thirtie bookes of *the welshbate* . and all the ballades that he hath printed of *the Traitours lately Arrayned at Winchester*. also YT IS ORDERED that he shall pay **xiij**s **iiij**d for a fine for printing the same book and ballad without Licence. And not to meddle with printing or selling any of the same bookes or ballades hereafter." A small fine "for breakinge order" was inflicted upon him in 1604, and in 1610 is this entry in reference to Dekker's *Shoemaker's Holiday*: "IT IS AGREED that **Valentyne Symms** shall haue the workmanshipp of the printinge thereof for the vse of the sayd **John wrighte** duringe his lyfe, yf he haue a printinge house of his owne." After his troublesome career his business seems to haue passed to Richard Badger, although six of his books were transferred to Edward Griffin in 1619.

Simmes printed the editions of *Richard II.* and *Richard III.* in 1597 and 1598 for Wise, *The Contention* in 1600 for Millington, *Much Ado* and 2 *Henry IV.* for Wise and Aspley, 1 *Henry IV.* in 1604 for Lawe, the 1607 *A Shrew* for Ling, and *The*

PUBLISHERS.

Nicholas Ling *(Continued)*.

1601 he was one of twenty-eight booksellers fined half-a-crown each "for their Disorders in buyinge of the bookes of *humours lettinge blood in the vayne* beinge newe printed after yt was first forbydden and burnt." This volume of Satires by Samuel Rowlands had been licensed to William White in 1600 (see p. 272). In April, 1603, with Edward White and others, he was fined about the King's book (see p. 271). This was a bad time for Ling, concerning whom and two others on December 5th of the same year it was "ORDERED that they shall pay xs. A pece for their fines for printinge a booke called *the wonderfull yere* without Aucthoritie or entrance. contrary to thordonnances for pryntinge. Also that they shall forbeare and neuer hereafter entermedle to printe or sell the same book or any parte thereof. Also that they shall presently bringe into the hall to be vsed accordinge to thordonnance in yat behalf so many of the said bookes as they or any to their vse haue left in their handes. And their ymprisonment for this offence is respited till further Consideracon and order herein be had." In the following year he was ffned £10 for an offence unnamed, or perhaps for declining to take office. He was probably dead in 1607 when some of Shakspere's plays, which he had received from Burby, were transferred to Smythick (see p. 79).

The editions of *Hamlet* in 1604 and 1605 and probably that in 1603 (see p. 135) were printed by Roberts, and the 1607 *A Shrew* by Simmes. Ling published in 1582 a book for Munday which John Charlwood printed, in 1590 with Busby

PRINTERS.

Valentine Simmes *(Continued)*.

Troublesome Raigne in 1611 for Helme. For Aspley he printed *A Warning for Fair Women* in 1599, and Marston's *Malcontent* in 1604. In 1599 he printed one of Chapman's plays, in 1600 he printed *Sir John Oldcastle* for Pavier, in 1604 *Faustus* for Thomas Bushell, and in 1604 and 1606 some of Ben Jonson's *Masques* for Blount and Thorp, for the latter of whom he printed Chapman's *Gentleman Usher* in 1606. He printed the undated *Patterne of peynfull aduentures* "for the Widow Newman" (see p. 159).

Simmes in 1595 was "dwelling in Adling street, at the signe of the white Swan, neare Bainards castel."

Richard Field.

1593 *Venus and Adonis*, p. 118.
1594 *Venus and Adonis*.
1594 *Lucrece*, p. 119.
1596 *Venus and Adonis*.

Henry Field, a tanner of Stratford-on-Avon, with whom John Shakspere had been officially brought into contact, sent two of his sons into business as stationers. Richard was apprenticed for seven years from Michaelmas, 1579, when "It is agreed yat this Apprentis shall serue ye first . vj. yeres of his apprentiship with ye said **vautrollier** to learne ye art of printinge . and ye vijth yere with ye said . **g. bisshop.**"

Richard, having been made free on February 6th, 1587, by George Bishop, took a few apprentices from 1589 to 1604, one of whom was his brother Jasper.

From 1588 to 1623, sometimes under

PUBLISHERS.

Nicholas Ling *(Continued)*.

he issued some of Greene's prose-works, one of which Thomas Orwin was employed to print, in 1594 Kyd's *Cornelia* printed by Roberts and in 1595 an edition by himself without printer's name and one of Nash's *Pierce Penilesse* which Creede printed and with Burby another book by Nash in 1599, by himself and with Edward White and John Flasket he published several of Drayton's works from 1596 to 1606, to print some of which Roberts and Short were employed, in 1600 he issued *Every Man out of his Humour*, *Kemps nine daies wonder* (see p. 155) printed by Edward Aldee, and, with Burby and Heyes, *England's Parnassus*, a popular book of poetical quotations. In 1605 and 1607 he published some of Greene's prose-works, one of which has Roberts's initials as printer. Probably about 1593, for in that year it was entered to them (see p. 77), Ling and Busby published Drayton's *Peirs Gaveston*, which was printed by Roberts.

At first Ling was living "in Paules Churchyarde, at the signe of the Maremaide" in Knightrider Street, formerly his master's place of business; but from 1591 to 1600 his shop is simply said to be "at the West end of Paules" or "at the little West doore of Poules," which he probably took when Busby left it; but in 1604 he had moved to a "shoppe vnder Saint Dunstons Church in Fleetstreet," near, if not at the actual place, where Busby had gone.

PRINTERS.

Richard Field *(Continued).*

the name of Ricardo del Campo, he printed a large number of books, among which were many French, Latin, and high-class books, as Vautrollier, whose widow Field married in 1588, and to whose business he succeeded, had a patent for Latin and school-books. Field in 1594 entered a book on the "sixpence in the £" arrangement.

In 1589 he was fined ten shillings for having "printed a booke Contrary to order," and half-a-crown for not presenting an apprentice at time of enrolment. He was received into the Livery in 1598, paying a fee of £2; and in the same year, and again in 1604, was chosen one of the three to represent the Company at the Lord Mayor's feast. In 1599 he was in trouble with Creede and others (see p. 270). In 1604 (when he paid £10 to escape acting as Renter) he was one of the Court of Assistants, and in the next year was Junior Warden. In 1611 and 1613 he was Senior Warden. At the official allowance of presses in 1615, Field was permitted to work two. He was Master of the Company in 1619 and 1622. About 1625 he was dead, and Mistress Field sold the business to George Miller (to whom she transferred many of her husband's copyrights on April 3rd, 1626) and Richard Badger (a native of Stratford-on-Avon), who seems also to have had an interest in the business which had been Simmes's.

Field probably printed all the above-named editions of Shakspere's poems for Harrison (see p. 269). Without publisher's name, Field printed in 1589 (Puttenham's) *The Arte of English Poesie*, interesting to Shakspere-students, being,

PUBLISHERS.

Sampson Clarke.

1591 *The Troublesome Raigne* (1), p. 95.

The record of Sampson Clarke's apprenticeship is amongst the lost papers of the Stationers' Company. When he was made free on March 26th, 1583, his sponsors were George Buck and William Browne.

A few apprentices served under him between 1587 and 1596. Of two in the last of those years it is said. "YT IS ORDERED that these twoo apprentises alowed to **Sampson clerk** shall not be putt to pryntinge bookeselling or any faculty perteyninge to the Art of Stationers."

Only a few books were entered to him from 1583 to 1589. An entry in 1587 is accompanied by this note: "Which as Master HARTWELL certyfyithe by his hande to the written Copie . my Lordes grace of CANTERBURY is content shall passe without anie thinge added to yt before it be pervsed."

Clarke was one of the booksellers against whom Edward White and others petitioned in 1585 (see p. 000). He was admitted into the Livery in 1598 with a fee of £2.

In 1584 Clarke employed Thomas East to print a prose-work by Lodge. The name of the printer of the 1597 *Troublesome Raigne* is not given, but the device on the title-page is apparently that of Thomas Orwin, who printed Greene's *Menaphon* for Clarke in 1589.

In 1584 Clarke had "his shop by Guyld Hall." In 1589 he was "behinde the Royall Exchange," where he was still in business in 1591.

PRINTERS.

Richard Field *(Continued).*

as Mr. Arber, in the Introduction to the Reprint in his Series, says, an "original and clever book on Poetry, Rhetoric, and Good Manners" in Elizabeth's time. In 1594 he printed for William Ponsonby a poem by Chapman.

In 1589 Field was "dwelling in the black-Friers, neere Ludgate," where Vautrollier had carried on business.

John Danter.

1597 *Romeo and Juliet* (1), p. 91.

John Danter, the son of an Oxfordshire weaver, was apprenticed from Michaelmas, 1582, to John Day for eight years, one of which was remitted. Day died in 1584 (see p. 271). On April 15th, 1588, Danter was "put ouer to the said **Robert Robinson** fromhensforthe vntill the feast of Sainct michas tharchangell in *Anno* 1589. And then to be made free And where there is another yere moore then to comme of his prentiship: that yere beinge the Eight yere conteined in his Indenture is frely Remitted by the consent of mistres **Day** *alias* **Stone.**" He received his freedom on September 30th, 1589.

When his only-recorded apprentice was made free in 1602, Danter then paid the entrance-fee, as his pupil "had serued out his prentiship without presentment."

Between 1591 and 1596 several books were entered to Danter, amongst them being *The Repentance of Robert Greene,* which was published by Burby in 1592 without printer's name. In 1594 he entered a play and a ballad about *Titus Andronicus* (see p. 59), and a ballad about

PUBLISHERS.

Thomas Heyes.

1600 *The Merchant of Venice* (8), p. 101.

The date of Thomas Heyes's original apprenticeship is lost. On January 8th, 1580, he was transferred to William Lownes, on account of the death of John Sheppard, his first master, and was made free on March 31st, 1584.

Between 1589 and 1601 there is a record of only three apprentices serving under him.

The few books entered to him were all from 1600 to 1602, when his entries were made in conjunction with Short.

In 1601 he was fined with Ling and others about Rowlands' book (see p. 275), and the following year was received into the Livery, paying a fee of £2. In 1605 he was dead. His son Lawrence (see p. 101) was made free of the Company on November 7th, 1614.

The Merchant of Venice published by Thomas Heyes was printed by Roberts. Also in 1600 Heyes was one of the publishers of *England's Parnassus* (see p. 276).

Thomas Heyes's place of business was "in Paules Church-yard, at the signe of the Greene Dragon."

William Leake.

1599 *Venus and Adonis,* p. 118.
1599 *The Passionate Pilgrim,* p. 120.
1602 *Venus and Adonis* (two).

The entry of William Leake's apprenticeship is in the lost portion of the Company's Registers. His master was probably Francis Coldock, by whom he was made free on October 6th, 1584, the day of Henry Chettle's enfranchisement

PRINTERS.

John Danter *(Continued)*.

The Jew of Malta. He entered *Green's Groatsworth of Wit* in 1596, in which year it was printed by Creede. On the "sixpence in the £" arrangement he then printed two books, one of which had belonged to Day, his former master.

During his apprenticeship Danter and some others got into trouble through printing a grammar, to the copyright of which they had no claim. They were to "henceforth be dysabled to prynte otherwise then as Journemen in pryntinge, and shall never hereafter keepe any printinge house to their or any of their owne behoof." This stringent order was, so far as Danter at least was concerned, relaxed in 1591, when he and Chettle were allowed to become partners with William Hoskins. In 1593, when he entered Greene's *Orlando Furioso*, which in the following year was put over to Burby, "PROUIDED ALWAIES, and yt is agreed that soe often as the same booke shalbe printed . the saide **John Danter** to haue thimpryntinge thereof," a warrant was issued for him; and in 1596 his press, man, "j forme" and "j heape" were brought to the hall; and in 1597 an order went forth that his "presses and l'res shalbe defaced and made vnserviceable for pryntinge;" and this in the year when, on September 6th, a book was entered to Burby, "Reservinge the Workmanship of the printing at all tymes to the said **John Danter**." He was dead before October 6th, 1600.

The 1597 *Romeo and Juliet* has no name of publisher. In 1592 and 1596 Danter printed two of Nash's books. He only printed for Burby the 1594 *Orlando Furioso*, and in the same year

PUBLISHERS.

William Leake *(Continued)*.

From 1588 to 1604 half-a-dozen apprentices entered under him.

From 1592 to 1602 he was busy in issuing books. In the earlier year it is said of one that it is "to be translated into Englishe, and after pervsed and lawfullye allowed before it be put to printe." As he was never the owner of a press, the entry in 1602 crediting him with printing a book by the "sixpence in the £" arrangement is probably a mistake. There are no entries of books to him after 1602, except one in 1614 in conjunction with others. In 1618 he appears as an officer of the Company.

In 1585 Leake was one of the alleged offenders against Edward White and others (see p. 271). He was fined fourpence in 1586 for opening his shop "contrary to order on the 19 (? 18) of October beinge holyday." In 1598 he Joined the Livery, paying a fee of £2, and in 1600 he was chosen one of the three "to goo to my lord maiors feast." He was amongst the twenty-eight booksellers who were fined in 1601 (see p. 275). In 1602 several books were transferred to him from Gabriel Cawood. In 1604 he paid £10 rather than serve the office of Renter, and in the same year he was Junior Warden and again in 1606, acting as Senior Warden in 1610 and 1614. In 1617 he passed over a large number of books to Barrett (see p. 105). In the following year he was Master of the Company.

Leake's editions of *Venus and Adonis* were issued without printer's name. The 1599 *Passionate Pilgrim* was printed by someone whom William Jaggard employed. Leake published in 1601 the two

PRINTERS.

John Danter *(Continued).*

he printed Lodge's *Wounds of Civil War* without name of publisher; but from the place at which it was to be sold, obviously for Thomas Gosson, the father of the publisher of *Pericles*. In 1595, for Ralph Hancocke and John Hardie, he printed Peele's *Old Wives' Tale.*

Danter carried on his business "dwelling in Hosier Lane neere Holburne Conduit."

Peter Short.

1594 *The Taming of A Shrew* (1), p. 97.
1595 *The True Tragedy* (1), p. 69.
1596 *The Taming of A Shrew* (1).
1598 *Lucrece*, p. 119.
1598 1 *Henry IV.* (1), p. 107.

Peter Short, on March 1st, 1589, became a member of the Stationers' Company by Redemption, for which he paid six shillings.

Amongst the four apprentices whose enrolment under him is recorded from 1592 to 1602 was Richard Badger from Stratford-on-Avon, who bought a share in the business which had belonged to his fellow-townsman Field. For keeping one of his apprentices "vnpresented aboue thappointed tyme" Short was fined one shilling in 1602.

From 1591 to 1602 he entered a tolerably large number of publications, among which were many music-books. His first entries were with Richard Yardley, with whom he was for a short time in partnership. In 1595 a license was granted to him for "the *prentize Indentures* to be printed for the Companie of Merchant tailours." For unlawfully printing these another stationer was fined in December,

PUBLISHERS.

William Leake *(Continued).*

parts of *Robin Hood* in which Munday and Chettle were concerned (see p. 227), and in 1606-7, 1609, and 1613 editions of *Euphues*.

In 1599 Leake was "at the Greyhound in Paules Churchyard," which may possibly have been the place of business of Harrison, from whom he received the copyright of *Venus and Adonis* (see p. 118). William Welby was publishing there in 1609. From 1606 Leake was "dwelling in Paules Churchyard, at the Signe of the Holy Ghost," a house formerly occupied by Gabriel Cawood.

The William Leake who was made free on July 22nd, 1623, and admitted to the Livery in 1628, and who in 1639 published editions of *Philaster* and of *A King and No King*, copyrights of which, with that of *Othello*, were transferred to him in that year, was probably the son of the first-named William Leake, and is thus referred to in *The Obituary of Richard Smyth* on February 12th, 1673, "Old Wm. Leake, stationer wthin Temple Barr in Fleet Street, buried."

John Busby.

1600 *Henry V.* (with Millington) (1), p. 117.

When John Busby, the son of a London cordwainer, was enrolled as an apprentice to Oliver Wilkes for nine years from Michaelmas, 1576, the following note was added: "MEMORANDUM yt is agreed yat this apprentice abouenamed shall serve his whole apprentishood with ANDREWE MANSELL Draper exercisinge tharte of a Stacioner." Busby was made free on November 8th, 1585.

Almost at once an apprentice was trans

PRINTERS.

Peter Short *(Continued).*

1596. In 1598 to one of his entries is appended a memorandum saying, "PROVIDED that this entrance shall not be effectuall if any other haue Right to this booke by any former entrance;" and to another, entering with others the works of Josephus, "To be translated out of French into Englishe . and to be their Copie to printe, bringinge better and sufficient aucthoryty for yt first and before they print yt." Towards the end of his printing career Short entered books with Heyes.

In 1598 he was received into the Livery with a fee of £2, and in the year following he was one of the fourteen concerned in the trouble referred to under Creede's name. In 1601 he was one of the three who "went to my Lord maiours feast." At some time (the date given in the 1636 "Succession of the Master-printers" must be wrong) Short seems, with John Windet, to have come into possession of Henry Denham's business. In 1603 Short was dead, and Humphrey Lownes took on the widow and the business.

Short printed *A Shrew* for Burby, *The True Tragedy* for Millington, *Lucrece* for Harrison, and 1 *Henry IV.* for Wise. In 1595 he printed Daniel's *Civil Wars* for Simon Waterson (see p. 63) and the Countess of Pembroke's *Antony* for William Ponsonby, in 1598 Drayton's *England's Heroical Epistles* for Ling and Meres's *Palladis Tamia* for Burby, in 1599 Daniel's *Cleopatra*, and in 1600 a work by Marlowe for Walter Burre.

Whilst partner with Yardley, and when working by himself, Short was "dwelling on Bread Street hill, at the Signe of the Starre."

PUBLISHERS.

John Busby *(Continued).*

ferred to him from Ling. The only other of whom there is a record entered in 1598.

From 1590 to 1614 several publications were entered to him. The earliest were with Ling (see p. 274). In 1595 he received "by assignement from **Elizabeth wynnyngton** wydowe of **John Wynnyngton** Staconer Deceased Three copies" which were "supposed to haue belonged to the said **John wynnington** . . . . PROVYDED ALWAIES that yf the said **Elizabeth** marrie againe to any of the Companie . That then she shall haue their copies againe as in her former estate PROVYDED ALWAIES that yf yt shall appere that these copies did apperteyne to any other man and not to the said **Wynnyngton** That then the said **John Busby** shall haue no Interest to them or any of them by force of this entrance." In 1599, with John Oxenbridge, Busby entered Heywood's *Edward IV.*, but before publication in 1600 he transferred his share to Humphrey Lownes. In 1602 he had somewhat similar dealings with *The Merry Wives of Windsor* (see p. 113). In 1606 to him and Trundell a comedy was entered, "PROVIDED that they are not to printe yt tell they bringe good aucthoritie and licence for the Doinge thereof." With Nathanael Butter he entered *Lear* in 1607 (see p. 149) and Heywood's *Lucrece* in 1608 (see p. 119).

The 1600 *Henry V.* was printed by Creede. Although Ling and Busby had entered Lodge's *Rosalynde*, it was published by Busby and Thomas Gubbin in 1590, when Thomas Orwin printed it. Busby published other of Lodge's books, employing various printers. He published in 1592 Nash's *Pierce Penilesse*

PRINTERS.

Thomas Purfoot.

1622 *Richard III.* (8), p. 87.
1622 1 *Henry IV.* (7), p. 107.

Thomas Purfoot, an original member of the Stationers' Company, around whose name gathers much of the greatest interest in connection with the history of printing, apprenticed his son Thomas, who printed some of the Shakspere Quartos, to Richard Collins for seven years from Midsummer, 1584, and admitted him to the freedom of the Company on October 8th, 1590, "*per patronagium.*"

He has only one enrolment of an apprentice, and then the following note was added: "MEMORANDUM that the said **Thomas purfoote** hath promised that yf his father hereafter Require to haue an Apprentise alowed vnto him . Then he shall haue this apprentise of his sons putt ouer vnto him in stede thereof."

Before 1606 there are only two entries of books to him, the first of which was with Blower. From then he had licenses for several publications. Twenty books that had belonged to his father, who was dead in 1615, were transferred to him in that year. Amongst these was included "The Imprintinge of *the breifes of all letters pattentes vnder the great seale of England for Causualties and losses by sea and by lande.*" This had originally been granted to his father in 1587, and from it many licenses arose.

In 1591 the newly-enfranchised son was "licensed by ye Company, vppon ye Archbishops letter to succeede his father;" but in 1599 he received the censure of the Company because he had

PUBLISHERS.

John Busby *(Continued).*

printed by Abel Jeffes, and probably in 1593 Peele's *Honour of the Garter,* the printer of which was "the Widdowe Charlewood" whom Roberts married. In 1594 with Ling he published Kyd's *Cornelia,* in 1598 he issued Marston's *Scourge of Villainy* (both printed by Roberts), a book by Dekker in 1609, and with others an edition of Drayton's *Poly-Olbion* in 1613.

In 1592 Busby's shop was "neere to the West doore of Paules." In 1596 he seems to have been in business "in S. Dunstan's churchyard in Fleet-street, at the little shop next Cliffords Inne." The 1600 *Henry V.* was to be sold "in Carter Lane, next the Powle head," which doubtless was Busby's house then, as Millington's place of business is stated in those books of which he was sole publisher.

Busby had a son (see p. 137) who was made free on June 15th, 1607, and who acted as Renter in 1630.

William Jones.

1602 *Thomas, Lord Cromwell* (2), p. 105.

There were two contemporary stationers named William Jones. One, a printer and always so distinguished in the Registers, was enfranchised on July 5th, 1596, and farmed Blower's business from the latter's widow. The publisher was the son of a Northamptonshire yeoman, and was apprenticed to John Judson for nine years from Michaelmas, 1578, becoming free on October 19th, 1587.

PRINTERS.

Thomas Purfoot *(Continued)*.

"betaken himself to another vocation," and had been "disorderly and obstinate." On September 3rd, 1604, he was fined a crown, half of which he paid the following April. Then, as will be seen above, he seems to have mended his ways. In 1615 he was authorised to work two presses. In 1617 he was one of the three "appointed to goe to my lord Mayours feast." He was Renter in 1620, Junior Warden in 1629, and Senior Warden in 1634. In 1635 he was one of the Referees "for Considering the Complaintes of the Jorneymen Printers," and in 1637 he was one of the twenty whom the Star-Chamber allowed to be Master-Printers.

Purfoot printed his two Shakspere plays for Lawe. Thomas Purfoot, either father or son, printed Marston's *Dutch Courtezan* for John Hodgets in 1605, and his *Parasitaster* for William Cotton in 1605, and the Pericles novel for Butter in 1608.

The father in 1567 was printing "in Paules Churcheyarde, at the Signe of the Lucrece." In 1580 his press was "in Newgate Market, within the new Rents, at the Signe of the Lucrece." In 1581 he had a shop, where he was selling books, "without Newgate, ouer against Saint Sepulchers Church;" but went on printing till 1591 at least in Newgate Market, and in 1598 his press is described as being "in St. Nicholas Shambles within the newe Rents."

PUBLISHERS.

William Jones *(Continued)*.

There is a record of three apprentices being entered to him from 1590 to 1600.

Many books were entered to him from 1590 to 1618, when he died. His widow then transferred *Mucedorus* and another book to John Wright. In 1590 one was licensed "PROVIDED ALWAIES that if it laufully belonge to any other man, Then this entrance to be void." Of one in 1597 it is said: "This entrance is condycionall that no other man haue Right to the seid booke."

In 1594 he was fined sixteen pence, probably for some such offence as Millington's connected with a psalm-book. He paid £2 as his fee when elected to the Livery in 1604, and in the following year he was one of the three "appointed to goo to my Lord Maiours feaste."

Jones published Marlowe's *Edward II.* in 1594 and 1598 (see p. 77), and in 1594 a book by Nash which Danter printed, Lyly's *Woman in the Moon* in 1597, Chapman's *Blind Beggar of Alexandria* in 1598 (entered to him in that year "vppon Condicon thatt yt belonge to noe other man"), and *Mucedorus* in 1598, 1610, 1613, and 1615, the last of which was printed by Okes.

All the time that William Jones was in business as a publisher he was "dwelling at the Signe of the Gun, neere Holburne Conduict."

PRINTERS.

William Jaggard.

1599 *The Passionate Pilgrim*, p. 120.
1612 *The Passionate Pilgrim*.

William Jaggard, described at the time of his apprenticeship and for some time after as Jagger, was the son of a barber-surgeon of London. He was apprenticed to Henry Denham for eight years from Michaelmas, 1584, and was made free on December 6th, 1591. His brother John, apprenticed in the same year to Richard Tottell, obtaining his freedom in 1593, became a publisher and, after having been elected into the Livery in 1602, was Junior Warden in 1619.

William received a few apprentices from 1595 to 1604, one of them being Thomas Cotes, the printer of the Second Folio.

From 1595 to 1622 William Jaggard had licenses for a large number of publications. In 1608 he availed himself of the "sixpence in the £" arrangement. In the same year, when Heywood's *Britain's Troy* (see p. 120) was entered to him, the following note was added: "PROVIDED that yf any question or trouble growe hereof . Then he shall answere and discharge yt at his owne Losse and costes."

On October 23rd, 1600, he and Blower were fined "for printinge without licence and contrary to order, a little booke of Sir ANTHONY SHERLLEies *voiage* And also that they shall presently accordinge to thordynance in yat behalf, forfayt and bringe into the hall all the said bookes so printed. And their Imprysonment for this offence is Referred ouer to another tyme" (see p. 252). Jaggard paid his

PUBLISHERS.

Andrew Wise.

1597 *Richard II.* (1), p. 81.
1597 *Richard III.* (1), p. 87.
1598 *Richard II.* (8).
1598 *Richard III.* (8).
1598 1 *Henry IV.* (1), p. 107.
1599 1 *Henry IV.* (7).
1600 *Much Ado about Nothing* (with Aspley) (8), p. 103.
1600 2 *Henry IV.* (with Aspley) (8), p. 111.
1602 *Richard III.* (8).

Andrew Wise, a Yorkshire yeoman's son, described at the time of his enrolment as Wythes, was apprenticed to Henry Smith for eight years from Lady Day, 1580, and re-apprenticed twelve months after for the same period to Thomas Bradshaw, by whom he was made free on May 26th, 1589.

From 1591 to 1598 three apprentices entered under him.

His name appears in connection with a few books only from 1596 to 1601. In 1595 a fine of forty shillings, which was reduced to five shillings, was inflicted upon him about a sermon which was licensed to him in the following year. The preacher of the sermon said, in the dedication of the authorised edition, "as much diuersitie as there is betweene yuorie and woode: so much there is betweene that Sermon which was first once preached, and that which was afterward twise printed."

Wise was fined with Ling and others in 1601 (see p. 275), and after being fined four shillings about *Basilicon Doron* (see p. 271) his apparently small stock-in-trade was transferred to Lawe (see p. 81).

Wise employed Simmes to print his

PRINTERS.

William Jaggard (*Continued*).

share on the 7th of the following September. From 1600 to 1623 he was Printer to the City of London. Having bought Roberts's business, he received nine of his copyrights in 1615, and was in that year officially allowed to work two presses. The 1623 Folio, printed by his son Isaac, who succeeded to his business, was issued partly at his charges.

The 1599 *Passionate Pilgrim*, published by Leake, does not seem to have been printed by Jaggard's press, but by some-one employed by him. He printed *A Woman Killed with Kindness* for John Hodgets in 1607, and in 1609, without publisher's name, Heywood's other book referred to above. William Jaggard probably worked at Roberts's place of business (see p. 269).

Ralph Blower.

1608 *A Yorkshire Tragedy* (4), p. 133.

Ralph Blower, the son of a Shropshire husbandman, was apprenticed to Richard Tottell for seven years from October 1st, 158;. Tottell, who was "Amerced according to thordenances for keping this Apprentise two yeres vnpresentid," made him free on November 3rd, 1594.

From 1595 to 1600 Blower had three apprentices. The first was "discharged from his master to serue out of this Company." The second died in 1600, when another was allowed in his place.

Blower entered a great many books from 1595 to 1614. In 1602 he was licensed "to printe, *all billes and peticons that are hereafter to be printed for the poore prisoners of the Gatehouse at Westminster,*

PUBLISHERS.

Andrew Wise (*Continued*).

two Quartos of *Richard II.* and his 1597 *Richard III.*, Short for the 1598 and Stafford for the 1599 1 *Henry IV.*, and Creede for the 1598 and 1602 *Richard III.* Simmes printed *Much Ado* and 2 *Henry IV.* for Wise and Aspley. In 1594 Wise issued a book by Nash.

Wise, during the whole time he was in business, had "his shop in Paules church yard at the signe of the Angel."

Thomas Millington.

1594 *The Contention* (1), p. 65.
1595 *The True Tragedy* (1), p. 69.
1600 *The Contention* (1).
1600 *The True Tragedy* (1).
1600 *Henry V.* (with Busby) (1), p. 117.

Thomas Millington, the son of an Oxfordshire husbandman, was apprenticed to Henry Carre for eight years from St. Bartholomew's Day, 1583, and was made free on November 8th, 1591.

Of one of his three apprentices between 1594 and 1598, a note was made that he was "gone from his master and neuer to be free."

Books were entered to Millington from 1594 to 1603. In the first of those years with Ling he entered *The Rich Jew of Malta*, and in the same year he received licenses for a book and ballads on the subject of the murder of Beech by Merry, the book possibly being the play written by Day and Haughton (see p. 247) In 1595 one that had received the authority of one of the wardens was licensed to him "Provided that before the printinge

PRINTERS.

Ralph Blower *(Continued).*

Ludgate, Newgate, bothe the Counters in London, The Counter in Southwark, The Clink, the Marshallsea, The kinges benche and White Lyon. PROVIDED that they be lawfull to be printed and apperteine to no other man by former entrance." In 1603 he printed on the "sixpence in the £" system. In 1614 to him and Leonard Snodham a law-book was "Entred (by the license of the Company to print one Impression of 1500 for master ASH paying to the Company at the finishing thereof either x^s, or one quartern of bookes)."

In 1599 Blower was one of those in trouble with Creede (see p. 270), and in 1600 he was fined with William Jaggard (see p. 284). In 1615 he was allowed one press by authority. Blower and George Shaw bought Thomas (not Henry, as given in the 1636 succession-list) Scarlet's business, but afterwards bought out Shaw. Blower's wife, who survived him, let the business to William Jones, the printer.

Blower printed the 1608 *Yorkshire Tragedy* for Pavier. He had printed other things for him in 1602 and 1605, and also an edition of Edward Webbe's *Trauailes;* but, considering the date of his enfranchisement, obviously not in 1590, as commonly thought. Blower had dealings with Pavier in 1615 about Scoggin's *Jests.*

Blower's printing press was doubtless worked at the establishment formerly occupied by Scarlet, which probably was "at the Flower de Luce, ouer against the Castle without Fleetbridge."

PUBLISHERS.

Thomas Millington *(Continued).*

thereof he get Master **Cawoodes** hande for further warraunt." In 1603 he had a conJoint license with Burby.

In 1594 he had to pay four pence as a fine "for a *psalmebook* the counterfet leaf taken out." In 1596 and 1597 he was fined small amounts for offences against the rules of the Company (see p. 155), one of them being a wrong done to Creede. But in 1603, after he had authority for Chettle's *England's Mourning Garment,* which Simmes printed for him, Lawe appropriated it, and was fined for doing so. It had been entered to Millington in these words: "This book is not to be entred to any but hym, nor to hym neither vnles he bring my Lord graces hand or my Lord of LONDONS hand, for Aucthoritie."

Millington's editions of *The Contention* in 1594 and 1600 were printed respectively by Creede and Simmes and those of *The True Tragedy* in 1595 and 1600 respectively by Short and William White. Creede printed for Millington the 1600 *Henry V.* and also Middleton's pageant of the entry of the King in 1603.

Millington had "his shop vnder saint Peters Church in Cornhil."

Cuthbert Burby.

1594 *The Taming of a Shrew* (1), p. 97.
1596 *Edward III.* (1), p. 93.
1596 *The Taming of a Shrew* (1).
1598 *Love's Labour's Lost* (6), p. 79.
1599 *Romeo and Juliet* (1), p. 91.
1599 *Edward III.* (1).

Cuthbert Burby, the son of a Bedford-

PRINTERS.

William Stansby.

N.D. *Hamlet* (8), p. 135.

William Stansby, the son of an Exeter cutler, was apprenticed from Christmas, 1590, for seven years to John Windet, by whom he was made free on January 7th, 1597.

The dates of his licenses extend from 1611 onwards. The first entry to him postponed printing for further authority, and a few months later the book was entered to him and Eld. In the same year he received the copyrights of a large number of books that had belonged to his master. An entry of three books reads thus: "and are ordered and appoynted alwayes hereafter to bee printed to the vse of the common stocke of the parteners in the Privileges &c. And it is granted that **william Stanesby** shall alwayes have the workmanshippe of the printinge thereof to that vse from tyme to tyme when the same shall be ordered and appoynted by the master and wardens to be printed." In 1626 the largest assignment of books up to that time recorded in the Registers was made to him by Snodham's widow.

Stansby in 1615 received permission to work two presses. He was one of the three "to goe to my lord Mayors feast" in 1628. He was dead in 1639. His widow then transferred his copies to Richard Bishop.

If the *Hamlet* which Stansby printed for Smythick is of the date 1607, it was the earliest known work on which he was engaged. From 1608 to 1630 he printed several of Greene's and Drayton's works for Smythick, who received

PUBLISHERS.

Cuthbert Burby *(Continued).*

shire husbandman, was apprenticed to William Wright for eight years from Christmas, 1583. He received his freedom on January 13th, 1592.

From 1592 to 1603 several apprentices were entered to him. The first, a transfer from Humphrey Lownes, had his "indenture cancelled and this apprentise neuer to be free." The same was also said of the second. In the case of the third it is said "his Indentures were neuer sealed and the said Apprentise is discharged and Dismissed." The fourth shared the same fate as the first two. For not presenting one of them Burby was fined half-a-crown in 1593. Of one in 1598 there is a "MEMORANDUM that the said **Cuthbert Burbye** hath promised never to putt this apprentise to the Stacioners trade nor printinge." For one made free in 1603 the presentment-fee was paid at the time of enfranchisement and Burby was fined ten shillings.

His record of licenses is from 1592 to 1602. Concerning some Sermons by Henry Smith (see p. 233), some of which Burby entered in 1595, it was ordered in 1599, when Short printed them for him, "that they may sell out this imp'ssion which they haue last printed (whereof they haue about a thousand left vnsold) at xx^d. the booke: And that all Imp'ssions thereof after this, they shall sell at ij shetes a penny and not aboue." In 1597 a book was entered to him "vppon condicon that yt be no other mans copie, and that vpon the translatinge thereof. he procure it to be Aucthorised and then Doo shew it at the hall to the mastre and wardens so aucthorised." *Patient Grissil* (see p. 235), entered to

PRINTERS.

William Stansby *(Continued).*

his freedom on the same day as Stansby; *Hero and Leander* in 1613 for Blunt and Barrett, Ben Jonson's Folio for Richard Meighen, the 1620 *Silent Woman* for John Browne, in 1622 Bacon's *History of King Henry VII.* for Matthew Lownes and Barrett, Lyly's Comedies in 1632 for Blunt, and apparently an edition of Meres's *Palladis Tamia* in 1634.

As Stansby became a master-printer in succession to Windet, to whom he had been apprenticed, his work was doubtless carried on at his master's last recorded place of business, "at Pauls wharf, at the signe of the Crosse-keyes."

Simon Stafford.

1599 *Edward III.* (1), p. 93.
1599 1 *Henry IV.* (7), p. 107.
1611 *Pericles* (8), p. 159.

On May 7th, 1599, Simon Stafford was sworn and admitted a freeman of the Stationers' Company, "beinge orderly putt ouer from the Companye of Drapers."

The Registers contain the record of one apprentice serving his time with Stafford.

From 1599 to 1614 he was busy at publications of a miscellaneous character. Twice he took advantage of the "six-pence in the £" arrangement, and in one year two old copies were entered to him. In 1604 a school-book was entered to him, "vppon this condicon that he shall neuer prynt the *A. B. C.* with yt to the hinderance either of the *prymmer* or *the spelling*. *A.B.C.* yf he doo contrary here-

PUBLISHERS.

Cuthbert Burby *(Continued).*

him in 1600, was not published till 1603, and then it did not bear his name in the imprint, but it was issued, if not from his place of business, from a shop next door. In the same year *Every Man in his Humour* and Nash's *Summer's Last Will and Testament* were both entered to him and Walter Burre, but both were issued without his name, although he had an interest in them (see p. 99).

In 1598 Burby was received into the Livery, paying the fee of £2. In 1601 he was fined with Ling and others (see p. 275); and in 1602, the year in which he was one of the three who "went to my lord Maiours feast," he had to pay twenty shillings for "A fine for printinge *the Englishe scholemaster* without alowance."

The editions of *A Shrew* which he published in 1594 and 1596 were printed by Short, the 1596 *Edward III.* has no printer's name, but for the 1599 edition he employed Stafford, *Love's Labour's Lost* was printed by William White and the 1599 *Romeo and Juliet* by Creede. Burby in 1592 issued two of Greene's prose-works, one of which was printed by Thomas Scarlet, who printed Lyly's *Mother Bombie* for him in 1594 (for his 1598 edition he employed Creede), and the other probably by Danter, to whom it was entered (see p. 278). In 1593 he published the Wagner-book (see p. 67), which Jeffes printed. In 1594 Danter printed Greene's *Orlando Furioso* and Wilson's *The Cobbler's Prophecy* for him. For the 1599 edition of *Orlando Furioso* he employed Stafford, who printed in the same year *George-a-Greene* for him. In 1594 he published a book by Nash which

PRINTERS.

Simon Stafford *(Continued).*

vnto Then this entrance to be void." His connection with the 1605 *Leir* is mentioned at p. 149. On June 30th, 1613, he entered "a ballad called *the sodayne Burninge of the 'Globe' on the Bankside in the Play tyme on Saint Peters day last* 1613." The next entry in the Registers is to Edward White of *A doleful ballad of the generall ouerthrowe of the famous theater on the Banksyde, called the 'Globe,' &c.* by WILLIAM PARRAT (see p. 183).

In 1596 Stafford's name appears over Gabriel Simpson's in an entry in the Registers. For printing books before having the freedom of the Stationers' Company he came into conflict with the Star-Chamber, and about March, 1598, his printing-apparatus was seized. Against this he appealed, and his "goods & stuffe" were re-delivered to him in March, 1599. His admission in the following May put an end to the controversy, and then he started business "by meanes of the Lady Stafford." In 1614 he sold his business to George Purslowe, who in 1615 received official permission to work one press.

Stafford printed *Edward III.* for Burby, and 1 *Henry IV.* for Wise. He printed *George-a-Greene* and *Orlando Furioso* for Burby in 1599, Dekker's *Old Fortunatus* for Apsley, and *Summer's Last Will and Testament* for Walter Burre in 1600, and the 1605 *Leir* for John Wright.

At one time of Stafford's work he was described as "dwelling on Adling Hill." In 1607 he was said to be "dwelling in the Cloth-fayre, neere the Red Lyon."

PUBLISHERS.

Cuthbert Burby *(Continued).*

Scarlet printed. He employed Adam Islip to print Lodge's *Wit's Misery* in 1596 and Short for Meres's *Palladis Tamia* in 1598. In 1599 he and Ling published a work by Nash without printer's name.

Burby's first place of business was "at the middle shop in the Poultry, vnder Saint Mildreds Church." From 1594 to 1599 he had "his shop at the Royall Exchange." In 1604 he was "in Paul's Church Yard, at the Signe of the Swanne."

Thomas Thorpe.

1609 *The Sonnets*, p. 121.

Thomas Thorpe, frequently described in the Registers as Throp, was the son of a Middlesex "Inholder" (Innkeeper: see Minsheu's *Guide into the Tongues*, 1627). He was apprenticed to Richard Wilkins for nine years from Midsummer, 1584, and admitted a freeman on February 4th, 1594.

His brother Richard was apprenticed to Martin Ensor in 1596, but did not become free.

Thomas Thorpe's entries in the Registers range from 1603 to 1618. In the first of those years, with Aspley, he entered a book which had, only a short time before, been entered to another. With Aspley he also entered in 1604-5 Marston's *Malcontent* and *Eastward Ho*, but his name does not appear in the imprint of either.

Thorpe employed Eld to print the *Sonnets*. In 1605 he published Ben Jonson's *Sejanus* (transferred to him

PRINTERS.

John Harrison.

1600 *Lucrece*, p. 119.

The fondness of the Harrison family for the Christian name of John makes it difficult occasionally to identify the person to whom reference is made in the Registers. There were four contemporary stationers named John Harrison. The most noted of the name was the publisher of the 1594 *Lucrece* (see p. 267). He had a brother with the same Christian name (*Transcript*, II., 32, 716), who was apprenticed to him in 1561, made free in 1569, who passed into the Livery in 1585, paid £5 in 1599 to avoid acting as Renter, was one of the Court of Assistants in 1603, and Junior Warden in 1612. He was a prominent member of the Company, publishing books at the Golden Anchor in Paternoster Row, and had two sons, Philip and Josias, who were made free respectively in 1603 and 1605.

The printer of the 1600 *Lucrece* was a son of the eldest John Harrison, who made him free by patrimony on July 9th, 1599.

Books were entered to him from 1600 to 1603. For one in 1602 he availed himself of the "sixpence in the £" arrangement, showing that, differing from his father and uncle, he was carrying on the business of a printer. He was dead before February, 1604. In that month an apprentice entered to him in 1601 was on that account transferred to his father, and in the following year was passed on to Humphrey Lownes. His only other apprentice was "discharged by order and neuer to be made free."

This John Harrison bought Thomas

PUBLISHERS.

Thomas Thorpe *(Continued)*.

from Blunt) printed by Eld and Chapman's *All Fools*, in 1606 one of Jonson's *Masques* and Chapman's *Gentleman's Usher* both printed by Simmes, in 1607 Marston's *What you Will* printed by Eld and Jonson's *Fox*, in 1608 Chapman's *Byron's Conspiracy* printed by Eld (Thorpe's name is also on the 1625 edition which Okes printed), in 1609 another of Jonson's *Masques*, in 1610 *Histrio-Mastix* (see p. 167), and a book by Nash in 1613.

Thorpe carried on his business "at the Tygers head in Paules Church-yard," which he probably took from Aspley, where he was probably succeeded by Lawrence Lisle.

John Smythick.

N.D. *Romeo and Juliet* (1), p. 91.
N.D. *Hamlet* (8), p. 135.
1609 *Romeo and Juliet* (1)
1611 *Hamlet* (8).

John Smythick, the son of a London draper, was apprenticed for nine years to Thomas Newman from Christmas, 1589, and admitted to the freedom by Mistress Newman on January 7th, 1597.

Smythick has a record of three apprentices from 1597 to 1601. Of the first it is said: "gone awaie and neuer to be made free," and, at the time of the enrolment of the last, Smythick was "to bring in thindenture of his former Apprentise to be cancelled."

Smythick's book-entries extend from 1597 to 1618. In 1605 one was in conjunction with John Jaggard. In 1607 he

PRINTERS.

John Harrison *(Continued).*

Judson's printing-plant on February 4th, 1600. As in the earlier part of his career Judson had been in partnership with John Windet, and that then their place of business was "in Adling street, at the signe of the White Beare, neere Baynards castle," it is probable that Judson continued there at the expiration of the partnership, when Windet went to the Cross Keys at Paul's Wharf (see p. 288), and that Harrison continued to work the press in the same place as Judson.

It is said that in 1606 his business was in the possession of Lionel and George Snodham; but there is much confusion about the Christian names of these stationers and about the dates. Lionel, not obviously a relation of the printer of the 1616 *Lucrece*, was apprenticed in 1597; but there is no record of his freedom. A John Snodon was made free in 1613. In one place in the *Transcript* he is described as L. Snodham.

On June 25th, 1600, another John Harrison was made free by the father of Philip and Josias. He passed through the various stages of honour in the Company, becoming Master in 1638.

There was also a John Harrison apprenticed in 1564.

George Eld.

1609 *The Sonnets*, p. 121.
1609 *Troilus and Cressida* (two), (8), p. 167.

George Eld, the son of a Derbyshire carpenter, was apprenticed for eight years from Christmas, 1592, to Robert Bolton, by whom he was made free on January 13th, 1600.

PUBLISHERS.

John Smythick *(Continued).*

received several books which had belonged to Ling (see p. 79).

In 1601 Smythick was fined with Ling and others (see p. 275), and with Ling and one other in 1603 (see p. 275), not paying till April, 1605. In 1614 and again in 1628 he was one of those who represented the Company at the Lord Mayor's dinner. In 1625 he was Renter, in 1631 Junior Warden, in 1635 Senior Warden and one of the Court of Assistants, and Master in 1639.

Of Smythick's four Shakspere quartos, the undated *Hamlet* printed by Stansby is the only one which bears a printer's name. From 1608 to 1637 Smythick published books by Drayton, and from 1611 to 1630 books by Greene, employing Stansby to print several of them. From 1609 to 1634 he issued at least four editions of Lodge's *Rosalynde*, and in 1635 Okes printed for him Ben Jonson's *Catiline* and Beaumont and Fletcher's *Knight of the Burning Pestle*.

In 1599 Smythick sold his books "at his shop in Fleetstreete, neare the Temple Gate," or, as it is described in 1600, "within Temple Barre," but afterwards had "his shop in Saint Dunstanes Churchyard, in Fleetestreete vnder the Dyall," which probably had been Ling's place of business.

Smythick was one of the four at whose charges the first Folio was printed.

PRINTERS.

George Eld (Continued).

He received two apprentices in 1604, for keeping one of whom "vnpresented contrary to order" he was fined one shilling.

From 1605 to 1623 many books were entered to him. In 1611 he entered a publication with Stansby, and in 1615 one with William White. From 1617 he was in partnership with Miles Fletcher. The first book entered to them conJointly had been assigned to them by its previous owner "by a bill of sale vnder his hand and seale." Fletcher, upon Eld's death, having paid "a valuable consideracon" "for the other moitie" of the business, was, after petition to the Archbishop of Canterbury, appointed "a master printer in the roome or place of the said **George Eld**," who died in 1624. On November 13th, 1664, it is recorded in *The Obituary of Richard Smyth* that "Mr. Miles Flesher, printer, died this morning, being well at 7 of ye clock; buried at Butolph's, Aldersgate, Novem. 17."

Eld seems also at one time to have had the business which had been held by William White in partnership with Gabriel Simpson (see p. 272), whose widow, having had a stationer also for her second husband, took Eld for her third. In 1615 Eld was allowed to have two presses at work.

The *Sonnets* were printed for Thorp, and *Troilus and Cressida* for Bonian and Walley. Eld printed Daniel's *Philotas* for Simon Waterson and Ben Jonson's *Sejanus* for Thorp in 1605, the 1606 *Return from Parnassus* for John Wright, for whom he printed Marlowe's *Faustus* in 1609 and 1611, in 1607 Marston's *What You Will* for Thorp, the *Northward Ho* of Dekker

PUBLISHERS.

William Aspley.

1600 *Much Ado about Nothing* (with Wise), (8), p. 103.

1600 2 *Henry IV.* (with Wise), (8), p. 111.

William Aspley, the son of a Cumberland clerk, was apprenticed to George Bishop for nine years from February 5th, 1588, and admitted a freeman on April 11th, 1597.

There is no record in the Registers of any of his apprentices, but it is known from *The Obituary of Richard Smyth* that one who was entered under him did not become a stationer, for in August, 1663, "Sim. Burton, an oyleman wth out Algate, sometime prentice to Mr. Aspley, bookseller, died."

Between 1598 and 1616 there are many book-entries to Aspley. The first of them was a comedy, and was followed by many other plays. Of a book entered to him in 1599 it is said: "PROVIDED that yf it Conteine any thinge offensive to thEstate of England Then this entrance to be void." Several of his entries were with other publishers, among them, besides Wise being Thorp, Blunt, Barrett, and Butter. In 1610 Aspley became owner of a twelfth part of Camden's *Britannia*.

In 1626 Aspley was Renter and one of the Court of Assistants in 1630. In 1632 and 1633 he was Junior Warden, in 1635 one of the Court of Assistants, in 1637 Senior Warden, and Master in 1640, in August of which year "Wm. Asply, bookseller, died."

The 1600 editions of *Much Ado* and 2 *Henry IV.* were printed by Simmes, who also in 1599 printed for Aspley *A*

PRINTERS.

George Eld (*Continued*).

and Webster, Tourneur's *Revenger's Tragedy* and *The Puritan* (entered in 1607 as *The Puritan Widow*—see p. 229), Chapman's *Byron's Conspiracy* for Thorp, and Middleton's *Trick to Catch the Old One* for Henry Rockett in 1608 and the latter again in 1616 for Thomas Langley, one of Chapman's *Masques* in 1613 for George Norton, in 1617 an edition of Lyly's *Euphues* for Barrett and Johnson, and for the latter *The Merry Devil of Edmonton* in 1617, and Field's *Amends for Ladies* for Matthew Walbanke in 1618.

Eld's house was "in Fleete-lane at the signe of the Printers-Presse." In 1621 he was said to be "dwelling in Little-Britaine."

Thomas Snodham.

1613 *Thomas, Lord Cromwell* (2), p. 105.
1616 *Lucrece*, p. 119.

Thomas Snodham, whose name appears in the Registers also as Snoden, Snodam, and Susden, was the son of a London draper, and was apprenticed to Thomas East for nine years from Midsummer, 1595, and by him made free on June 28th, 1602.

Scarcely anything was entered to him before 1609, when an assignment was made to him of several high-class books, the copyrights of which had belonged to his master, who was then dead, and who had bequeathed the business to Snodham. In 1611 several of East's music-books were passed over to Snodham and two others. A large transfer of copies that had been Welby's was made to him in 1618 (see p. 93), in which year "halfe a Booke" was assigned to him. His last

PUBLISHERS.

William Aspley (*Continued*).

Warning for Fair Women, which Richard Simpson included in his *School of Shakspere* as it was a play acted by the Lord Chamberlain's servants. In 1600 Aspley published Dekker's *Old Fortunatus* printed by Stafford, in 1604 two editions of Marston's *Malcontent* printed by Simmes, in 1605 *Eastward Ho*, and in 1607 Chapman's *Bussy d'Ambois*. Aspley's name appears on some of the 1609 copies of the *Sonnets*.

Aspley, who had "his shop in Paules Church-yard, at the signe of the Tygers head," which Thorp probably took when Aspley moved to the sign of the Parrot, was one of the four who bore the expense of printing the First Folio.

John Trundell.

1603 *Hamlet* (with Ling), (8), p. 135.

John Trundell, the son of a Hertfordshire yeoman, was apprenticed to Ralph Hancock for eight years from Midsummer, 1589, and was made free by him on October 29th, 1597.

There were several entries of books to him from 1603 onwards, several of which were in conJunction with other stationers, including Busby, Butter, and Gosson. In 1605 he entered the book about Gamaliel Ratsey, which contains (see Halliwell-Phillipps's *Outlines*, Vol. I., pp. 299, 300) an unmistakeable reference to Shakspere, mentioning *Hamlet*, with the publication of which Trundell had been connected two years before. Another book in the same year was entered to him "yf he gett sufficient Aucthoritie . . . And shewe his aucthority to the wardens

PRINTERS.

Thomas Snodham *(Continued).*

entry was in 1623, and soon after that time he died; for in 1626 his widow transferred a large number of copies to Stansby (see p. 287).

A torn page of the Registers shows that in 1605 Snodham was one of the "suters to be in master **wryghtes** priuiledg." In 1615 he was allowed to have two presses. In 1618, and again in 1622, he was one of the three who represented the Company at the Lord Mayor's feast. A late record, which is a deficient authority at least in the matter of dates, says his business passed to George Wood and William Lee.

The 1613 *Thomas, Lord Cromwell* Snodham probably printed for John Browne, to whom it was assigned in 1611. The 1616 *Lucrece* was printed for Jackson. In 1612 Snodham printed Ben Jonson's *Alchemist* for Walter Burre, and for John Budge a poem by Chapman, whose *Revenge of Bussy d'Ambois* he printed for Helme in 1613, and in the same year Marston's *Insatiate Countess* for Thomas Archer, in 1615 Speed's *Description of England and Wales* for John Sudbury and George Humble, and one of Munday's pageants in 1623.

Thomas Snodham probably printed "in Aldersgate streete, over against the signe of the George," which was East's latest place of business.

Nicholas Okes.

1607 *Lucrece*, p. 119.
1622 *Othello* (8), p. 143.

Nicholas Okes was the son of a London "**horner.**" (Cotgrave gives "Corneur: *A*

PUBLISHERS.

John Trundell *(Continued).*

Then yt is to be entred for his copy Or yf any other bringe the Aucthority. yet it is to be the said **John Trundelles** copy;" and of another it was said that it was "to be staid for **John Trundel** till he bringe further aucthority for yt;" and in after years there were somewhat similar deferred orders. In 1614 one was licensed to him "with this Caution that if any exceptions be taken he shall stand to the perrill thereof himself." In 1623 he assigned some books to John Wright.

But few of Trundell's published works are extant. He issued without date *Nobody and Somebody*, which had been entered to him in 1606, and which is given by Simpson in *The School of Shakspere.* In 1614 he published Cooke's *City Gallant*, which is reprinted in Hazlitt's *Dodsley*, and in 1617 *A Fair Quarrel* by Middleton and William Rowley. *Westward for Smelts*, which he issued in 1620, has been often thought to have supplied Shakspere with part of the story of *Cymbeline.* But as it was licensed to Trundell in the year he published it, and no earlier edition is known, it should be removed from the fanciful list of sources to which it has been imagined Shakspere was indebted.

Trundell carried on business "at his shop in Barbican, at the signe of Nobody."

Roger Jackson.

1616 *Lucrece*, p. 119.

Roger Jackson, the son of a Yorkshire yeoman, was apprenticed for eight years from Midsummer, 1591, to Ralph New-

PRINTERS.

Nicholas Okes (*Continued*).

Horner; a winder of a Horne"; but here it most probably signifies "one that works in horn, and sells horn," or, as in the *Promptorium Parvulorum*, a "horne maker.") He was apprenticed to William King for eight years from Lady Day, 1596; but on December 5th, 1603, was admitted to his freedom by Field.

From 1607 onwards many books were entered to him. His first venture was printing "an old copye" on the "sixpence in the £" arrangement. A book entered to him in 1612 was soon after "put out by order of A court," and then entered to Waterson.

There is a record that Okes was admitted a Master-Printer on April 19th, 1606. Most likely this meant that he was allowed to take the place of John Harrison (see pp. 290, 292). At the granting of presses to the Master-Printers in 1615, Okes received permission to have one. After having succeeded to the business which Lionel and George Snodham had taken from John Harrison (see p. 291), he took John Norton as a partner, who is said to have paid him £70 for the share of the business then acquired.

The printing of the 1607 *Lucrece* by Okes for John Harrison is accounted for by the fact that he was in possession of the business formerly held by Harrison's son, who had printed the previous edition. The 1622 *Othello* was printed for Thomas Walkley. Okes printed one of Ben Jonson's *Masques* in 1609 for Bonian and Walley, works by Webster in 1612 for William Welby and in 1613 for Thomas Archer and in 1623 (see p. 165) for John Waterson, in 1612 Heywood's *Apology for Actors*, at the end of which is a letter from

PUBLISHERS.

Roger Jackson (*Continued*).

berry, who made him free on August 20th, 1599.

Richard Gosson, brother of the publisher of the 1609 *Pericles*, was apprenticed to him in 1604.

Beginning in 1603, he entered many books, amongst which were several sermons.

Jackson employed Snodham to print *Lucrece* in 1616. In 1602, with John North, who had been a fellow-apprentice, he published a prose-work about Greene.

Jackson's shop was "neere the Conduit in Fleet-street."

Thomas Fisher.

1600 *A Midsummer-Night's Dream* (8), p. 85.

Thomas Fisher was one of twelve who, paying three shillings and fourpence each, were on June 3rd, 1600, "Sworne and admitted ffreemen of this Companye by Translation hither ffrom the Companye of the Drapers, by Consent of bothe Companies, Accordinge to the Constitutions of the Citie."

In 1602 an enrolment of an apprentice to him is supplemented by this note: "Thapprentise gone away. And thindentures neuer sealid and a newe Aprentise alowid in stede of him." Of the successor it is said: "The sealing of these Indentures to be stayed for a tyme."

Fisher was fined with Ling and others in 1601 (see p. 275).

Marston's *Antonio and Mellida* was published by Fisher in conJunction with

PRINTERS.

Nicholas Okes *(Continued).*

the author to him (see p. 120), in 1615 an edition of *Mucedorus* for Wiliam Jones, an edition of *Greene's Groatsworth of Wit* for Henry Bell in 1621, in 1623 Daniel's *Cleopatra* and his complete works both for Simon Waterson, *The Duchess of Malfi* in 1623 for John Waterson, Chapman's *Byron's Conspiracy* in 1625 for Thorp, for Smythick in 1655 Jonson's *Catiline* and *The Knight of the Burning Pestle* by Beaumont and Fletcher, and in 1637 *Hero and Leander* for Leake's son.

Okes probably worked his press at first at Harrison's place (see p. 291).

Okes had a son John, who was made free on January 14th, 1627. In 1636 they were together "dwelling in Little St. Bartholomewes."

Augustine Matthews.

1622 *The Troublesome Raigne* (7), p. 95.

Augustine Matthews was admitted to the Freedom of the Company on May 9th, 1615.

At first he was not the actual possessor of printing-plant, as in one place it is said that he "farmed his printing house of John White," the son of William White (see p. 273), and in another place that he had his business "by composicon from White."

Beginning about 1619, he printed a great many books. One was entered to him in 1622, "PROVIDED it Doth not preiudice any other mans Copie."

In 1637, in a note about authorised printers, occurs this: "**Augustine: Mathewes**. he was taken reprinting of *ye holy table*. **Marmaduke Parsons** hath

PUBLISHERS.

Thomas Fisher *(Continued).*

Matthew Lownes in 1602. *Antonio's Revenge* in the same year bears Fisher's name only in the imprint.

Fisher had his "shoppe at the Signe of the White Hart, in Fleetestreete." The Marston plays, with Fisher's device, were sold at Lownes's place of business.

Matthew Lawe.

1604 1 *Henry IV.* (7), p. 107.
1605 *Richard III.* (8), p. 87.
1608 *Richard II.* (two), (8), p. 81.
1608 1 *Henry IV.* (7).
1612 *Richard III.* (8).
1613 1 *Henry IV.* (7).
1615 *Richard II.* (8).
1622 *Richard III.* (8).
1622 1 *Henry IV.* (7).

Matthew Lawe was admitted with Fisher and others from the Drapers' Company on June 3rd, 1600 (see p. 295).

The Registers contain the record of one apprentice he had in 1603.

From 1600 there are entries of many publications to him; but very few between 1606 and 1614, and between 1616 and 1623. A large number of his publications consisted of sermons.

In 1601 and 1603 he was joined with Ling and others in fines (see p. 275); and in the latter year it was "ORDERED that he shall presently pay **xx**s for a fine for printinge contrary to order A book called *Englandes mourning garment* beinge **Thomas Millingtons** copie. And that he shall bring into the hall as forfayted by thordonnance all such numbers of the said bookes as now remayne in his handes vnsold which he say are 100.

PRINTERS.

Augustine Matthews *(Continued).*

long had his presse and priuledg made over to him and is most fitt to be in his Roome;" and about this time "pauper" appears after his name in the Registers.

Matthews printed the 1622 *Troublesome Raigne* for Dewe, for whom in the same year he printed *A Fair Quarrel* by Middleton and William Rowley, in 1623 John Grismand employed him for Webster's *Devil's Law-case*, for Richard Hawkins he printed *Philaster* and *A King and No King* by Beaumont and Fletcher in 1628 and 1630 and *Hero and Leander* in 1629, George Wilkins's *Miseries of Enforced Marriage* in 1629 for Richard Thrale, Massinger's *Renegado* for John Waterson in 1630, in 1631 a work by Drayton for William Lee and *A Woman will have her Will* (see p. 247) for Thrale, and in 1635 works by Beaumont and Fletcher without publishers' names.

PUBLISHERS.

Matthew Lawe *(Continued).*

he brought in . 3 quarterns or thereaboutes. and vs of the fine is gyven back to him." And he was also fined with Wise, from whom he then received a transfer of copyrights (see p. 81). In 1604 he was fined two shillings "for opening his shop on a holy Day contrary to order. and for nonne apperance on the quarter Day," and in the next year he was fined half-a-crown for disobedience. In 1610 he was one of the three who "went to my Lord Maiours dynner." In 1617 he acted as Renter.

Lawe seems to have almost entirely confined his dramatic publications to the Shakspere-quartos. More of his are in existence than any other bookseller's.

Lawe throughout his business-career had "his shop in Paules Church-yard, neare vnto S. Augustines gate, at the signe of the Foxe."

PUBLISHERS.

Thomas Pavier.

1602 *Henry V.* (1), p. 117.
1608 *Henry V.* (1).
1608 *A Yorkshire Tragedy* (4), p. 133.
1619 *The Whole Contention* (8), p. 65.
1619 *A Yorkshire Tragedy* (7).
1619 *Pericles* (7), p. 159.

Thomas Pavier came over from the Drapers' to the Stationers' Company on June 3rd, 1600 (see p. 295).

He at once got into a publishing business, and for the next twenty years at least had licenses for many publications, of which several, perhaps most, were ballads. Two months after he received his freedom a dozen copies were entered to him at once (see p. 117). In 1602 he had an assignment from Millington (see p. 59). In 1605 he entered a ballad about Ratsey (see p. 293), and in the same year obtained some copies through a bill of sale. In 1620 with John Wright he had a large assignment from Edward White (see p. 67), the son of the publisher of *Titus Andronicus*.

In 1601 Pavier was fined with Ling and others (see p. 275), and in 1602 a fine of thirteen shillings and fourpence, reduced

PUBLISHERS.

Thomas Pavier (*Continued*).

to six shillings and eightpence, was imposed upon him "for causinge **Edward aldee** to print" a book contrary to order, and in the following year he offended about the second edition of *Basilicon Doron* (see p. 271). In 1604, the year in which he was received into the Livery with a fee of £2, he was, probably for declining to take an office, fined forty shillings, ten of which were remitted. In 1605 Pavier's name occurs with Snodham's in a torn entry (see p. 294). In 1619 he was one of the Court of Assistants, and in 1622 Junior Warden.

Pavier employed Creede to print the 1602 *Henry V.*, Blower to print the 1608 *Yorkshire Tragedy*. In the case of the others no printer's name is given. At p. 133 I have given T. P. as the printer of the 1619 *Yorkshire Tragedy*; he was the publisher. In 1600 Pavier published *Sir John Oldcastle* printed by Simmes, in 1602 Lodge and Greene's *Looking Glass* which Creede printed and Kyd's *Spanish Tragedy* which was printed by William White, in 1605 the same author's (see p. 245) *Jeronimo*, and in 1610 Thomas Heywood's *If you Know not Me, You Know Nobody*, the copyright of which was Butter's.

Pavier carried on business "at his shop in Cornhill, at the signe of the Cat and Parrets neare the Exchange," otherwise described as "at the entring into the Exchange." It was in Cornhill "ouer against Popes head alley."

Arthur Johnson.

1602 *The Merry Wives of Windsor* (8), p. 113.

1619 *The Merry Wives of Windsor* (7).

On May 3rd, 1594, the Court of Assistants passed the following resolution: "WHEREAS **Arthur Johnson** son of THOMAS JOHNSON of PARKHALL in the county of DERBY husbandman hath serued ij yeres with WILLIAM YONG Draper Vsinge the trade of bookselling and thereby should in tyme be free of the Company of drapers yf Remedy to the contrary should not be Provided. and is put ouer to **Robert Dexter** a freman of this Company, yt is therfore thought mete and ordered by a Court holden this Day that to thend he may be free of this Company, the said **Robert Dexter** shall Receaue hym to be his apprentise for vij yeres from mydsomer next." Johnson was made free by Dexter on July 3rd, 1601. There is a notice of one apprentice he received in 1602.

His first entry in the Registers is in connection with *The Merry Wives of Windsor* (see p. 113). From that date to 1621 he was very busy. In 1606 one of his copies had the frequent deferred order attached to it, and in that year with Busby he received a transfer from Trundell. In 1614 he had from Samuel Macham a large assignment of Dr. Hall's books, which in the following year were transferred to Henry Fetherstone.

The 1602 *Merry Wives* was printed by Creede. The 1619 edition has no printer's name. Smythick's device is on the title-page, but Smythick was not a printer. In 1607 Johnson published Middleton's *Phœnix* printed by Edward Aldee, and in 1608, 1612, and 1617 editions of *The Merry Devil of Edmonton* (see p. 237), which were

PUBLISHERS.

Arthur Johnson *(Continued).*

printed respectively by Henry Ballard, Creede, and Eld. On October 22nd, 1607, the latter play had been entered to Johnson, and not to Joseph Hunt and Thomas Archer as stated in Hazlitt's *Dodsley* and elsewhere.

In 1602 Johnson had "his shop in Powles Church yard, at the signe of the Flower de Leuse and the Crowne," where he was succeeded by Francis Burton, but from 1608 to 1617 he was "dwelling at the signe of the White-horse in Paules Church-yard, ouer against the great North doore of Paules."

Henry Gosson.

1609 *Pericles* (two) (8), p. 159.

Henry Gosson received his freedom on August 3rd, 1601, "*per patrimonium*," through his mother "**Alice Gosson** Late Wyfe of **Thomas Gosson**," a stationer who had been made free in 1577 after serving an apprenticeship to the elder Purfoot.

In 1604 an apprentice was entered to Henry Gosson.

An entry of one of his books in 1603 said that it was "to be staied and not entred to any but hym when he hathe Aucthority for it." He entered no more books till 1606, but from that time he was continually entering publications, mostly ballads, and many of them the works of John Taylor, the water-poet. With John Wright he entered two books in 1608. In 1610 a work by John Day was entered to Gosson. Probably this was a lost play. Joseph Hunt, with whom a conjoint entry was made in 1613, had been also associated with Henry Gosson's father (see p. 97). From 1618 to 1623 Henry Gosson at times entered books with Trundell, and seems to have been in business till 1636.

Henry Gosson carried on his business "at the signe of the Sunne in Pater-noster row," where his father had been.

Thomas Gosson had two other sons, Edward and Richard. Edward was apprenticed to Roberts in 1601, becoming free in 1607, when he was described as Edmund. Richard was apprenticed to Jackson in 1604, but does not seem to have received his freedom.

John Wright.

1609 *The Sonnets*, p. 121.

John Wright, the son of a Northamptonshire yeoman, was apprenticed to Edward White for eight years from Midsummer, 1594, and was made free on June 28th, 1602. The note "*per patrimonium*," accompanying the record of his enfranchisement, must be an error. He was not the son of William Wright, who probably died about 1605 (see p. 294).

His brothers Cuthbert and Edward became stationers. Cuthbert was apprenticed in 1603 to Felix Kingston, and became free in 1610. Edward was apprenticed to John in 1604, and received his freedom in 1611.

PUBLISHERS.

John Wright *(Continued)*.

John Wright's first entry was the transaction about *Lear* in 1605 (see p. 149). In 1608 he entered books in conjunction with Gosson. In 1610 he was associated with Simmes (see p. 275), and in the same year he had an assignment of two books from Thomas Busshell (see p. 67). He entered a book with Busshell in 1613 and with his brother Edward in 1615. In 1618 the widow of William Jones, the publisher, assigned *Mucedorus* (see p. 214) to him. In 1620 to Pavier and him there was an assignment of books from his old master's son (see p. 67), and in 1623 both singly and with his brother Cuthbert he received copyrights from Trundell. *The Obituary of Richard Smyth* contains this statement: "John Wright, bookseller, in ye Old Bayly, buried" May 11th, 1658.

The *Sonnets* were printed by Eld employed through Thorp. Wright published in 1605 the *Leir* Chronicle History, which according to the condition in the entry (see p. 149) was printed by Stafford, in 1606 *The Return from Parnassus* which Eld printed, in 1607 *The Travels of Three English Brothers* written by Day, Wilkins, and William Rowley (see p. 252), six editions of *Faustus* between 1609 and 1631, two of which Eld printed, the others have no printer's name as is the case with the four editions of *Mucedorus* which Wright issued between 1619 and 1634.

Wright's place of business was described in 1605 as "his shop at Christ Church dore, next Newgate-Market," in 1606-12 it is merely "at Christ Church gate" or "neere Christ Church doore," and in 1616 it is "his shop without Newgate, at the signe of the Bible." These may all refer to the same house. In 1647 he was "at the Kings Head in the old Bayley."

Nathanael Butter.

1605 *The London Prodigal* (8), p. 127.

1608 *Lear* (two) (5 and 8), p. 149.

Nathanael Butter, the son of Thomas Butter, a stationer, was made free "*per patrimonium*" on November 20th, 1604, by his mother, then Mistress Newberry, who had carried on for a time the business of her first husband.

Nathanael's first license was in 1604, and a great many books published by him between that date and 1640 are extant. In 1605 he was interested in a play about the events of the reign of Henry VIII. (see p. 183) and in some of the literature about Calverley's Yorkshire tragedy (see p. 133). In 1612 one of his entries is accompanied by the condition: "PROUIDED that the sheetes be severally broughte to master Doctor MOKETT to viewe as they are printed." This was a book giving the reasons which prompted some one to leave the Church of Rome for the Church of England. Some of Butter's books were entered with Trundell (1607), Busby (two in 1608), and Aspley (1613). One of his books in the latter year was *The travails of Sir* ANTHONY SHERLEY, one of the three brothers the story of whose Journeyings was dramatised by Day, Wilkins, and William

PUBLISHERS.

Nathaniel Butter *(Continued)*.

Rowley (see pp. 252, 284, 300). Many of Butter's entries were of a serial publication, in the form of a newspaper, which was called by various names, such as "A Currant of newes," "The certaine newes of this weeke," or "The Affaires of the world, for this present weeke." The earliest of the entries is dated June 7th, 1622, and on October 10th, 1623, the first of a second series of fifty was begun.

Nathanael Butter served the office of Renter in 1629, and was one of the Court of Assistants in 1633. On February 22nd, 1664, "Nath. Butter, an old stationer, died very poore."

The London Prodigal was printed by Creede. Butter employed Edward Aldee in 1606 to print Dekker's *Seven Deadly Sins of London* (reprinted in Arber's series), and published other works by Dekker in 1609 and 1630; in 1608 the Pericles novel printed by Purfoot, the first part of Heywood's *If You Know not Me, You Know Nobody* in 1606, 1608, 1613, 1623, 1632, and the second part in 1606 and 1609, the 1630 and 1638 editions of Heywood's *Lucrece* which had been licensed to him and Busby in 1608 (see p. 116), and Samuel Rowley's *When You See Me You Know Me* in 1613 and 1632 (see p. 251). In 1616 Butter employed Field to print Chapman's "*Homers Odisses 24 bookes*," having also issued "*The Iliads of Homer Prince of Poets*" in an edition without date.

Butter carried on his business "in Pauls Church-yard at the signe of the Pide Bull neere St Austins Gate."

William Barrett.

1617 *Venus and Adonis*, p. 118.

William Barrett, the son of a Lincolnshire yeoman, was apprenticed for eight years from Christmas, 1597, to Bonham Norton, who in June of the following year was fined eighteenpence because he had bound Barrett "without firste presentinge him accordinge to the orders of this Companie." Barrett was made free on January 21st, 1606.

From 1607 to 1624 he was fairly busy without much intermission, entering books by himself and in conJunction with others. One in 1608 was a deferred license. Some books he entered with Aspley (1607) and Blunt (1610–12). With the latter in 1611 he entered *The delightfull history of the witty knighte Don* QUISHOTE (see p. 157); Blunt seems to have been the publisher of it. In 1617 he had a large assignment of copyrights from Leake (see p. 105), many of which he passed on to Parker in 1620 (see p. 118), in which year one book was licensed to him, "PROUIDED that if hereafter it be found to belong to any other man, that then he to giue him satisfaction for the same."

In 1613 Barrett was one of the three "appointed to goe to my Lord Mayours to Dinner."

Barrett and Blunt issued editions of *Hero and Leander* in 1609 and 1613, the latter of which Stansby printed; and in 1617 an edition of *Euphues* was printed for Barrett by Eld, and sold by Johnson.

PUBLISHERS.

William Barrett *(Continued).*

In 1622, with Matthew Lownes, he published Bacon's *History of King Henry the Seventh*, which Stansby printed for them.

The *Hero and Leander* in which Barrett was concerned was "sold in Pauls Church-yard, at the signe of the Blacke Beare."

John Helme.

1611 *The Troublesome Raigne* (3), p. 95.

John Helme, the son of a London tailor, was apprenticed to Ling for nine years from February 2nd, 1599, and was made free on June 15th, 1607.

He was publishing books from 1607 to 1616. Two were entered with young Busby. Helme was dead in 1620.

The 1611 *Troublesome Raigne* was printed by Simmes. In 1608 Helme published plays by Day and by Middleton, in 1613 Chapman's *Revenge of Bussy D'Ambois* which Snodham printed, and with others Drayton's *Poly-Olbion* which was printed by Humphrey Lownes.

Helme had "his Shop in Saint Dunstons Church-yard in Fleetestreet."

Richard Bonian.

1609 *Troilus and Cressida* (two with Walley) (8), p. 167.

Richard Bonian, the son of a Middlesex yeoman, was apprenticed to Richard Watkins for eight years from Christmas, 1598; but was re-entered to Simon Waterson for eight and a half years from Midsummer, 1599. He was made free on August 6th, 1607.

His record of book-entries extends only from 1607 to 1611. Most of them were with Walley. For *The Case is Altered* (1609) Sutton's name was added in the entry less than six months after the first register, and the edition bore Sutton's name only.

The editions of *Troilus and Cressida* were printed by Eld. About 1607 Bonian published Middleton's *Your Five Gallants*, In 1609 Bonian and Walley published Ben Jonson's *Masque of Queens* printed by Okes, a poem by Chapman printed by Humphrey Lownes, and perhaps in the same year Fletcher's *Faithful Shepherdess*.

Bonian and Walley had their place of business "at the spred Eagle in Paules Church-yeard, ouer against the great North doore."

Henry Walley.

1609 *Troilus and Cressida* (two with Bonian) (8), p. 167.

As there is no record of Henry Walley's apprenticeship, it is probable that his freedom, obtained on December 5th, 1608, came by patrimony, as there were earlier stationers of the name of Walley.

Henry Walley's entries of books are

PUBLISHERS.

Henry Walley *(Continued).*

only in the years 1608 and 1609, and each time with Bonian.

After this time he probably became a permanent official of the Company. It is known that he was clerk of the Company in 1635 (see *Calendar of State Papers.* Domestic. 1635, p. 205 and Arber's *Transcript.* IV. 24) and in *The Obituary of Richard Smyth* it is recorded that on April 30th, 1660, "Mr. Walley, once clerk of Stationers' Hall, died in ye country."

John Parker.

1620 *Venus and Adonis*, p. 118.

John Parker received his freedom on March 1st, 1617.

For many years he was an active member of the Company. In 1620 he received a large assignment from Barrett (see p. 118).

Parker was one of the Livery in 1621, and one of the Court of Assistants in 1637. He was Senior Warden in 1645, during an agitation for a reform of the Company. On July 30th, 1648, "Mr. John Parker, stationer, died."

In 1623 he published an edition of *Euphues*, which John Beale printed.

Thomas Walkley.

1622 *Othello* (8), p. 143.

Thomas Walkley took up his freedom on January 29th, 1618, and did a large business on to 1640, publishing, amongst other things, Beaumont and Fletcher's *A King and No King* in 1619 (see p. 153) and 1625, *Philaster* in 1620 and 1622 (see p. 147), Ben Jonson's *Love's Triumph* and Massinger's *Picture* in 1630, both printed by John North.

The Quarto of *Othello* was printed by Okes and sold by Walkley, "at his shop, at the Eagle and Child, in Brittans Bursse."

Thomas Dewe.

1622 *The Troublesome Raigne* (7), p. 95.

Thomas Dewe became free of the Company on March 5th, 1621.

One work entered to him in 1622 was "PROUIDED it belong to noe other man."

In 1624 he was received into the Livery.

He published in 1622 Cooke's *City Gallant* and *A Fair Quarrel* by Middleton and William Rowley, both of which he had received from Trundell the year before (see p. 294). The latter was printed by Matthews, whom he had also employed for *The Troublesome Raigne.* In the same year Dewe issued, with others, the second part of Drayton's *Poly-Olbion.* He probably took Helme's business. Not only did they both publish *The Troublesome Raigne*, but their books were issued from the same place (see p. 302).

The First Folio.[1]

On November 8th, 1623, an entry was made in the Stationers' Registers of a book, the thoughts and phrases of which have become a part of the lives of English-speaking people to a greater extent than those of any volume published before or since, if the Authorised Version of the Bible and the Book of Common Prayer be excepted. Published seven years after the author's death, and three months after his widow died, this volume[2] includes all the plays, except *Pericles,* which are named in the lists at the beginning of this chapter, but in some cases in a very different form, and in addition is the earliest authority for 1 *Henry VI.,*[3] *The Comedy of Errors, The Two Gentlemen of Verona, As You Like It, Twelfth Night, Julius Cæsar, All's Well that Ends Well, Measure for Measure, Macbeth, Antony and Cleopatra, Coriolanus, Timon of Athens, Cymbeline, The Tempest, The Winter's Tale, Henry VIII.*

If the scheme of work recommended at pp. 18-19 be divided into two equal parts, it will be seen that of the plays in the first part only three had to wait till the Folio for their first publication,[4] whilst in the second half there are thirteen. This can scarcely be a matter of chance, and the explanation of it might form an interesting subject for enquiry.[5]

1 Much interesting detail about this and the succeeding editions will be found in a series of articles by Mr. J. Parker Norris in Vols. II.—V. of *Shakespeariana.*

2 It was sold at £1. The price is now much higher. At Mr. George Daniel's sale a copy sold for £714.

3 In the entry called The Third Part.

4 Taking for granted that there are no earlier editions to be discovered.

5 On p. 163 I have in Suggestion 1 put the question forward as one for discussion.

The entry of the Folio in the Registers is thus worded:

1623 November 8.

Master **Blounte**
Isaak Jaggard.

Entred for their Copie vnder the hands of Master Doctor WORRALL and Master **Cole** warden Master WILLIAM SHAKSPEERS *Comedyes, Histories, and Tragedyes* soe manie of the said Copies as are not formerly entred to other men. *vizt.* **vijs.**[1]

COMEDYES.

The Tempest
The two gentlemen of Verona
Measure for Measure
The Comedy of Errors
As you like it
All's well that ends well
Twelfe night
The winters tale

HISTORIES

The thirde parte of HENRY ye SIXT
HENRY the EIGHT

TRAGEDIES.

CORIOLANUS
TIMON of Athens
JULIUS CÆSAR
MACKBETH
ANTHONIE and CLEOPATRA
CYMBELINE

The title-page of the book has simply the words: "Mr. William Shakespeare's Comedies, Histories, & Tragedies. Published according to the True Originall Copies. London Printed by Isaac Iaggard, and Ed. Blount. 1623." A large portion of the page is taken up with the author's Portrait, concerning which some lines by Ben Jonson are placed opposite. The book was dedicated "To

[1] From the number of plays entered, it looks as if the sum should have been eight shillings.

the Most Noble And Incomparable Paire of Brethren . William Earle of Pembroke, &c., Lord Chamberlaine to the Kings most Excellent Maiesty. And Philip Earle of Montgomery, &c., Gentleman of his Maiesties Bed-Chamber. Both Knights of the most Noble Order of the Garter, and our singular good Lords."[1] The dedication, in which the plays are called "these trifles," is signed by the Editors, John Heminge and Henry Condell, who had been fellow-actors with Shakspere. They also give an address "To the great Variety of Readers," in which reference is made to the earlier editions as "stolne, and surreptitious copies, maimed, and deformed"[2]; but these are said to have been "cur'd" and made "perfect."

The plays printed for the first time, the editors say, are presented "as he conceiued thē," and so little alteration had been made in writing that they "scarse receiued from him a blot in his papers." The public are counselled, with much vehemence, to buy the book and well to read it "againe, and againe"; and then, in words suitable to the present days, they say: if "you doe not like him, surely you are in some manifest danger, not to vnderstand him." Following this are some commendatory verses by Ben Jonson, L. Digges, T. M., and Hugh Holland. The Table of Contents, called "A Catalogve," and "The Names of the Principall Actors in all these Playes," come next.[3]

In the book itself, in which the plays are printed in the order unfortunately adopted by the "Globe" and by most modern editors, there are some peculiarities of pagination which should be noticed. At the end of the last play the volume is said to have been

[1] See pp. 231-2.
[2] See pp. 222, 258.
[3] The order of this preliminary matter is not the same in all copies.

"Printed at the Charges of W. Jaggard, Ed. Blount, I. Smithweeke, and W. Aspley." There are none of the poems in the Folio.

There is no division of Acts or Scenes in 2 *Henry VI.*, 3 *Henry VI.*, *Troilus and Cressida, Romeo and Juliet, Timon of Athens*, or *Antony and Cleopatra*. All the others have some division of Acts or of Acts and Scenes. The arrangement, which is not Shakspere's, is capable of improvement.[1]

The Second Folio.

This, published in 1632, contains the same plays as the 1623 edition, but with some slight alterations in the text.

The Third Folio.

This is the name by which the editions of 1663 and 1664 are known. Some errors in the preceding editions are corrected, and some fresh ones made. The 1664 copies have the plays of the other folios and *Pericles*, and also the following, now looked upon as doubtful or pseudo-Shaksperian plays:—*The London Prodigal* (see p. 127), *Thomas, Lord Cromwell* (see p. 105), *Sir John Oldcastle*, (see p. 228), *The Puritan Widow* (see p. 293), *A Yorkshire Tragedy* (see p. 133), and *Locrine* (see p. 89).

The Fourth Folio.

This, issued in 1685, has the same matter as the Third Folio, from which it differs mainly in adopting a more modern spelling. It removed the final "e" in the author's name.

[1] See New Shakspere Society's *Transactions*, 1877-9, Part I. and 1880-2, Part I. The subject, as a whole, is worth investigation.

ROWE'S EDITION.

There was no new edition till 1709, when appeared in 8vo "The Works of Mr. William Shakespear: in Six Volumes. Adorn'd with Cuts. Revis'd and Corrected, with an Account of the Life and Writings of the Author. By N. Rowe, Esq." This contains the doubtful plays of the Third Folio, and is the first of the editions with explanatory matter. The poems are not included, but for the first time there are lists of the *dramatis personæ*. In 1710 a book purporting to be a supplement to Rowe's edition was published with the title—"The Works of Mr. William Shakespear. Volume the Seventh. Containing Venus & Adonis, Tarquin & Lucrece And His Miscellany Poems. With Critical Remarks on his Plays, &c., to which is Prefix'd an Essay on the Art, Rise and Progress of the Stage in Greece, Rome and England." Rowe issued a second edition of his work in 1714, then in eight volumes. The other volume, which was without Rowe's authority, was then published as "Volume the Ninth."

Rowe, born in 1673, was intended for the Bar, but, being a man of means, devoted himself to literature, writing several plays and poems. He also filled several Government offices. He died in 1718, and was buried in Westminster Abbey.

POPE'S EDITION.

The next Editor of Shakspere was Alexander Pope, who in 1725 brought out in quarto "The Works of Shakespear. In Six Volumes. Collated and Corrected by the former Editions. By Mr. Pope." This has only the First Folio plays, which the Editor dealt with freely in the way of alteration and excision. He reprinted Rowe's Life of the Poet, added a preface of his own, and gave the locality of the scenes. Pope's edition, which brought out a supplemental volume similar to Rowe's, reached a second edition in 1728, a third in 1731, a fourth in 1735, a fifth in 1766, and a sixth in 1768. These were not published in the same form as the first.

Pope was born in 1688, and died in 1744.

THEOBALD'S EDITION.

Lewis Theobald, a prolific play-writer, was induced to enter the field of Shaksperian editing by a desire to rescue the text of the plays from the emendations of Pope. His first venture was a small book in 1726, with an examination of Pope's version of *Hamlet*. In revenge, Pope gave Theobald a place in *The Dunciad*. In 1733 came "The Works of Shakespeare: in Seven Volumes. Collated with the Oldest Copies, and Corrected; With Notes, Explanatory, and Critical: By Mr. Theobald." The Editor's preface dealt with various matters of Shaksperian criticism. He emended freely, his most successful venture being the "babbled of green fields" (*Henry V.*, II. iii. 17). The edition was very popular, and was reprinted in 1740, 1752, 1757, 1762, 1767, 1772, and 1773.

Theobald, who was born about 1692, was a barrister in early life. He died in 1744.

HANMER'S EDITION.

Sir Thomas Hanmer issued in 1744, in quarto, "The Works of Shakespear. In Six Volumes. Carefully Revised and Corrected by the former Editions, and Adorned with Sculptures designed and executed by the best hands." Hanmer's name did not appear, but the edition was at once recognised as his. It had, of course, some extra emendations, a short preface, a glossary, and included some of the introductory matter of previous editions. It was published again in 1747, 1750-1, 1760, 1770-1, in differing sizes and number of volumes.

Sir Thomas, who was born in 1677, became Speaker of the House of Commons in 1713, and died in 1746.

Warburton's Edition.

William Warburton was a great friend of Pope. In 1747, three years after Pope's death, he issued in 8vo "The Works of Shakespear in Eight Volumes. The Genuine Text (collated with all the former Editions, and then corrected and emended) is here settled; Being restored from the Blunders of the first Editors, and the Interpolations of the two Last; with a Comment and Notes, Critical and Explanatory. By Mr. Pope and Mr. Warburton." In addition to much of the matter given by other editors, there was a new preface, a quantity of reckless emendations, and a list of the plays in an order of merit. The edition evoked much adverse criticism in books, which are interesting to the curious. The edition was reprinted in another form in the same year.

Warburton, who was born in 1698, disliking the bar, was ordained in 1723, and became Dean of Bristol in 1757, and Bishop of Gloucester in 1760, where he died in 1779.

Johnson's Edition.

The great lexicographer was the next who essayed to correct the plays of Shakspere. Having begun in 1745 with a Review of Hanmer's Edition, he put forth in 1765 in 8vo "The Plays of William Shakespeare, in Eight Volumes, with the Corrections and Illustrations of Various commentators; To which are added Notes by Sam. Johnson." His preface deals with the previous editions, and to some of their introductory matter he adds many of the notes of the other commentators in the form adopted by later editors. He altered the order of printing the plays, but it is not known on what system. The edition was reprinted in 1768.

Dr. Samuel Johnson was born in Lichfield in 1709. He died in 1784, and was buried in Westminster Abbey.

Capell's Edition.

Edward Capell, who was born in 1713, soon after 1736 became Deputy-Inspector of Plays. Upon the death of his father he inherited a large fortune. In 1758 he prepared, with Garrick, an abridgement of *Antony and Cleopatra* for acting purposes, following in 1767 with "Mr. William Shakespeare his Comedies, Histories, and Tragedies, set out by himself in quarto, or by the Players his Fellows in folio, and now faithfully republish'd from those Editions in ten Volumes octavo; with an Introduction: Whereunto will be added, in some other Volumes, Notes, critical and explanatory, and a Body of Various Readings entire." In his Introduction he pays particular attention to the quartos, and gives a list of those then known, with their imprints. He improved the descriptions of the scene-localities and the stage-directions. Capell made a further contribution to Shaksperian criticism by his three volumes of *Notes* published after his death, which took place in 1781. He had a large collection of the quartos, which he left to Trinity College, Cambridge.

Steevens's Edition.

George Steevens was born in 1736. His principal service to Shaksperian study was the publication in 1766 of "Twenty of the plays of Shakespeare, Being the whole Number printed in Quarto During his Life-time, or before the Restoration, Collated where there were different Copies, and Publish'd from the Originals, By George Steevens, Esq: In Four Volumes." As this work can still be obtained without much difficulty, and may be the most accessible form in which many may be able to see the early editions, the list is here given in the two sections of before and after the Folio, and arranged in the order of study recommended:

1611 *Titus Andronicus.*	1613 1 *Henry IV.*
1619 *Whole Contention.*	1600 2 *Henry IV.*
1615 *Richard II.*	1619 *Merry Wives of Windsor.*
1600 *Midsummer-Night's Dream* (Roberts).	1608 *Henry V.*
1612 *Richard III.*	1609 *Sonnets.*
1597 *Romeo and Juliet.*	1611 *Hamlet.*
1609 *Romeo and Juliet.*	1622 *Othello.*
1611 *Troublesome Raigne.*	1605 *Leir.*
1600 *Merchant of Venice* (Roberts).	1608 *Lear.*
1600 *Much Ado about Nothing.*	1609 *Troilus and Cressida.*

1631 *Love's Labour's Lost.*	1631 *Taming of the Shrew.*

1630 *Merry Wives of Windsor.*

These were of great service, as the Editor collated them with such other quartos as he was able to obtain. In 1773 Steevens issued in

8vo "The Plays of William Shakspeare. In Ten Volumes. With the Corrections and Illustrations of Various Commentators; To which are added Notes by Samuel Johnson and George Steevens." It followed with some slight departures the lines of its predecessors. The deviations consisted in adding some personal information about the poet and his family, and a list of translations from the Classics which were in existence in Shakspere's time. In 1778 a second edition was published, "Revised and Augmented." It included Malone's "Attempt to ascertain the order in which the plays attributed to Shakespeare were written." Isaac Reed in 1785 edited a third edition, which was little more than a reprint. In 1793 Steevens issued a fourth edition in fifteen volumes. This contained much more prefatory matter than his previous editions, including, for the first time, extracts from the Stationers' Registers, with the well-known essays by Farmer on Shakspere's learning, and by Malone on the history of the Stage. It had also a glossary prepared by Reed. Steevens's text was preferably that of the Second Folio. He died in 1800, and lies buried in Poplar Chapel, London.

Reed superintended the fifth edition in 1803 and the sixth in 1813, each in twenty-one volumes. In the editions for which Reed was responsible the principal alterations were in the quantity of notes.

Malone's Edition.

Edmond Malone's Shaksperian work has had a more enduring fame than that of any of the other editions of the eighteenth century. Like many of his fellow-workers, he was called to the bar; and, like them, he gave up its practice upon coming into possession of wealth. His first contribution to Shaksperian literature was in 1780, when he issued two volumes as a Supplement to the edition by Johnson and Steevens. These contained notes, the Poems and Sonnets, and the doubtful plays from the 1664 Folio. The Supplement received an additional volume in 1783, and in 1790 appeared in 8vo.: "The Plays and Poems of William Shakspeare, in Ten Volumes; Collated *verbatim* with the most authentick Copies, and revised: with the Corrections and Illustrations of various Commentators; to which are added, an Essay on the Chronological Order of his Plays; an Essay relative to Shakspeare and Jonson; a Dissertation on the three Parts of King Henry VI.; an Historical Account of the English Stage; and Notes; By Edmond Malone." In it he printed much of the editorial matter of his predecessors, and added fresh information on dramatic subjects and valuable illustrative notes to the text. Malone rendered valuable service in helping to expose the forgeries of Samuel Ireland and his son William Henry, who pretended to have discovered not only documents referring to Shakspere in his own handwriting and in that of some of his contemporaries, but a lost play by the poet called *Vortigern and Rowena*.[1]

Malone was born in 1741, and lived till 1812, when, having accumulated large stores of fresh information on the Elizabethan drama, he constituted James Boswell, the son of Dr. Johnson's biographer, his literary executor, who, in 1821, brought out in twenty-one volumes the edition known as "the 1821 Variorum," or "Boswell's Malone," which has been the resort of every other Editor down to the present day, and who has found it a treasure-

[1] The literature evoked by these frauds is named in the *Bibliographer's Manual* under the title of "Ireland Forgeries and Controversy."

house of unrivalled illustration on the dramatic times and obscurities of Shakspere.

Between Rowe's edition and this later issue there were other editions, mostly following Steevens's text; but of these and of the countless editions that have succeeded that of 1821 it is not necessary to say much in detail. Boydell's venture in nine Folio volumes in 1802 presented the text of Shakspere printed in a style of excellence previously unattempted. "The Story of the Boydell Shakespeare" is told at length in Vol. IV. of *Shakespeariana*, 1887. Chalmers, who believed in the Ireland-forgeries, issued an edition in nine volumes in 1805. In 1807 a Folio Reprint of the 1623 Edition was issued.[1] The Rev. William Harness, to whom after-generations owe a debt of gratitude for founding a Triennial Prize at Cambridge, which has recently produced two books for which Shakspere-students are grateful,[2] edited an eight-volume edition in 1825. S. W. Singer was responsible for a ten-volume edition in 1826, with later issues of which W. Watkiss Lloyd's Essays were incorporated. Valpy, in 1832-4, issued an edition in fifteen volumes. Charles Knight's Pictorial Edition in eight volumes, having much explanatory matter, came out in 1843, and his National Edition in six volumes in 1851-2. John Payne Collier's first edition in eight volumes, an excellently printed book, was completed in 1844, and re-issued in six volumes in 1858. One useful feature in it is, that he gives the actual words of the title-pages of the Quartos. Collier's

[1] For some references to this, see *Notes and Queries*, 1853 and 1865. In addition to the reprints mentioned at p. 46, Day and Son published in 1866 a photo-lithographic *facsimile* under the direction of Howard Staunton.

[2] The Rev. H. P. Stokes's *Chronological Order of Shakespeare's Plays*, 1877, and *Two Essays on the First Quarto Edition of Hamlet* by Messrs. C. H. Herford and W. H. Widgery, 1880.

work in the elucidation of Shakspere-obscurities was enormous; but it is unfortunately marred by that inexplicable taste for literary forgery which he at one time developed, and which has left a deplorable taint upon all his research that has not been verified by other workers. His dealings with the text of Shakspere, dating from his *Notes and Emendations*, and with the documents to which he had access, have provoked a considerable literature. The student who wishes to investigate this painful but interesting episode in literature will find enough to satisfy in a consideration of the books named under "Shakespeariana-Collier Controversy" in the *Bibliographer's Manual.*[1]

Our kinsfolk in the United States, who have been such ardent students of Shakspere, often putting those in the old country to shame, were represented in 1851-6 by an excellent edition by the Rev. H. N. Hudson in three volumes. The Rev. Alexander Dyce issued a valuable edition in six volumes in 1857. Howard Staunton's three-volume edition, with Gilbert's illustrations, which contain much of the Spirit of the Shakspere-life, was first published in 1858-60. Charles and Mary Cowden-Clarke, who have been loving students of the poet, edited a four-volume edition in 1864. Begun in 1853, and ended in 1865, the sixteen-volume Folio edition of J. O. Halliwell [Phillipps] surpassed all its predecessors in the wealth of comment it supplied upon biographical, archæological, and kindred points. Richard Grant White, an acute American scholar, completed in 1866 his twelve-volume edition; and at the same time the editors

[1] Articles on the subject will be found in *Blackwood's Magazine*, August, September, and October, 1853, *Edinburgh Review*, April, 1856, *Quarterly Review*, January, 1859, *Fraser's Magazine*, January, February, and May, 1860. The investigation should be aided by Dr. Ingleby's *Shakspere Controversy* and Mr. H. B. Wheatley's book, referred to at p. 200.

of the 'Cambridge' *Shakespeare* issued their carefully-collated text in nine volumes, with footnotes showing, of the conjectural emendations that have been suggested, all those that are the least worthy of notice. The last great edition of the complete works, excepting the 'Henry Irving' *Shakespeare*, which is not quite completed, is that which comes from across the Atlantic, edited in twenty volumes by W. J. Rolfe. Both these are pleasant and helpful, and have distinctive characteristics. One-volume editions, of which the 'Globe' and the 'Leopold' are most useful to the student, are innumerable, as are also the editions of separate plays which have been, and are constantly being, issued. As many of these are desirable helps, I append a list, including the other plays of the scheme of study, and giving the prices, to save the enquirer much trouble. Some are of value even to the advanced scholar, and others are of service only to the merest beginner. But in their notes or introductions they all contain something of use or interest. Additions are doubtless intended to be made in several of the series.

Members of Shakspere-Societies who wish for a copy they can freely mark cannot do better than get the plays published by Ward and Lock at a penny each. They are fairly well printed on tolerable paper, and have a good text. Not only are they convenient for carrying in the pocket and for recording notes for critical purposes, but they will also be found exceedingly useful upon those occasions of reading when much expurgation is required. The secretary should, in as many copies as may be necessary, score through all the parts that have to be left out. If each member will read from a copy so marked, many an uncomfortable pause will be avoided.

	Furness' Edition.	Rolfe's Classics.[1]	Hudson's School Shakespeare.[2]	Clarendon Press.	Pitt Press.	London Series of English Classics.	Rugby Edition.	Collins' Series.	University Shakespeare.	Hunter's Annotated Shakespeare.	Longman's Modern Series.	English Classics for Indian Students.	"Falcon" Edition.	Pseudo-Shakespearian Plays.	Household Shakespeare.[3]	Blackie's School Classics.	Victoria Library.[4]	Cassell's National Library.[5]
Alchemist	...	...	...	...	...	...	...	...	...	...	...	...	...	...	...	...	...	...
All's Well that Ends Well ...	...	2/4	...	...	...	...	...	...	...	1/-	...	...	...	...	...	...	...	...
Antonio and Mellida	...	...	...	...	...	...	...	...	...	...	...	...	...	...	...	...	...	...
Antonio's Revenge	...	...	...	...	...	...	...	...	...	...	...	...	...	...	...	...	...	...
Antony and Cleopatra	...	2/4	1/6	...	...	...	...	...	...	1/-	...	...	...	...	...	...	...	-/6
As You Like It	...	2/4	1/6	1/6	...	...	2/-	1/-	...	1/-	...	...	...	...	1/-	-/8	...	-/6
Birth of Merlin	...	...	...	...	...	...	...	...	...	...	...	...	...	2/-	...	...	1/-	...
Campaspe	...	...	...	...	...	...	...	...	...	...	...	...	...	...	...	...	...	...
Comedy of Errors...	...	2/4	...	...	...	...	...	...	...	1/-	...	...	...	...	...	...	...	-/6
Coriolanus	...	2/4	1/6	2/6	...	...	2/6	1/-	...	1/-	1/-	...	...	...	1/-	...	...	-/6
Cymbeline	...	2/4	1/6	...	...	...	...	...	...	1/-	...	2/6	...	...	...	...	...	-/6
Duchess of Malfi	...	...	...	...	...	...	...	...	...	...	...	...	...	...	...	...	...	...
Duke of Milan	...	...	...	...	...	...	...	...	...	...	...	...	...	...	...	...	...	...
Edward II.	...	...	...	3/-	...	...	...	1/-	...	...	...	...	...	...	...	...	...	...
Edward III.	...	...	...	...	...	...	...	...	...	...	...	...	...	2/-	...	...	...	...
Every Man in his Humour ...	...	...	...	...	...	2/6	...	...	...	...	...	...	...	...	...	...	...	...
Faustus	...	...	...	}6/6	...	2/-	...	...	...	...	...	...	...	...	...	...	...	...
Friar Bacon	...	...	...		...	...	...	...	...	...	...	...	...	...	...	...	...	...
Hamlet	36/-	2/4	1/6	2/-	...	...	2/6	1/-	...	1/-	...	...	...	...	1/6	...	...	-/6
1 Henry IV.	...	2/4	1/6	...	...	...	...	...	...	1/-	...	...	1/6	...	...	...	...	-/6
2 Henry IV.	...	2/4	1/6	...	...	...	...	...	...	1/-	...	...	...	...	...	...	...	-/6
Henry V.	...	2/4	1/6	2/-	...	...	2/-	1/-	1/-	1/-	...	2/6	...	...	1/-	...	...	-/6
1 Henry VI.	...	2/4	...	...	...	...	...	...	...	1/-	...	...	...	...	...	...	...	-/6
2 Henry VI.	...	2/4	...	...	...	...	...	...	...	1/-	...	...	...	...	...	...	...	-/6
3 Henry VI.	...	2/4	...	...	...	...	...	...	...	1/-	...	...	...	...	...	...	...	-/6
Henry VIII.	...	2/4	1/6	...	...	...	...	1/-	...	1/-	...	...	...	...	1/-	-/8	...	-/6
John	...	2/4	1/6	1/6	...	...	2/-	1/-	1/-	1/-	1/-	...	...	...	1/-	-/8	...	-/6
Julius Cæsar	...	2/4	1/6	2/-	...	...	...	1/-	...	1/-	1/-	...	1/6	...	1/-	-/8	...	-/6
King and No King	...	...	...	...	...	...	...	...	...	...	...	...	...	...	...	...	...	...
King David	...	...	...	...	...	...	...	...	...	...	...	...	...	...	...	...	...	...
Knight of the Burning Pestle	...	...	...	...	...	...	...	...	...	...	...	...	...	...	...	...	...	...

1 Each volume is published in cloth at 56 cents., in paper at 40 cents.
2 Also issued in paper at 1/-.
3 Also issued in limp covers at -/2 less for each play.
4 The two plays of this series are in one volume.
5 Issued in paper at -/3.

	Furness' Edition.	Rolfe's Classics.[1]	Hudson's School Shakespeare.[2]	Clarendon Press.	Pitt Press.	London Series of English Classics.	Rugby Edition.	Collins' Series.	University Shakespeare.	Hunter's Annotated Shakespeare.	Longman's Modern Series.	English Classics for Indian Students.	"Falcon" Edition.	Pseudo-Shakespearian Plays.	Household Shakespeare.[3]	Blackie's School Classics.	Victoria Library.[4]	Cassell's National Library.[5]
Lear	18/-	2/4	1/6	1/6	...	...	2/6	1/-	...	1/-	...	...	...	...	1/3	...	...	-/6
Locrine	...	...	...	...	...	...	...	...	...	...	...	...	...	...	...	...	...	...
London Prodigal	...	...	...	...	...	...	...	...	...	...	...	...	...	...	...	...	...	...
Love's Labour's Lost	...	2/4	...	...	...	...	...	...	...	1/-	...	...	...	...	...	...	...	-/6
Macbeth	18/-	2/4	1/6	1/6	...	...	2/-	1/-	...	1/-	...	...	...	...	1/-	-/8	...	-/6
Measure for Measure	...	2/4	...	...	...	...	...	...	...	1/-	...	...	...	...	...	...	...	...
Merchant of Venice	18/-	2/4	1/6	1/-	...	...	...	1/-	...	1/-	1/-	...	1/6	...	1/-	-/8	...	-/6
Merry Wives of Windsor ...	...	2/4	...	...	...	...	...	...	...	1/-	...	...	...	...	...	...	...	...
Midsummer-Night's Dream ..	...	2/4	1/6	1/6	...	...	2/-	1/-	1/-	1/-	...	...	...	...	1/-	...	...	-/6
Much Ado about Nothing ...	...	2/4	1/6	...	...	...	...	...	...	1/-	...	2/-	...	...	...	...	...	-/6
New Way to Pay Old Debts.	...	...	...	...	...	...	...	...	...	...	...	...	...	...	...	...	...	...
Othello	18/-	2/4	1/6	...	...	...	...	...	...	1/-	...	2/6	...	...	...	...	...	-/6
Pericles	...	2/4	...	...	...	...	...	...	...	...	...	...	...	...	...	...	...	...
Philaster	...	...	...	...	...	...	...	...	...	...	...	...	...	...	...	...	...	...
Richard II.	...	2/4	1/6	1/6	...	...	...	1/-	...	1/-	1/-	...	...	...	1/-	-/8	...	-/6
Richard III.	...	2/4	1/6	2/6	...	...	...	1/-	...	1/-	...	2/6	2/-	...	1/-	...	...	-/6
Romeo and Juliet	18/-	2/4	1/6	...	...	...	2/-	1/-	...	1/-	...	...	...	...	...	...	...	-/6
Silent Woman	...	...	...	...	...	...	...	...	...	...	...	...	...	...	...	...	...	...
Taming of the Shrew	...	2/4	...	...	...	...	...	...	...	1/-	...	...	...	...	...	...	...	-/6
Tempest	...	2/4	1/6	1/6	...	...	2/-	1/-	...	1/-	...	1/6	...	...	1/-	-/8	...	-/6
Thomas, Lord Cromwell ...	...	...	...	...	...	...	...	...	...	...	...	...	...	...	...	...	1/-	...
Timon of Athens	...	2/4	...	...	...	...	...	...	...	1/-	...	...	...	...	...	...	...	-/6
Titus Andronicus	...	2/4	...	...	...	...	...	...	...	...	...	...	...	...	...	...	...	-/6
Troilus and Cressida	...	2/4	...	...	...	...	...	...	...	1/-	...	...	...	...	...	...	...	-/6
Twelfth Night	...	2/4	1/6	1/6	...	...	...	...	...	1/-	...	...	1/6	...	...	...	...	-/6
Two Gentlemen of Verona ...	...	2/4	...	...	...	...	...	...	...	1/-	...	...	...	...	...	...	...	-/6
Two Noble Kinsmen	...	2/4	...	...	3/6	...	...	...	...	...	...	...	...	...	...	...	...	...
Virgin-Martyr	...	...	...	...	...	...	...	...	...	...	...	...	...	...	...	...	...	...
Winter's Tale	...	2/4	1/6	...	...	...	...	...	...	1/-	...	2/6	...	...	...	...	...	-/6
Woman Killed with Kindness	...	...	...	...	...	...	...	...	...	...	...	...	...	...	...	...	...	...
Yorkshire Tragedy	...	...	...	...	...	...	...	...	...	...	...	...	...	...	...	...	...	...

1 Each volume is published in cloth at 56 cents., in paper at 40 cents.
2 Also issued in paper at 1/-.
3 Also issued in limp covers at -/2 less for each play.
4 The two plays of this series are in one volume.
5 Issued in paper at -/3.

CHAPTER XII.

The Actors of Shakspere's Time.

"A fellowship in a cry of players.'
Hamlet, III. ii. 289.

NOT later than the early part of the thirteenth century the English clergy, fearing that the people would become demoralised by the frivolities of the itinerant mummers, proscribed the entertainments and excommunicated the performers. As there was then the beginning of a national dramatic instinct, this course failed in its intention. So the religious authorities determined to rival that which they could not suppress, and by way of competition instituted the Sacred Drama, in which they themselves were the actors. This, which formed a welcome entertainment to the people and supplied the clergy with a ready method of instruction, became very popular, and held its ground till it was succeeded by the Morality, a form of drama in which impersonated Virtues and Vices took the places of scriptural or ecclesiastical characters; and this in turn was superseded by the Interlude and Chronicle-History, the immediate precursors of the vigorous and multiform Elizabethan drama, with which still existed occasional forms of the older stage-representations.

As institutions other than the monasteries were founded for the promotion of learning, the regular acting of plays extended to universities,[1] colleges, and schools. From the middle of the sixteenth century till after Shakspere's time, plays were often acted at Oxford and Cambridge and by the law-students at the Inns of Court.[2] The trade-guilds also had dramatic representations of their own. For a long period the singing-boys and scholars in abbeys and priories had acted plays.[3] There was considerable outside discontent at the amount of time which was taken from school-work and devoted to acting.[4] In addition to the two principal companies of children—those of St. Paul's Cathedral-School and of the Chapel Royal—the children of Westminster (Jonson's school-fellows) and the children of Windsor occasionally played at Court. These boy-actors became so popular that they were serious rivals to the professional men-players. Shakspere, by the words of Rosencrantz, gives one view of them. "The tragedians of the city" had to become strolling companies because there was "an aery of children, little eyases, that cry out on the top of question, and are most tyrannically clapped for 't: these are now the fashion."[5] Some more information will be given about them under their re-

1 Polonius had played Julius Cæsar in the University (*Hamlet*, III. ii. 103-9).

2 At Clement's Inn Master Shallow had played Sir Dagonet in Arthur's Show (2 *Henry IV.*, III. ii. 299), and the earliest reference to *Twelfth Night* is the record of its performance in the Middle Temple Hall (see p. 129).

3 The earliest date is 1378. The practice at Westminster still survives.

4 "They make all their scholars play-boys! Is 't not a fine sight to see all our children made interluders? Do we pay our money for this? We send them to learn their grammar and their Terence, and they learn their play-books!" (Ben Jonson's *Staple of News*, III. ii.)

5 See the whole passage, *Hamlet*, II. ii. 341-79, and the comments thereon in the Preface to the Clarendon Press edition of the play.

spective titles. Many of the best known plays, especially Lyly's, were first acted by these boy-players, some of whom afterwards passed into the men's companies. This partly accounts for the excellence of many of the Elizabethan and Jacobean actors.

From the time of Edward IV. there are records that bands of professional players were recognised by Court authority,[1] and contemporaneously several noblemen also kept companies of actors. Up to 1542 and occasionally afterwards plays were acted in churches. In 1547, when Gardiner, Bishop of Winchester, was directing "a solemn dirge and mass for the late King," he said that the players in Southwark were going to have at the same time "a solemne playe to trye who shal have most resorte, they in game, or I in ernest."[2] In 1549, 1551, 1553, and at other times, there were very definite and strict royal warrants directed against players.[3] At the beginning of Elizabeth's reign, plays were acted mostly in large inns or on temporary scaffolds or on open stages. In 1559, in terms much less severe than those of Edward VI. and of Mary, Elizabeth issued a proclamation[4] regulating the time, the place, and the manner of playing interludes. In 1560 a Royal payment was made to the players of Lord Robert Dudley (afterwards Earl of

[1] In 1494 each of the King's players of Interludes received a payment of five marks yearly for his wages, and later £1 3*s.* 4*d.* a year was added for his livery (see *Calendar of State Papers*. Domestic. 1547-1580, p. 40).

[2] See *Calendar of State Papers*. Domestic. 1547-1580, p. 1.

[3] For reprints of these and many other interesting papers see *The English Drama and Stage* (1543-1664), 1869. In 1556 orders were issued "against players and pipers strolling through the Kingdom, disseminating seditions and heresies" (*Calendar of State Papers*. Domestic. 1547-1580, p. 82.

[4] Copies are in the British Museum and the Bodleian, and a reprint in the work mentioned above. Some of these royal proclamations were no doubt intended to prevent the assembly of crowds and the consequent spread of the plague.

Leicester).[1] It is thought that Elizabeth never attended a public theatre, yet she was exceedingly fond of dramatic representations, which were often given before her.

It is clear from the 1559 Proclamation that early in Elizabeth's reign various noblemen had companies of actors under their patronage. In 1571-2 a statute was passed enjoining that all common players not belonging to such were, if they wandered abroad, unless under a certain special license, to be adjudged rogues and vagabonds. In 1574 the Queen granted a license to five servants of the Earl of Leicester as actors of stage plays "throughout o[r] Realme of England." This license must have accorded them other privileges than this permission, which would have been, in some measure at least, already secured to them by the statute of 1571-2. The official recognition, which is probably the first privy seal recognition of a company of players, no doubt gave them a position much superior to that of other companies. All dramatic entertainments were under the general supervision of the Master of the Revels.[2] In 1575 Leicester entertained the Queen at Kenilworth for nineteen days with great magnificence, of which histrionic representation formed a large part, and of some of which it has been suggested that Shakspere, then eleven years old, was a spectator. About this time the Lord Mayor and Common Council of London, adopting the views of the Puritans, endeavoured to

[1] For a copy of the entry made in the Office-books of the Treasurers of the Chamber, and much other information in reference to some of the early companies, see *Extracts from the Accounts of the Revels at Court*, edited by Peter Cunningham for the Shakespeare Society, 1842, pp. xxviii.-xlv.

[2] This functionary dated his existence from 1546. Sir Thomas Cawarden held the office from 1546 to 1560; Sir Thomas Benger, from 1560 to 1577 (see p. 198); Thomas Blagrave, from 1577 to 1579; Edmund Tylney, from 1579 to 1610; Sir George Bucke from 1610 to 1622 (see p. 177).

considerably limit the doings of the players. A petition from "the Queenes Maties poore Players" was presented in 1575 to the Privy Council, praying for a relaxation of some of the restrictions under which they were suffering. In 1576 the house known as The Theatre[1] was built by James Burbage, and in 1577 The Curtain theatre was erected. They were both outside the City jurisdiction, being in Shoreditch, in the part now known as Holywell Lane. Many communications referring to players passed between the City Authorities and the Privy Council, and on the 24th of December, 1578, the latter "required the Lord Mayor 'to suffer the children of her Majesty's Chapel, the servants of the Lord Chamberlain,[2] of the Earl of Warwick, of the Earl of Leicester, of the Earl of Essex, and the children of Paul's and no companies else to exercise plays within the city.'" The Privy Council was not, however, entirely antagonistic to the religious scruples of those whom the Lord Mayor represented. It made determined and repeated efforts to prevent the acting of plays in Lent, and even tried to do away with Sunday performances,[3] except in the case of the Court, where plays were acted on that day down to the time of Charles I. By 1580 there were places, not always theatres, set apart for the performance of plays. That at Black-

[1] In the Royal Historical Society's *Transactions*, Vol. X., Mr. Fleay has a painstaking paper "On the History of Theatres in London, from their First Opening in 1576 to their Closing in 1642." An interesting series of articles on "London Theatres," by Mr. T. Fairman Ordish, will be found in *The Antiquary* from March, 1885, to December, 1887.

[2] At that time, the Earl of Sussex.

[3] This was rendered more easy by the effect on public opinion resulting from a serious accident to a large number of the audience at Paris Garden on a Sunday in 1582. Records of many of the cases treated at St. Thomas's Hospital are given in *The Young Chirurgion's Practice*, quoted by Mr. Rendle in *The Antiquary* for September, 1889.

friars[1] was the most noteworthy, being used for various purposes, including rehearsals in connection with dramatic representations at Court and other aristocratic festivities. In 1583 from some of the noblemen's actors Elizabeth formed, under her own immediate patronage, a company of players who were known as the Queen's Majesty's servants. The Puritan writers and preachers about this time inveighed in the most severe terms against the corrupting influences of the theatre and the practices of theatre-goers. Even deducting a considerable amount for exaggeration and bigotry, there was doubtless enough left to justify Elizabeth in appointing a Commission in 1589 for revising plays.[2]

It is perhaps not too much to say that at this time the future of the stage and of dramatic literature was determined. Plays had to such a large extent become mere outlets for personal and political abuse that it was necessary for State-purposes to place them under serious restrictions, and contemporaneously with this came, in the person of Shakspere, one who by the supreme excellence of his work was enabled to raise dramatic writing to a level which, a few short years before, it would have seemed impossible to reach. Although the satirising of individuals was still carried on—and sometimes freely so—yet it sank into comparative insignificance, and, being in a more disguised form, it lost its virulence and soon ceased to be a political danger. The State-reform was not without its good influence on Shakspere. As by it an improved tone had been given to the stage, there was no temptation for him to debase his mighty powers by writing down to a depraved popular taste: but at the beginning of his literary career, knowing only an upward

[1] It was here that some of Lyly's plays were acted.

[2] 1821 *Variorum*, Vol. III. p. 457.

tendency, his energies instinctively went to encourage it; and although the stage and drama were afterwards subject to most pernicious influences, to which Shakspere unfortunately yielded at times, yet he impressed them so favourably that writers of every shade of thought agree in pronouncing the spirit of his plays to be essentially elevating, pure, and ennobling. His own words, written in connection with an entirely different matter, will express the general result of his work:

"'Fair, kind, and true,' is all my argument,
'Fair, kind, and true,' varying to other words;
And in this change is my invention spent.
Three themes in one, which wondrous scope affords.
'Fair, kind, and true,' have often lived alone,
Which three till now never kept seat in one."

Some little time before 1592, Henslowe was managing the Rose theätre, which, being on the south side of the Thames, in Southwark, was outside the authority of the Lord Mayor, and which probably had been only just built near Paris Garden,[1] the scene of bear-baitings and other noisy sports.[2] In Henslowe's *Diary* the first entry of the acting of a play at the Rose is on February 19th, 1592. It was here that Shakspere's first plays were performed.[3]

During the greater part of 1593 the theatres were closed in consequence of the extent of the plague. In December, 1594, Shakspere acted with the Lord Chamberlain's servants before the Queen at Greenwich Palace. From this time most of the history of the stage, so far as the work of a Shakspere-society is con-

[1] Mr. William Rendle has a full account of this and the Bankside neighbourhood generally in Appendix I. of Part II. of the New Shakspere Society's edition of Harrison's *Description of England*. This and the other two parts are full of interest to the Shakspere-student.

[2] See *Henry VIII.*, V. iv. 2.

[3] See pp. 59, 63.

cerned, is the history of the several companies of actors, as will be hereafter briefly stated. It will be sufficient to record here that in 1596 or 1597 James Burbage, not without a local protest, converted the Blackfriars premises, alluded to at p. 325, into a theatre,[1] which stood in the present Playhouse Yard near *The Times* office; that in 1599 the Globe theatre on the Bankside, on ground now occupied by the brewery of Messrs. Barclay and Perkins, was built by the Burbages partly from the materials of The Theatre, which was then pulled down, and that the Fortune theatre in St. Giles's, Cripplegate, in the street now known as Playhouse Yard, between Whitecross Street and Golden Lane, was built very soon after by Henslowe and his son-in-law, Edward Alleyn,[2] the great rival of James Burbage's son, Richard. Henslowe became the manager of the Fortune, and Alleyn its leading actor. There were several other but minor theatres about this time, and on June 22nd, 1600, the Privy Council endeavoured to control their number by issuing an order limiting them to the Fortune for the north side of the Thames and the Globe for the Surrey side. This order was not carried into effect, and at the end of 1601 a more stringent order was issued. In 1603 the stage found in the person of the new monarch a warm supporter. In a special license which on May 17th, 1603, he gave to the actors then known as the Lord Chamberlain's servants, of whom Shakspere was one, it is seen that they were occupying "theire now usuall howse called the Globe."

Soon after the accession of James, the companies of players under the patronage of various noblemen were absorbed into "the

[1] This was on a site exempt from the Jurisdiction of the City Authorities.

[2] Alleyn, who was the principal holder of the property, became the founder of Dulwich College.

three companies of plaiers to the King, Queene and Prince," and in April, 1604, there went out from the Privy Council to the Lord Mayor and the county magistrates, an order, the signatories to which included the Lord Admiral and the Earl of Worcester, two of the patrons of prominent companies, that the newly-organised bodies were "publicklie to exercise their plaies in ther severall and usuall howses for that purpose and noe other; viz., the Globe scituate in Maiden Lane on the Banckside in the countie of Surrey, the Fortune in Goldinge Lane, and the Curtaine in Hollywelle in the cowntie of Midlesex,[1] without any lett or interrupption in respect of any former Lettres of Prohibition heertofore written by us to your Lordship, except ther shall happen weeklie to die of the plague above the number of thirtie within the Cittie of London and the Liberties thereof, att which time wee thinke itt fitt they shall cease and forbeare any further publicklie to playe untill the sicknes be againe decreaced to the saide number." In 1605-6 an Act of Parliament was passed which forbade in stage-plays the jesting or profane use of "the holy Name of God or of Christ Jesus, or of the Holy Ghost or of the Trinitie." Effects of this are to be seen in the plays, and are of help in fixing the dates of passages either original or altered.

In 1613 the Globe theatre was burned down, and at once rebuilt with greater ornamentation. James I. in 1615 gave permission for the erection of a second theatre in Blackfriars, but of which advantage was not taken. In 1619 the City of London Corporation endeavoured to suppress the Blackfriars theatre because "the owner of the said playehowse within the Blackfryers under the name of a

[1] The Globe was occupied by the King's servants, the Fortune by the Prince's servants, and the Curtain by the Queen's servants (see *Calendar of State Papers.* Domestic. Addenda. 1623—1625, p. 530).

private howse hath converted the same to a publique playhowse," one of the results of the consequent obstructive traffic being that the minister and people were "disturbed at the administracion of the Sacrament of Baptisme and publique prayers in the afteer-noones." How far this effort of the City Authorities was successful may be seen from the license granted by the King in 1620, which empowered his servants to act "when the infection of the plague shall not weekely exceed the nomber of Fortie by the certificate of the Lord Mayor of London for the time being, as well within theis two their now usuall Houses called the Globe within or Countie of Surrey and their private House scituate in the precincts of the Blackfriers within our Citty of London, As also within any Towne Halls, or Moute-halls, or other convenient places within the liberties and freedom of any other Cittie, Universitie, Towne, or Burrough whatsoever within or said Realmes and Domynions;" and not only were no hindrances to be placed in their way, but they were to be aided and assisted, and to be allowed "such former curtesies as hath byn given to men of their place and qualitie." In 1621 the Fortune theatre was burned down, and rebuilt in the following year. Other authorities must be consulted for the history of the stage from this time till 1642, when the theatres were closed on account of "the distressed estate of Ireland, steeped in her own blood, and the distracted estate of England, threatened with a cloud of blood by a civil war," and because "public sports do not well agree with public calamities, nor public stage-plays with the seasons of humiliation" then enjoined by the Long Parliament, which in 1648 issued an order for "the utter suppression and abolishing of all Stage-Playes and Interludes. With the Penalties to be inflicted upon the Actors and Spectators." With the Restoration came a drama influenced by, and almost re-created on, French lines of thought and manner.

The notes that follow are on the theatrical companies[1] that acted the plays which form the Society's course of study. There were some others to which incidental reference will be made.

The Children of Paul's.

The scholars or choristers of St. Paul's Cathedral had from the fourteenth century been engaged in dramatic representation. In 1378 they petitioned Richard II. to protect their interests, which they feared would be injured by competition. At that time they were of course acting Mysteries. They however kept pace with, and probably developed, the taste for other forms of drama, and in the sixteenth century they had become very popular actors. Commonly they performed in the School-room of St. Paul's, but they also played before the Court and often went out of London to act. In 1544 they played at Hatfield before Princess Elizabeth, when she was there visited by Queen Mary. In 1559 they appeared again before Elizabeth, when as Queen she was entertained by Lord Arundel at Nonsuch in Surrey. 1563 is the earliest date in the Council-registers when they were paid for performing at Court. They acted Lyly's *Campaspe* in 1584. There seems to be no record of any play acted by them between 1594 and 1600. Soon after this

[1] The fullest contribution to their history is in Mr. Fleay's paper "On the Actor Lists, 1578-1642," in Vol. IX. of the Royal Historical Society's *Transactions*. Vol. III. of the 1821 *Variorum* is full of interesting details of the history of the Stage, to which later writers have not added much that is material. *Historia Histrionica*, 1699, reprinted in Hazlitt's *Dodsley*, and, with much caution, Collier's *History of Dramatic Literature* and *Memoirs of Actors*, should be consulted.

they acted *Antoñio and Mellida* and *Antonio's Revenge* (see pp. 109, 115). For part, if not all, of this period they were prevented from playing by official interdict, but from the latter date to 1608 several plays are mentioned as having been performed by them.

It is not at all improbable that about this date, after which nothing is heard of the Children of Paul's, James took them under his patronage, and that they became the company known as The Children of the King's Revels. The audiences in their school-room differed from those at the theatres, consisting principally of gentlemen and scholars.[1] This will account for the character and expressions of many of the plays that were written specially for them.

When the Paul's Children played Chapman's *Bussy d'Ambois* (perhaps in 1602), Nathaniel Field played the title *rôle*.

A company known as The Servants of his Majesty's Revels played *The Virgin-Martyr* at the Red Bull about 1620.

The Children of the Chapel.

Judging from the dramatic history of the Children of Paul's, it will probably be safe to conclude that the singing-boys of the Chapel Royal had been for some time in the habit of acting plays. Quite in the early part of her reign, when Richard Edwards was their master, they played before Queen Elizabeth. Up to 1569, and perhaps afterwards, they acted in the Chapel itself.[2] From that year onwards there are in the Council-books records of payments made to them for performances. They occasionally acted in

1 See 1821 *Variorum*, Vol. II., pp. 192-6.
See Drake's *Shakspeare and his Times*, Paris ed. 1838, p. 442.

the Blackfriars house,[1] and from the time it was converted into a theatre they seem to have had it as their regular dramatic home till it was occupied by the King's servants in 1609. In 1604 they formed almost, if not quite, entirely the newly-formed Children of the Revels (see p. 232). After this they were but rarely known by their former title.[2]

In 1600, when they played Ben Jonson's *Cynthia's Revels* (see p. 210), Nathaniel Field (see p. 252), Salathiel Pavy, Thomas Day, John Underwood,[3] Robert Baxter, and John Frost belonged to the company; but in the following year, in the list of *dramatis personæ* of the *Poetaster*, the names of the first four are given with those of William Ostler[3] and Thomas Marton.

The Children of the Revels played *The Silent Woman* (see p. 137) in 1609. Field was a member of the company, and his is the only one of the 1600 and 1601 names of the Chapel-Children. Pavy was dead.[4] The other names are William Barksted, Giles Carey, William Penn, Hugh Attawel, Richard Allin, John Smith, and John Blaney.

The Lord Admiral's Servants.

Lord William Howard, who was created Lord Howard of Effingham and who was Lord High Admiral during the greater part of Mary's reign, holding the post between the two terms of

[1] See p. 325. They acted Lyly's *Campaspe* there (see p. 61).

[2] See 1821 *Variorum*, Vol. III., p. 428. A company called The Children of the Chapel acted in 1612-13 (see Cunningham's *Revels at Court*, p. xlii.)

[3] Afterwards with the King's servants.

[4] See Ben Jonson's poem on Pavy. Epigra cxx.

office of Edward the 9th Lord Clinton, does not seem to have had a company of players. Upon his death in 1573 his son Charles succeeded to the title, and was appointed Lord Admiral in 1585, upon the death of the Earl of Lincoln, the title bestowed on Lord Clinton in 1572. Lord Howard's band of actors seems to be first noticed in 1576, when they played before the Queen at Hampton Court.[1] When they acted two interludes before her Majesty on the Sunday after Christmas, 1588, they were described as the Lord Admiral's servants.[2] In November, 1589, they obeyed the Lord Mayor's order "to forbere playinge" within the city.[3] At the end of 1590 and in the beginning of 1591 they acted two plays at Court.[4] In May, 1594, they were with Henslowe; and in the following month, with the Lord Chamberlain's men, they began an engagement under him at Newington.[5] In 1597 their patron was created Earl of Nottingham. They were sometimes known under the new title from that date till they became the theatrical servants of Henry, Prince of Wales, in 1603. They were playing by themselves from October, 1596, to July, 1597 (see *Diary*, pp. 82—90). From October 21st, 1597, to March 4th, 1598, they seem to have been

[1] See 1821 *Variorum*, Vol. III., p. 387, and Cunningham's *Revels at Court*, p. 102.

[2] 1821 *Variorum*, Vol. III., pp. 448-9. In the Royal Historical Society's *Transactions*, Vol. X., p. 131, Mr. Fleay states, without giving any reference, that there was a company known as the Admiral's in 1583. If so, it must have been under the patronage of the Earl of Lincoln. I cannot understand Mr. Fleay's statement (*Op. cit.*, p. 114, and *Introduction to Shakespearian Study*, p. 53) about the Lord Chamberlain and the Lord Admiral. Philip Howard never held either of these offices. Beatson's *Political Index* and Burke's works on the Peerage will supply all the information necessary on these points.

[3] See *English Drama and Stage*, p. 34

[4] See 1821 *Variorum*, Vol. III., p. 449.

[5] *Diary*, pp. 34-5. During this engagement *Titus Andronicus* and *Faustus* were played, the former probably by the Chamberlain's men only and the latter by the Admiral's.

acting with Lord Pembroke's men (see *Diary*, pp. 102-103). From March 10th, 1598, it would appear they were again playing by themselves, for Henslowe then took inventories of their properties.[1] At this time was the performance of *Faustus* referred to in the title-page of the 1604 edition (see page 67). Soon after these performances, which were at the Rose, they moved to the Fortune (see p. 327).

Henslowe's *Diary* shows that between 1594 and 1602 the company included Edward Alleyn[2] (see p. 327), John Singer, Richard Jones,[3] Thomas Towne, Martin Slater, Edward Juby, Thomas Downton,[4] James Dunstan,[5] William Bird (or Borne), Gabriel Spencer[6] (see p. 207), Robert Shaw,[4] Humphrey Jeffes,[7] Anthony Jeffes, Charles Massey, Samuel Rowley (see p. 251), Wilson, Flower, Price, and Day. When they became Prince Henry's servants the names of Singer and Jones are wanting, but others are added.[8] After the Prince's death in 1612 the actors, passing under the patronage of

[1] See Appendix to *Diary*.

[2] Alleyn had belonged to Lord Worcester's company in 1586. In 1593 he was one of Lord Strange's men. Alleyn was an actor of the leading parts, amongst which he played Faustus (see p. 67). For references to others of his parts see *Memoirs of Edward Alleyn*, pp. 7, 8, 198—213, and Thomas Heywood's Dedication to the 1633 Edition of Marlowe's *Jew of Malta*. He was absent from the stage from 1597 to 1601. Ben Jonson (ed. Cunningham, p. 242) adds his testimony concerning Alleyn's histrionic ability.

[3] Jones was a member of Lord Worcester's company in 1586.

[4] Shaw and Downton were prominent members of the company in 1598 (see 1821 *Variorum*, Vol. III., p. 450). Shaw became one of Lord Worcester's men in 1602.

[5] Perhaps the Tunstall of Lord Worcester's company in 1586.

[6] Probably this is the actor who played the Messenger in 3 *Henry VI.* (see 1623 Folio, "Histories," p. 150).

[7] This is probably the player of the Second Keeper in 3 *Henry VI.* (see 1623 Folio, "Histories," p. 158).

[8] See 1821 *Variorum*, Vol. III., p. 444, and New Shakspere Society's *Transactions*, 1877-79, Part III., Appendix II.

the Lady Elizabeth and her husband, the Elector Palatine,[1] became known as the Palsgrave's men.[2]

The Earl of Sussex's Servants.

It is known that this set of actors, whose first patron perhaps was Thomas Ratcliffe, the 3rd Earl, played before the Queen in 1577, 1580, and 1592.[3] The Earl of Sussex succeeded the first Lord Howard of Effingham as Lord Chamberlain[4] in 1573, and held the office till he died in June, 1583. The players up to that time were sometimes known by his private, and sometimes by his official, title (see p. 337). In their earlier days it is probable that they acted at the Curtain. The performance at Court in 1592 was when they were the servants of their earliest patron's brother Henry, the 4th Earl, who lived till April, 1593. Henslowe in his *Diary* (pp. 31-4) shows that with other companies they were acting for him at the Rose from December, 1593, till the following April. During this engagement they played *Titus Andronicus*[5] (see p. 59). They must then have been under the protection of Robert, the son of the previous Earl. After this date there is no information about them. At the dispersion consequent upon the death of the Earl of Derby (Lord Strange) in 1594, they probably ceased to exist as a separate company.

[1] See p. 103.

[2] See Collier's *History of Dramatic Literature*, Vol. I., p. 381; 1821 *Variorum*, Vol. III., p. 59.

[3] See 1821 *Variorum*, Vol. III., pp. 446-9.

[4] The Lord Mayor and Corporation of London wrote to him in that capacity in 1574 in reference to theatrical performances (see *English Drama and Stage*, pp. 23-4).

[5] The other plays at that time are mentioned by Henslowe.

The Earl of Derby's Servants.

It is not known when these were formed;[1] but on Sunday, the 14th of February, 1580, they acted a play before the Queen. It has been thought that their theatrical home was at the Curtain. Their patron, Henry, the 4th Earl, died on September 25th, 1593. Probably for some time before this, his eldest son, Ferdinando, known as Lord Strange, had become their nominal head.[2] In 1591-3, as Lord Strange's servants, they played before Elizabeth at Whitehall and at Hampton Court. From February to June, 1592, they were acting under Henslowe's management at the Rose (see *Diary*, pp. 20-8). At this time they played Greene's *Friar Bacon*, which was afterwards acted by the Queen's men (see p. 73). Their repertory, of which Henslowe gives a full list, included a play known as *Henry VI.* (see p. 63). On May 6th, 1593, Lord Strange's men included Edward Alleyn (see p. 334), William Kempe[3] (see pp. 155, 338), Thomas Pope,[4] John Heminge (see p. 306), Augustine Phillipps (see p. 81), and George Bryan.[4] Lord Strange did not live long to enjoy the earldom; and before his death, in April, 1594, the company became dispersed. Alleyn stayed with Henslowe and the Lord Admiral's men; the others joined the Lord Chamberlain's servants.

[1] Collier (*Shakespeare*, ed. 1858, Vol. I., p. 17) says the Earl of Derby had a company of players about 1532-6.

[2] See *English Drama and Stage*, p. 34. Lord Strange's men, who were at Stratford in 1579 (see 1821 *Variorum*, Vol. II., p. 150), were probably his company of tumblers who appeared at Court in 1580-1 (*Op. cit.*, Vol. III., pp. 448-9).

[3] While Kempe was one of Lord Strange's men he did the comic business in *A Knack to Know A Knave* (reprinted in Hazlitt's *Dodsley*). Kempe had been with the Queen's men in 1588.

[4] Pope and Bryan were amongst the English players who were acting at the Courts of Denmark and Saxony in 1585-6 (see p. 75 and Cohn's *Shakespeare in Germany*, p. xxiii.) Pope played comic parts.

Lord Strange's brother, who succeeded to the title, had a company of actors who played before the Queen in 1600. *Titus Andronicus* (see p. 59) and Heywood's *Edward IV.* (see p. 87) were acted by the Earl of Derby's servants.

The Lord Chamberlain's Servants.

Under this designation a company acted from 1574.[1] Then and till his death, in June, 1583, the Earl of Sussex was Lord Chamberlain (see p. 335). He was succeeded by Charles, the 2nd Lord Howard of Effingham;[2] but in 1585 Henry Carey, the 1st Lord Hunsdon, and cousin to Elizabeth, who had a company that acted a comedy before the Queen in 1582,[3] was Lord Chamberlain. His players then took the official title, being the company that afterwards acted most of Shakspere's plays. In 1594 they were reinforced by some of the actors who had played under Lord Strange's name. In that year, whilst acting in conjunction with the Lord Admiral's men,[4] they played *Titus Andronicus* (see p. 59), and by themselves they played before Elizabeth at Greenwich, when Shakspere was one of the party. When the Queen's servants broke up in 1594 coincident with the death of Lord Strange, it seems reasonable, in the absence of direct information, to believe that the Chamberlain's servants acted at The Curtain till they went to the Globe in 1599 (see p. 327). In July, 1596, Lord Hunsdon died, and William Brooke, the 7th

[1] See 1821 *Variorum*, Vol. III., p. 382, and Cunningham's *Revels at Court*, p. 87.

[2] See *Calendar of State Papers*. Domestic. 1581—1590, pp. 163-4.

[3] See 1821 *Variorum*, Vol. III., p. 405, and Cunningham, *Op. cit.*, p. 176.

[4] See p. 333. Henslowe's record of this double engagement is so vague, that it is impossible to say whether the many plays he mentions *(Diary*, p. 35 *et seq.)* were acted by the companies singly or together. The record ends about the time of the first Lord Hunsdon's death.

Lord Cobham, was appointed to the office; and the players, passing to the patronage of George Carey, who succeeded his father in the title, again became known as Lord Hunsdon's servants.[1] Upon Lord Cobham's death, the 2nd Lord Hunsdon became Lord Chamberlain, in March, 1597, and the players resumed the official designation, retaining it till James's accession, soon after which they went to form the King's servants.

In 1598, when the Lord Chamberlain's servants played *Every Man in his Humour*, the company included William Shakspere,[2] Richard Burbage,[3] Augustine Phillipps (see pp. 81, 336), Heminge[4] (see pp. 306, 336), Henry Condell (see p. 306), Thomas Pope[4] (see p. 336), William Sly, Christopher Beeston, William Kempe[5] (see p. 336), and John Duke. In the following year, when the company played *Every Man out of his Humour*, the names of Shakspere, Beeston,[6] Kempe,[6] and Duke[6] are wanting. About this time Richard Cowley must have been a member of the company.[7] In 1603 the Chamberlain's servants acted *Sejanus*, in the cast of which were Burbage, Shakspere, Phillipps, Heminge, Sly, Condell, John Lowin,[8]

[1] During this period they acted *Romeo and Juliet* (see p. 91).

[2] Supposed to have acted old Knowell, and to be represented in that character in the First Folio Portrait.

[3] Son of James Burbage (see p. 327). Richard's position in the company can be inferred from the fact that Richard III., Hamlet, Othello, and Lear were among his parts.

[4] Heminge and Pope were often the business-representatives of the company (see 1821 *Variorum*, Vol. III., p. 450).

[5] Kempe played Dogberry in *Much Ado* (see 1600 Quarto and 1623 Folio "Comedies," p. 116), and Peter in *Romeo and Juliet* (see 1599 Quarto). The Folio also states that Balthazar in *Much Ado* was played by "Jack Wilson."

[6] Beeston, Kempe, and Duke Joined Lord Worcester's players (see Henslowe's *Diary*, pp. 236-7).

[7] He played Verges in *Much Ado* (see 1600 Quarto and 1623 Folio "Comedies," p. 116).

[8] Lowin had previously belonged to Lord Worcester's players. Later on he acted Falstaff, Morose in *The Silent Woman*, and Mammon in *The Alchemist*.

and Alexander Cooke. On May 17th of that year they lost their title of the Lord Chamberlain's servants, and by the Royal License of that date became the King's servants.

Of the plays given in Chapter IX. for study it is known that the Lord Chamberlain's servants acted *Titus Andronicus* (see p. 59), *Richard II.* (see p. 81), *A Midsummer-Night's Dream* (see p. 85), *Richard III.* (see p. 87), *Romeo and Juliet* (see page 91), *The Merchant of Venice* (see p. 101), *Much Ado About Nothing* (see p. 103), *Thomas, Lord Cromwell* (see p. 105), 2 *Henry IV.* (see p. 111), *The Merry Wives of Windsor* (see p. 113), and *Henry V.* (see p. 117).

The Queen's Servants.

Attached to the Court, and continued from the time of Henry VII., there were performers who acted interludes (see p. 322), and who in Elizabeth's time were known as the Queen's players.[1] As these, however, were "very poore and ignorant" in comparison with the "very skilfull and exquisite Actors . . . . entertained into the seruice of diuers great Lords,"[2] Elizabeth determined not to be behind the age; so Edmund Tylney, who was Master of the Revels from 1579 to 1610, was "sente for to the Courte by letter from Mr. Secretary dated the xth of Marche 1582 [1583] To choose out a companie of players for her Matie."[3] In Stow's *Chronicle* (*loc. cit.*) it is said that this was done by choosing twelve of the principal

[1] They acted at Stratford in 1569, and probably again in 1587, 1592, 1593, and 1596.

[2] Stow's *Chronicle*, ed. 1631, p. 698.

[3] Cunningham's *Revels at Court*, p. 186. Fleay (*Introduction to Shakespearian Study*, p. 54) says that "there was only one Queen's company in Elizabeth's time." He is undoubtedly right in stating (Royal Historical Society's *Transactions*, Vol. IX., p. 47) that the actors led by the Duttons and Lanham were one company. But he seems to have forgotten the Interluders.

actors from various existing companies. Fleay says that "the Earl of Warwick's and the Earl of Leicester's companies were dissolved and Queen Elizabeth's men were formed out of them." But the earlier authority must be right, as visits to Stratford were made by Warwick's players[1] in 1584 and by Leicester's[2] in 1587 (see 1821 *Variorum*, Vol. II., p. 151). Leicester also probably took his company to Holland in 1585 (see p. 193). The newly-formed company had its home at The Theatre[3] (see p. 324). From 1586 to 1591 there are entries in the Council-Registers of payments being made to her Majesty's players.[4] Not later than 1591 the Queen's players acted *The Troublesome Raigne* (see p. 95), which was not played by any other company before 1611. For a week in April, 1594, the Queen's men were acting with those of the Earl of Sussex,[5] when Greene's *Friar Bacon* was among the plays performed. After that nothing is known of them. Probably they became absorbed into other companies. Lord Strange's death in 1594 seems to have led to a general re-arrangement of the acting companies.

Amongst the Queen's servants were included Thomas (? Robert) Wilson and Richard Tarleton,[6] Lawrence Dutton, John Dutton,

[1] Warwick's players had acted before the Queen in 1564 and in 1576, when Lawrence Dutton (who was at the head of Sir Robert Lane's players in 1573) and John Dutton were the chiefs of the party.

[2] Leicester, when Lord Dudley, had a set of actors who performed at Court in 1562. In 1574, when he received the special license (see p. 323), James Burbage, John Perkyn, John Lanham, William Johnson, and Robert Wilson were the players mentioned in it.

[3] It is almost certain that Leicester's company had acted there, as James Burbage one of its leading members, was the builder of the house.

[4] These were doubtless the 1583 company. The Registers from June 26th, 1582, to February 14th, 1586, are lost.

[5] Henslowe's *Diary*, pp. 33-4.

[6] Stow, *loc. cit.*

and John Lanham (its leaders in 1589-90), and perhaps the others mentioned in Leicester's patent of 1574. Upon Tarleton's death in 1588, his place as comedian was taken by William Kempe.[1]

At the beginning of the reign of James I., the company adopted as the Queen's servants had been previously under the patronage of the Earl of Worcester.[2] Amongst them were Richard Perkins, John Duke,[3] Christopher Beeston,[3] Thomas Heywood (see p. 213), and Robert Pallant, as mentioned in Henslowe's *Diary*, pp. 235-45. When adopted by the Queen, the names of Thomas Greene,[4] Thomas Swinnerton, James Hoe, and Robert Beeston are found in addition. They then occupied the Curtain.

This later company of Queen's servants played *A Woman Killed with Kindness* (see p. 123), which upon its first production had been acted by the Earl of Worcester's players.

The Earl of Pembroke's Servants.

It seems that it was on St. John's Day, 1592, that the Earl of Pembroke's servants acted for the first time before the Queen at Court.[5] It was probably not much before this date that the

1 Kempe was one of Lord Strange's men in 1593, in 1598 one of the Lord Chamberlain's servants, and in 1602 one of Lord Worcester's players.

2 Worcester's players were at Stratford in 1569 and at Leicester in 1586 (see 1821 *Variorum*, Vol. II., p. 150, and Shakespeare Society's *Papers*, Vol. IV., p. 145). In the latter year the company included Robert Browne (who became one of the leaders of the Earl of Derby's servants in 1600), James Tunstall, Edward Alleyn, William Harrison, Thomas Cooke, Richard Jones, Edward Browne, and Richard Andrews. Alleyn and Jones, and perhaps Tunstall (Dunstan), became members of the Lord Admiral's company.

3 Duke and Beeston were with the Lord Chamberlain's men in 1598 (see p. 338).

4 See *Calendar of State Papers*. Domestic. Addenda. 1623—1625, p. 530.

5 See 1821 *Variorum*, Vol. III., p. 450.

company had been formed under the patronage of the father of William Herbert (see p. 231). The names of the players are at present unknown. Not later than 1594 they acted *A Shrew*[1] (see p. 97) and *Edward II.*[2] (see p. 77). They also played *The True Tragedy* (see p. 69) and *Titus Andronicus* (see p. 59), of which it seems, from the order of the companies given on its title-page, they were the first possessors. Under Henslowe's management they were acting with the Lord Admiral's servants at the Rose from October 21st, 1597, to March 4th, 1598,[3] and by themselves for a short time, beginning October, 1600.[4] When the Earl of Pembroke died in 1601, it is not at all unlikely that they were taken into the Earl of Worcester's company,[5] acting with Henslowe.

The King's Servants.

The company of actors to which James I. gave his personal patronage soon after he came to the throne consisted principally, if not entirely, of the Lord Chamberlain's servants. Lawrence Fletcher,[6] Shakspere, Burbage, Phillipps, Heminge, Condell, Sly, Robert Armin, Cowley, and others unnamed, received from the King a license on May 17th, 1603, ten days after his arrival in

[1] In 1607, to judge from the title-page of the edition of that year, the play had not been acted by any other company.

[2] The 1612 *Edward II.* bore their name alone as its performers. Attention should be given to Prof. Dowden's article on Marlowe in *The Fortnightly Review*, January, 1870.

[3] See *Diary*, pp. 102-3.

[4] See *Diary*, p. 181.

[5] *Edward II.* was afterwards acted by the servants to the Queen, who had taken over Lord Worcester's players.

[6] Fletcher had come from Scotland with James. On account of his eminence as an actor, the freedom of the city of Aberdeen had been conferred upon him in 1601.

London, by which the company became the King's servants. In the following year they acted Marston's *Malcontent*, in which (as appears from the Induction) Sly, John Sincklo,[1] Burbage, Condell, and Lowin were engaged. On March 15th, 1604, when the virulence of the plague had somewhat abated, the Coronation-procession from the Tower to Westminster took place,[2] and for the occasion the King gave to each of the players named in the Royal license four and a half yards of red cloth.[3] When the company acted Ben Jonson's *Fox* in 1605, Burbage, Heminge, Condell, Lowin, Sly, and Cooke are mentioned as having taken parts. Phillipps died in that year, and in his will[4] left gifts to his servant, Christopher Beeston, and to his fellows, Shakspere, Condell, Fletcher, Armin, Cowley, Cooke, Heminge, Burbage, and Sly, the last three of whom he appointed his executors. In 1610 Burbage, Heminge, Lowin, Ostler (see p. 332), Condell, Underwood (see p. 332), Cooke, Nicholas Tooley, Armin, and William Ecclestone were amongst those who had parts in *The Alchemist*. The same names, with Richard Robinson in the place of Armin, appear as actors in *Catiline* in the following year. Before 1611 they played *Titus Andronicus* (see p. 59). About 1616 they acted *The Duchess of Malfi*, when are found the names of Burbage (Ferdinand), Condell (Cardinal), Ostler (Antonio), Underwood (Delio and Madman), Lowin (Bosola), John

[1] Sincklo played the First Keeper in 3 *Henry VI.* (see 1623 Folio "Histories," p. 158), one of the Players in the Induction to *The Shrew* (see 1623 Folio "Comedies," p. 209), and the First Beadle in 2 *Henry IV.* (see 1600 Quarto).

[2] Ben Jonson and Dekker were engaged in the preparation of the Pageant.

[3] See an extract from the Lord Chamberlain's Records given in the New Shakspere Society's *Transactions*, 1877-9, Part III. The material was for making a cloak and cape. Afterwards the grant became a biennial one (see 1821 *Variorum*, Vol. III., pp. 60-1).

[4] See 1821 *Variorum*, Vol. III., pp. 470-3.

Rice (Pescara), Thomas Pollard (Silvio), Pallant (Doctor and Cariola), Tooley (Madman), Richard Sharp (Duchess), and John Thomas (Julia). In 1623, when the play was again acted by them, the parts of Ferdinand, the Cardinal, and Antonio were taken by Joseph Taylor,[1] Robinson, and Robert Benfield. Field (see p. 332) was a late member of the company. The names also of Samuel Cross, Samuel Gilburne,[2] Robert Gough, and John Shancke appear in the First Folio list of "The Names of the Principall Actors in all these Playes."[3] Mr. Fleay (Royal Historical Society's *Transactions*, Vol. IX.) gives the names of the members of the company who had parts in many of Beaumont and Fletcher's plays, and much other information concerning them on to the closing of the theatres.

The King's servants played at the Globe, and in 1609 they also used the Blackfriars theatre.

It is recorded that the King's servants acted *Richard II.* (see p. 81), *Richard III.* (see p. 87), *Romeo and Juliet* (see p. 91), *Much Ado about Nothing* (see p. 103), *Thomas, Lord Cromwell* (see p. 105), perhaps 1 *Henry IV.* (see p. 107), *The Merry Wives of Windsor* (see pp. 103, 113), *The London Prodigal* (see p. 127), *A Yorkshire Tragedy* (see p. 133), *Hamlet* (see p. 135), *The Alchemist* (see p. 103), *Othello*, (see p. 143), *Philaster* (see p. 147), *Lear* (see p. 149), *A King and No King* (see pp. 103, 153), *Pericles* (see p. 159), *The Duchess of Malfi* (see p. 165), *Troilus and Cressida* (see p. 167), *The Duke of Milan* (see p. 175), *The Winter's Tale* (see pp. 103, 177), and *The Tempest* (see pp. 103, 179).

[1] Burbage died in 1619. Taylor acted Hamlet, Iago, Truewit in *The Silent Woman*, and Face in *The Alchemist*.

[2] Gilburne is mentioned in Phillipps's will as his "late apprentice."

[3] Shakspere bequeathed to Heminge, Burbage, and Condell £1 : 6 : 8 "a peece to buy them ringes."

Familiarity with the customs of the theatres in Shakspere's times, both on the stage and in the audience, is necessary for understanding many passages in the plays. The theatres are usually described as "private" and "public." The exact significance of these terms is, however, not clear, as the general public were admitted to both.[1] The announcement of the play was made by bills[2] or posters. The hour for beginning the performance varied from one to three o'clock, getting later as years went on. At some theatres admission could be obtained for a penny, and probably the best place could be secured for a shilling.[3] The doors seem to have been opened some considerable time before the acting began, and this interval was occupied by the audience with a variety of diversions, in which card-playing and the consumption of cheap and portable refreshments bore a conspicuous place. Tobacco-smoking, to which it is strange that Shakspere has no reference, seems to have been indulged in then and through the performance. During the waiting-time there was often some rough play by the more noisy portion of the audience,[4] including scrambling for partly-consumed fruits. There was an orchestra provided, whose purpose was the same as now. In the earlier period of the Elizabethan drama some portion of the drama was suggested by the presentation of a dumb-show.[5] This became less a practice, and the Prologue[6] became

[1] The Globe was called a public, and the Blackfriars a private, theatre.

[2] The transfer of copyright from Charlwood to Roberts in 1594 (see p. 267) included "*The billes for plaies.*"

[3] At some theatres accommodation for a limited number of spectators was afforded on the stage (see the address "To the great Variety of Readers" in the 1623 Folio), and for this an extra charge was made.

[4] See *Henry VIII.*, V. iv. 63-4.

[5] See *Locrine*, the play-scene in *Hamlet*, and *Pericles*.

[6] Much of interest has been gathered together by G. S. B. in *The Prologue and Epilogue in English Literature*.

a sort of substitute for it. Shakspere occasionally conformed to the custom of the Prologue, but was evidently not very tolerant of the practice.[1] Usually only one play was presented at a performance, and the average time occupied in this was about two hours.[2] Instead of the single play, several very short ones were given occasionally.[3] There has been much misunderstanding about the amount of scenery and stage-properties used in the Elizabethan plays. There can be no doubt that these were such as the age could produce.[4] The dresses of the performers were often of a costly character,[5] and bore a disproportionate relation to the remuneration of the author. This varied from about £6 to £20. Some of the writers and principal actors were "sharers"[6] in the theatre, and from this source derived considerable income.[7] The actors or "hirelings" were paid a weekly wage.[8] It must be borne in mind that on to the middle of the seventeenth century women's parts were acted by boys or men, and actors playing clowns' parts at times introduced some "extempore wit,"[9] for their ability in which they often received high commendation. Although Shakspere seems to have been more favourably disposed to the Epilogue than to the Prologue, he used it only sparingly. It was spoken at times by one who was not of

1 See *A Midsummer-Night's Dream*, III. i. 17-36, V. i. 108-52; *Romeo and Juliet*, I. iv. 1-10; and *Hamlet*, III. ii. 151-2.

2 See Prologues to *Romeo and Juliet*, *The Alchemist*, and *Henry VIII*.

3 See Suggestion 2 on *A Yorkshire Tragedy*, p. 133.

4 Many of Ben Jonson's *Masques* must have severely taxed the resources of the mechanicians.

5 For one instance see p. 123.

6 See *Hamlet*, III. ii. 290-1.

7 Burbage, Alleyn, Shakspere, Phillipps, Heminge, Condell, Underwood, Tooley, Pope, were all well off. Copies of their wills are given in Vol. III. of the 1821 *Variorum*.

8 See pp. 213-14.

9 See *Hamlet*, III. ii. 42-50.

the *dramatis personæ*,[1] and immediately after it, it was frequently the custom to offer a prayer on behalf of the Sovereign,[2] or, in private performances, for the patron of the Company.

The foregoing is only intended as a mere sketch of some of the more prominent customs of the theatre. The reader who wishes to know more of these interesting points is referred to Vols. II. and III. of the 1821 *Variorum*, where the notes contain numerous quotations from contemporary literature illustrating the various practices.

[1] See *As You Like It*. [2] See 2 *Henry IV*.

CHAPTER XIII.

Metrical Tests.

"The true concord of well-tuned sounds."
Sonnets, VIII. 5.

THERE are many persons who think that the chronological sequence of Shakspere's plays can be determined by their metrical characteristics.

Entirely opposed to these are people who are horrified at the bare mention of such a matter-of-fact, arithmetical test in connection with work "of imagination all compact."

Again, there are others who, seeing the vast metrical differences existing in many of Shakspere's plays, cannot ignore the fact that a poet must to a certain extent concern himself with the mechanical structure of his verse, and that it is only reasonable to suppose that with his maturer powers his versification would take a freer form.

It is principally of late years that verse-tests have been brought into prominence, although their determining value was recognised by earlier students.[1] The evidence afforded by these tests is too strong

[1] Malone in 1821 *Variorum*, Vol. II., p. 323, *et passim*, and Bathurst's *Remarks on the Differences in Shakespeare's Versification in Different Periods of his Life*, 1857.

to be set aside by attempts to ridicule them or the hopeless endeavour to ignore them. It is not necessary to concede that they prove as much as some would desire; but it is certain that in some cases they are strikingly confirmatory of known external evidence. If then, in reference to those plays about which the external evidence is certain, metrical tests are corroborative of the chronological position, they are surely, in those instances where no external evidence exists, not only entitled to respectful consideration, but should be welcomed as very material aids, if not absolute certainties, in the solution of many complicated problems in the question of determining the sequence of Shakspere's work. But no one verse-test must be set to do more than can reasonably be expected of it. It is demanding too much to think that any test of this kind can fix the exact chronological order of the plays, and it is unfair to discard the test altogether because it fails to do this. In Shakspere's plays the most we can expect verse-tests to show is that at different periods of his work he adopted, consciously or unconsciously, certain metrical forms which classify his plays into fairly well-defined periods.[1] If such arrangement does not contradict the definite external evidence, the verse-tests by which it has been made have established a claim for investigation which no intelligent student can afford to put on one side. It will be apparent that such is the case if attention be given to some details. Several tests of this kind have been employed.

(1) **Weak and light endings.** Many lines end in a weak or light monosyllable, and thus require the voice to be carried on almost without pause to the next line. Such endings scarcely exist in the

[1] In those plays parts of which were written at perhaps long intervals, and in which there is conjoint authorship, a further complication is introduced.

plays which are universally acknowledged to be early, and become frequent in those which are obviously later. Mr. J. K. Ingram has dealt fully with the application of this test in the New Shakspere Society's *Transactions*, 1874, Part II.

(2) **Double endings.** Shakspere in his later plays frequently employed lines which have a redundant syllable at the end. These are comparatively rare in the earlier plays. The percentage varies from 4 in *Love's Labour's Lost* to 33 in *The Tempest*. For a full consideration of this test, reference should be made to Fleay's *Shakespeare Manual*, where there is a full record of his investigations, and to the table from Hertzberg quoted in Dowden's *Shakspere Primer*.

(3) **Rhyme.** The presence of rhyming lines has been held to be evidence of early work. The application of this test brings out some very striking results, but its use is complicated by the fact that for certain purposes a writer would be very likely to use rhymes deliberately, although he may in a general sense have emancipated himself from the limitations which they impose. But even with this qualifying consideration, a test which shows a proportion of rhyme-lines to those of blank-verse varying from about 1 to 3 in a group of plays well-known to be early to about 1 in 50 in a group of plays equally well-known to be late makes it clear that the existence of rhyme must be of considerable service in determining the chronological position of a play. Mr. Fleay, who has been the hardest worker at investigating this test not only in Shakspere's plays but in many contemporary writers, has papers on the subject in the New Shakspere Society's *Transactions*, 1874, Part I.

(4) **Stopped and unstopped lines.** Stopped lines—those in which the pause occurs at the end of the line—are frequent in the early

plays, whereas in the later plays unstopped lines—those in which the sentence is "run on" to the next line—are much more common. Dr. Furnivall has paid considerable attention to this test, the great value of which can be seen from the following examples he gives in the Introduction to the 'Leopold' *Shakspere*, p. xx.:

PROPORTION OF UNSTOPPED TO STOPPED LINES.

Love's Labour's Lost - - -	1 in 18.14	*The Tempest* -	1 in 3.02
The Comedy of Errors - - -	1 in 10.7	*Cymbeline* - -	1 in 2.52
The Two Gentlemen of Verona -	1 in 10.	*The Winter's Tale*	1 in 2.12

The frequency of Alexandrines and the position of the cæsura ("the pause-test") have also been suggested as indications of the chronological order. But there are not enough statistics on these points to ensure accuracy.

When preparing the tables given in Chapter IX., I was struck with the varying discrepancy between the totals of printed lines and the totals of the lines when reckoned as verse. This discrepancy means that frequently Shakspere breaks up a verse-line between two or more speakers. It is obvious that such a practice gives a writer much more freedom than invariably making a speech close at the end of a line, and that it would be probable that he would use this freedom to a greater extent as time went on and he felt more sure of his powers. It occurred to me that this should supply another metrical test; and feeling sure that its significance would not have been overlooked, I searched my accessible authorities, but could only find that Professor Pulling, following up a suggestion by Professor Ingram, had, in the New Shakspere Society's *Transactions* for 1877-9, Part III., applied to twenty of Shakspere's plays that which has been called the "speech-ending test." That deals with the numerical proportion which speeches ending in the middle of line bear to the total verse-speeches, and may perhaps, if carried out in its entirety, be of more value than mine, which takes into consideration the proportionate frequency of split verse-lines and may be called "the split-verse test." It is clear that the application of this test must not be made to the total lines[1] in a play, but only to verse-lines in which split lines are possible. All solo-verse must be excluded, and dialogue-verse only must be taken into consideration. The apparent misplacement of some of the plays made by the split-verse test can be explained by other considerations. In a revision Shakspere may have introduced only a small quantity of new matter, and the force of the test is of course lessened in those plays in which he was only partly concerned. (See pp. 19, 20).

The differences of the two totals in the Reading-Tables do not always give the number of split lines, because sometimes a line of verse is occupied by more than two speakers and sometimes a line is spoken by two or more persons at once.

The efficacy of this test can readily be seen if the thirty-seven plays be taken in the order which I have recommended for study, and which represents in the main the accepted chronology, and then divided into two portions as nearly equal as possible.

Taking the first nineteen of the suggested chronological order, it will be observed that, with the exception of changing *As You Like It* for *Much Ado*, the test indicates the same plays to represent the first half of Shakspere's work. The first five plays are the same in both orders. All the plays mentioned by Meres (see p. 8) come in this division. The most serious dislocations are *Love's Labour's Lost*[2] and *Henry V*.

[1] For some observations on the preparation of the table on the opposite page, see preface.

[2] On the chronological position of this play see p. 19.

Chronological Order for Study (see pp. 18-9).	Order indicated by Split-verse Test.	Name of Play.	Total Lines.	Prose.	Verse.	Solo-verse.	Dialogue-verse.	Split-verse.	Percentage of Split-verse in Dialogue-verse.
4	1	*3 Henry VI.*	2905	3	2902	284	2618	11	.42
3	2	*2 Henry VI.*	3161	550	2611	247	2364	16	.67
2	3	*1 Henry VI.*	2678	10	2668	147	2521	18	.71
1	4	*Titus Andronicus*	2523	39	2484	137	2347	21	.89
5		*Comedy of Errors*	1778	237	1541	65	1476	20	1.35
8	5	*Richard II.*	2755	3	2752	79	2673	41	1.53
19	7	*Henry V.*	3380	1466	1914	343	1571	30	1.9
10	8	*Richard III.*	3618	75	3543	422	3121	60	1.92
13	9	*Taming of Shrew*	2648	561	2087	53	2034	47	2.31
17	10	*2 Henry IV.*	3446	1679	1767	89	1678	40	2.38
6	11	*Two Gentlemen of Verona*	2294	656	1638	239	1399	34	2.43
16	12	*1 Henry IV.*	3177	1496	1681	55	1626	41	2.52
12	13	*John*	2570	0	2570	116	2454	65	2.64
9	14	*Midsummer-Night's Dream*	2180	465	1715	322	1393	37	2.65
18	15	*Merry Wives of Windsor*	3019	2681	338	32	306	10	3.26
11	16	*Romeo and Juliet*	3053	455	2598	364	2234	86	3.84
20	17	*As You Like It*	2867	1682	1185	200	985	38	3.85
14	18	*Merchant of Venice*	2662	634	2028	56	1972	80	4.05
7	19	*Love's Labour's Lost*	2789	979	1810	157	1653	72	4.35
15	20	*Much Ado about Nothing*	2829	2094	735	57	678	34	5.01
21	21	*Twelfth Night*	2692	1740	952	146	806	47	5.83
22	22	*Julius Cæsar*	2480	186	2294	142	2152	126	5.85
32	23	*Troilus and Cressida*	3496	1195	2301	108	2193	132	6.01
30	24	Pericles	2391	454	1937	536	1401	106	7.56
23	25	*Hamlet*	3930	1174	2756	417	2339	197	8.42
26	26	*Measure for Measure*	2821	1151	1670	117	1553	147	9.46
27	27	*Lear*	3336	921	2415	244	2171	229	10.54
28	28	*Timon of Athens*	2373	680	1693	217	1476	161	10.9
25	29	*Othello*	3317	672	2645	206	2439	267	10.94
24	30	*All's Well that Ends Well*	2966	1485	1481	136	1345	154	11.44
29	31	*Macbeth*	2109	159	1950	170	1780	244	13.7
33	32	*Coriolanus*	3410	848	2562	45	2517	389	15.45
37	33	*Henry VIII.*	2822	82	2740	110	2630	408	15.51
36	34	*Tempest*	2065	461	1604	158	1446	231	15.97
35	35	*Winter's Tale*	3074	887	2187	146	2041	332	16.26
34	36	*Cymbeline*	3341	507	2834	476	2358	409	17.34
31	37	*Antony and Cleopatra*	3063	312	2751	101	2650	465	17.54

In the second division—that of the last eighteen plays—the coincidences are very close. Among the plays of this division, unless it be *Antony and Cleopatra*, there is no material difference, except with those piecemeal plays, *All's Well that Ends Well*, *Pericles*, and *Troilus and Cressida*.

If, in the joint-authorship plays, the generally-acknowledged Shakspere-parts only were subjected to the test, the results might be even more striking.

Bearing in mind the reservation as to the power of any one metrical test mentioned at p. 349, I think it will be conceded that the results given in the table are clear evidence that a test of this description is of great value in determining the order of the plays.

I may add that, long before I had any idea of applying this test, I had arranged the order of study recommended at pp. 18—19, and that the order does not differ very materially from that given by competent critics of the present day.

The overwhelming evidence afforded by these various verse-tests is of such a character, that their most determined opponent must acknowledge that in them may be found a substantial, if not essential, help for the intelligent comprehension of the poet's growing powers and one which no wise student can afford to despise.

CHAPTER XIV.

A National Requirement.

"Society, saith the text, is the happiness of life."
Love's Labour's Lost, IV. ii. 167-8.

TWICE in this century there have been in England attempts at a National Shakspere Society. But neither of them has been exactly what is required to popularise and foster the study of Shakspere. They have both catered too exclusively for the specialist, and have erred in taking for granted the existence of a general intelligent admiration of the poet. The Shakespeare Society founded in 1841 and the New Shakspere Society dating its life from 1874 have both rendered excellent service to the student, whom they have laid under a perpetual obligation for the reprints they have issued. Such a Society as that which I think is required might live alongside the present Shakspere Society, with whose work it need not in the least interfere. As societies multiply there will be required a bond of union to link them together and provide means of inter-communication. The New Shakspere Society has done, and is doing, something in this direction, but from its constitution it is unable to effect that which is really required. For supplying to subscribing societies copies of its papers before they are issued in the occasional volumes of Transactions, and for receiving from such local societies papers that have been read there and reading them at its own meetings, and at times printing them, it deserves and should receive great credit. But a Society that is to really introduce and encourage Shakspere-study among people who are at present indifferent or lukewarm must be formed upon a more popular basis. In the British Isles[1] the Society should be called the British Shakspere Association, and it should have these distinguishing features:

1. There should be a general meeting of its members once a year.

> This would be in accordance with the practice of many other societies and congresses. The annual meeting should consist of two day-meetings, at which papers could be read. One of the evenings might be devoted to a conversazione, including the exhibition of things of Shaksperian interest, and the other to a dinner. A third day could be devoted to excursions to places of suitable attraction in the neighbourhood.

2. The President should be an annual one, being of course a local person interested in the work of the Society.

3. The general members to consist of two classes: guinea subscribers, entitled to all the privileges of the Society; and half-guinea subscribers, who could attend the annual meeting, and who would receive a copy of its transactions.

[1] In each country where Shakspere-Societies exist there should be a central Society bringing all together.

4. The Society to be managed by a council consisting of representatives from the branch societies forming part of the central Association, and such other persons as may be thought desirable.

The meetings of this committee to be held at Stratford-ou-Avon, which is fairly central.

5. The appointment of local secretaries for counties or large towns or combined districts.

The business of these to be the gathering in of subscribers and the formation of local branches—semi-independent—for rational Shakspere-work.

6. The issue of a monthly Shakspere-magazine.

This, which should have existed long ago in Shakspere's own country, would be of great interest, and would afford an opportunity for wide circulation, not only of important articles, but of small points of correspondence on Shaksperian matters, direct and indirect.

7. Possibly the issue of Parallel Texts of all Quarto and Folio versions, to be published at special charges.

These are much needed.

CHAPTER XV.

Chronicle of Events Connected with Shakspere-work.

"The abstract and brief chronicles of the time."
Hamlet, II. ii. 548-9.

THIS chapter is not to be taken as a full record of the events with which Shakspere-students should concern themselves. It is literally a "brief chronicle," and is only intended to indicate the salient points to which special attention must be directed. The reader can easily make any additions thought desirable. Before the birth of Shakspere there are many things to be considered which prepared the way for the Elizabethan Drama, and after his death the results of his influence must be gauged. No mention is made of the entry or publication of any of Shakspere's plays. Doubtful dates are printed in *Italic*.

1564 Birth of William Shakspere
1565 First edition of *Gorboduc*
1566 Entry of *Roister Doister* in Stationers' Registers
1574 License to Leicester's servants
1575 Kenilworth festivities
1576 Building of The Theatre
1577 Building of The Curtain
1579 Publication of *Euphues*
1579 Gosson's *School of Abuse*
1580 Lodge's *Defence of Poetry*

1580 Birth of William Herbert
1582 William Shakspere's marriage
1583 Formation of the Queen's servants
1584 First edition of *Campaspe*
1586 Date of *Tamburlaine*
1587 Greene's *Menaphon* with Nash's preface
1588 Date of *Faustus*
1589 Commission for revising plays
1589 Lord Mayor forbids two companies to act
1589 Date of *Friar Bacon*
1591 Henslowe manages The Rose
1592 Daniel's *Sonnets*
1592 Greene's references to Shakspere
1592 Entry of *The Spanish Tragedy* in Stationers' Registers
1592 Death of Greene
1592 Date of *Edward II.*
1593 Earliest edition of *Venus and Adonis*
1593 Death of Marlowe
1593 Theatres closed on account of plague
1594 Shakspere acting with Lord Chamberlain's servants
1594 Date of *King David*
1596 Earliest record of Thomas Heywood as a writer
1596 Drayton's historical poems
1596 Death of Peele
1596 Institution of the Blackfriars theatre
1597 Shakspere's purchase of New Place
1598 Performance of *Every Man in his Humour*
1598 Meres's literary references
1598 Dekker begins writing for Henslowe
1598 Publication of first part of Chapman's *Homer*
1599 Building of the Globe theatre

1600 Beaumont enters literary life
1600 Building of the Fortune theatre
1601 Webster begins writing plays
1601 Death of John Shakspere
1602 Middleton begins writing for Henslowe
1602 Date of *Antonio and Mellida*
1603 Shakspere becomes one of the King's servants
1603 Acting of *A Woman Killed with Kindness*
1604 Company of the Children of the Revels established
1606 Death of Lyly
1606 Parliament limits the use of the Divine Name in plays
1607 Death of Mary Shakspere
1607 Marston ceases dramatic writing
1607 Literary partnership of Beaumont and Fletcher
1608 Performance of *Philaster*
1609 Acting and publication of *The Silent Woman*
1610 Entry of *The Alchemist* in the Stationers' Registers
1611 Acting of *The Knight of the Burning Pestle*
1612 Performance of *The Duchess of Malfi*
1613 Acting of *A King and No King*
1613 Massinger has dealings with Henslowe
1613 Destruction of the Globe theatre
1614 Opening of the new Globe theatre
1616 Death of Beaumont
1616 Death of William Shakspere

INDEX.

Many references, being more conveniently given in the text, are not repeated in the Index.

Compound figures (*e.g.* 140–1) indicate the position of Reading-Table and general comments on play.

LIBRARY OF THE UNIVERSITY OF

J. W. ARROWSMITH, PRINTER, 11 QUAY STREET, BRISTOL.

Arrowsmith's Bristol Library.

Fcap. 8vo, stiff covers, 1/-; cloth, 1/6.

Saturday Review speaks of ARROWSMITH'S BRISTOL LIBRARY "as necessary the traveller as a rug in winter and a dust-coat in summer."

VOL.		
1.	**CALLED BACK**	HUGH CONWAY.
2.	**BROWN EYES**	MAY CROMMELIN.
3.	**DARK DAYS**	HUGH CONWAY.
4.	**FORT MINSTER, M.P.**	Sir E. J. REED, K.C.B., M.P.
5.	**THE RED CARDINAL**	Mrs. FRANCES ELLIOT.
6.	**THE TINTED VENUS**	F. ANSTEY.
7.	**JONATHAN'S HOME**	ALAN DALE.
8.	**SLINGS AND ARROWS**	HUGH CONWAY.
9.	**OUT OF THE MISTS**	DANIEL DORMER.
10.	**KATE PERCIVAL.**	Mrs. J. COMYNS CARR.
11.	**KALEE'S SHRINE**	GRANT ALLEN.
12.	**CARRISTON'S GIFT**	HUGH CONWAY.
13.	**THE MARK OF CAIN**	ANDREW LANG.
14.	**PLUCK**	J. STRANGE WINTER.
15.	**DEAR LIFE**	Mrs. J. E. PANTON
16.	**GLADYS' PERIL**	JOHN COLEMAN and JOHN C. CHUTE.
17.	**WHOSE HAND?** or, The Mystery of No Man's Heath	W. G. WILLS and The Hon. Mrs. GREENE.
18.	**THAT WINTER NIGHT.**	ROBERT BUCHANAN.
19.	**THE GUILTY RIVER**	WILKIE COLLINS.
20.	**FATAL SHADOWS**	Mrs. L. L. LEWIS.
21.	**THE LOVELY WANG**	Hon. L. WINGFIELD.
22.	**PATTY'S PARTNER**	JEAN MIDDLEMASS.
23.	**"V.R."** A Comedy of Errors	EDWARD ROSE.
24.	**THE PARK LANE MYSTERY.** A Story of Love and Magic	JOSEPH HATTON.
25.	**FRIEND MAC DONALD**	MAX O'RELL.
26.	**KATHARINE REGINA**	WALTER BESANT.
27.	**JAN VERCLOOTZ**	MATTHEW STRONG.
28.	**THE CLIFF MYSTERY**	HAMILTON AÏDÉ.
29.	**AS A BIRD TO THE SNARE.**	GERTRUDE WARDEN.
30.	**TRACKED OUT:** A Secret of the Guillotine	ARTHUR À BECKETT.
31.	**A SOCIETY CLOWN**	GEORGE GROSSMITH.
32.	**CHECK & COUNTER-CHECK**	BRANDER MATTHEWS and GEORGE H. JESSOP.
33.	**THE INNER HOUSE**	WALTER BESANT.
34.	**A VAGABOND WILL**	W. G. WATERS.
35.	**PHARAOH'S DAUGHTER**	EDGAR LEE.
36.	**TROLLOPE'S DILEMMA.**	ST. AUBYN.
37.	**JACQUES BONHOMME.**	MAX O'RELL.
38.	**THE DOUBTS OF DIVES**	WALTER BESANT.

Bristol: J. W. ARROWSMITH, 11 Quay Street.
London: SIMPKIN, MARSHALL, HAMILTON, KENT & CO. LIMITED.

ARROWSMITH'S 2/- SERIES

Crown 8vo. Boards.

VOL. I.

Dead Men's Dollars. By MAY CROMMELIN.

Author of "BROWN EYES."

"The tale is told with an intensity of feeling."—*Daily Chronicle.*

"A very bright and readable novel, full of incident and 'go.'"—*Daily News.*

VOL. II.

On the Wrong Tack. By A. E. WILTON.

"Is a smartly written story, the conversations are well managed and full of sprightliness, and the plot is interesting."—*Literary World.*

VOL. III.

The Truth about Clement Ker.

Being an account of some curious circumstances connected with the life and death of the late Sir Clement Ker, Bart., of Brae House, Peebleshire, told by his second cousin, GEOFFREY KER, of London. Edited by GEORGE FLEMING.

VOL. IV.

Elizabeth Morley.

By KATHARINE S. MACQUOID.

Authoress of "PATTY," "AT THE RED GLOVE," &c.

"Some charming pictures of life in out-of-the-way foreign places give additional attraction to an interesting and altogether sympathetic story."—*Graphic.*

VOL. V.

Francis and Frances; or, An Unexplainable Phenomenon.

"The complications that would naturally arise out of an alternate existence such as that described . . . are set forth in a manner that is always logical, generally humorous, and occasionally thrilling. . . . The inquisitive Mrs. Winterly, who constantly overreaches herself; Dr. Ditchburn, the good genius of the plot, and his impulsive colleague; Austin, a good-humoured Hercules of a medical student—these characters have all vitality and freshness about them."
Athenæum.

"The idea on which it is founded is, so far as our experience goes, quite unique."—*Western Figaro.*

"A most readable and enjoyable story."—*The Bookseller.*

VOL. VI. [*Nearly Ready.*]

Lal. By LORIN LATHROP and ANNIE WAKEMAN

THIS BOOK IS DUE ON THE LAST DATE STAMPED BELOW

AN INITIAL FINE OF 25 CENTS
WILL BE ASSESSED FOR FAILURE TO RETURN THIS BOOK ON THE DATE DUE. THE PENALTY WILL INCREASE TO 50 CENTS ON THE FOURTH DAY AND TO $1.00 ON THE SEVENTH DAY OVERDUE.

JUN 11 1935	29 MAR 01
DEC 12 1936	REC'D LD
NOV 1 1938	MAR 15 1963
SEP 28 1940	
18 Apr'56	
APR - 4 1956 LU	
24 May '57	
REC'D LD	
MAY 10 1957	

LD 21-50m-1,'33

Lightning Source UK Ltd.
Milton Keynes UK
UKHW012225271118
333084UK00009B/536/P

9 781330 703915